Reversible Destiny

Reversible Destiny

Mafia, Antimafia,
and the Struggle for Palermo

Jane C. Schneider

Peter T. Schneider

UNIVERSITY OF CALIFORNIA PRESS
Berkeley · Los Angeles · London

University of California Press
Berkeley and Los Angeles, California

University of California Press, Ltd.
London, England

© 2003 by the Regents of the University of California

Library of Congress Cataloging-in-Publication Data

Schneider, Jane, 1938–
  Reversible destiny : mafia, antimafia, and the struggle
for Palermo / Jane C. Schneider and Peter T. Schneider.
      p.   cm.
  Includes bibliographical references and index.
  ISBN 0-520-22100-1 (cloth : alk. paper).—ISBN
0-520-23609-2 (pbk. : alk. paper)
  1. Mafia—Italy—Palmero—History.   2. Palmero
(Italy)—History.   3. Palermo (Italy)—Politics and government. I. Schneider, Peter T., 1933– II. Title.

HV6453.I83 M376432 2003
364.1'06'0945823—dc21

                                        2002013905

Manufactured in the United States of America

10 09 08 07 06 05 04 03 02 01
10 9 8 7 6 5 4 3 2 1

In Memory of Eric R. Wolf
Scholar, Teacher, and Friend

Contents

Illustrations

Acknowledgments

We were fortunate to reside in Palermo off and on between 1987 and 2000, while pursuing the research for this book. Numerous friends and colleagues took excellent care of us—helping us locate interesting places to live, mediating introductions to public figures, answering our interminable questions. Knowing of our desire to chart transformations in the relationship between mafia and antimafia in the Palermo region, many went out of their way to contribute. They suggested books and journals to read, alerted us to events and controversies of interest, invited us to meetings and discussion groups, and included us in the rounds of their everyday lives. Perhaps needless to say, people who assisted in these ways are concentrated on the antimafia side of the mafia–antimafia equation (although we have in the past also known mafiosi in rural Sicily). We particularly want to thank Ginni Albegiani, Orazio and Nina Barrese, Letizia Battaglia, Daniele Billiteri, Raimondo Catanzaro, Augusto Cavadi, Alessandro Cestelli, Marta Cimino, Gabriella Callari, Donatella Di Natoli, Giusi Ferrara, Renata Feruzza, Giuseppe and Vivi Fici, Giovanna Fiume, Gabriella Gribaudi, Angela Locanto, Salvatore Lupo, Rosario Mangiameli, Pasquale Marchese, Wanda Mollica, Franco and Rita Nicastro, Giovanni Oddo, Letizia Paoli, Anna Puglisi, Marina and Santi Rizzo, Sergio Russo, the late Giuliana Saladino, Umberto Santino, Cesare Scardula, Paola Sconzo, Cosimo Scordato, Mary Taylor Simeti, Paolo Viola, Emanuele Villa, and Francesco Vinci.

Letizia Paoli, Umberto Santino, Mary Taylor Simeti, and Paolo Viola also read an early draft of the manuscript, corrected errors of omission and commission, and raised questions that were extremely important to our revisions. We gladly assume responsibility for the final outcome, knowing how much it has improved over this earlier version. In the United States, the following persons read and criticized the early draft as well: Michael Blim, Sally Booth, Jeffrey Cole, Marc Edelman, Shirley Lindenbaum, Sarah Munro, Ray Montgomery, and Reg Potterton. Thanks to their generosity, we were provoked to clarify arguments and consider new sources, comparisons, and analytical strategies in nearly every chapter. Julia Schneider generously (and mercilessly) made editorial comments.

We are grateful to Benjamin Orlove for bringing our work to the attention of the University of California Press and to Juliane Brand, Cindy Fulton, and Sheila Levine at the press. Two external readers, Judith Chubb and David Kertzer, both long-time students of Italy, offered extended comments, at the same time encouraging us to consider the wider implications of our case. We much appreciate their thoughtful and constructive suggestions. Finally, we thank the Harry Frank Guggenheim Foundation, the National Science Foundation, the Wenner Gren Foundation, and the faculty fellowship programs of the City University of New York and Fordham University for financial support of the fieldwork.

Reversible Destiny was essentially complete before September 11, 2001. The events of that morning have cast it in another light. The Sicilian mafia, although not ideologically driven, is a secretive organization whose loosely networked "families" nurture violence. After the breakup of the French Connection in the 1970s, in the context of Sicily becoming a crossroads of global narcotics trafficking, the mafia turned to terrorism, with a rising toll of shootings and bombings directed against state power. The massacres of the Palermo Prefect Carlo Alberto dalla Chiesa in 1982, and the prosecutors Giovanni Falcone and Paolo Borsellino in 1992, provoked waves of especially intense reaction—high points in a multifaceted *lotta contro la mafia* (struggle against the mafia). Notwithstanding its history as the "mafia capital," Palermo, the fulcrum of this struggle, is today internationally recognized for a series of experiments in civility and legality. Perhaps, we believe, aspects of the Sicilian experience are relevant to the pending struggle against terrorism in other parts of the world.

In particular, the Sicilian experience suggests a way to frame the pending struggle in criminal justice rather than mainly in military terms. Doing so means calling attention to the role of creative and transnational police, intelligence, and investigative work aimed at uncovering not only terrorist networks and "cells" but also the corrupt elements of states and financial institutions that give these organizations their cover. It means highlighting the role of citizens' social movements supporting this work while at the same time monitoring the unstable boundary between protecting society from violent criminality and guaranteeing its civil liberties. Finally, it means recognizing that a credible strategy must also address poverty, unemployment, and severe dislocation—and not merely as secondary concerns to be taken up when the emergency is over.

We have shared these thoughts with numerous friends and colleagues, including several of the people who are thanked above. Their responses encourage us to think that the efforts of Sicilian citizens to reverse their "destiny" have lessons to impart that transcend the struggle against the mafia and political corruption in Italy. With this book we seek to acknowledge those efforts.

PORT

Foro Italico

Cala

Via del Porto

Santa Maria
dello Spasimo

Palazzo Steri

Piazza
Marina

Piazza San Domenico,
Church of San Domenico

Via   Roma

Central
RR Station

Corso Vittorio Emanuele

Via Maqueda

Teatro Massimo

The Quatro Canti della Città
(The Four Corners of the City)

Palazzo di Giustizia
(Palace of Justice)

Palazzo
Sciafani

Cattedrale
(Cathedral)

Palazzo dei Normani
(Norman Palace)

San Giovanni
degli Eremiti

Map 1. The historic center of Palermo

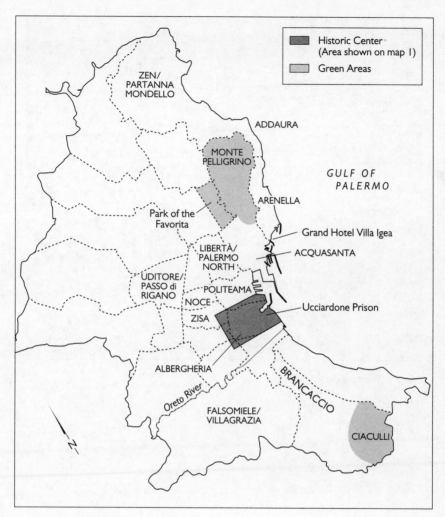

Map 2. The neighborhoods of Palermo

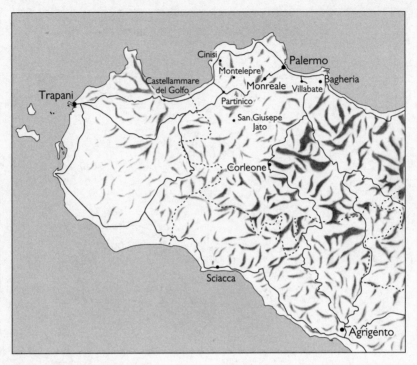

Map 3. Western Sicily

CHAPTER I

The Palermo Crucible

The Piazza Marina is situated behind a row of antique *palazzi* facing the gulf in Palermo's historic center. In the middle is an acre of garden called the Villa Garibaldi, which is surrounded by a handsome Art Nouveau, wrought iron fence depicting animals of the hunt. A gigantic *Ficus magnoloides* tree dominates one quadrant of the garden, each enormous branch sending shoots to the ground like elephants' trunks, creating a labyrinth of arched chambers underneath. The Piazza Marina was the center of elegance in eighteenth- and early nineteenth-century Palermo. Here men and women of baronial and princely pedigree gathered nightly, clothes and carriages on display, to eat jasmine petal ices and gossip (Eberstadt 1991: 48). After the unification of Italy in 1860, however, the city's northward expansion diminished the importance of this luxurious scene, creating new piazzas and boulevards as places for the elite to be seen. That the Piazza Marina was the scene of the 1909 murder of New York City police officer Joe Petrosino, sent to Palermo to pursue mafiosi, did nothing to enhance its reputation.

Near the end of World War II, Allied bombers destroyed many of the waterfront *palazzi,* and by the mid-1960s the Piazza Marina was somewhere to avoid, a place where you had to step over garbage, be vigilant against pickpockets and purse snatchers, and wonder whether the magnolia tree, abandoned to the surrounding patch of weeds, hid something sinister in its gothic roots. In a 1991 *New Yorker* article describing the neighborhood around the piazza, Fernanda Eberstadt vividly captured its degraded yet vibrant quality: "a row of bombed out buildings inhabited by cavernous little bodegas outfitted with altars to the Madonna and posters of local football stars; and a fishmonger's outdoor stall, auto repair shops, and a stand selling *semenza* (lentils and seeds) served in brown paper cones." Her hosts warned her about being robbed on the streets.

Since the early 1990s, however, several buildings surrounding the Piazza Marina have been restored, as has the intricate fence around the Villa Garibaldi. The garden itself, now cleaned and replanted, has become the site of a small playground with brightly colored swings. Children playing hide and seek under the tree contribute to the sense of rejuvenation, as do the trendy outdoor restaurants and a popular Sunday flea and antiques market that enliven the piazza's perimeter.

Palermo's large historic center, formerly neglected and abandoned by many, a shabby symbol of degradation and decay, sprang to life in the 1990s with many such recuperation projects. A second spectacular example is the refurbished Teatro Massimo, the third largest opera house in Europe after those in Paris and Vienna. Reopened in 1997 after twenty-three years of haunting silence during which pigeons nested in the rafters and water leaked through the roof, this structure is at the ceremonial center of the renewal. In June 1999, it served as the stage for Hillary Clinton's address to an international audience on the subject of "educating for legality." In December 2000, it hosted the opening ceremony of the United Nations Convention Against Transnational Organized Crime, during which speakers from Kofi Annan, to the presidents of Italy and Poland, to Pino Arlacchi, the United Nations' under secretary for drug control and crime prevention, praised what they called the Palermo Renaissance. The city that was once the "capital of the mafia" now offers itself to the world as the "capital of the antimafia," its people having suppressed, according to official rhetoric, a "crime-friendly culture" of indifference and cynicism in favor of a "law-abiding culture" of civic pride.

Integral to this reversal of images is Palermo's liberation from the "long 1980s," the period from 1978 to 1992 when its streets were bloodied by unprecedented violence. At the outset, a group of notoriously aggressive mafiosi originally from the mountain town of Corleone waged a takeover of the city's established mafia "families." The aggressors' strategy included murdering public officials—police and Carabinieri officers, magistrates and political leaders. With a population of around 700,000, Palermo lost 100 or more persons annually to assassination, not counting disappearances (Chinnici and Santino 1989; Santino 1988: 238). Underlying this exceptional violence was the mafia's assumption of a strategic role in global heroin trafficking, yet Sicilian organized crime was about much more than narcotics. Because the mafia was rooted in the regional society and intertwined with national as well as regional and local politics, many considered it Sicily's "destiny." As the violence associated with drugs intensified, police and judicial repression and a Palermo-centered antimafia social movement joined together in a concerted effort to reverse what seemed inevitable. This book examines the interrelated histories of the mafia and the antimafia since World War II.

Defining what the mafia "is," where it leaves off and not-mafia begins, and the location of responsibility for "it" becomes a major challenge in writing such a book. Since its nineteenth-century inception, interpretations of the mafia's causes have swung between "things Sicilian"—the regional culture—and "things Italian"—the Italian nation-state. The differences are not trivial. Participants in the antimafia process grapple constantly with ambiguity as they seek to confront an institution whose contours are partly unknown and whose descent into murder and mayhem was tolerated and often abetted by regional, national, and international political leaders.

The dilemmas of interpretation notwithstanding, the antimafia movement has energetically propagated a set of values loosely associated with building "civil society." Among its many projects, this study concentrates on two: efforts to recuperate the city's built environment, and efforts to "culturally re-educate" children according to the civil society ideal. One detects the effectiveness of these and related initiatives in the emergence of a backlash—an anti-antimafia discourse—which, although expressive of the old "destiny," is not simply the propaganda arm of the mafia.

Antimafia activists, who are generally middle-class, find it very difficult to reach working-class audiences, who, it turns out, have many reasons to be skeptical about reform. In substantial measure, Palermo's working-class people, the *popolo,* identify their livelihoods with the (corrupt and mafia-infiltrated) construction industry, which for a long time has been the largest employer in the city. The antimafia process has coincided with, and in part promoted, this industry's decline. Our concluding chapter considers the implications for Palermo's future of poor people's perception that "too much legality" spells the end of a way of life.

Although this book would at first appear to have two parts, one devoted to the mafia and the other to the antimafia, we hope the reader will not come away with a sense of two separate stories in one binding. We describe and analyze a complex struggle between contending social forces that do not face off on opposite sides of a battlefield as identifiable armies. Rather, this struggle is embodied in the divergent attitudes and practices of people who occupy the same social spaces—households, neighborhoods, workplaces, unions, government and professional offices—and who are at times themselves unsure which banner they are carrying. Nor is the outcome certain. The destiny of the mafia is reversible; it has not been reversed.

Four propositions underlie this claim to "reversibility" (our metaphor for profound change). First, contrary to the conviction of many, the mafia is both a recent social formation, dating only to the nineteenth century, and separable as a subculture from its surrounding milieu. Not an age-old outgrowth of "things Sicilian," its status as Sicily's destiny is questionable. Second, both the police-judicial crackdown and the social movement of the past two decades can be traced to the modernization of Sicilian society after World War II, and with this the proliferation of urban, educated, and professionalized social groups, above all in Palermo. Third, through a process of extended political and cultural work, these social groups have challenged local practices favorable to organized crime—for example, how public contracts are bid—while replacing a discourse that characterizes the mafia as inevitable and mafiosi as "men of honor" with a new language that refers to these men as criminal and prosecutable. Fourth, all of this has occurred during a time of monumental transformation in the geopolitical and political-economic arrangements of the world. In particular, with the end of the Cold War, the Italian and U.S. governments can no longer justify sanctioning organized crime in Sicily as a bulwark against communism while the European Union, a newly powerful structure of significance for Sicily and Italy, is committing substantial resources to the fight against organized crime.[1] What lies behind Palermo's possibility of change is the synergy between local citizens' activism and the opening provided by the shift in the national and international context.

This larger context may also create an obstacle to the antimafia process, however, because of the operations of the new global economy. Emerging from the response of capitalist states, markets, and financial institutions to the oil shock of the 1970s, and subsequently benefiting from the "collapse" of communism, this economic system is premised upon the mobility of capital, unfettered by local and national measures that protect, among other amenities, decent jobs. More to the point, in the world without communism, the modality for managing capitalism depends ever less on "social democratic" constraints—employment security, welfare benefits, seniority systems, and pensions. Rather, the new economic system seeks legitimacy and peace through what might be called civil democracy—institutions and practices founded on the rights of individual citizens and their respect for the rule of law. In breaking up the mafia's monopolies in the Palermo economy and promoting civil society, antimafia activists have, not necessarily with intention, mirrored this broader change in the operations of world capitalism. What remains to be seen is whether Palermo's less privileged classes, cut loose from their moorings in the old economy with as yet no substitute livelihood, can in fact embrace the civil democracy ideal.

International audiences watching the new Palermo present itself from the stage of the Teatro Massimo want to know whether the city is indeed a laboratory for fighting organized crime. There is a temptation on the part of Palermo's image makers to package its hard-won changes in a formulaic language, as if a model now exists for replication elsewhere. Rather than present Palermo as an unambiguous success story, we will extrapolate from its history some useful lessons, elements of complexity and contradiction that might be significant beyond this particular case. Our concluding chapter sketches what these might be.

To arrive at these general contradictions and dilemmas, we must first appreciate Palermo as a particular place where the mafia and the antimafia, each with its appropriations of urban space and understandings of the urban community, have clashed dramatically. In the remainder of this chapter, we describe the city as a whole, both its rich architectural patrimony and its many wounds, as a prelude to understanding the deep commitment of the antimafia process to urban recuperation and renewal. In the last section, we locate ourselves as researchers in the urban landscape.

THE LAYERS OF A DISTANT PAST

Palermo's "most lucid and concentrated moment," its most brilliant epoch, occurred during the Middle Ages, when the conquering Normans made it the capital of their autonomous Kingdom of Sicily (Eberstadt 1991: 42). Drawing upon the organizational innovations and artistic achievements of the Tunisian-based emirate that governed Sicily in the ninth century, the Normans commissioned great works that rendered the city one of the most glorious courts of Europe. In the later Middle Ages, Catalan and then Aragonese conquerors demoted Sicily to vice-royal status. Remaining the capital city, however, Palermo became magnificent again with the lavish investments of Counter-Reformation viceroys in the seventeenth and eighteenth centuries. Aristocratic families and ecclesiastical institutions, overlords of the great wheat and pastoral latifundia that dominated the island's interior, clamored to be close to (if only to controvert) the vice-royal authority. Like their counterparts in Naples (and Mexico City), they registered their exuberance in urban palaces that dripped with what Eberstadt calls "a frenzy of ornamentation and whimsical baroque." Straight lines were submerged in a riot of bulbous windows and serpentine balconies and staircases (1991: 66).

Baroque dominates Palermo's historic center. Facades in this style, reaching five and six high stories, line both sides of the two principal arteries. One, the medieval "Cassaro," renamed Corso Vittorio Emanuele for the Piedmontese king under whom Italy was unified, runs from east to west, linking the mountains to the port. The other, a north-south route, was laid down by the Spanish viceroy, the Duke of Maqueda, in 1600 and continues to bear his name. They cross at the *Quattro Canti,* the Four Corners, where the oblique angle of each facing building offers several tiers of festooned and columned niches, which, like miniature stage sets, frame statues of the four seasons, four Spanish kings, and the four patron saints of the adjacent *mandamenti* (administrative divisions). Tall Baroque *palazzi* interspersed with late medieval examples also flank the nearby streets, which are much narrower (see fig. 1 and 2). Here, balconies constitute a scaffolding for the often-photographed laundry lines, their flapping sheets, in Eberstadt's image, "like backdrops for puppet shows."

A consequence of forceful urban planning, Baroque Palermo demolished older structures and styles, rotating the city's east-west axis by 90 degrees so that it stretched to the north and south along the waterfront (Lo Picolo 1996: 73–74). The new Via Maqueda maximized the streetfront along which ecclesiastical and lay overlords, drawn to the court, could invest their mounting rural revenues in urban real estate (La Duca 1994: 32). In the 1570s, the Spanish viceroys, rattled by the Ottomans' growing presence in the Mediterranean, built massive ramparts along the old medieval walls. Yet, although much earlier construction was erased, spectacular residues remain, creating a rich and varied architectural patrimony to curate for the future. The palace of the medieval Norman kings, now the seat of the regional government and before that the vice-

Figure 1. Palermo of the *popolo* before the 1968 earthquake. Photograph by Nicola Scafidi.

royal headquarters, is the largest and most important. Inside is an exquisite chapel, completed in the 1130s, whose total decoration in gold leaf mosaics captures the synthesis of Crusading, Arabic, and Byzantine cultures created under King Roger. Dating to the same period are the Zisa, an imposing Arab pleasure palace used by the Norman kings, another less well-preserved Arab palace, the Cuba, and, located in the now

Figure 2. Palermo of the aristocracy. Interior of Palazzo Ganci, ca. 1976.
Photograph ©Letizia Battaglia, from *Letizia Battaglia: Passion, Justice,
Freedom—Photographs of Sicily,* Aperture, 1999.

working-class neighborhood of Brancaccio, a somewhat crumbling Arab
castle called Maredolce ("Sweetwater") because it was built alongside an
artificial lake.

Although Palermo's historic churches have undergone periodic transformations so that what is now Baroque might once have been Ro-
manesque or Gothic, a number of Arab-Norman and Catalan Gothic
treasures remain. In two enchanting smaller complexes—the attached
churches of San Cataldo and Santa Maria dell'Amiraglio, and the convent and cloister of San Giovanni degli Eremiti—medieval Gothic
stonework competes for attention with rosy cupolas evoking Muslim
worship. Among the Gothic palaces to have survived the Baroque
makeover is Palazzo Steri, the residence of the fourteenth century's most
prepotent of feudal lords, the Chiaramonte. Located in the Piazza Marina, it was the seat of the Sicilian Inquisition from 1601 to 1782. Today
it houses the rectorate of the University of Palermo, which has been
restoring it for over two decades. Palazzo Steri is matched in scale by the
enormous (also Gothic) palace of the Chiaramonte's rival, the Sclafani

family, situated at the opposite, western end of the old city, and largely behind scaffolding as of this writing.

All of these highlights of the distant past were of course built over yet deeper layers of history. Palermo was originally a Phoenician city—a fact still evident in its maritime location and port development—and it was, as well, the site of early Christian settlement. A vast third-century Christian catacomb consisting of underground galleries and niches near the cathedral attests to this. When Allied planes conducted their raids in 1943, the catacomb served as a bomb shelter, a safe place where parents could distract their frightened children with legends of the Beati Paoli, a mythical eighteenth-century sect that, according to popular lore, was a forerunner of the mafia. People think that another underground space in the neighborhood of Capo, one of the three large popular markets in the historic center, may have been the sect's meeting place; the market's principal street is named for the Beati Paoli. According to the urbanist Rosario La Duca, "This grotto-courtroom was connected to other subterranean cavities by means of tortuous tunnels . . . forming part of the complex of Christian catacombs." But, La Duca adds, the people of Palermo attribute the presence of the Beati Paoli to any subterranean openings, including cavities created by recent excavations for construction materials (La Duca 1994: 293–94). Meanwhile, the catacombs of the Capuchin order continue to preserve—and in surprisingly good condition—the well-dressed and embalmed corpses of about eight thousand members of Palermo society who, in the 1860s and 1870s, could afford to be buried there.

PALERMO BEYOND THE WALLS

Toward the end of the eighteenth century, Palermo's resident aristocrats, now chafing under viceroys of the Bourbon kingdom in Naples, competitively extended their high society into a lush zone of *villeggiatura* beyond the city walls, constructing elegant villas with formal gardens set amid orchards and citrus groves. Covering the Piana dei Colli (Plain of the Hills) in the north, and stretching to include the coastal town of Bagheria in the east, a newly verdant landscape sprang forth, tended by sharecroppers and laborers from nearby hamlets and villages (see La Duca 1994: 38). (Of Palermo's 200,000 inhabitants in 1861, 27,000 lived in these outlying communities [Lupo 1993: 47]). To the west, a similar zone of intensive cultivation climbed the surrounding mountainside to the height of the extravagantly wealthy bishop's seat at Monreale.

Whether watching the sunset from Zisa palace in Palermo, whose windows perfectly frame Monte Cuccio, the highest western peak, or gazing down from the terraces of the brilliantly decorated Monreale cathedral and cloister, visitors immediately grasp that Palermo is surrounded by a "golden shell," the famous Conca D'Oro.

The development of this Conca D'Oro was consonant with the Bourbons' major projects of beautification in Palermo, in particular the Villa Giulia, a large public park and botanical garden on the southern edge of the historic center, and the renovation by King Ferdinand IV, in flight from Napoleon's invasion of Naples, of the Favorita—an immense park and hunting preserve in the northern Piana dei Colli. Here Ferdinand and his family found refuge in an eccentric "Chinese" palace built in the preceding decade to indulge the intense romanticism of a local notable and judge. Thereafter, the Bourbon kingdom's most significant public works in Palermo was the immense walled Ucciardone prison, begun north of the old walls in 1837. It became the site of the dramatic maxitrial of over four hundred mafiosi in the mid-1980s, although it had earlier been known as the mafia's hotel.

BOURGEOIS EXUBERANCE

Immediately following Italian unification and the end of Bourbon rule, Sicily and its regional capital fell on hard times, but by the 1870s new investments were being made in roads, railroads, education, and the development of the shipping interests and an improved port. The Florio family was Palermo's foremost exemplar of an emergent capitalist bourgeoisie. In the early years of the nineteenth century, Vincenzo Florio, a spice merchant with British backing, had pioneered two industries for which Sicily is still famous: Marsala wine making and tuna fishing. His son, Ignazio, greatly leveraged by the state's involvement in the economy after 1868, not only expanded the wineries and fisheries, he also moved into banking and finance, married a baroness, headed the Palermo Chamber of Commerce, and became a major shipbuilder. Other families of the Florio circle included the English Whitakers, the noble Gulì who owned a Palermo textile mill, and a few components of the local aristocracy such as the Tasca, Mazzarino, and Trabia families—all Anglophiles who attended the funeral of Queen Victoria in 1901 (see Cancila 1988: 317).

Bourgeois exuberance lasted in Palermo into and through the end of the century, finding expression in the built environment. For one thing, the city population grew rapidly, from 194,463 in 1861 to 305,716 by 1901, and 336,148 by 1911—an increase of 73 percent as against 59 percent for Sicily as a whole. Some of this increase derived from new arrivals: university students and upwardly mobile gentry landowners, the so-called *civili*, who acquired large estates with the transition from feudalism to capitalism in the countryside. In imitation of the nobility with whom they sought marriage alliances, the most affluent of this group considered having a residence in Palermo to be a condition of social arrival. Palermo, however, had to compete for immigrants with America, the preferred destination for casualties of the agrarian crises that capitalism also produced in interior Sicily from the 1880s forward (see Schneider and Schneider 1996). Hence, most of the city's demographic expansion was attributable not to immigration but to natural increase.

Whatever its cause, the growing density of population set off a hydra-headed process in the historic center that vexes urban planners to this day. On the one hand, large and modest-sized *palazzi* were fragmented through multiple heirship, creating countless small, oddly shaped apartments whose confines are not coherently defined spaces. On the other hand, single-room, single-story dwellings known as *catoi* were cobbled together to create added space for multiple inhabitants. Influenced by the discussions of hygiene and health taking place all over Europe since the remake of Paris, planners of the time were appalled. Sometimes excavated below street level, the humid dwellings of poor people received air and light only through a single entrance; they were paved with porous earthen tiles impossible to clean; and a latrine and conduit for waste immediately beneath the floor were breeding grounds for infection, the more so as the alleyways and courtyards outside were virtually without sun for nine months of the year. Whole quarters, "putrid" and miserable, seemed to fulfill the Malthusian nightmare of too many bodies crowded onto too little ground (see Cancila 1988: 298–99). New construction, mostly in the form of super-elevations on the tops of older buildings, further darkened the narrow streets.

A menacing cholera epidemic in Naples in 1884 and another in Palermo in 1887 added to the pressure for large-scale projects of *risanamento*—urban rehabilitation. Palermo's first Urban Plan (*Piano Regolatore Generale,* or PRG), formulated under the engineer Felice Giarrusso in 1885, guided the demolition of the old city walls and bastions (the present-day courthouse occupies one of the spaces thus created) and the opening of another road that ran straight through the historic center, parallel to the Via Maqueda. Called the Via Roma in homage to Rome's

having become the capital of Italy in 1870, the new road begins at the
principal railroad station at the southern edge of the old center and continues north into the new Palermo. That the line is in fact interrupted reflects modifications allowed by Giarrusso to favor the Marchese of
Arezzo, whose *palazzo* was in the way, as well as to avoid demolishing
another recently built *palazzo* and theater. As in Paris, both housing and
monumental structures succumbed to rational planning, but not to the
same degree (La Duca 1975: 108). The embroiled politics surrounding
the investigation into these clientelistic deviations from the plan offered
a tiny taste of what was to come (Cancila 1988: 260).

Throughout the late nineteenth century, the historic center remained
vibrant if teeming, a magnet for professionals who worked in offices and
merchants who owned small shops (ibid.: 300–301). The city beyond the
walls was also growing, however, absorbing perhaps half of the population increase, according to some estimates (ibid.: 301). For example,
hugging the harbor and coastline immediately to the north of the old
walls, the one-time fishing and tannery communities of Borgo Santa Lu-
cia, Acquasanta, and Arenella filled up with dockworkers, shipbuilders,
and tuna fishermen responding to the investments of the Florio family.

Consonant with the Paris-inspired principles of openness and light in
architecture, and with the Europe-wide aesthetic movement of arts and
crafts, or Art Nouveau, the haute bourgeoisie of late nineteenth-century
Palermo spearheaded the construction of new villas and *palazzi*. Already
in 1870, the Florios had built a neo-Gothic Venetian villa, prompting a
string of variations on the theme. Several of these were along an entirely
new corridor, the Viale della Libertà, a wide, sycamore-lined boulevard
that extended the Via Maqueda to the north, evoking the Champs
Elysées. At the same time, northwest of the historic center, the neighborhoods of Noce and Zisa—the latter dominated by the Arab pleasure
palace of the same name—became home to the factories of the English
Whitakers, the French Ducrot, the Italian Gulì, whose textiles, furniture,
ironwork, and glasswork supported the Belle Epoque, called Liberty
Style in Palermo.

With time, expansion to the north reoriented the city's social and cultural life away from the aristocracy's favorite gathering place, the waterfront esplanade of the old center and its adjacent Piazza Marina.
Newly landscaped gardens, including the very large "English Garden,"
contributed, as did the construction of two great theaters, the imposing
Teatro Massimo and the Politeama. The Massimo, designed by Palermo
architect Giovanni Battista Filippo Basile and built between 1875 and

1897, occupies the "top" of the Via Maqueda. Its construction was controversial, not only because of the expense to a poor city that many believed should have built a new hospital, but because three monasteries and a densely populated neighborhood had to be razed to make way for it. (Closed for "restorations" in 1974, the Massimo's failure to reopen within a reasonable time placed it high on the list of urban disasters that the antimafia movement sought to redress.) The Politeama, a smaller-scaled rotunda at the "bottom" of the Viale della Libertà, went up between 1867 and 1874. Hotels and cafés followed, such as the luxurious Hotel of the Palms, which opened in the 1870s as a remodeled *palazzo* along the Via Roma, and the Excelsior Hotel, bordering the English Garden. Among the Florios' many palaces and villas, the Villa Igea at the north end of Palermo's harbor in Acquasanta blossomed as a world-renowned centerpiece of Art Nouveau decoration and is to this day the fanciest hotel in the city. Here the Florios entertained a succession of cosmopolitan elites: royalty from all over Europe, Russia, Egypt, and Zanzibar, plus the Vanderbilts and Pierpont Morgan from the United States.[2]

Unlike artists and architects patronized by the old nobility, the designers and decorators behind these wonders looked beyond the historic center for aesthetic validation. Most, indeed, lived in the new zone of gardens and bourgeois amenities known today as *Palermo per bene* (the best Palermo) but which we will call, for simplicity, Palermo north. For example, Ernesto Basile, son of the much-praised architect of the Teatro Massimo and himself the designer of the Villa Igea, took up residence there while Giarrusso, author of the 1885 Urban Plan, lived in Acquasanta. All were involved in promoting Palermo as the site of the Fourth National Exhibition in 1891–92. Occupying vacant land along the Viale della Libertà, this event motivated further investment in new properties, including a secondary railroad station on the Via Lolli, soon to be renamed the Via Notarbartolo after a martyred official of that name (and eventually the street of the celebrated antimafia prosecutor, Giovanni Falcone).

So exciting was the new pole of worldly life and comfort that a few noble families gave up the patina of the historic center, turned over their *palazzi* to the rental market, and moved northward, enjoying their "last season as the dominant social class" by mixing with the bourgeoisie (ibid.: 317). After 1900, even their clubs moved north. According to historian Orazio Cancila, it was "as if Palermo were divided in two" (ibid.: 310). The old half, still viable for shops and offices, increasingly housed people who were poor and/or economically obsolete, whereas the new city attracted younger, more prosperous, and more "progressive" residents. At the same time, however, the Viale della Libertà promised to bring within the city's orbit some important legacies of the feudal past: the eighteenth-century villas of the grandest nobility that dotted the Piana dei Colli and the beautiful park and watering place of the Bourbons in exile, the Favorita.

Looking south from the historic center, the picture is somewhat different. Older maps recall a mix of fishing and industry. Metal products and railroad cars were manufactured before World War II, and after the war, space was increasingly devoted to fabricating and warehousing construction materials. Except for a silversmith's firm in Brancaccio, the zone expanded in an "economical" way, that is without the high-end artisanal works in support of Liberty Style arts and crafts or the growing presence of stylish and costly architecture characteristic of Palermo north (ibid.: 306).

THE "SACK" OF PALERMO

More than other cities of Western Europe—certainly more than other Italian cities—Palermo was damaged by its rush into modernism after World War II. Sadly distorted because unregulated and undercapitalized, and further warped by the aggressive involvement of mafiosi in real estate speculation and construction, the modernist transformation of the 1950s through the mid-1980s is now referred to by many as the *scempio,* or "sack," of the city. The years from 1957 to 1963 were the high point in private construction, followed in the 1970s and 1980s by a greater emphasis on public works (see Chubb 1982: 132, 150–51). Overall, the rhythm reflected the rapid urbanization of Sicily after World War II, as a land reform and resultant mechanization of agriculture created a massive peasant exodus, and as rural landlords moved their investments into urban real estate. In the same period, an expanding national welfare state made cities attractive as a source of public employment. Palermo, which in 1946 became the capital of the new, autonomous Region of Sicily, grew from a citizenry of 503,000 in 1951 to 709,000 in 1981, an increase of 41 percent. Although an urban plan mandated by the regional government was developed in 1962, it had little effect on large and small investors, who hoped to profit from the resulting demand for housing and office space.

Uniquely unhappy events further distorted the postwar construction boom. Bombed by Allied forces in 1943, the city's historic center lost its moorings. More heavily damaged than any other southern Italian city, 70,000 rooms were lost, leaving nearly 150,000 people condemned to live in crowded slums, shantytowns, and even caves (ibid.: 129). Opulent *palazzi* were severely affected, so much so that their noble owners, rattled by the pending land reform, abandoned them to leaking roofs and damaged interiors. Vandals removed architectural embellishments from their empty carcasses—statues, columns, fountains, even the plumbing. Meanwhile, the opportunistic city administration collected the rubble from crumbling walls as landfill, dumping it along the coast. If the late nineteenth-century florescence of Palermo north had not already seduced the city away from its beautiful waterfront, the unsightly piles of junk on the beach would have been the coup de grace. Along the former avenue of elegance lining the old port, the landfill became an amusement park. This "lunar landscape" of Ferris wheels and bumper cars served as a focus of Sunday entertainment for Palermo's working classes, but to other citizens' groups it "mortified" its architectural surroundings. In addition to the Teatro Massimo, it was one of the most violated spaces that the antimafia movement hoped to fix.

Bombing raids had also affected the poor neighborhoods of the historic center. Here precarious buildings, at risk of falling, had either been demolished or were stabilized by densely crisscrossed wooden beams at the level of the upper stories, propping them up against facing structures. To this day, walking the narrow streets one enters the shadows of these overhead "bridges." Ferns sprout from abandoned stone balconies like "pale-green moustaches," writes Eberstadt, and because there is no preservation, everything "is either ruining or mutating from mineral to vegetable" (1991: 67). With time, a growing number of immigrants from Africa and Asia moved into condemned buildings; cloisters and courtyards were turned into parking lots, depots for construction materials and stolen goods, or artisans' noisy workshops; and empty quarters of all kinds lent themselves to prostitution and the retail sale of drugs (see Cannarozzo 1996; Lo Picolo 1996).

More serious than the destruction of the old city was the political decision to turn away from its restoration in favor of building a "new Palermo," at first concentrated at the northern end, beyond the Art Nouveau neighborhood of nineteenth-century expansion, then in other peripheral zones to the west and south. Here the built environment spread over, and obliterated, if sometimes oddly and in patches, the Conca d'Oro's orchards, villas, and hamlets. Aristocratic landowners were, apparently, as eager to sell their orchards as to sell their latifundia and this fact accelerated the cementification of what was formerly green. Many middle-class people of Palermo north remember the 1960s as a decade when the orchard you saw out your bedroom window or played in on your way home from school could disappear within days before your very eyes. In the words of urbanist Rosario La Duca, "Speculation prevailed over good sense" (1994: 48).

The remaining traces betray the violence: abandoned and crumbling villas totally suffocated by surrounding apartment houses several times their height; villas restored like movie sets for wedding receptions that are, however, hemmed in by the incongruous high-rises; and isolated overgrown gardens, their broken statues the humbled survivors of the orgy of clearing (see fig. 3). In one case, near the Via Notarbartolo, a double row of widely spaced palms that once lined the stately entrance to a villa was left standing, only to be intersected, at right angles, by a busy two-way thoroughfare. Cars using this road must wait their turn to pass between the trees that grow through the asphalt. In the farthest periphery, former rural hamlets are today the commercial centers of new suburbs. Modest owners of the houses and commercial buildings that line their main streets have eagerly sold out to speculative investors who either super-elevate or demolish and begin anew. The resulting mix of shapes and styles overlays a past of architectural coherence. At the same time, the automobile, multiplying in tandem with the suburban population, has turned these once sleepy village streets into quagmires of congestion.

Nor was this the worst of the *scempio*. The thinking of the 1960s was that the buildings of the historic center should be left to die; eventually they could be leveled to create space for a thoroughly modern, New York–inspired downtown. City investments in outlying public housing and roads, including a ring road projected in the 1950s, enticed private housing developers to the outskirts, although neither they nor the city provided the necessary infrastructure—gas, water, electricity, transportation, and schools (Chubb 1982: 151–56). Then, in 1968, an earthquake in the Belice Valley south of Palermo shook the old center one more time. The reaction to the disaster replicated the established pattern: the city would cover more orchards with tracts of public housing and relocate center-city residents rather than attempt to repair their compromised buildings. Numbering 125,000 in 1951, the population of the historic center fell to fewer than 40,000 over the next thirty years (Cole 1997: 30).

Hence peripheral Palermo's vast expanses of multi-story condominium and rental slabs, laid out in block after monotonous block, dis-

Figure 3. The "sack" of Palermo, showing the vestiges of a villa and its gate amid high-rises. Photograph by Alessandro Fucarini, Labruzzo Agenzia, Palermo.

tinguished from their Eastern European equivalents mainly by the pro-
fusion of cacti and geraniums that overflow the balconies. Some of the
slabs have penetrated the historic center, lighting upon spaces that happened to be cheaply available. Wherever one encounters them, they seem
shabby, both for their flaking and chipping cement surfaces and because
a heavy reliance on iron rods and railings for support and decoration has
produced, over the years, the stains of spreading rust.

Some blame the *scempio* partly on "the times," recollecting from
personal experience how attractive modernism seemed. Given Palermo's pattern of postwar growth, a large proportion of the consumers
of new housing were formerly rural people encouraged by the land reform, or by work stints in Northern Europe, to dream of escaping from
"backwardness"—to imagine becoming, in their terms, *evoluto,* or
modern. Easy credit, commingled with migrants' remittances, facilitated
their project. Anyone wanting to purchase an apartment could get away
with a down payment of less than 3 million lire (about $2000), with the
builder negotiating a bank loan for the difference. For employees of the
regional government, low-cost loans were a standard benefit (Chubb
1982: 129). In such an atmosphere, even many native Palermitans got
the idea that anything old was unworthy. The Art Nouveau decorative
arts were a particular casualty of this attitude. Younger people felt repulsed by them, calling them oppressive and outmoded. Little imagining their eventual value, they told their parents to throw out Liberty
fruitwood furniture and sell their turn-of-the-century apartments for
housing that was spanking new. When, in 1960, Palermo's one and only
"skyscraper" was completed—a mini-office tower in the middle of
what was once the Liberty quarter—these modernists raced with excitement to see its crowning red light go on for the very first time. In ret-
rospect, they confess, Prague would have been a better model than New
York.

But blaming what happened on the power of style—on the desire to
be modern—only goes so far. Narratives of the construction boom are
far more likely to point to the corrupt *intreccio,* or interweaving between political, economic, and mafia interests. Christian Democratic
politicians owed their success in local and regional elections to votes
that were mobilized by mafiosi, particularly those who had their roots
in the zones of urban expansion. Formerly agriculturalists, mafiosi in
these zones flooded into activities associated with construction—hauling materials, pouring cement, speculating on land, building apartments
for family, friends, and profit. Their role and the role of the politicians

in mutilating the postwar development of Palermo cannot be over-stated.

However one accounts for it, Palermo remained "two cities," socially and urbanistically in dramatic contrast. In La Duca's words, one was a *città fantasma* of war wounds and degradation, the other "monstrous for its abnormal volume of construction and lack of necessary green" (1994: 48). Urban sociologist Vincenzo Guarrasi calls this outcome "hyperurbanization" (Guarrasi 1981; see also Booth 1997: 174–86).

RESEARCH IN PALERMO

We lived in Palermo during seven summers between 1987 and 1999 and for six months in 1996. During the first two summers, we shared an apartment with a friend and fellow academic who had been involved in the earliest moments of the antimafia movement. This was followed by two summers in the borrowed apartment of another friend. Both were located in Palermo north, a comfortable base from which to travel the city, interviewing key actors in the antimafia process, attending meetings, conferences, and symposia, and observing public demonstrations, small group conversations, and intense debates among friends. In 1996, we rented a small apartment in the Albergheria quarter of the historic center (our home, as well, in the summer of 1989) from January until June. Long a "popular quarter" of Palermo, this location hosts a mix of underemployed Sicilians and new immigrants—Tunisians, Moroccans, Sri Lankans, Filippinos, Ghanians, and many others for whom Sicily is the gateway to Europe (see Cole 1997). Walking the quarter's narrow streets, shopping in its lively street market of Ballarò, entering homes that ranged from humble ground-floor dwellings to a sixteenth-century *palazzo*, and monitoring our physical surroundings for signs of change, we developed an appreciation for the challenges involved in restoring the old center without harming its residents.

Our residence during the summer of 1999 was just beyond the old city walls, along the road toward Monreale. Then, and in 1996, we studied antimafia interventions to "recuperate" the urban landscape of Palermo and antimafia programs of cultural "re-education" in the schools. Of particular help in pursuing the latter were the principals and teachers of four middle schools, located in the peripheral and more or less troubled neighborhoods of ZEN (Zone of Expansion North) to the far north, Noce and Uditore to the west, and Falsomiele to the southeast. Each school invited us to observe its various antimafia programs, to interview a sample of parents with children in attendance, and to be with the children themselves.

From 1965 to 1967, and again in 1977, we lived in and studied a rural community of western Sicily, set amid vast latifundia in the mountainous interior. More a town than a village, its approximately 7,500 residents were arrayed in a social hierarchy that included wealthy landowners, government officials, professionals, artisans, well-off and very poor peasants. Thanks to this experience, we well appreciate how closely rural Sicily is tied to Palermo, not only through the exchange of commodities and services but through its residents' multiple, ongoing relationships with urban kin and contacts. The town had a local mafia "family," or *cosca* (plural *cosche*), and, although studying the mafia was not our immediate purpose, because interacting with mafiosi was then a normal part of everyday life, we inevitably learned a bit about them. Having experienced this situation, we are burdened with a more nuanced moral map of who is good and who is bad than are some of today's antimafia activists, whether because they are much younger than we are, have always lived in the city, or both. A few activists have never been exposed to rural Sicily, let alone the rural mafia. In some ways we are at once outsiders and, ironically, more inside than they are.

Since the "long 1980s" it is no longer feasible or ethically uncomplicated for us to experience the mafia at first hand, but secondhand sources have multiplied. In addition to the historians' accounts noted above are the depositions of the so-called *pentiti*, mafiosi who have turned state's witness. Insignificant in the past, the number of justice collaborators against the mafia grew to more than 350 by 1997 (430 according to Santino 2000: 379). Their statements are obviously constructed documents, the joint product of an investigating magistrate eager to prosecute and a mafioso whose motives for talking may have little to do with confessing "the truth." Nevertheless, these depositions are of enormous value for their autobiographical detail, accounts of the production of violence within the mafia, and descriptions of organizational structure, norms, and etiquette. There are also judicial reports, obtainable through the press, as published books, or from the courts, which contain police and investigative information converging on the *pentiti* statements. Often they reveal the state of the evidence for relationships between the mafia and particular local and national, political and economic elites. We have memories of entering Palermo's handful of bookstores in the 1960s to ask for publications on the mafia and being made to feel intrusive and embarrassed. Today there are many more bookstores and in nearly all of them a vast assortment of "mafiology" is on display, the output of an awakened scholarly interest and insatiable demand for journalists' accounts. This book, *Reversible Destiny,* captures our own sense of the depth of transformation that Sicily has witnessed since 1965.

CHAPTER 2

The Genesis of the Mafia

To place the article "the" before the word "mafia," as in "The Genesis of the Mafia," is to risk attributing a misplaced concreteness to an elusive phenomenon. There is, however, another risk that must also be considered: underestimating the institutional energy and coherence of Sicilian organized crime. This does not mean that the mafia is an age-old institution. There is a growing historiography of mafia formation, all of which points to a relatively shallow time frame. The mafia dates to the second half of the nineteenth century, when it emerged out of the "transition" from feudalism to capitalism in (especially western) Sicily, and out of the politics surrounding the fall of the ancien régime of the Bourbons and its replacement by the Italian nation-state. This very history is a brief for defining the mafia as inherently ambiguous—both more of a "thing" than it appears, yet less of one than numerous authorities have made it out to be. An overview of bandit and criminal formations in other times and places reinforces the central argument about ambiguity. The chapter concludes with a preliminary assessment of what, in spite of necessary caution, we think the mafia "is" at this point, a sketch that will be amplified in the chapters to follow.

INCIPIENT MAFIA FORMATION: 1815 TO 1859

Sicily entered the nineteenth century as a vice-royalty of the Bourbon Kingdom of Naples but ended up in British hands when southern Italy was occupied by French soldiers spreading the French Revolution. After Napoleon's defeat at Waterloo in 1815, the restored Bourbons recaptured the island, hastening the reform of its feudal institutions along paths laid down by the increasingly powerful, and imperial, British and French states. Decrees passed between 1807 and 1810 had already attacked the use rights of local residents to gather wood and pasture animals on common land and cultivated fields after the harvest. Now feudal privileges were abolished, a land market created, and common lands enclosed, their use diverted from (collective) pasture to (private) cultivation.

Paralleling these reforms, the Bourbons attempted to impose an administrative hierarchy. In the eighteenth century, they had governed Sicily without provincial capitals, relying instead on extraordinary commissioners dispatched to deal with local elites directly. Already insubordinate, these elites grew headstrong during the British occupation. In contrast to the Code Napoléon, promoted in southern Italy, the Anglo-Sicilian Constitution of the time gave few prerogatives to the executive, vesting power rather in a parliament and twenty-three administrative districts. The restored monarchy consolidated these districts into seven provinces, each headed by a centrally appointed prefect, but a paucity of roads and financial resources undermined the prefects' efficacy.

As is typically the case when a land market is created, winners and losers appeared. Excluded peasants were promised compensation through the division and sale of the commons, but in the end, an emergent class of nonaristocratic owners, known as the *civili,* or gentry, received the lion's share—so much so that the number of substantial landholders increased in Sicily from 2,000 to 20,000 between 1812 and 1865 (Mack Smith 1968: 203). Apart from marrying into noble families and acquiring minor titles, the most effective way for members of this new class to appropriate land—that sine qua non of social worth—was to seize upon the administrative reforms and divert them to private ends. Becoming the (appointed) mayors, (elected) councilors, national guardsmen, and tax collectors of their respective rural towns, called *comuni,* they used these positions to usurp once common holdings and block judicial inquiries into the usurpations. In fractious competition with each other, they also favored their kin and clients in the distribution of public works contracts and municipal employment, drew up personalized electoral lists so as to keep their enemies out of power, and evaded taxation. Based on local archival research, Giovanna Fiume concludes that the prize of factional conflict was a monopoly of communal offices "run to accumulate, supplement, and consolidate family wealth through the looting of the public purse" (quoted in Riall 1998: 53).

Already suffering from oppressive and humiliating class relations under feudalism, peasants saw their situation deteriorate as feudalism was declared at an end. Rebellion flared accordingly. Well before 1860, police and judicial archives were rife with complaints about rural disorder. At the same time, Sicily, like southern Italy and indeed much of Europe, harbored secret societies, lodges of Freemasons and liberal intellectuals, plotting insurrection against an absolute monarchy—in this case, the Bourbons. Insurrections in 1820 and 1848 quickly became vehicles for expressing peasants' resentment and their desire for vindication. Indeed, the revolutionary turmoil that engulfed much of Europe in 1848, spreading to Latin America, was launched in January from Sicily. Then and in 1860, when they joined up as irregulars following Garibaldi, peasants burned tax records, cut telegraph lines, held up the mail, and attacked outposts of military and police authority. In between they spawned bands that kidnapped landlords, rustled livestock, and preyed on commodities moving through the countryside. Historian Lucy Riall uses *squadre* for the revolutionary formations aimed at state power, *bande* for the rural thieves and kidnappers, and "armed gangs" for less specialized groups comprised of former prisoners and persons escaping arrest. But, she insists, the lines were never clear. Quests for retributive justice and revenge motivated all manner of strong men—bandits, ruffians, gang members, and revolutionaries (ibid.).

Peasant disturbances were island-wide; however, as historian James Fentress emphasizes, in the western provinces they were more violent, more likely to incorporate acts of theft, arson, and homicide (2000: 60–61). This surely reflects the divergent agrarian histories of the western and eastern regions. In eastern Sicily, large wheat-producing estates occupied the plain of the Simeto River but left both the coast and the higher elevations to the specialized cultivation of orchards, olive groves, and fruit trees on smaller, more intensively exploited holdings. In the west, orchards developed around Palermo and vineyards near the coast, but much of the rest of the territory, regardless of altitude or accessibility, betrayed a long exposure to *latifondismo*—a regime of far-flung properties (latifundia) characterized in Sicily not only by their vast size but by the extensive way they were farmed. Dedicated to wheat, they also supported large herds of sheep and cattle, which were driven from pasture to pasture according to season. In addition to impinging on fields planted in cereals, this practice of transhumant pastoralism required deforestation, its legacy a landscape of forbidding desolation. As the Bourbon reforms abrogated rights of pasturage, and as Sicily's population grew in the nineteenth century, abusive grazing and animal theft became more frequent. Fentress refers to the interior mountains between Palermo and the southern coast as a "brigand corridor" (ibid.: 132). Here the *comuni* were "off the grid," each a nucleated rural settlement whose depopulated surroundings eased the clandestine movement of beasts to city markets. The lawlessness of this corridor is part of the reason why the mafia would gain a particular foothold in western Sicily.

Another part has to do with the significance of Palermo in Sicily's periodic insurrections. Paradigmatically, in 1848, revolutionary leaders—a mix of anti-Bourbon noblemen, intellectuals, and romantics—anticipated that urban rebels would attack the centers of royal administration and police stations in the capital, then be reinforced by country people from nearby rural towns, ready to deploy their knives, muskets, and hunting rifles against the retreating Bourbons (ibid.: 55). Although temporarily successful, such plans ultimately backfired, leading to the arrest and imprisonment, deportation and exile, and sometimes execution of the most important leaders (ibid.: 80–87; Riall 1998). But taken as a whole, the insurrections consolidated relationships between the rural and urban forces of disorder in the western half of the island. Anchoring this western bias in proto-mafia development was the Ucciardone prison in Palermo, completed by the Bourbons in the 1840s. A nerve center for the interpenetration of banditry and revolution—of the dangerous and the influential classes—it enabled arrested intellectuals and romantics to learn from arrested "outlaws" and vice versa (Fentress 2000: 149–50, 156).

ITALY'S UNIFICATION AND ITS AFTERMATH

In 1859, Francesco Crispi, a lawyer and revolutionary leader exiled after 1848, returned to Palermo in disguise to reignite the struggle against the Bourbons. This time, however, the rural contingent would be mobilized by a revolutionary from the Continent, Giuseppe Garibaldi, whose larger project was to draw Sicily into the Risorgimento, the movement to unify Italy. With an army of about a thousand, Garibaldi landed in Marsala, a small port in the southwest, gathered another three thousand supporters in a march toward Palermo, and entered the city by an unexpected footpath (ibid.: 102–5). Citizens created barricades with mattresses and furniture; Garibaldi's army seized the police barricades, city hall, the archbishop's palace, and the cathedral. English and American, French and Piedmontese consuls announced support, and on June 6, 1860, the Bourbons surrendered. By October, Sicilians were voting a plebiscite to accept the constitution of Piedmont and join the new nation, Italy.

During his brief "dictatorship," Garibaldi abolished the hated grist tax on milling grain, but this and other democratizing reforms were at odds with the Moderate Party of Piedmont, which, under the leadership of Camillo di Cavour, was the Risorgimento's preeminent political force. The governors whom they dispatched to Sicily connected with the landed classes, Bourbon sympathizers included, dismissing advocates of the common people as unreliable (see Mack Smith 1968: 438–41; Riall 1998: 129–30). Not only did Sicily receive Piedmont's flag and currency, the Piedmontese imposed their tax code, their military draft, and their anticlerical legislation. After 1862, 163,000 hectares of ecclesiastical holdings in Sicily plus 27,000 hectares of common land were sold at auction to pay off debts incurred by the new nation-state. As with the Bourbon reforms, local councils administered the land sales. Cliques of elites dominated the councils, scaring away bidders and flaunting the authority of prefects who dared to object. A parliamentary inquest of 1878 determined that 93 percent of the distributed land went to those "who were already rich," leaving thousands of peasants precariously close to landlessness and, in material terms, worse off than they had been before (Brancato 1977: 145–46; Clark 1984: 17–18; Corleo 1871; La Rosa 1977).

Understandably, the colossal problem of peasant unrest worsened, and with it the confusing mix of criminal and revolutionary activity. As Richard Tombs has observed, "Those most likely to participate in revolution were also those most likely to indulge in crime, for crime and revolution were symptoms of the same disease" (quoted in Riall 1998: 187). Now, in addition to the struggle for land, protestors had as targets the mounting unfairness of the tax burden and the new government's enforcement of conscription. Squads of rebels continued to form, and with them attacks on municipal offices, Carabinieri outposts, the government's telegraph lines, and prisons (Riall 1998: 163–78). Released and amnestied prisoners continued to join these squads or coalesce as "gangs." And bandits continued to kidnap landlords, make off with livestock, and commit highway robbery, at times with the aim of funding the rebels or embarrassing the government on behalf of the "revolution." The government's detachments in Sicily, in "vexed frustration and bewilderment" (ibid.: 177), began to see all Sicilians, including those who should have been their allies, as impenetrably "barbarian" or "other."

This mix of criminal disorder and political insurrection culminated in an antigovernment uprising in Palermo in the fall of 1866. Riall's survey of those arrested indicates that the rebel groups were not, as the authorities believed, rabble fired up by Bourbon and/or Republican conspirators but artisans and family men driven into the streets by a convergence of urban dislocations: the introduction of competing Piedmontese manufactures, the abolition of the guild system by legislative fiat, the simultaneous abolition of the religious orders (founts of artisanal employment as well as charity), the spread of cholera, and the attempt to enforce conscription (ibid.: 205–11). As in 1848 and 1860, bands and squads descended upon the city from the surrounding mountains, already energized by parallel revolts. Anticipating the Paris Commune, these rebels attempted to storm the Ucciardone, where 2,500 inmates were imprisoned, among them Giuseppe Badia, a fiery revolutionary leader (Fentress 2000: 145). Representatives of the new national government declared a state of siege, rounded up alleged instigators for trial in military courts, put suspicious persons under surveillance, exiling vagrants and idlers, and suspended freedoms of association and press. As might be expected, with their cells overflowing, the prisons became ever more a locus for the organization of rebel/criminal groups (Riall 1998: 212–20).

DEMOCRATIZATION AND BOSSISM: THE 1870S TO WORLD WAR I

Eventually, in 1876, a new regime, the "historic left," superseded the "historic right" (that is the Piedmontese Moderates) at the national level, with important implications for the south. By 1871, the national capital had been moved to Rome, a location both culturally and geographically closer to the Mezzogiorno. In contrast to the historic right, dominated by the elite state-makers of Piedmont, the historic left grew out of the democratic forces of the Risorgimento, among them a number of southern notables and lawyers such as Crispi (Clark 1984: 61–63). For the first decade after 1876, left and right made many compromises, arrived at through back-room exchanges, known as *trasformismo*, over which the prime minister, Agostino Depretis (of northern background), presided. In 1887, Depretis was succeeded by Crispi, who, after returning to Palermo from exile in 1859, had joined the national parliament. Defining himself as the Italian Bismarck, Crispi held the prime ministership until 1891, and again between 1893 and 1896, a period marked by

Italy's tortuous attempt to acquire colonies in Africa and by a massive peasant revolt in Sicily, known as the Sicilian *fasci*. He has gone down in history for bungling the colonial project and severely suppressing the revolt, in the aftermath of which Sicilian emigration to America swelled in earnest.

All told, 1876 initiated the absorption of the south into the Italian polity; southern deputies gained access to the state's resources, some of them becoming ministers or friends of ministers. "The Mezzogiorno found its state," writes Lupo (1993: 37–38). At the same time, state initiatives to build schools and railroads in the disadvantaged provinces and to encourage financial investment in their economies intensified. Support flowed to the Palermo Chamber of Commerce, whose members spawned a navigation company owning thirteen medium-sized ships, enough to bid on naval and other shipyard contracts. Commodity warehouses mushroomed near the port, which, undergoing improvements, became one of Italy's largest. And completing a transformation begun by the Bourbons, monasteries and convents were converted to state use as schools and police stations (see Schneider and Schneider 1996: 70–72). All were measures that laid the foundation for Palermo's Belle Epoque, described in chapter 1.

Competing with the postal savings system and the Italian National Bank, the Bank of Sicily and other Sicilian financial institutions mounted a banking and credit system that went beyond the traditional roles of public finance and short-term loans to cover bad harvests and weddings (Brancato 1977; Giuffrida 1973, 1980; Pillitteri 1981). In the early 1800s, English investors had opened up the island's sulfur mines, but otherwise, until the 1870s, overly cautious governments did little to develop resources. Now, two sectors—these sulfur mines in south-central Sicily and the vineyards of the westernmost province of Trapani—received a particular boost (Schneider and Schneider 1996: 69–74). Land in market gardens and orchards, much of it surrounding Palermo, expanded from less than 8,000 hectares in 1853 to nearly 27,000 hectares in the early 1880s (Bevilacqua 1993: 44; Scrofani 1977). Yet the growing state presence seemed to exacerbate rather than ameliorate Sicily's governance problems. Until just before World War I, when the suffrage was extended to all adult males, Italy had no mass political parties with the exception of a small but growing Socialist Party. Rather, restricted parties of "liberal" elites and "democrats"—formerly the historic right and the historic left—competed for ministerial positions at the national level. Parliamentary deputies from Sicily made themselves clients of ministers who dispensed the state's patronage, while local bosses, as "grand electors," both distributed this patronage and delivered the deputies' votes.

In the rural towns, *civili* landowners and notables took unconscionable advantage of this patron-client system. Arranging themselves into two or three factions structured by allegiances to the national "parties," they competed to dominate the municipal council, junta, and office of mayor. Whichever faction won used the state's police powers and largesse to enhance its following, usurp public resources, and weaken the factions that were "out." In effect, the police and the National Guard became the factionalized *bravi* of the most powerful landowners. The archival records of Villamaura, a pseudonym for the rural town we studied in the 1960s, offer a vivid picture of the scandals that ensued. To take only one example, in 1891 a newly elected mayor, allied with the ascendant national "party" of Giovanni Giolitti, struck the names of seventy-nine voters from the electoral roll and entered fifty new names. He then caused the records of literacy tests that purportedly justified these changes to disappear. Telegrams from the prefect urging restoration of the missing documents were of no help to his opponents, who twice appealed their case in court and lost.

Throughout the period of boss power, which lasted until the installation of tighter state controls under fascism, prefects and subprefects seemed ephemeral. Technically they could annul the deliberations of a local council or junta, point up irregularities in the budget, question new appointments, and order the reinstatement of dismissed personnel. They could require explanations for why a town ignored certain of its debtors but spent vast sums prosecuting others, or indeed why it granted its tax-collecting franchise to crooked contractors who extorted favorable terms by scaring off potential competitors. The prefects could even propose that the town administration be taken over by the state. But the council bosses had their own connections in Rome who could in turn "annul" the deliberations of the prefecture, declaring that the prefect was ill informed, out of order, "arbitrary and impetuous." In 1881, Villamaura's council wrote to the minister of justice to accuse a circuit judge—then prosecuting the town's secretary for graft—of having "spilt bile on the local administration" (see Schneider and Schneider 1976: 155–57).

Especially in the mountainous interior, Sicily was still plagued by a lower ratio of roads and railroads to territory than most of the rest of Italy, and this deficiency had a debilitating effect on the administration of justice. In 1876, the council of Villamaura requested in vain that an appeals court be established in the district capital, the provincial capital being too far away; decades later it pleaded for a local circuit court, deed registry, and notary public on the grounds that sixteen kilometers of miserable road and insecure countryside to reach these seats of justice were responsible for the "rancor and dissidence that eats away at families and at the community as a whole" (ibid.: 160–63, 174–75). Rural towns considered the comparable lapse in resources for policing to be even worse. To restrict animal theft, for example, livestock had to be registered, but mayors authenticated false documents that the rustlers used to market stolen animals. National officials accused local authorities of neglecting their obligation to maintain an armed, mounted guard, but local officials angrily complained of inadequate funds for arms, horses, and uniforms. In the end the town councils contracted with private guards, conceding to them the right to collect fees from property holders in exchange for protection against loss or damage (ibid.: 175).

Nor were the state-supported district police units more convincing. According to a famous 1876 inquest conducted by Tuscan parliamentarian Leopoldo Franchetti, typical district policemen spent hours in the inns and taverns of the towns on their itinerary where, setting their rifles down in the corner, they drank with "muleteers, traveling merchants . . . people of every type" (Franchetti 1925: 46; see also Blok 1974; Recupero 1987: 315–18; Schneider and Schneider 1976). During times of "high brigandage," outlaw bands kidnapped wealthy landowners for ransom and were not above executing their enemies, leaving their victims ritually mutilated to send a message (Pezzino 1995: 46–49). Yet even the most audacious bandits enjoyed the support of kin and neighbors, landed elites and notables, and the police.

FROM BANDITRY TO MAFIA IN THE BRIGAND CORRIDOR

The Italian state launched no brigand war in Sicily comparable to its military campaign against banditry in southern Italy. Nevertheless, after the historic left displaced the right in 1876, a new minister of the interior, Giovanni Nicotera, a leader of the southern left, and Antonio Malusardi, the prefect he appointed in Palermo, undertook to shame Sicilian elites into delivering brigands to the authorities. Several of the most celebrated outlaws were captured, and in 1886 a police delegate, Giuseppe Alongi, declared that "classical banditry" had come to an end (Lupo 1990: 135; 1993: 42–43). But although audacious kidnappings subsided, crimes against property continued; indeed, animal rustling flourished with the growth of urban markets. As Pezzino has suggested, banditry and its lore were by then endemic aspects of property relations in Sicily, marked as they were by chronic episodes of trespass, abusive grazing, sheep stealing, and crop theft (see 1995: 55–60). Early mafiosi arose, it seems, from the interstices of this situation, among an incipient entrepreneurial class of carters, muleteers, itinerant merchants, bandits, and herders. Forming themselves into *fratellanze,* or "brotherhoods," also called *cosche* (singular, *cosca*) after the tightly bundled leaves of the artichoke, they offered protection for a price. Property owners resorted for security to these nascent groups, engaging them as estate guards, rentiers, and all-around henchmen. To quote Lupo (1993: 11), "The threat of brigandage was used to convince landowners that the protection of their land should be entrusted to mafiosi."

Acting as private avengers and judges, mafiosi claimed to restore order, yet, a leitmotif of their ambiguous status, they were also a source of disorder, going beyond protecting property to protecting outlaws as well. When damage or loss occurred, they were able to negotiate a settlement because they knew or could trace the perpetrators, often having maneuvered them in the first place. The duplicity did not end here. Powerful elites—aristocratic and *civili* landowners occupying important political positions—protected mafiosi as they had earlier protected bandits, shielding them from prosecution by the state. This relationship could take two forms—*favoreggiamento* and *manutengolismo.* The former refers to "favoring" bandits or mafiosi with patronage, alibis, places to hide, and so on; the latter to directing or "using" them to accomplish one's own ends.

There are interesting differences between the mafia and banditry, as social forms. Whereas the economics of banditry revolved around theft and kidnapping, mafiosi deployed violence or the threat of violence to regulate or eliminate competition in otherwise legitimate activities, such as milling grain. Claiming to restore order and protect property within definable territories, they also extorted a regular tribute, or *pizzo*— literally, a "beakful," the word referring to the right of overseers to scoop a portion of the grain being threshed by the peasants—from activities controlled by others. In the transition from banditry to mafia, writes Pezzino, extortion became an industry of "expansive and monopolistic character" (1995: 47). Characteristically, those who protected mafiosi were more involved than the protectors of bandits in the criminal enterprise, more likely to make the move from *favoreggiamento* to *manutengolismo.*[1]

Anticipating arrests and even convictions as their cost of doing business, from the 1870s forward, mafiosi consolidated a network of territorially based mutual aid societies. Variously named (for example, the Fratuzzi, Stuppagghieri, Pugnalatori, Malfattori, Fontana Nuova), they were incipient *cosche* that enforced members' silence vis-à-vis the law while helping them avoid, escape, or endure imprisonment. Banditry was less institutionalized. Moreover, operating "outside the law," bandits depended for protection upon powerful elites who considered them an embarrassment and were capable of withdrawing support at critical moments. Mafiosi, by contrast, developed an *intreccio,* that is, a dense interweaving with the state. Although there is considerable overlap between banditry and the mafia, particularly before the 1870s and in certain places to this day, of the two, only the mafia aimed for a non-conflictual relationship with state authorities, so much so that *manutengolismo governativo* must be seen as an element of what the mafia "is" (Crisantino 2000: 90; Pezzino 1995: 46–47).

VARIETIES OF MAFIA FORMATION

Recent historical research has questioned the centrality of the latifundium to the mafia's history, privileging the towns and hamlets of the Conca d'Oro surrounding Palermo and Palermo city itself. All were loci of intense commercial activity linking Sicily with European and transatlantic markets for fruit and wine (see Crisantino 2000; Fiume 1991; Lupo 1984; Pezzino 1995). Over several decades, moreover, the rural towns of the orchard zone had sent armed squads into the city to reinforce rebel attacks on the symbols and properties of government. State investigators of the 1870s, inclined to blur the boundary between crime and insurrection, accused precisely these towns of harboring criminal sects, replete with secret rites of initiation (Fentress 2000). And perhaps they did. On the receiving end of state repression, "disorderly" persons from these towns had unique opportunities to interact with intellectuals and Freemasons in the Palermo jails. It is surely significant that in 1863 Sicilian dramatists Giuseppe Rizzotto and Gaspare Mosca produced a play, *I Mafiusi della Vicaria,* in which the word *mafiusi* referred to a group of prisoners in the Vicaria prison. Defining themselves as "men of respect," these characters exacted deference from the other prisoners, one of whom was Crispi, jailed for being a political conspirator.

The new historiography of the mafia includes case studies of local mafias in the area around Palermo in which we see, up close, how ambiguous this intimacy with insurrection could be. Apparently, some of the brotherhoods that developed after 1870 intimidated or sought to eliminate the revolutionary squads of an earlier time (ibid.: 200–211). In a study of the Bishopric of Monreale, Amelia Crisantino found that, whatever their provenience, local armed men deployed violence primarily for a different reason. They wanted to gain monopoly control of the most important local resource, ever more precious as the orchard economy expanded: water for irrigation. Sensitive to the limitations of police records for historical reconstruction, Crisantino questions their portrait of a highly structured and purposeful if occult political-criminal nexus, at the same time as she appreciates the examples they provide of specific state officials—policemen included—colluding to foster the integration of entrepreneurship and violence (Crisantino 2000).

It is not necessary to minimize the place of the brigand corridor, and with it the latifundium, in the genesis of the mafia, but it seems a reasonable hypothesis that the Palermo mafia—or better, the mafia of the Palermo orchards—overlapped to a greater extent with political insurrection than with banditry (assuming these phenomena can even be disaggregated). As will become apparent below, the Palermo region itself has long experienced tension between two modalities of the mafia, one oriented toward the latifundist interior, the other toward the port.

THE MAFIA AND POLITICS

Whether in the orchards or the brigand corridor, the most powerful mafiosi became the "grand electors" of parliamentary deputies, gaining influence in national government circles and a strategic role in the emergence of mass politics in the late nineteenth and twentieth centuries. Reciprocally, the political patrons, or *favoreggiatori,* provided access to public resources and a scandalous degree of immunity from criminal prosecution. This mafia-state reciprocity, which historian Francesco Renda (1987: 201–2) calls "that wicked deal," made it easy for mafiosi to acquire and carry weapons, intimidate witnesses, and fix trials. Famously, it insured that older, established *capi* (heads) would rarely go to jail, attempts to prosecute them ending in absolution for technical error or lack of proof; that younger *picciotti,* or soldiers, would experience incarceration as no more than a perfunctory interruption of their business and everyday affairs; and that mafiosi who successfully manipulated the courts and prisons would thereby enhance their credibility as "men of honor."

But the term *intreccio* signifies more than a simple reciprocity between the mafia and the state; it points to a vast gray area where it is impossible to determine where one leaves off and the other begins. To understand this, it helps to recognize that the state is not unitary. In Italy, indeed, it is common to use the expression "pieces of the state," which immediately conveys a generally high level of internal inconsistency and the possibility that, through a kind of relay system, one state element might engage with fractious local groups to gain advantage over another. Significantly, many of the earliest references to local *cosche* emphasize their relationships to "parties," not the state.

The first such official reference dates to an 1838 report of a Bourbon magistrate, Pietro Calà Ulloa, who noted that in the western province of Trapani, many local communities supported small "brotherhoods"—"types of sect called *partiti*"—that had powerful patrons and deployed common funds to influence judicial proceedings. Witnesses never talked and highly placed magistrates did not want them to (Blok 1974: 95; Lupo 1993: 23). This phenomenon was not officially named until 1865, when, for the first time in an official document, the prefect of Palermo Province, Filippo Gualterio, referred to the "so-called Maffia," which he defined as a criminal association (probably with statutes). It was "growing in audacity," he declared, thanks to support from powerful patrons: feudal lords at first and then "the political parties" (Gualterio, in Pezzino 1995: 29–31). In subsequent police reports "the mafia" appears as a network of "politically protected extortion rings" or "groups of criminals who terrorized a local community, living off extortion and other illegal gains, and controlling access to jobs and local markets." The groups were "always connected to local political parties and factions, whom they supported, and from whom they drew protection" (quoted in Fentress and Wickham 1992:189).

Beyond *favoreggiatori* and *manutengoli* (respectively, persons who favor and persons who make use of mafiosi) the reports refer to the figure of the *mandante,* who "orders" or initiates particular crimes, creating the phenomenon of "sponsored criminality" (Santino 1988: 205). In the words of Gualterio, organized criminals had not only "valid protectors and efficacious defenders" but also a "hand that directed them" *(una mano dirigente)* (Gualterio, in Pezzino 1995: 31). All of which points to a murky moral-political map. Did mafiosi help politicians accumulate political clout and economic resources? Did they conveniently eliminate annoying rivals? And/or, were those who accused politicians of this *using the issue* to advance their own "party" or faction? The notorious murder of Emanuele Notarbartolo in 1893 illustrates two fundamental aspects of the mafia and politics: how conflicting "pieces of the state" play out their antagonisms around local fault lines, and how conflicts of interpretation inevitably swirl around an accused *manutengolo* or *mandante*.

THE MURDER OF NOTARBARTOLO

The 1880s was the decade of the first great capitalist depression, the effects of which in Italy and Sicily were severe. American wheat, now transported to foreign ports by steamship, undermined Sicily's position as a wheat exporter and turned many of its landowners into protectionists. For the most part exponents of the historic left, their position was favored at the national level so long as Crispi was prime minister. In 1887, in 1888, and again in 1894, Parliament raised the wheat tariff. Responding to northern Italian interests, it also raised tariffs on steel and textiles, provoking a trade war with France, which countered by interdicting Sicily's recently developed export trade in wine, wine grapes, and fruits.

Crispi's commitment to protectionism was supported in Palermo by a coalition of parvenu *civili* landlords with residences in Palermo, a faction of the aristocracy, and the city's growing commercial and industrial bourgeoisie. At the center of this coalition was the grand bourgeois, Ignazio Florio, heir of shipyards, wineries, tuna fisheries, and the Villa Igea, who lost money in poorly timed investments as the depression deepened into a trade war in the early 1890s. Florio retained a capomafioso to guard his neo-Gothic villa in the elegant Olivuzza neighborhood of Palermo north but claimed never to have heard of "the mafia"—anyone who said there were criminal associations that involved themselves in elections was spreading lies about Sicily! When state authorities appointed by the historic right accused the Florios of being steeped in vile and cowardly relations with criminals, it only provoked the counteraccusation that, having failed to guarantee the elementary rights of Sicilians, these authorities were wrongly criminalizing persons who happened to be their political enemies and who were victims, not perpetrators, of extortion and intimidation (Lupo 1990: 149).

Arrayed against the Florio group were heirs of the right who, retaining the liberal, "free trade" orientation of the Risorgimento era, took a different approach to the agrarian crisis. When a foreign shipping company, the Italo-Britannica, proposed to redirect Sicily's lost trade with

France toward English ports, they responded eagerly, an affront to the
Florio group, which was keen on retaining its Sicilian monopolies. The
two clusters of interests were also at loggerheads over broader investment strategy in which the right, fearful of inflation, wanted to rein in
risky speculation, whereas the left (whose constituents would be called
crony capitalists today) resented this cautious stance.

Both factions were destabilized by the popular classes' response to the
agrarian crisis. Between 1891 and 1893 perhaps as many as 200,000 day
laborers, sharecroppers, artisans, and students, women and children
among them, joined the revolutionary squads called *fasci* (the word
means bundle or sheaf, as in a sheaf of wheat) in the cities and rural
towns of (primarily) western Sicily. Encouraged by the nascent Italian
Socialist Party, the squads staged flag-waving parades and noisy demonstrations against oppressive taxes, launched cultural projects to promote
literacy, and, in the summer of 1893, organized a massive agrarian strike
for higher wages and lower rents on the large estates. On January 3,
1894, shortly after returning to power, Crispi declared a state of emergency, ordered the dissolution of the *fasci,* and sent a royal commissioner
to Sicily to oversee the trial of their leaders in a military tribunal. More
than a thousand presumed activists were deported and the Socialist Party
dissolved on the national level (see Clark 1984: 102–3; Santino 2000:
43, 77–79).

Not surprisingly, authorities of both the left and the right claimed that
the *fasci* were a haven for criminals and delinquents. With a few exceptions, however, local histories suggest a growing divergence between
peasant insurrection and organized crime by this time. Sicilian sociologist, statistician, and political leader Napoleone Colajanni, himself involved in the Palermo *fascio,* was decisive about this in his turn-of-the-
century writings. Although of humble origins, he argued, mafia leaders
had established multiple connections with the landed and political
classes, which made them antagonists or potential antagonists of the
peasants' struggle. To proclaim otherwise was to obscure the real issues—
landlessness, oppressive taxes, and immiseration—that motivated the
fasci revolt (see ibid.: 36, 68–71).

The conflict between left and right elites in Palermo came to a head
on February 1, 1893, when Notarbartolo, former mayor of Palermo
(1873–76) and director general of the Bank of Sicily (1876–90), was
stabbed to death on a train en route to a town southeast of the city. Suspicion fell on two mafiosi from the nearby *cosca* of Villabate, yet no one
thought that responsibility for the crime ended with them. Notarbartolo

was a conservative of aristocratic background and European experience, a member of the historic right who, as bank director and then advisor to a subsequent director, had exposed a corruption ring in the bank: persons using bank funds were artificially inflating the value of shares in the General Navigation Company of Sicily, then taking advantage of the sale of these shares on the Milan and Genoa exchanges, all the while working behind the scenes to defeat the Italo-Britannica Company. At the center of these practices was Raffaele Palizzolo, an influential member of the bank's council.

Allied with Crispi, Palizzolo was a parliamentary deputy from the electoral district that includes Villabate, home of the supposed mafia assassins. As an important landholder in this district, he inevitably had close relations with mafiosi, not to mention an immense electoral clientele (Lupo 1993: 75–76). Political analyst Gaetano Mosca wrote of him that "his house was open without distinction to gentlemen and *bricconi* . . . of every type and class. He promised things to everyone, shook everyone's hand, gossiped tirelessly with everyone" (quoted in ibid.: 76). Palizzolo was one of those figures, Lupo argues, who "related to politics and property as an element of connection between the *cosche* . . . a grand coordinator on a subprovincial scale" (ibid.: 79). In the midst of Notarbartolo's tenure as bank head, he precipitated the crisis that led Crispi to dissolve the administration of the Bank of Sicily, naming Giulio Benso, the Duke of Verdura, as the new director (Lupo 1990). Shortly thereafter, however, Giolitti replaced Crispi as prime minister. Restoring the open-market position of the historic right, the new government sent a special envoy to investigate the bank. Notarbartolo knew this envoy, advised him, and was perhaps about to resume the bank's directorship when he was assassinated.

Many signs pointed to Palizzolo as the *mandante* of this crime, among them the work of the freshly appointed police chief of Palermo, Ermanno Sangiorgi, who, between 1898 and 1900, wrote a 500-page report detailing a "vast association of evildoers, organized in sections, divided into groups, each group regulated by a capo." Without sparing the names of the people involved, it paints a picture of dense interconnections between security guards and traffickers, landowners, rentiers, and political personages in the Palermo region (see ibid.).

In 1902 Palizzolo was tried and convicted in the Courts of Assizes in Bologna, but the highest court, the Court of Cassation in Rome, annulled the ruling on technical grounds—an outcome that would later occur regularly in mafia cases. This led in 1904 to a retrial in Florence that

absolved Palizzolo of responsibility for the killing. In the interim, the
Duke of Verdura organized a committee, Pro Sicilia, to collect money for
Palizzolo's defense. Its mantra, propagated by *L'Ora,* a new Palermo
daily owned by the Florios, was that by investigating mafia collusion,
Notarbartolo had sullied Sicily's reputation. There was, however, an antimafia committee even then. Headed by the Prince of Camporeale, it
sponsored the erection of a bronze bust of Notarbartolo that, together
with the avenue that bears his name, still commemorates his courage in
Palermo (see Lupo 1990; Notarbartolo 1977).

The Notarbartolo affair was a script for later developments, from the
powerful *intreccio* between the mafia and politics, to the divided role of
the judiciary in prosecuting mafia crimes, to the off-stage drama of a
peasant uprising, to the battle over interpretations. Even today, there are
scholars who doubt Palizzolo's guilt on the grounds that his initial trial
was influenced by the court of public opinion in northern Italy, which
was angry with Crispi and his close associates for Italy's failed effort at
colonial expansion in Africa and brutal repression of the *fasci.* The as-
sassin used a knife, they point out, which is the weapon of "crimes of
passion" in Sicily, not a shotgun, the so-called signature weapon of the
mafia (see Fentress 2000: 239–52).

The affair also revealed a geographical line of demarcation that
would reappear in subsequent mafia conflicts. Lupo uses Sangiorgi's report to reconstruct two grand coalitions *(schieramenti),* each with its
own political economy. The *cosche* of the orchard areas to the north and
west were geographically closer to, and heavily involved in, the city's
produce markets and port. Members supported politicians in local elections and received protection from them, but they organized their own,
inter-*cosca* relations more or less independently of this political shield.
At times these relations reached the level of a coordinated federation, although the individual *cosche* remained strongly territorial in orientation,
specializing in guarding property and crops and in the control and distribution of water for irrigation. And individual *cosca* members engaged
in commercial mediation, above all of orchard produce.

In contrast, the *cosche* of the south and east appeared less coherent.
Much of this zone was also given over to orchards and gardens, but these
were interspersed with large towns—rural towns of the sort that characterize the latifundist interior. Moreover, the entire zone was a gateway
to the interior, the main pathway over which rustlers and bandits drove
stolen livestock for clandestine butchering and sale in Palermo. Significantly, robbery, kidnapping, and animal theft were the premier crimes

of this zone, as opposed to the dominant crime of extortion in the city's hinterland to the north and west. Elastic relationships between local mafias articulated well with these crimes, as did the lesser concern of mafiosi with strictly territorial activity. At another level, the political figure of Palizzolo was the single interlocutor for the southern and eastern mafias, enabling a certain degree of integration among them (see Lupo 1993: 81–85).

While laying out these differences, Lupo warns against exaggerating them. Crimes that were typical of one zone were also found in the other (ibid.: 85). Anticipating the "commission" that united mafia groups in the 1960s through 1980s, leaders of the families of the two zones attempted a common command structure at the turn of the century, the *Conferenza*. Yet the division lived on as an economic and ecological substrate of mafia formation, resurfacing in the twentieth-century "mafia wars" as described in chapter 3.

INTERPRETING THE MAFIA: CONTESTED MEANINGS

The difficulty of defining the mafia derives not only from the ambiguities inherent in its relationships to society and the state, but also from the contradictory discourses that surround it. For, at the same time as police reports began to depict a secret, conspiratorial association, clearly bounded and sworn to *omertà*, the dialect word for silence in the face of "unjust" laws, they were countered by theories of a mafia-friendly Sicilian character, diffuse and ages old. The latter tendency to posit Sicilian culture as the locus of the mafia took two different forms, however. One was explicitly racist: all Sicilians are *delinquenti* at heart. The other amounted to a defensive attempt to render the mafia benign and romantic, "not a criminal association but the sum of Sicily's values," which outsiders can never understand (see Santino 2000: 91–92).

Following Unification in 1860, writers, policy makers, and public intellectuals (not a few of whom were southerners) increasingly represented all of Italy south of Rome as homogeneous and inferior (Petrusewicz 1998). In Nelson Moe's words, this new national discourse, the "Southern Question," added up to a "moral geography" of the new nation, in which all manner of social problems were located in a single region that was not only spatially but also culturally the farthest from Northern Europe—and the closest to Africa (Moe 1998). Moe analyzes Franchetti's 1876 report on the conditions of law and order in Sicily as a text in this vein, noting how it likened Sicilian peasants to the "sav-

ages" of North America, incapable of civilization unless guided by outsiders. To the influential Franchetti, interior Sicily of the 1870s was a
malign place where dangerous brigands and marauders dotted the "bare
and monotonous" landscape as if some "mysterious and malicious
power" weighed on it. As one approached the groves and orchards
surrounding Palermo, tales of violent crime transformed the scent of or-
ange and lemon blossoms into the "smell of rotting corpses" (quoted in
ibid.: 65).

This sinister image gave rise to commonplace descriptions of Sicily as
"a paradise inhabited by devils," a "cancer on the foot of Italy," a "coven
of mafiosi" where "neither customs nor laws can be civil" (Lupo 1990:
152). In the 1880s and 1890s, Europe's first "scientific" criminologists—
the Italians Cesare Lombroso, Enrico Ferri, and Giuseppe Sergi—applied
the theory of English Social Darwinist Herbert Spencer to their country
and its respective regions. Lacking capitalist industries and colonies, Italy
compared unfavorably to Britain, they argued, attributing the gap to a
compromised biology. Although each criminologist resorted to his own
distinctive classificatory scheme, as a group they propagated the idea that
southern Italians and Sicilians carried inferior Mediterranean-type genes
that threatened to dilute the progressive northerners' European endow-
ment (Alpine, Aryan, or Celtic). Most perniciously, the new criminologists sought to prove that Calabrian and Sicilian men were predisposed
to crime, using the variable "congenital Latin decadence" to account for
the southern crime rate (see Gibson 1998).

Against such racialized thinking, Colajanni presented his analysis of
the *fasci,* which attributed everyday crime or delinquency to the poverty
and suffering of Sicilian peasants and artisans who, he further argued,
were capable of organizing a collective movement outside of, if not
everywhere opposed to, the mafia. Among the Sicilian voices countering
northerners' racism, however, his was not the voice that prevailed. According to Lupo, Sicilian elites of the late nineteenth century, seeking to
gain acceptance from the *national* ruling class, promoted the idea of the
mafia as an "honored society." *Omertà* was based on the root *omu,*
meaning "man" or "human being," and could even be rendered as
umiltà—humility—according to this version. Turn-of-the century figures
like the physician and ethnologist Giuseppe Pitré, a leader of the Pro Sicilia defense of Notarbartolo, were exemplary. A prolific collector of
folklore, Pitré wrote that "mafia" meant "beauty, grace, perfection and
excellence of its kind . . . the idea of . . . superiority and skill in the best
meaning of the word" (quoted in Lupo 1993: 6).

Still today, vendors hawking their wares in crowded street markets use the word "mafia" *(che mafioso!)* to describe an extraordinary specimen of something—a perfectly formed, full, round cabbage, for example. Applying it to men, Pitré added this meaning: "the awareness of being a man, self-assertion, and more than that, bravery, but never bravery in a bad sense, never arrogance, never haughtiness." The mafioso, he insisted, "is simply a courageous and skillful man, who does not bear a fly on his nose . . . (who) wants to be respected and almost always respects others. If he is offended, he does not resort to Justice, he does not rely on the Law," for to obtain one's rights in this way is considered *schifusu* (disreputable) or *'nfami* (unworthy) (quoted in Paoli 1997: 31; see also Pezzino 1995: 24, 50–55, 123–29). Folding the mafia into a generalized cultural "atmosphere," blurring its definition by assimilating it to Sicilians' presumed exaggeration of self—of individual force or efficacy—constitutes a kind of Sicilianism. We will encounter it again in later chapters.

THE MYTH OF THE BEATI PAOLI

Romantic accounts of the mafia are, of course, close to the ways in which mafiosi represent themselves—as "men of honor" who solve problems (their own and others') without resorting to state-authorized law. In the mid-1960s, we were told by a mafioso that, if we wanted to understand "the true spirit of the mafia," we should read *I Beati Paoli* (The Blessed Paulists), a book he had been given as a young man. Authored by Luigi Natoli, a Sicilian publicist, under the pen name William Galt, it was first published in 239 installments in the *Giornale di Sicilia,* Palermo's main daily, between May 1909 and January 1910. A best seller, it attracted a readership in all social classes from the aristocracy to the illiterate peasants, who heard others read it aloud. Successive editions up to Flaccovio's two-volume issue of 1984 attest to its continued popularity (La Duca 1984; see also Natoli 1984).

I Beati Paoli narrates the adventures of an eighteenth-century Palermitan secret society whose members were *giustizieri*—literally, carriers of justice. Dressed in black sackcloth with hooded heads and masked faces, they met at night in the galleries and tunnels that honeycomb the city's underground. Here they staged trials of evil persons, pronounced them guilty, and dispatched some of their number to execute punishment, including death. The sect's claim to legitimacy rested upon the charisma of its members and their presumed religious authority.[2] Sicily's ruling class, a feudal aristocracy of awesome power and privilege, supplied a quintessentially evil character to the plot line, one Don Raimondo, who usurped his dead brother's dukedom by poisoning his young widow and robbing her baby son of his birthright. Honest common folk of Palermo adopted this abandoned child, knowing nothing of his noble origins. The intervention of the Beati Paoli on his behalf constitutes the central act of retributive justice in the novel.

In an intriguing introduction to the 1984 edition of *I Beati Paoli*, Umberto Eco points out that Natoli's colorful descriptions of occult meetings among masked men in underground caves and tunnels were written precisely as a thesis of antecedents, an act of legitimation, and should be understood as a charter myth for the mafia. Locating the novel in a genre of popular romances such as *The Three Musketeers* of Alexandre Dumas, Eco further draws our attention to its powerful images of unfair dealings, not only between the brothers of the ducal house, but also between the aristocracy and the commoners. Just as the Beati Paoli could right the wrongs that an evil duke perpetrated against his disinherited nephew, so they could intervene, piecemeal, on behalf of the dominated classes. For Natoli, and in mafia ideology, however, these ministers of justice were themselves outside the social hierarchy. The novel, indeed, makes explicit that the Beati Paoli came from all ranks of society, their individual status dissolving in uniform costumes and unifying rituals. Nor is this opposition to hierarchy a mere instrument of sectarian solidarity; under Natoli's crafting it becomes the reason why justice is possible. Acting without recourse to interested parties, representing no particular class interest, the Beati Paoli arrive at fair and impartial sentences under the tutelage of spiritual forces. Because at times their sentences sustain the poor against the rich, the oppressed against their oppressors, the weak against the strong, Eco is moved to draw a comparison with socialism, which, in the two decades before the Natoli serial appeared, had spread widely and been suppressed in Sicily.

The comparison is instructive. Rather than lead the victims of dispossession and social injustice in class struggle, the Beati Paoli rendered them the passive beneficiaries of swift justice carried out on their behalf by the sect's executioners. Although the people's lives sometimes improved, the significant interventions that made this possible took place beyond their control, above their heads, at times without their knowledge. Eco concludes that the producers and disseminators of mafia ideology wanted its social side to speak to inequality and class injustice—but to speak the language of autogenerative heroism in which clairvoyant superheroes punish evil transgressors, sidestepping any discussion of reorganizing property relations.

In depicting the Beati Paoli as ministers of justice, Natoli went to some lengths to minimize their possible interest in accumulating wealth or power. To the contrary, his narrative passes over other, already existing legends about the sect, removing precisely the element of personal gain. There are, it turns out, several nineteenth-century stories, plays, and diary entries from which to construct an image of the Blessed Paulists as cutthroat murderers acting for their own advantage rather than as altruistic and just executioners. An example is Benedetto Naselli's 1864 play characterizing the chief of the Beati Paoli as a scheming artist who had a rival artist brought up before the nocturnal tribunal for dishonoring a poor virgin, and yet another rival sent out to administer the punishment. Not only was the first rival executed, but the second, presumably because the police were tipped off, was arrested while committing the murder. He conveniently died in prison, leaving the field of fresco contracts open to the villainous Paulist artist (Naselli 1864).

In other words, the myth of the mafia as distilled by Natoli consists of two interrelated elements: that an occult sect of supermen can be trusted to execute sentences piecemeal against social as well as private wrongs; and that its members perform their services in the absence of any self-interest.

BETWEEN CRIME AND CRIMINALIZATION

For anyone attempting to grasp what the mafia "is," comfort resides in knowing that similar phenomena in other times and places are also suspended between conflicting interpretations. And no wonder, given their histories. In his "outlaw" survey, Thomas Gallant establishes that banditry is a frequent corollary of what Marxists call "primitive accumulation" (we prefer the term "primary accumulation")—seizures of land through military conquest, the legislated creation of private property, the exaction of tribute at gunpoint. The reason is hardly obscure. People resent being dislodged from the resources that form the basis of their livelihood and may take up arms to vindicate this wrong, above all if demobilized soldiers are part of their universe or arms are otherwise available. Rough countrysides—the difficult-to-police terrain of forests, deserts, and mountains—and a state's overall "thinness" on the ground further enable poaching, rustling, highway robbery, and other predatory endeavors, just as the high seas enable "rule" by pirates; these phenomena have an ecology and a geography (Gallant 1999; see also Armao 2000: 119–23; Birkbeck 1991; Herzfeld 1985). So do urban gangs, whose members share a similar trajectory of economic marginalization.

Primary accumulation is almost always defended by ideological justifications that deny self-interested motivation. Claiming legitimacy in the name of overarching principles—authenticity, the rule of law, divine command, manifest destiny, "competitiveness"—mega-predators tacitly "impute non-partisanship" and a "mutuality of benefits" (to borrow two phrases from Gouldner 1970) to their aggressive acts. Those who respond also seek legitimacy, in their case through a discourse of retributive justice, "taking back." The extent to which bandits and their organized crime successors express "legitimate" resistance to dispossession is, however, controversial, as illustrated by the debates surrounding Eric Hobsbawm's 1959 book, *Primitive Rebels,* whose concept "social bandits" depicted these rogue figures, the earliest Sicilian mafiosi among them, as an expression of peasant protest. An early critic was Anton Blok, a Dutch anthropologist studying the mafia. Far from being romantic heroes, Blok argued, bandits preyed on peasants as well as landlords (Blok 1972; Hobsbawm [responding] 1972). Similarly to Blok, Paul Vanderwood, an historian of Mexico, eschewed the Robin Hood image, defining bandits as "self-interested individuals and their followers who found themselves excluded from the possibilities and opportunities, not to mention the benefits, of society at large, and who promoted disorder as a lever to enter a system reserved for a few . . . the majority did not seek justice for others but opportunity for themselves" (1992: xvi). To these and other "revisionist" scholars, bandits depended for their viability far more on the protection of the wealthy and powerful than on the peasant world (see Joseph 1990).

A third, more complicated understanding was pursued by Ranajit Guha (1983) in his study of peasant insurgency in colonial India. Here we see that what bandits do is inconstant; they can be Robin Hoods in one time or place and terrorists in another. Most important, the meanings of their actions depend upon who is speaking. Whereas peasant observers might think of them as mythic champions of justice, to those with property and state power they are dangerous, a threat to public order. Conflating political protesters with robbers, cutpurses, and assassins is, to quote Vanderwood, "an ideal means of drawing attention away from any genuine peasant grievances [that] bandits might represent and of defaming or belittling political adversaries" (1992: xxxiii). In other words, states deploy labeling techniques to criminalize entire panoplies of inchoate defiance, the better to repress what threatens them politically or embarrasses their claim to rule (see Joseph 1990: 21–22).

A concern raised by this otherwise compelling approach is how little scope it allows for the actuality of organized crime as a vital social force in its own right. Theft and extortion are treated *either* as manifestations of resistance, mislabeled as criminal by those in charge, *or* as the work of real "criminals," understood as wicked, sick, or marginal to society— the concern of mainstream criminology but not of general social theory. *Whigs and Hunters* (1975), Edward Thompson's study of the politics of the Black Acts—a series of draconian punishments that the eighteenth-century English state imposed on poachers who blackened their faces for camouflage—hints at a middle road. In assessing the poachers' legal status, Thompson rejects the definitions "of those who own property, control the state, and pass the laws which 'name' what shall be crimes" (ibid.: 194). At the same time, however, he warns that just "because we can show that the offenders were victims of economic and social oppression, and were defending certain rights, this does not make them instantly into good and worthy 'social' criminals, hermetically sealed off from other kinds of crime" (ibid.: 193). Moreover, there may "have been something in the nature of a direct tradition, stretching across centuries, of secret poaching fraternities or associations in forest areas" (ibid.: 58). Newspaper accounts and letters of the time claimed that the blackened poachers took secret oaths, were organized into a confederacy, and swore loyalty to a quasi-monarchical organization headed by a king [!] (ibid.: 81–82). That these documents are, in Thompson's terms, folkloric and not evidentiary does not contradict the likelihood that elements of them were "true."

This possible middle road, pointing to self-organization among "criminals," has surfaced most recently in relation to Russia, whose post–Cold War privatization process has been accompanied by an increased presence of organized crime, often glossed as "mafia." To some observers (see Backman 1998; Verdery 1996), the problem has been exaggerated, on the one hand by Westerners who need to demonize Russia but no longer have a ready target in communism, and on the other hand by Russians who believe that markets inevitably provoke criminal epidemics. Others (for example, Gambetta 1993; Ledeneva 1998) believe that "mafia talk" references a troubling reality: the abrupt privatization of resources in the absence of a supportive institutional matrix renders the emergence of protection rackets inevitable. How else would the winners shelter their gain from the grasping and sometimes violent losers?

Like Thompson, Caroline Humphrey challenges the straightforward functionalism implicit in this model; the protection racket arises in each case from particular values, symbolism, and legitimacy, which develop from particular *criminal traditions*. Rather than "seeing racketeers only as agents who happen to have appeared on the scene," or who are labeled mafiosi by others, she argues, it behooves us to examine "the historical dynamic of a criminal culture that has its own momentum and attracts certain people to take part in it" (1999: 201). As "culturally distinctive groupings," the new Russian rackets use techniques of predation and patronage that "evolved from historically earlier Soviet contexts" (ibid.: 201). Specifically, peasant bandits, although they participated in the Bolshevik Revolution, were jailed for thieving by the Soviet authorities and, within the prison system, went on to generate a paramilitary culture with exclusive codes and rituals stressing honor (Handelman 1995; Humphrey 1999).

In other words, although criminalized, organized crime groups take pride in charting the means to a reproducible livelihood through crime. If anything, time in prison serves to enhance their skills and deepen their traditions. This mode of analysis, between crime and criminalization, informs the following preliminary assessment of what the Sicilian mafia "is."

WHAT, THEN, *IS* THE SICILIAN MAFIA?

Sicilian mafiosi, in the most general sense, mediate illegal traffics or use illegal means, including violence, to gain a foothold in legal activities. To operate in this fashion, they have to be entrepreneurial, opportunistic, aggressive, capable of violence. As such they share with bandits both a preparedness to murder, if necessary, and a sensitivity to retributive justice. As we will see in the following chapters, concerns with equity—with a "just" or proportionate distribution of benefits—drives mafiosi to rivalry and even "war" among themselves, at the same time as it energizes their continued push to penetrate new domains. An expansionist institution capable of reproducing itself over time, the mafia also draws energy from its organizational form and political connections.

For the most part, mafiosi recruit and socialize appropriate members, and look out for their interests, through local fraternal sodalities—the *cosche*. Legitimated through a charter myth and ideology of honor, these mutual aid fraternities obligate their members to be "silent before the law," while supporting them through whatever brushes they may have with the police, the judiciary, and the prisons. Rural towns in the western provinces, and the neighborhoods of the western cities, have generally harbored one such group—two if its factions were unable to coexist.

Consistent with this territorial grounding, mafia organization is to a large extent decentralized, yet constituents of the various "families" are in constant communication and share a sense of common membership. More to the point, Palermo and its hinterland have long been the center of gravity for the mafia, the locus for efforts at coordination in Notar- bartolo's day, and for the establishment, since 1957, of an admittedly fragile overarching "Commission." It should be noted that scholars of the 1960s (ourselves among them) questioned this extent of unicity or "thingness," so much so that Charles Tilly, in his introduction to Blok's 1974 *The Mafia of a Sicilian Village,* flatly wrote the following: "Sicily has never had any single organization one could properly call The Mafia. The Mafia supergang is a simplifying fiction, invented by publicists and by Fascist officials charged with eliminating Southern Italian lawlessness. On the other hand, there really are *mafiosi*—men wielding power through the systematic use of private violence. The sum of their actions makes up the phenomenon called *mafia*" (Tilly 1974: xiv; see also Hess 1998 [1970]).

In the 1960s, there was also widespread skepticism that initiation rites existed. To acknowledge them gave too much credence to the model of the mafia developed by the fascist prefect, Cesare Mori, whose police actions (referenced in chapter 3) were based on the premise that mafiosi were members of an *associazione a delinquere*—a criminal organization with clearly defined boundaries, rules, and goals (see Blok 1974: 144–45; Duggan 1986: 65–70). Both the depositions of the *pentiti* and recent archival studies (see Pezzino 1995: 89–119) have prompted a reassessment, describing in detail how novices hold the burning image of a saint while their sponsor pricks their finger and, mixing the symbolically laden blood and ashes, gets them to swear an oath of life-long loyalty and silence before outsiders. The new generation of historians, moreover, has traced this rite, and its associated commitment to secrecy, to the covert masonic lodges of the nineteenth century's liberation struggles (Pezzino 1992: 47–58; 1995: 5–7, 71–72; see also Fentress 2000: 26, 217; Lupo 1993: 182; Recupero 1987: 313–14).

To this extent, what we now understand the mafia to be is not inconsistent with police reports such as that of Sangiorgi. Although presenting their own problems of interpretation (discussed in chapter 6), today's "justice collaborators" lend retrospective credibility to these reports, which were, after all, based on informer testimony. We do, however, continue to question the tendency for police and prosecutorial models to represent the *cosca* and the coordinating bodies as super-secret, clearly bounded, and, like conspiracies, acting in concert, for this underplays the systematic practice of single mafiosi to cultivate strategic relationships in a wider social and political universe. Among these relationships, the most important are with various "pieces" of the state. Umberto Santino's insistence that the mafia's *intreccio* is the key to its economy and system of power is compelling (2000: 381). In this respect, the prototypical nucleus of Sicilian organized crime consists of loose, at times shifting coalitions between leading mafiosi (select *capi*) and corrupt elites (regional and national politicians, administrators, professionals, and businessmen) engaged in the accumulation of power and wealth (ibid.: 150)—not the overly conjured *cosca* or Commission. Chapter 3, which takes up the mafia's development after World War II, makes ample reference to such coalitions.

CHAPTER 3

The Mafia and the Cold War

Many people are convinced that, once suppressed by Mussolini's "Iron Prefect," Mori, the mafia was then given the kiss of life by the Allied military authorities during their seven-month occupation of Sicily in the period 1943–44. One vivid detail has long been emblematic of this scenario: that American intelligence agents, after negotiating with New York (and Sicilian) mobster Lucky Luciano, dropped a yellow silk foulard bearing Luciano's monogram from a plane flying over the small rural town of Villalba, signaling the onset of the Allied invasion. Surrounded by latifundia, Villalba was the home of the charismatic capomafia Don Calogero Vizzini. The story originated with a well-known journalist, Michele Pantaleone, a socialist enemy of Don Calò who was from a landowning family of the same town. According to Pantaleone (writing in 1962), after receiving the Americans' signal, Vizzini alerted his mafia colleague, Don Giuseppe Genco Russo of Misilmeri, near Palermo, to prepare logistic support for the advancing American and British troops. In return, Don Calò and other mafiosi received favored treatment from the provisional military government, AMGOT.

There is now substantial scholarship questioning the accuracy of this story, while at the same time pointing to a more nuanced relationship between American interests and the mafia as the Cold War took shape. *Pentito* testimony, journalists' accounts, and recent historical research together suggest that the postwar mafia was able to reconstitute its *intreccio* with the state and to penetrate the modern domains of urban con-

struction and drug trafficking, in part because of anticommunism—
American as well as Italian. This chapter retraces the steps and the violence that accompanied them, on the one hand among mafiosi, on the
other hand against those "pieces of the state" that dared to object. In its
concluding sections, we consider this license for violence in relation to a
covert political-financial shield, a network of super-secret masonic
lodges, secret services, and money-laundering channels spawned by the
Cold War. Although necessarily sketchy, accounts of this hidden territory help us understand why the end of the Cold War and the "fall" of
Italy's First Republic in 1992 have constituted so critical a turning point
in the antimafia process.

THE ALLIED OCCUPATION REVISITED

Following Crispi's repression of the *fasci* in the early 1890s, Sicilians em-
igrated in massive numbers—150,000 per year by the peak in 1913—the
vast majority to the United States, others to South America and Aus-
tralia. By returning, which perhaps a third did, and by remitting wages,
the migrants enabled their kinfolk in Sicily to acquire small parcels of
land and enhance their standard of living. Following World War I, however, the United States severely restricted the flow of Italian migrants,
while in Italy the fascist regime, consolidating power after 1922, declared emigration (unless to North Africa as colonial settlers) shameful
and strengthened its border patrols. Rekindling the peasant movement
was impossible under fascism, but frustrated claims to land and a decent
life continued to simmer below the surface.

For the most part, fascism was a northern Italian political development with less resonance in the south or Sicily, yet it was consequential
for the mafia. Viewing organized crime as a competing system of power
and a source of unauthorized violence, Mussolini empowered his
Palermo prefect, Mori, a veteran of other Sicilian administrative posts,
to devise measures to eliminate it. A few hundred mafiosi escaped the
heat by migrating clandestinely to America or Tunisia, and many others
operated illegal monopolies and extortion rings as before. Nor did the
mafia's *favoreggiatori* and *manutengoli* become targets of repression.
But there were controversial round-ups and arrests leading to exile or imprisonment, and the prisons ceased to operate like "mafia hotels" (see
Duggan 1986).

Before invading Sicily, the Allied forces had only very general information about the island, much of it outdated (Mangiameli 1994). This

heightened their dependence on persons of influence who could act as interlocutors with the local population—"prominent families" and representatives of the Church. The fact that a number of mafiosi and their associates, including Vizzini, were indeed appointed to positions of authority by the military government is partly attributable to their connections with these notables rather than any prior arrangement with U.S. intelligence personnel. Maurice Neufeld, then second officer to the American commander Charles Polletti and now a retired Cornell labor historian, remembers (personal communication) getting particularly thorough advice from Count Lucio Tasca Bordonaro, a major landowner in the province of Caltanissetta, where Villalba is located, and AMGOT's choice for mayor of Palermo.

Neufeld further recalls the command's alarm over conditions in the countryside, where, amid severe food shortages and peasant agitation for improved agrarian contracts and land, armed bands rustled livestock, preyed on rationed grain supplies, kidnapped people for ransom, and killed numerous Carabinieri and police officers (see also Santino 1997: 135–44). If the contrabandists and grain thieves continued to disrupt the system of rationing inherited from the fascists, starving people might riot. Mafiosi were among the bandits and black marketeers; they could also be presumed to be able to control them. The reports of an American captain, Scotten, suggest that this fact discouraged the Allies from contemplating the arrest and deportation of mafia leaders (Santino 2000: 133–34).

RECONSTITUTING THE *INTRECCIO*

Once the story of the Allied landing and occupation is shorn of the element of a "pact with the devil," one can also surmise that the mafia's rebirth did not require Allied intervention. In Lupo's words, the mafia "grew in strength because . . . it offered . . . a means of controlling the growing (postwar) problems of banditry and peasant protests while at the same time providing critical support for the political expansion of the Christian Democrats" (1997: 28). Both aspects—the deflection of peasant protest and the support of the nascent Christian Democratic Party (the *Democristiani,* or DC)—dovetailed with America's Cold War foreign policy.

American advisors contributed to the drafting of Italy's postwar constitution establishing the First Italian Republic as a parliamentary democracy. Subsequently, Americans helped set the parameters for this regime's approach to the Italian Communist Party (the *Partito Comu-nista Italiano,* or PCI), the largest Communist Party in Western Europe. Caricatured as "Bulgaria of the West," Italy seemed as worrisome to America as Greece and a strategic place for the installation of military bases. In addition, U.S. policy makers combined covert funding of the Christian Democrats with threats to withhold Marshall Plan aid if the Communists were to win national elections (Ginsborg 1990: 100–101, 146–52; Mancini 2000: 128). According to Patrick McCarthy, the DC, the Catholic Church, and their satellites, as well as the majority of Ital-ian voters, welcomed the Americans' sometimes "irksome" intervention but manipulated it for their own ends, leaving the United States "often exasperated by its inability to get its way" (1995: 44; see also Tarrow 1989: 38–39). (One imagines that the leaders of the Soviet Union, which consistently provided financial aid to the PCI, found themselves in the same boat—able to assure the Party's continued friendship but unable to determine its policy, especially after 1968, when Soviet tanks rolled into Prague.)[1]

The postwar Italian government was founded on the principle of uni-versal suffrage and proportional representation, and there emerged an array of "mass" political parties. Beside the two largest—the Christian Democrats and the Communists—the list included Socialists and Social Democrats, Republicans and Liberals, remnant fascists and monarchists. Five parties—the DC, the Socialists (PSI), the Republicans (PRI), the Lib-erals (PL), and the Social Democrats (PSDI)—made up the *partitocrazia,* or "party-ocracy," that dominated the governing regime. Over the nearly half century of its existence, the First Republic saw governments rise and fall, form and re-form, but in each case, the new prime minister and cabinet were drawn from an alliance of these parties that pivoted around the DC, with the Communists excluded.

In Sicily, the mafia built and maintained a reliable electoral base for this regime. As in the time of Notarbartolo, some voters were impressed merely to see local and regional politicians walking arm in arm with capomafiosi in the evening *passeggiata* (della Porta and Vannucci 1994). Beyond this, at election time mafiosi were among the party hustlers *(ga-loppini),* who rounded up the voters. According to one of the earliest *pentiti,* Antonino Calderone, between friends and kin an average mafioso of postwar Sicily could guarantee the loyalty of 40 to 50 per-sons. As there were some 1,500 to 2,000 men of honor in the province of Palermo, that would add up to from 75,000 to 100,000 "friendly" votes in that province alone.[2]

Generally mafiosi endorsed the centrist parties, the "democratic" parties, which, they believed, guaranteed a degree of political stasis that was "good for mafia." In Calderone's words, it was "always known that we could not get along with the Left . . . that we have nothing in common with the Communists." The neofascist MSI *(Movimento Sociale Italiano)* was also "off limits," in memory of the Mori experience. By contrast, many politicians of the center, above all among the Christian Democrats, became "representatives of the mafia" thanks to its voting power (Calderone, in Arlacchi 1993: 182–84; Rossetti 1994: 183–84). The favor was returned in the criminal justice sector, where aggressive police officers suddenly found themselves transferred to far off jurisdictions, forensic artifacts and incriminating documents unaccountably disappeared, and criminal trials were moved to different venues at critical moments for unexplained reasons. When convictions were obtained, they were often overturned or the sentences reduced on appeal.

In mafia lore, these outcomes, already common in the nineteenth century, are referred to as "adjusting trials" *(aggiustare processi),* and, as many *pentito* depositions now confirm, they were considered the most important quid pro quo for political support. Powerful persons "above suspicion" and operating at the national level clearly pulled some strings, let slip some words, whispered some off-stage advice or consent as their part of "that wicked deal." Many antimafia activists and prosecutors refer to such persons as the hidden "third level" of the mafia (above the first-level "soldiers" and second-level "bosses") and hold them in varying degrees responsible for the postwar power of organized crime.

THE RURAL-TO-URBAN TRAJECTORY OF THE POSTWAR MAFIA

In the late 1940s, peasant protest in Sicily and southern Italy was galvanized anew through local organizations whose leaders belonged to, or were supported by, the Italian Communist Party. Inevitably, the ideology of anticommunism informed the Italian state's response to the peasants' struggle for land and social justice. In 1963, the Communist Party section of Palermo calculated that, since the end of the war, twenty-seven union activists, Communists, and farm laborers had been killed by the mafia in Palermo Province; fifty-seven in western Sicily as a whole (Paoli 1997: 282).[3] The killers, however, were not often apprehended and, if prosecuted, were absolved for lack of proof.

In 1945, landed elites sympathetic to, and attempting to manipulate, a social movement for Sicilian separation from Italy created a Voluntary Army for Sicilian Independence (*Esercito Volontario Indipendenza Siciliana,* or EVIS). Having emerged before 1943 as a response to fascist repression, the movement became a vehicle for expressing landowners' fear of Italy's postfascist democratization and commitment to land reform (see Santino 1997). Among the "volunteer" bandits recruited by EVIS was Salvatore Giuliano, a black marketeer from Montelepre, nestled at the foot of a rock-strewn pass on the other side of the mountains ringing Palermo. On May Day 1947, Giuliano's band fired on a crowd of peasants—men, women, and children—gathered at the gateway to this pass, Portella della Ginestra, to celebrate the Festival of Labor. Twelve were killed and thirty-three wounded, yet relevant investigations were not pursued. Giuliano himself was subsequently murdered, in 1950, most probably by the mafia of the zone. Many are convinced that his assassination was at the behest of the separatist landowners with the tacit assent of the minister of interior in Rome, their motive being to silence this rogue figure before he revealed, as he threatened to do, who had "ordered" the Portella massacre. Adding to the mystery, Giuliano's material killer, although caught and convicted, was poisoned to death in his jail cell in 1954 (ibid.: 143–44).

Never having had a genuine popular base, after the assassination of Giuliano, the separatist movement dissolved, its major backers allying themselves with the Christian Democratic Party. Subsequent manifestations of separatist sentiment—most notably on the part of the scandal-ridden banker Michele Sindona, discussed below—have also lacked a following and fizzled out. Sicily was, however, one of only three Italian regions granted autonomy with its own president and parliament in 1946.

The separatists were not alone to disappear. By 1950, events like Portella della Ginestra had derailed the possibility of a broad, antifascist or popular front, leaving the DC-led Italian government to respond to peasant distress in a more limited way. Only abandoned and poorly cultivated large estates were targeted for division under a land reform that also advanced cheap credit for the purchase of agricultural machinery. At the same time, a generous "fund for the South" *(Cassa per il Mezzogiorno)* was set up to finance industrial and commercial development. Reflecting the success of mechanization in agriculture and the failure of industrial development, emigration picked up again, this time focused on Northern Europe. In the twenty years between 1951 and 1971, more than a million people, out of a population of 4.5 million, departed from

Sicily, not counting the thousands who merely left the countryside for the city (Santino 2000: 185).Remarkably, mafiosi infiltrated the offices that administered the new resources, defining them as preserves to be milked not only for themselves but on behalf of their many clients. Local bosses won contracts to work on roads and dams, to haul construction materials to building sites, and to organize the cooperatives that purchased the government-financed harvesters, threshers, and combines. Continuing, as before, to be involved in the commerce of agricultural produce, including the sale of stolen meat, now they also trafficked in jobs—stable, white collar government jobs, replete with health benefits and pensions.

They also thrived impressively on Palermo's growth as the regional capital and primary point of absorption for peasants leaving agriculture. In particular, the bosses of the orchards set about brokering relationships between public officials and construction entrepreneurs as the Conca d'Oro succumbed to urban sprawl. Bribes to politicians, rigged bidding, and collusion between firms that entered false bids or withdrew from the competition to "fix" the outcome were rampant. This, of course, can happen anywhere, but mafiosi introduced the threat of violent retaliation should anyone resist the way the deals were "piloted." And mafiosi influenced the eventual execution of the work, its final inspection and approval. Indebted contractors and subcontractors, not to mention politicians, obligingly employed clients of the mafia, thereby increasing its influence over voters. The result was the re-emergence in Palermo of the prefascist system of continuous and organic exchanges between organized crime and members of the local and regional political class (della Porta and Vannucci 1994).

From the mid-1950s through the 1970s, a clique of young Christian Democratic politicians affiliated with the national DC leader, Amintore Fanfani, rode the crest of this development, ousting old guard politicians from city government. The most notorious of the newcomers, Vito Ciancimino and Salvo Lima, were of modest background but had good connections. Lima's father was a Palermo mafioso, although he himself was not a "made member"; Ciancimino had been a black marketeer and small businessman in Corleone and was close to its mafia (Chubb 1982: 146). When Lima, having been the commissioner of public works, became the mayor in 1958, Ciancimino took over the Public Works Department. Together they gave a huge boost to mafia-allied building contractors, who, by one estimate, held 80 percent of the construction licenses even though four-fifths of them lacked the capital and technical qualifications to bid the contracts (Lupo 1993: 175). High up in Lima's "inner circle" were the up and coming La Barbera brothers, deeply involved in the building boom and protagonists in one of the mafia "wars" described below (Jamieson 2000: 21).

Another insider was Francesco Vassallo, who began his adult life as a cart driver hauling sand and stone in a *borgata* (suburb) northwest of Palermo. Helped by easy credit from friendly banks, he became a major builder of private housing after 1958 and, along with his banker allies, reaped a huge windfall from rising real estate values. He exemplified disrespect for the building code, erecting private buildings in public spaces and greatly exceeding their allowed volume (see Chubb 1982: 135–38). Of course, such personages mobilized electoral support for Ciancimino and Lima. As Chubb has put it, "The ascent of the new DC leadership in Palermo . . . cannot be adequately understood without consideration of the critical role played by key real-estate and construction interests in the consolidation of its power" (ibid.: 128; see also Crisantino 1990: 181, 221–39; Lupo 1993: 189; Santino and La Fiura 1990: 366–91, 455–63).

Lima and his friends presided over the robust investment of national monies in Sicily, part of the Italian state's "extraordinary intervention" in the south, which, like the United States' Marshall Plan aid to Italy, was motivated by the conviction that modernizing "backward" regions was the best inoculation against the spread of communism. Some of the funds went into public housing, a critical domain of "collusion in the speculative development of the city" (Chubb 1982: 130, 193–94). Others were invested in the extension of roads, water, sewage, and electricity to new neighborhoods, often not in time for occupancy but driving up land values nonetheless. Chubb estimates that between 1957 and 1963—boom years for the construction of both public and private housing—speculators made over $650 million in profit on real estate investments in Palermo (ibid.: 132).

In 1968, Salvo Lima became a national parliamentary deputy, but only after breaking with the DC's Fanfani faction to follow the competing, less intransigently anticommunist current of Giulio Andreotti (see fig. 4). Ciancimino, still a "Fanfaniano" and with three indictments hanging over his head, became mayor for a brief period in 1970 (ibid.: 146–47). By this time, Lima had arranged that an unusually lucrative concession to collect the taxes for all of Sicily be granted to two friends of his administration, the prosperous mafioso cousins of the rural town of Salemi (province of Trapani), Antonino (Nino) and Ignazio Salvo. In exchange for their loyalty to Lima and the Andreotti current of the DC, the Salvos' company, SATRIS, was guaranteed 10 percent of the take—

Figure 4. Giulio Andreotti and Salvo Lima in the 1980s. Photograph by Alessandro Fucarini, Labruzzo Agenzia, Palermo.

approximately three times the national average of 3.3 percent (Stille 1995: 55).

CHANGING SOCIAL HIERARCHIES

Once dominated by its grand aristocrats, Palermo had been modestly reshaped during the Belle Epoque as its grand bourgeoisie, exemplified by the Florios, relocated the city's architectural center toward the north. Now a less grand middle stratum, enriched through the nexus of politics, state funds, real estate speculation, and construction, was pushing out in every direction, "sacking" the city, it is said. How unsettling for the former ruling groups to have watched an expanded suffrage, a land reform, and the state's considerable investment in development put persons with "no heritage" in charge—middle-class professionals, state functionaries, Christian Democratic politicians like Lima and Ciancimino. Surely the old guard disdained these upstarts, even as they abandoned their antique residences for modern apartments themselves.

Yet the parvenues of the postwar era could not resist knocking on the doors of older elites, seeking entry to their fashionable cafés and shops, their clubs and social circles, and occupying the most modern of apartments in Palermo north. Recent depositions of the justice collaborators suggest there were several sites where these diverse elements could interact, among them the masonic lodges. According to Paoli, a few mafiosi (such as the Grecos, described below) could be seen in "the most exclusive circles of the Palermitan bourgeoisie," for example, the Press Club and the Trap Shooting Club (1997: 312). Eventually drug profits supplemented government largesse as a foundation for class climbing. Between 1951 and 1982, the number of bank teller counters multiplied in Sicily by 124 percent, compared to a national increase of 64 percent (Santino 1988: 230). The increase was no doubt higher in Palermo, which, although last among Italian cities in per capita income, assumed fifth place in consumer spending (Mercadante 1986: 89–90; see also Roldan 1999 on the "miracle" of Medellin).

At the same time as Palermo seemed to be shedding the most rigid aspects of its social hierarchy, the social distance was growing between the city and its hinterland—so much so that rural mafiosi, who had earlier enjoyed considerable clout within the ecology of rural-urban relations, risked losing position. The old Palermo, the baronial Palermo, was on a cultural continuum with interior towns like Corleone. Although flaunting an astonishingly opulent life style, pursued in extravagant palaces, it was not different in quality from what local elites pretended to all over the island (see Schneider and Schneider 1996). By contrast, postwar Palermo projected a different, modern image that redefined the island's interior, and indeed the historic center of the city, as backward, inferior, and unworthy—less "evolved" *(evoluto)* was the operative term. Mafia families of the interior towns acutely sensed the slight. In the words of Giovanni Brusca, a recent *pentito* from San Giuseppe Jato, high in the mountains between Palermo and Corleone, the urban mafiosi "considered [us] small town folk . . . rustic, not presentable in (polite) society" (Brusca, in Lodato: 1999: 50, 53).

Vincenzo Marsala, another rural mafioso, once told a prosecutor, *"Signor Giudice* . . . if you do not begin with the rural towns, this evil plant will never become extinct. The reservoir of the mafia is in the hinterland" (quoted in Lupo 1993: 205). Weapons are surely the instrument that makes this so. In the following synopsis of the mafia "wars," it is worth remembering that a critical ingredient was the disrespect that the Palermo-based bosses visited upon their rural cousins. As we will see, in a succession of conflicts over newly emerging urban opportunities, victory went to the party that was originally marginal to the city but also the most audacious at wielding violence.

EARLY WARNINGS

Palermo's mode of expansion during the 1950s created an uneven field of challenges and opportunities for the mafia families of the city and its surroundings. Mafiosi of the northern and western hamlets and villages that were fast becoming city suburbs were the immediate beneficiaries of the new developments in real estate and construction, to the envy and consternation of mafiosi to the south and east, who desired to right this imbalance. Communities in both directions were further torn by intra-*cosca* rivalries that elevated young, militant, and aggressive risk takers to leadership positions. The most important example was Corleone where a politically well-connected physician, Michele Navarra, took charge of the local *cosca* at the end of the War. Under Navarra's tutelage, Luciano Liggio (also spelled Leggio), reputed to be a *sanguinoso* (bloodthirsty) youth, got his start in animal rustling and clandestine butchering, then as an estate guard *(campiere)* on a latifundium. By age 20 he had risen to be the (youngest ever) *gabelloto* or rentier of this estate (Lupo 1993: 166–67; Paoli 1997: 309–11; see fig. 5).

Both Navarra and Liggio were connected to the murder of the socialist trade union leader and advocate for agrarian reform, Placido Rizzotto, whose body was found in March, 1948, near Busambra Rock, an outcropping above the town with the sinister history of concealing the skeletons of humans as well as sheep. An 11 year-old shepherd boy, Giuseppe Letizia, came forward to report that he had seen a man being hanged there. Apparently, he was so upset by the experience that he was taken to the hospital, a fief of Dr. Navarra, who is reported to have given him an injection from which he died (Chilanti and Farinella 1964: 44; Lupo 1993: 167; Pantaleone 1962: 134). Liggio was subsequently tried for killing Rizzotto as well as for several other assassinations, but not convicted of any of them, his apparent immunity before the bar enhancing his prestige (Pezzino 1995: 204–206).

The convergence of interests between Navarra and Liggio was to be short-lived. With the Agrarian Reform, Navarra and his friends were upset by the construction of a dam and irrigation system that threatened their monopoly over artesian wells, whereas Liggio, in a position to sell construction materials and truck them to the dam site, supported it (ibid.). In June 1958, Navarra's people made an unsuccessful attempt to kill Liggio.

Figure 5. Luciano Liggio, mafia boss of Corleone, enters the courtroom where he will be judged, 1978. Photograph ©Letizia Battaglia, from *Letizia Battaglia: Passion, Justice, Freedom—Photographs of Sicily,* Aperture, 1999.

In August, Liggio and his affiliates murdered Navarra and another doctor who happened to be in his car. Reciprocal killings continued until 1963 (Chilanti and Farinella 1964), during which time Liggio disappeared, having been condemned for the Navarra murders. Even as a fugitive, he managed the Corleone mafia from 1948 until his arrest and imprisonment in 1964. Mysteriously escaping from custody five years later, he was recaptured in 1974 and subsequently died behind bars (Paoli 1997: 310–11).

As was typical for mafiosi, prison for Liggio was less a confinement than a platform for continued activity, which, in his case, included the acquisition of a substantial property in the territory of Corleone and coaching Salvatore (Totò) Riina, a man slightly older than himself, as his protégé-capo. (Born in Corleone in 1930, Riina had participated in the assassination of Navarra and was on a path to becoming the most violent leader in the history of the mafia [Paoli 1997: 282].)

Another locus of trouble was the hamlet of Ciaculli on Palermo's southeastern edge, home to the extended Greco family of prominent mafiosi (Chilanti and Farinella 1964: 86–88; Lupo 1993: 198–99). Alexander Stille offers this account of the most famous of them, Michele Greco (nicknamed *Il Papa,* "the Pope"; see fig. 6), as he appropriated the fortune of his noble landlord, the count of Tagliavia: "In desperate need

Figure 6. Capomafioso of Ciaculli, Michele "the Pope" Greco, February 1991. Photograph by Alessandro Fucarini, Labruzzo Agenzia, Palermo.

of cash, the aristocrats tried to put the land up for sale. Only one buyer stepped forward. . . . But then, the buyer, despite being one of Palermo's leading real estate developers, pulled out of the deal, forfeiting his deposit. . . . [M]embers of Greco's mafia family bought it for a fraction of the original price" (1995: 174).

Politically well connected, Michele Greco tapped into government money for digging wells on this land and selling what should have been public water to the city of Palermo for profit. "In the hottest months of summer," Stille writes, "when water was particularly scarce and badly needed for the irrigation of crops, Greco sold water in canisters at exorbitant prices. The perpetual water crisis was maintained, in part, by Greco and his friends in city hall" (ibid.: 62).

In 1955, the city of Palermo relocated its wholesale fruit and vegetable market from the neighborhood of Zisa to Acquasanta near the port, provoking a ferocious encounter between the Acquasanta mafia and the "classical mafia" of Ciaculli, led by the Grecos. For the Acquasanta *cosca* to exert the expected territorial control, it had to prevent the Ciaculli bosses from reconstituting their prior domination of the market by anticipating payments to growers. Francesco Greco, a major Ciaculli wholesaler of fruit and vegetables, died in this skirmish. Presaging the eventual takeover of Palermo by the bosses to the south and east, however, the Acquasanta *cosca* lost two of its capi in rapid succession, and a third was then murdered in Como in northern Italy.

There is also to consider the urban and suburban *cosche* of the north and west, for which the construction boom of the postwar years was pivotal. In the northwestern *borgata* of Partanna-Mondello, for example, the sons of an itinerant charcoal burner and vendor, Angelo and Salvatore La Barbera, were on the move, bent on transcending the indignities of their poverty. Angelo, in particular, became the protégé of a local capo, and by 1952 he and his brother had organized a building supply company. He then murdered the right-hand man to Salvatore Moncada, a contractor, so that he could become the construction impresario's lieutenant. Well positioned to participate in the frenzied expansion of Palermo, by 1955 Angelo had become the vice-capo and de facto head of the Palermo Centro *cosca*.

Still in his thirties, Angelo La Barbera began acting like a man of affairs, acquiring bulldozers, trucks, and other construction equipment as well as apartment buildings. Generous and charming, he assumed the life style of a Chicago gangster of the 1930s, with new cars, luxurious clothes, and frequent visits to Milan and Rome, where he stayed in the best hotels, surrounded by beautiful women. Far from shunning his hotheaded past, however, he attracted audacious killers to his group, disturbing the delicate political-economic equilibrium that other mafiosi, especially the "peripheral" groups of Ciaculli and Corleone, hoped to foster in Palermo. The first of the recent *pentiti*, Tommaso Buscetta remembers him as arrogant and "uppity" (Arlacchi 1994: 115).

THE INVENTION OF THE "COMMISSION"

In 1957, Sicilian-American boss Joe Bonanno initiated a meeting in Palermo's nineteenth-century Grand Hotel of the Palms, where he mobilized the heads of several Sicilian *cosche* to create a translocal coordinating "commission," similar to that of organized crime families in New York (Bonanno 1983; Stille 1995: 102). Like several other transatlantic mafiosi with roots in the area between Palermo and Trapani, Bonanno was already deeply involved in the transport through Sicily to the United States of heroin that had been refined in Marseilles or Milan. As Lupo explains, Sicilian immigrant networks, dense with ties of kinship and friendship, were adaptable as conduits for heroin traffic, as were the businesses that exported olive oil, cheese, sardines, anchovies, and fruit. The *cosche* of towns on or near the western coast—Castellammare, Terrasini, Salemi, Alcamo, Partinico, Cinisi—several of them in the province of Trapani, participated disproportionately in the linkages, both because they were places where these exports were processed and packed and because they had launched the clandestine emigration of mafiosi to America under fascism. Apparently the mafiosi of Ciaculli and Corleone had many fewer American connections of which to boast. Even the La Barberas of Palermo had no American relatives who "counted" (Lupo 1993: 190–97, 212; see also Pezzino 1995: 219).

This is not to say that these families were disinterested in drugs. Lucky Luciano, dealing in drugs since the 1930s, had contacts with the La Barberas, who, along with Buscetta, became significant exporters. So did one of the Grecos, Salvatore, "the Engineer," who, as a former tobacco smuggler, set up a European channel of his own (Lupo 1993: 192–95; Pezzino 1995: 211–12, 219–20). More to the point, the syndicates that organized transatlantic shipments of heroin were self-consciously inclusive. Although the various capi, in deciding who would take part, favored affiliates who were closest to them, they also invited participation from a wide range of investors, among other reasons because it was imagined that the return of lucrative profits would serve to heal old wounds (Paoli 1997: 317–18; Pezzino 1995: 211–12, 297). It is even likely that Bonanno promoted the concept of a Sicilian Commission with the goal of suppressing the apparent division between the south and east and the north and west, a division that threatened the smooth flow of narcotics to America. The fall of Havana to the Cuban revolutionaries in 1959, and its consequent loss as a critical node in drug trafficking, soon peaked his interest in facilitating this flow (Lupo 1993: 196).

As if reaching for peace, the early Commission members came from all sides of the conflicts. Salvatore "Chicchiteddu" Greco of Ciaculli, Luciano Liggio of Corleone, and Angelo La Barbera's brother, Salvatore, all had seats. So did Gaetano Badalamenti, a powerful boss with a drug-trafficking brother in Detroit who hailed from Cinisi, Palermo's airport town just north and west of the city. Yet despite this attempt to achieve equilibrium, the new organization developed along lines that favored Palermo's southern and eastern hinterland, that is, the families that were somewhat marginal both to the export of contraband and to the building boom. For one thing, the Commission was provincial, not Sicily-wide. Representing the province of Palermo, it left out families from the Trapani towns whose Sicilian-American connections were well developed. Second, after a brief hiatus, in which it was unclear whether the Commission could elect a leader, the position went to the "southeast-erner," the Salvatore Greco nicknamed "Chicchiteddu" (Little Bird).

The nominal functions of the Commission were to settle jurisdictional disputes between the *cosche,* punish violations of the code of *omertà,* and regulate the use of violence. Presumably, the murder of a police officer, magistrate, politician, or journalist—sure to bring tremendous heat on mafiosi everywhere—had to be approved by unanimous decision of all the Commission members. Cross-*cosca* murders also required Commission approval, although *cosca* chiefs could authorize intra-*cosca* acts of violence in their own territories (Paoli 1997: 189). Many mafiosi were concerned that the Commission would become an instrument of one or another faction. Angelo La Barbera, the ambitious and glitzy boss of the Palermo Centro *cosca,* refused to recognize its authority altogether. When the contractor Moncada (formerly La Barbera's patron) complained before the Commission that Angelo was overcharging him on building supplies, the commissioners decided in Moncada's favor and "ordered" La Barbera to give up his headship of the Palermo Centro family—which he refused to do.

THE FIRST MAFIA "WAR"

By 1962 the stage was set for a protracted conflict whose principal protagonists were the La Barberas of central Palermo and the Grecos of Ciaculli. Known as the first mafia war, it was precipitated by a dispute over a drug transaction in which both had invested money, anticipating a profit. Two Palermo bosses, Calcedonio Di Pisa and Rosario Anselmo, entrusted a large shipment of heroin from Egypt to a waiter on a transat-

lantic steamer for delivery to dealers in the United States. When the cash
payment came back, it was significantly less than the agreed upon
amount, the Americans claiming that the shipment had been short. Suspicion fell on Di Pisa and Anselmo. Called before a special meeting of the
Commission, they successfully pleaded their innocence, but the La Barbera brothers remained unconvinced (almost certainly because Di Pisa
was a rival in the construction business, being close to the contractor,
Moncada). When Di Pisa was then assassinated, the Greco-led Commission, already hostile to the La Barberas, proclaimed that they were responsible for the "war," and ordered that they be murdered (Barrese
1999; Pezzino 1995: 219–20; Chinnici and Santino 1989: 256ff). Salvatore disappeared in January 1963 (his burned out car was discovered a
few days later in the province of Agrigento [Barrese 1999]). One of their
principal allies, Buscetta, and his entire *cosca* were expelled from the
mafia, ostensibly for too much drug trafficking with outsiders.[4] After a
series of reciprocal homicides and attempted homicides, two attempts
were made on Angelo, one in the streets of Milan. He escaped both but
was killed in prison in 1975 (ibid.; Santino 1989: 257).

The *pentito* Buscetta has offered a yet more convoluted version of
these events. Although the Grecos blamed Angelo La Barbera for Di
Pisa's death, according to Buscetta the murder was actually carried out
by Michele Cavataio, head of the Acquasanta *cosca*. Having his own
problems with Di Pisa and wanting him out of the way—and on bad
terms with the La Barberas, as well—Cavataio contrived Di Pisa's murder so that the La Barberas would appear responsible, an act of double
revenge (see Arlacchi 1994: 115–41; Paoli 1997: 189–90). Cavataio then
participated, along with Buscetta and another Acquasanta capo, in several car bomb attacks on the Grecos and their allies, considered enemies
because of their intrusion in the wholesale produce market (see Pezzino
1995: 223–28).

THE MASSACRE OF CIACULLI

One of these attacks, a car bomb planted in Ciaculli on June 30, 1963,
marked an important turning point in postwar mafia/antimafia history.
Seven police and Carabinieri officers called to inspect the suspicious-
looking car accidentally detonated its explosive payload and were blown
up. This event, the massacre, or *strage,* of Ciaculli, was the most shocking of a cumulative series of provocations that finally led to 1,200 arrests, a major trial (held in Catanzaro, Calabria), and the activation of

the Parliamentary Antimafia Commission. Meanwhile, the *mafia's* Commission for Palermo Province, already destabilized by internecine conflict, was dissolved, its members and their affiliates becoming fugitives from justice—a few to Brazil, Argentina, Venezuela, Canada, and the United States, where they opened other branches of the Sicilian narcotics traffic (Lupo 1993: 205–6).

Thanks to the mafia's ability to "adjust trials," by the years 1968–69 most of the defendants in the Catanzaro courtroom had either been acquitted or been granted reduced sentences on appeal. At the same time, it soon became evident that the new Parliamentary Antimafia Commission would disappoint its advocates by investigating only "small fish" (Pezzino 1995: 235–36). In apparent celebration of these outcomes, the mafia altered its posture of "laying low." Having discovered Cavataio's probable machinations in the 1962 murder of Di Pisa, the Commission's former leaders ordered his elimination, accomplished by a team of gunmen disguised as police officers who conducted a messy shootout in Moncada's office in December 1969 (Brusca, in Lodato 1999: 48; Calderone, in Arlacchi 1993; Lupo 1993: 189–90). Significantly, two of the shooters, Stefano Bontade and Salvatore Riina, would be on opposite sides in the second mafia "war."

Antonino Calderone has now told the world in his published "confession" that after 1969 the mafia was reduced to "starvation," then "saved by drugs." According to Calderone, the up-and-coming Corleone boss Riina "cried when he told me that his mother couldn't come visit him in prison . . . because she couldn't pay for the train ticket. . . . Then we all became millionaires; suddenly, within a couple of years, thanks to drugs" (Calderone, in Arlacchi 1993: 75–76). Because the mafia's involvement in extortion, the construction industry, and produce markets continued with little interruption, and because mafiosi had long participated in the smuggling of both tobacco and heroin, this claim is surely exaggerated. Yet international narcotics trafficking after 1970 presented a new and wildly lucrative opportunity for Sicilian organized crime.

Badalamenti was among the first to leap. With properties in Cinisi near the airport, a deep involvement in that facility's post–World War II construction and operations, and the gangster brother in Detroit, he had a longstanding logistical advantage. Stefano Bontade, son of a prosperous mafioso of the orchards, was another early entrant. Reconstituting the northern-western alliance after the demise of the La Barberas, he mobilized support from Badalamenti and from Giuseppe Inzerillo of Uditore and his up-and-coming son, Salvatore, of the neighboring *borgata* of Passo di Rigano. Conveniently, the Inzerillos had drug-dealing cousins (Rosario Spatola and Carlo Gambino) in America (Lupo 1993: 212).

Still attempting a balance of forces, the Commission was reinstated under the joint leadership of Badalamenti and Luciano Liggio of Corleone. When Liggio was recaptured in 1974, both his Commission seat and the leadership of the Corleone *cosca* went to his protégé, Riina (Paoli 1997: 189–90). Another Commission leader was Stefano Bontade. For a while "the so-called triumvirate Badalamenti-Bontade-Riina governed Cosa Nostra," writes Brusca, for whom the term CN, or "Our Thing," evokes the highest level of mafia coordination. The *cupola*—another favored term for the coordinating commission—was like "a happy family. . . . There were exchanges of favors (including) possibly committing a homicide to give a hand to whoever might be in difficulty with someone." So, for example, as a favor to Badalamenti, the Corleonesi helped him "clean up" his town of Cinisi (Brusca, in Lodato 1999: 49). But the apparent, fragile harmony was to be short lived.

THE *SCALATA* (ESCALATION) TO POWER OF THE CORLEONESI

During the early 1970s, French and American authorities broke up the "French Connection," after which Middle Eastern morphine base, previously refined into heroin in Marseilles, was channeled through seven clandestine laboratories established (with the help of French chemists) in Palermo and its hinterland. As was regularly the case with expanding opportunities, the new resource did not take the edge off existing quarrels; on the contrary, it worsened them. Along the southern and eastern side of the old fault line, in Ciaculli and Corleone, mafiosi nursed a growing resentment, believing themselves still at risk of losing out to the *cosche* of central Palermo and the northwest suburbs over narcotics, real estate, and construction. In particular, Liggio and Riina suspected Stefano Bontade of excluding them from the richest heroin deals, as if they were "country hicks" (Brusca, in Lodato 1999: 49–50). Maneuvering to prevent Badalamenti and his allies from monopolizing key positions on the newly reconstituted Commission, they strategized to raise the capital needed to become major narco-players on their own. Their aggression was especially evident in a series of kidnappings for ransom, committed without the approval of the Badalamenti group and against the Commission's rules, which forbade "men of honor" to engage in acts that the general public found reprehensible, such as prostitution and kidnapping (Paoli 1997: 141–42, 231–32). Not only were the targets rich men, they were construction impresarios who were closely allied to the northern-western alliance.[5] As prophylaxis against reprisals, the Corleonesi infil-trated the most powerful Palermo families, enlisting the support of per-sons within them (often also excluded from drug deals and feeling resentful) in order to take over the Commission. In the 1975 election for the Commission head, Michele Greco, "the Pope," close to the Corleone mafia, unseated Badalamenti, who in 1977 was "expelled," presumably for his American orientation and unseemly enrichment through drugs (Lupo 1993: 207).

It has been argued that the first volley of the second mafia war was fired in 1977, when the Corleonesi killed Carabiniere Colonel Giuseppe Russo (Pezzino 1995: 256, 263–64). The motive, as clarified by Brusca, was their strong suspicion that Bontade's group "had this colonel in hand," ate dinner with him, and were not above setting him up to arrest competing mafiosi. Riina, in particular, felt burned by this possibility, "after all the favors (i.e., murders) we did for them?" (Brusca, in Lodato 1999: 49–51). Brusca's father had maintained an arsenal for Riina on his land outside of San Giuseppe Jato. Although initially friendly with all sides, he eventually gravitated toward Riina. Brusca himself, a young man at the time, was recruited to the group of six, led by Riina and his Corleonese brother-in-law Leoluca Bagarella, that assassinated Colonel Russo.

Russo's killing was a major insult to those Commission members who were outside the Corleonesi faction and who had not been informed be-fore the event. The Corleonesi, however, quickly sought and won Com-mission head Michele Greco's blessing for the deed and in May 1978 were throwing down the gauntlet again, killing Giuseppe Di Cristina, a mafioso from the interior town of Riesi in the province of Caltanissetta, who was suspected of being a confidant of Colonel Russo (ibid.: 55–56). Di Cristina was a close friend of the Bontades and Inzerillos, and his murder, also without prior warning to the Commission members, took place while he was visiting Salvatore Inzerillo in Palermo. Indeed, he was mowed down in a drive-by shooting at a bus stop in Passo di Rigano, Inzerillo's very territory (Pezzino 1995: 267–68). Again Michele Greco backed the Corleonesi, spurning the protests of Bontade and company (Brusca, in Lodato 1999: 57).

By 1978, the Corleonesi no longer had to depend on clandestine lab-oratories in the Palermo area serving the Bontade coalition; they could get their heroin refined in new labs in Mazara del Vallo and Alcamo, in Trapani Province, in San Giuseppe Jato, and on a property owned by

Michele Greco (Pezzino 1995: 300–301). Over the next two years, between four and five tons of pure heroin worth $600 million in annual
profits and meeting roughly 30 percent of United States demand were
produced each year in Sicily (Paoli 1997: 317–18). In such a context, the
Corleonesi became contemptuous of the mafia's usual pattern of accommodation with the state. According to Calderone, the late 1970s was
a turning point in the political process, after which mafiosi felt superior
to politicians—that the politicians could "not refuse" their requests for
favors. Outright bribes and threats took the place of the earlier reciprocities. In the words of another justice collaborator, "We obviously
give votes to politicians of our choice after a previous agreement with
them, but they have to do what we say, otherwise we break their horns"
(quoted in Paoli 1997: 344).

Most dramatic, the group around Riina opted for a scorched earth
policy toward officers of the state: those who got in the way of the
mafia's expansion were to be wiped out. Like their earlier resort to kidnapping to raise investment capital, this decision violated the mafia's
own rules, according to which killing any public official, professional, or
journalist required the unanimous consent of the whole Commission. In
1979, without warning those Commission members who were out of the
loop, the Corleonesi killed Boris Giuliano, a police captain who was
tracking the new heroin laboratories. The next victims were two Christian Democratic leaders, Michele Reina in 1979 and Piersanti Mattarella
in 1980, the first because he was embroiled in construction contracts, the
second because, as president of the Region of Sicily, he was threatening
to become a reformer. Judge Cesare Terranova, promoter of antimafia
investigations, was also killed in 1979, followed in 1980 by antimafia investigator Carabiniere Captain Emanuele Basile. Then, in 1982, the Corleonesi murdered the state-appointed high commissioner against the
mafia, General Carlo Alberto dalla Chiesa, and the leader of the regional
Communist Party, Pio La Torre. La Torre had been a preeminent antimafia leader and ally of Terranova in pushing for effective police investigations and stronger antimafia laws. The next target, in July 1983, was
Judge Rocco Chinnici, head of the "pool" of antimafia magistrates in
Palermo. Referred to in the press as the "excellent cadavers," some fifteen magistrates, public prosecutors, and police inspectors were assassinated between 1979 and 1983, in almost every case because they were
engaged in the early stages of a renewed state effort to prosecute the
mafia and contain its narcotics enterprise.

Again, the point was not simply to remove inconvenient obstacles to

the free play of criminal activity. The ascendant Corleonesi, authors of
the great majority of these killings, contrived to commit several of them
in the territories of their rivals so as to focus the predictable heat of the
criminal justice apparatus on them. The provocation was enormous. It
drove one preeminent rival, Salvatore Inzerillo, to order the execution of
the prosecutor Gaetano Costa on August 6, 1980, in Porta Nuova, the
territory of Pippo Calò, an ally of Riina. Here, two motives were in play:
first, Costa had issued arrest warrants for Inzerillo and several of his
men; and second, Inzerillo felt compelled to prove that he too could stage
an outrageous murder in a rival's territory, and in violation of the mafia's
own rules (Paoli 1997: 248).

Meanwhile, the ruthless Riina ordered the assassination of none
other than Bontade (April 23, 1981), Inzerillo (May 11, 1981), and several of Buscetta's relatives—with the covert assistance of some of the victims' most trusted friends and lieutenants. One spectacular instance of
such duplicity concerns Rosario Riccobono of San Lorenzo, a *borgata*
northwest of Palermo. Initially close to Bontade, he "turned" to favor
the Corleonesi without other Bontade allies knowing about it. One of the
latter, Emanuele D'Agostino, innocently mentioned to him that Bontade
was hatching a plan to kill Riina during a plenary meeting of the Commission. Riccobono allowed D'Agostino to think that he supported this
strategy but then revealed it to Riina, after which D'Agostino disappeared without a trace (*Panorama*, December 17, 1985).

Eventually Riina set out to eliminate those members of rival *cosche*
who earlier had helped him on the grounds that, having demonstrated
their capacity to betray a former leader (on his behalf), they might now
betray him as well. Dozing off after a Christmas feast hosted by Michele
Greco, "Riccobono was awakened by a group of killers with a cord in
their hands" who told him, "Saro (his diminutive name), your story is
over," and strangled him on the spot (Stille 1995: 112).[6]

Between 1981 and 1982, two hundred mafiosi were killed in Palermo
Province and several others disappeared by means of the *lupara bianca*
(literally, the "white shot," i.e., leaving no trace of a corpse). By 1983,
the figure was five hundred for Sicily (Lupo 1993: 212–14).[7] One victim,
Inzerillo's brother Pietro, was found in New York with dollar bills
stuffed in his mouth and around his genitals as a sign that he had been
gorging on too much money. In Lupo's analysis, the "power syndicate"
of the more traditional mafia (the southern and eastern *schieramento*, or
"coalition") was "suppressing the enterprise syndicate, cutting out the
Sicilian-American axis and taking over the narcotics profits for itself"

(1993: 212–14). That these profits were at once substantial, irregular, and accessible to players on the bottom further destabilized the situation (ibid.).

Throughout the "long 1980s," the bloodshed continued with several additional victims. Allies of Riina decimated the investigative arm of the police, the *Squadra Mobile* (see chapter 6). In 1988, they killed a former mayor of Palermo, Giuseppe Insalaco, whose notes, found after his death, indicated his thorough knowledge of corruption in the city's construction industry. By this time the "maxi-trial" of over four hundred mafiosi in Palermo had ended with an impressive number of convictions. Later in the year, Antonio Saetta, the judge assigned to the first-stage appeal of this trial, was felled. All of which pointed to the crisis years of 1992–93. In 1992, the *Cassazione* (Supreme Court) upheld a majority of the maxi convictions. Signaling their keen sense of betrayal, the Corleonesi immediately murdered their former protector, Salvo Lima, and a few months later the tax collector, Ignazio Salvo. They then orchestrated the savage bombings that killed two of the most important antimafia prosecutors, Giovanni Falcone on May 23, 1992, and Paolo Borsellino on July 19, 1992. Two bomb blasts intended to destroy artistic monuments, one in Rome and the other in Florence, followed in May 1993, as did bombings in Rome and Milan in July (we return to these events in chapter 6).

The undisputed head of the Provincial Commission and of a new Regional Commission during these acts of terrorism, Riina called the *cupola* into session ever less frequently, making key decisions about violence in consultation with a shrinking circle of collaborators. As Paoli notes, in 1992 he ordered the tragic death of Falcone with another Corleone boss, Bernardo Provenzano, as his only sounding board (and Provenzano did not agree!). This, and the subsequent decision to kill Borsellino, was possible because, perhaps without precedent in mafia history, Riina had built a "firing squad" that would answer only to him. A master, too, at encouraging mafiosi to betray their own *cosca* leaders, at provoking rivalries within families to weaken them, at organizing disinformation campaigns to mislead the police, he had become a power-crazed dictator by the time of his arrest in January 1993 (Paoli 1997: 157–58, 249–53).

And to what end? The golden age of narco-trafficking did not last long for Sicilian mafiosi. The antimafia operations of the mid-1980s, the growing popularity and availability of Andean cocaine, and the global trend toward processing drugs closer to their point of production relegated them to a minor and less lucrative role. Nevertheless, the moment of accumulation enabled the Corleonesi to capitalize several construction firms, broaching their postwar ambition of directing the construction sector of the Palermo, and regional, economy (Centorrino 1986: 89–90). Based on DIA *(Direzione Italiana Antimafia)* evidence, Paoli argues that public works became a privileged locus for reinvesting drug profits, the goal being "complete control and the substantial internal conditioning of the entrepreneurial world" in this sector (DIA, quoted in Paoli 1997: 319).

In the past, each *cosca* had been free to impose kickbacks on contractors working within its territory, but now the Corleonesi sought exclusive claims over these relations regardless of place, engaging Angelo Siino, a wealthy businessman from Brusca's town of San Giuseppe Jato, as coordinator. Siino (described in the press as Riina's "minister of public works") articulated the "winning" families with local coalitions of businessmen, politicians, and public officials whose hands were on the system of parceling out bids at auction. Classically, the *cosca* of the territory where the work was being done skimmed 2–3 percent of the contract and was permitted to determine the subcontractors, the suppliers, and the pick-up work force, if necessary backing its requests with letters of extortion or menacing fires. By "piloting" which companies would win, in what order, and under what terms, Siino spread the rewards as evenhandedly as possible, enhancing the mafia's reputation for "taking care of its people."[8] And this at the very time when Riina was lurching into a reign of terror that would disgust even some of the hard-core Corleonesi (Paoli 1997: 320–21).

THE COLD WAR AND ITS COVERT STRUCTURES OF POWER

Situated at the crossroads of the Mediterranean, Sicily had long been favored by geography to mediate all manner of contraband.[9] Over and above its established smuggling networks, it had a century-long history of emigration to the United States and waves of migration to northern Italy and Northern Europe in the 1960s. Drug couriers could easily be recruited from among the thousands who traveled regularly to these destinations, their bona fides vouched for by ties of licit business and kinship. And Sicily had the mafia, an institution tailored for organizing illegal traffics. If a trafficker who mobilized the investments of others to finance a particular shipment failed to pay the promised return, mafia leaders could punish him, possibly with death. More to the point, in addition to policing drug deals, the mafia policed the state, both by eliminating troublesome officials intent on investigations and by its inter-twining with "third-level" officials and politicians. Indeed, what is most upsetting to the antimafia forces is that the entry of the mafia into nar-cotics trafficking took place with the studied ignorance—if not the out-right encouragement—of elements of the Italian state. In political ana-lyst Carlo Giuseppe Rossetti's words, the governing class of Italy sustained a "substantially passive attitude" toward the advances of the drug mafia, for a long time offering no "organic legislative strategy to counter the menace." Rather, with a few exceptions, the establish-ment—the governmental regime, Parliament, mass media, and intellec-tuals—"consented that criminal potentates (would) prosper." This vir-tual absence of countermeasures, says Rossetti, "is an index of the indirect complicity of the political class" (1994: 84–85).

In the climate of the antimafia investigations of the last decade, and in light of the quest for transparency associated with the end of the Cold War, shreds of evidence are accumulating that point to complicitous re-lations transcending even this class. According to a 1994 report by the Ministry of the Interior, in a section entitled "The Mafia and the Social System," the "long 1980s" saw a "progressive decline of consent from civil society" such that the mafia had to increase "the invisibility of its modus operandi and . . . ever more take recourse, when compared to the past, to a network of clandestine relations" (Ministry of the Interior 1994; see also Paoli 1996: 18; 1997). Coordinating the illegal and global traffic in heroin in particular required more rarified forms of collusion, facilitated by covert masonic lodges, provocateurs, and spies (Ministry of the Interior 1994; see also Paoli 1996: 8). The following pages attempt to reconstruct what is now known about this extraordinary aspect of the Cold War decades. It might be noted, in passing, that the apogee of this period in the late 1980s coincided with the spreading intellectual fash-ion of extreme epistemological doubt—with the conviction that we can never "know" reality or, indeed, that reality, apart from people's claims about it, does not exist.

As the organized crime groups of southern Italy and Sicily were nur-turing their relationship with the Christian Democratic Party after World War II, nuclei of former fascists, secret service operatives, and military personnel were weaving a different, but eventually overlapping, Cold War structure of power in the north. This web resembled the covert cliques of army officers and secret service personnel that staged coups d'etat in Greece and several Latin American countries during the 1960s and 1970s. Indeed, both the CIA and NATO had contingency plans for

Italy similar to those deployed in Greece and Chile should a popular front or Communist-Socialist alliance succeed in forming a government. No wonder, perhaps, that the colonels' coup in Greece and the coup against Allende in Chile were taken as object lessons by many leading Italian Communists and Socialists, who, in different degrees, moved toward the center beginning in the 1970s (see Ginsborg 1990: 258–59, 333–35; McCarthy 1995: 7, 44–45; Treverton 1987: 38–39).

Right-wing counterrevolutionaries actually attempted to mount such a coup in Italy, first in 1964, then again in 1970, and although the turbid plans failed to materialize, the plotters were later accused of other deeds (see Paoli 1996: 27, for reference to a further, 1974 plot). Agostino Cordova, an investigating magistrate in Palmi, Calabria, has conducted an exhaustive study of a rash of terrorist acts from 1969 to 1974, as well as of the bombing of the Bologna railroad station in 1980 in which 85 people died and 200 were wounded. Although ultra-left terrorist groups were also operating in these years, his 1993 report argues that these particular incidents had "germinated in the 'humus' of right-wing secret associations" (see Commissione Parlamentare Antimafia 1993; Paoli 1996: 30–31). Still being pursued are answers to a series of deeper questions: Were the center and right-wing currents of the Christian Democratic Party complicitous in the 1978 assassination of Aldo Moro, the Christian Democratic prime minister who was kidnapped by terrorists of the extreme left just as he was about to forge an "historic compromise" with the Communist Party? Can other terrorist bombings taking place between 1979 and 1981 be attributed to the occult network of coup plotters outlined above? And did the bombings utilize explosives stolen from secret weapons caches that NATO had "left behind" in Europe, in case of a Soviet invasion? NATO's "Project Stay Behind," known as "Gladio" in Italy, had supposedly been dismantled in 1972, but not all of the arms and munitions could be located when the covert training of militias finally came to an end.

Italy harbors a rich array of secretive organizations whose legal status was won—and lost, then won again—in the course of an historic struggle. For example, the historic right of the late nineteenth century banned the religious fraternity of the Knights of the Holy Sepulchre, but the organization is now sanctioned as a prestigious meeting ground for right-wing Catholics. So is Opus Dei, thought to have seventy thousand Italian adherents as well as a presence in some fifty countries (*Il Manifesto*, January 18, 1997). But of all Italian secret societies, Freemasonry is the most important. This fraternal organization, declared by Clement

XII to be incompatible with Catholic doctrine, was interdicted by the Vatican in 1738. Masonic lodges persisted, however, playing a critical role in the Risorgimento. They were then persecuted by Mussolini, with masons sympathetic to the fascist regime voluntarily giving up membership. Other masons went underground, reconstituting themselves after the war into two divisions: the English-affiliated *Grande Oriente d'Italia,* consisting of some 600 lodges, and the *Gran Loggia d'Italia,* a smaller network of 250 chapters oriented toward France and Belgium (Forgione and Mondani 1994; Mola 1992). Recruiting "liberal-minded" elites committed to the right of "free association," Italian masons were estimated to number some fifteen thousand in the 1980s (Di Bernardo 1987). They are, they insist, "neither a religion, nor a philosophy, nor a political ideology or socio-economic program; but rather *a meeting place for persons who would otherwise not be able to encounter each other*" (added emphasis; Mola 1992: 757).

Apparently, the plotters of the 1970 coup—the so-called Borghese Coup—forged their anticommunist alliance by transforming certain masonic lodges into meeting places for a more diverse than usual representation of elites, including some skilled in the use of violence. In the language of the Italian press, these branches of transformed Freemasonry were "covert" or "deviated." The model was the infamous lodge *Propaganda Due,* or P2, founded by a former Tuscan fascist and dual citizen of Italy and Argentina, Licio Gelli, in the mid-1960s. Gelli was prodigious at enrolling like-minded men of the military, the police, and the secret services, as well as highly placed personages in government, business, and the professions (De Lutiis 1991: 284–87). A police raid of his Arezzo villa in March 1981 uncovered a list that included several such members and evidence that the lodge had developed a so-called strategy of tension during the 1970s, aimed at using systematic blackmail, bribes, promises of advancement, and intimidation to displace left-of-center forces from the government (Nicastro 1993: 166).

In postwar Sicily as in Italy, various elites—doctors, lawyers, businessmen, government officials, and heads of institutions—joined masonic lodges in large numbers. According to Buscetta, however, in his day it was "absolutely prohibited for a man of honor to be a member of a masonic order . . . their aims were totally different and in part incompatible" (Quoted in ibid.: 33). Calderone says the same, but from a different angle. Many judges were masons, he reports, which tempted the mafia to want a relationship, yet the masons considered mafiosi "too cunning to be inducted." For a mafioso to join, moreover, would have meant to serve two masters—with the potential to betray one or the other (Calderone, in Arlacchi 1993: 178–79). And yet, sharing a similar logic of secrecy, initiation, and fraternal solidarity, there was a certain affinity between the two institutions, and some mafiosi did participate in Freemasonry. Supposedly, the important boss Salvatore Greco, nick-named "The Engineer," joined the Garibaldi Lodge in Palermo in 1946. His relative, Antonino Cottone of Villabate, was a member of another lodge, the Lux, from 1944 until 1956. A significant mafioso-mason was Nino Salvo, who, as noted above, held the lucrative tax-collecting fran-chise for all of Sicily in the postwar decades and whose brother Alberto also belonged (Nicastro 1993: 190). As the Corleonesi gained ascen-dancy in the 1980s, Riina engaged a Palermitan, Pino Mandalari, as his accountant and business advisor. Both Mandalari and Siino, his "minis-ter of public works," were at once masons and collusive with the mafia (ibid.: 188–94).

Calderone reports that in planning for the attempted coup of 1970, the nucleus of plotters approached certain "men of honor" to engage their participation in the installation of new prefects, but the mafia only entertained the idea as a bluff, hoping to "adjust" several trials without actually having to do anything (Calderone, in Arlacchi 1993: 83–86). The coup having failed, Gelli and the inner circle of *Propaganda Due* elaborated their "strategy of tension." In 1977, Stefano Bontade, a for-midable player in the expansion of narco-trafficking, announced that certain masons wanted to form a coalition with the mafia's highest-ranking members, two or three from each province. Michele Greco (cousin of Salvatore) and Bontade himself were chosen from the province of Palermo, Pippo Calderone (Antonino's brother) from Catania (Calderone in Arlacchi 1993: 178–79; Nicastro 1993: 188). According to the former grandmaster of the *Grande Oriente,* Giuliano Di Bernardo, during the years 1976–80, mafiosi competed to become masons (Di Bernardo 1987; see also Paoli 1996); it was the drug mafia's way of ap-proaching and infiltrating power (Ministry of the Interior 1994).

As the boundary between the mafia and the masons became blurred in the late 1970s, newspapers reported a growing rift in Sicilian masonry between an older faction, loyal to its traditions, and a new, brazen group that admitted anyone. Whereas masonry had once been exclusive, re-stricted to bankers, professionals, and leading businessmen seeking to create a nucleus of power, in the new, "squalid situation," regardless of their place in society, ideologues were joining the super-secret lodges and so were mafiosi. As Calderone put it, the initiative for an alliance with mafiosi came from a new secret lodge whose actions were hidden, even from the members of Freemasonry itself (Calderone, in Arlacchi 1993: 178–79).

Thanks to recent investigations, it is now known that masonic lodges of varying degrees of "deviation" multiplied in Sicily during the "long 1980s"; indeed, the names of some of them became familiar watchwords in the press. Readers know, for example, that the sign, *"Centro Socio-logico Italiano,"* posted on the door of a *palazzo* in Palermo's Via Roma, is actually a cover for five lodges that hold their meetings inside. The secret lodges in Trapani, the second most significant "mafia city," meet under the cover of the *Circolo Scontrino* (Di Bernardo 1987; Ministry of Interior 1993; Nicastro 1993). According to the 1986 report of the Parliamentary Antimafia Commission, there were "2,441 men of honor . . . distributed among 113 lodges in Sicily." Of these, 33 were indicted or convicted, and another 335 figured in various police records (see Ministry of Interior 1994). In his 1997 testimony as a justice collaborator, Siino mapped out the covert lodges where bosses and politicians, businessmen and bureaucrats, sat around a table *(il "tavolino")* to divide up the public works contracts, juggling the input of a wider circle of elected officials, "red" cooperatives, Carabinieri, magistrates, and north Italian entrepreneurs. In such a world, he claimed, "one loses the distinction between the bosses and the representatives of the institutions" (*Giornale di Sicilia,* May 18, 2002). Clearly, masonry "opened roads to a certain level" (Nicastro 1993: 187–88).[10]

The "long 1980s" also witnessed a growing entanglement between "mafia-masons" and the state-authorized secret services (see De Lutiis 1991; *Il Manifesto,* February 5, 1997; Nicastro 1993; Paoli 1996). As noted above, members of Italy's military secret service, SID, later called SISMI, appeared on Gelli's list of P2 associates. According to the journalist Nicastro, by the end of the 1970s, SISMI had developed close ties to P2, having become a "sort of super-SISMI," more secretive and restricted than before. An all-purpose man of affairs *(faccendiere)* and SISMI informer, Francesco Pazienza, close to the Rome-based mafioso of the Corleonesi faction, Pippo Calò, participated in this alliance (Nicastro 1993: 166–71; Di Lutiis 1991). The deposition of *pentito* Pino Marchese cites these relationships and describes, as well, a close connection between another Salvatore Greco, nicknamed "the Senator," and Bruno Contrada, a high-ranking officer in the secret services. Pondering how this association might have been born, Marchese cites Greco's membership in "some masonic lodge," where he "entered into

relationships with many important persons of the most diverse circles,"
and Greco's friendships, through masonry, with "magistrates, Carabinieri, policemen" (Nicastro 1993: 41–42). Early in 1997, Contrada
was convicted of having aided the bloody ascendancy of the Corleonesi
by tipping them off to pending police actions, along with other favors.
The long trial was highly controversial, and in 2001 the conviction was
overturned on appeal.

SECRET NETWORKS AND MONEY LAUNDERING

Not surprisingly, P2 held within its orbit a number of shadow speculators adapted for the money-laundering function. An early example was
the Sicilian financier Michele Sindona, a close personal friend of Gelli
and a founding member of that covert lodge. Having received a law degree from the University of Messina in 1938, Sindona made a killing in
black market grain sales at the end of the war, then moved in 1946 to
Milan, where he used the profits to buy up land in zones of urban expansion. By 1950 he had made enough from land speculation to buy
whole firms; by 1960 he had acquired the capstone piece of his "empire"—major shares in the Banca Privata Finanziaria (renamed Italiana),
a small Milan bank. A fortuitous marriage of his cousin to a Vatican
Bank insider led to relationships that furthered this meteoric rise, including one with the British bank Hambros (Galli 1995). Reputed for his
cleverness and charm, Sindona was soon upstaging another important
Sicilian banker, Enrico Cuccia, the "Calvinist" head of Mediobanca who
was closely allied to the Agnellis and other northern Italian industrial
families, all of whom scorned Sindona (as would have Notarbartolo).
Word of this rivalry spread through U.S. and European financial circles,
often to the benefit of Sindona's reputation.

But Sindona, succumbing to the global financial turmoil of 1973–74,
did not remain a winner. As many American readers will know, he purchased the Franklin National Bank in New York in 1973 in order to loot
some $45 million from its coffers, driving it into bankruptcy by 1974
(Wall Street Journal, May 7, 1984; see also Santino 1988: 215; Spero
1980). Perhaps it was his losses that whetted his appetite for narco-
profits, which he allegedly invested in real estate deals in Aruba, on behalf of mafiosi allied with Inzerillo and Bontade. Grandiose and overex-
tended, his operations nevertheless failed. In the summer of 1979, just
prior to his conviction for bank fraud in Italy, he attempted to flee American jurisdiction by staging his own bogus kidnapping on the streets of

New York and his subsequent wounding at the hands of his (mason) doctor in Palermo. Two *pentiti* of the early 1990s have revealed how several bosses, dependent on Sindona to launder their drug profits, were exasperated by his troubles and wanted his head (Arlacchi 1995: 40–47).

In the summer of 1979, attorney Giorgio Ambrosoli was murdered in circumstances that were reminiscent of the Notarbartolo assassination. He had been appointed to investigate Sindona's affairs and preside over the liquidation of the Banca Privata, which went bankrupt along with the Franklin Bank in 1974. Sindona was convicted of ordering this murder and threatening other crimes (including a threat in 1977 to kidnap Cuccia's son). Also convicted on the charge of fraudulent bankruptcy, he died after drinking a cup of poisoned coffee in a Milan prison in 1986. (Italian authorities have not been able to determine whether his death was a suicide or a homicide.) It is widely believed in antimafia circles that affiliates of P2 attempted to obstruct his prosecution with the help of some of the highest officials of the Italian state, including Andreotti (Arlacchi 1995: 31–40; Jamieson 2000: 218–20; Mola 1992).

In the late 1970s, as Sindona's house of cards was collapsing, Roberto Calvi, another banker friend of Gelli's and a member of P2, became engaged with the Corleonesi.[11] At first an ally of Sindona, Calvi turned into his enemy, competing for, among other things, high-level connections in the Vatican Bank (Piazzesi and Bonsanti 1984). On June 18, 1981, his body was found dangling beneath Blackfriar's Bridge in London, weighed down by pieces of concrete, with British authorities unable to determine how he got, or was placed, there. Significantly, the bridge, near London's financial district, is rich with masonic symbolism. In 1996, *pentito* Francesco Di Carlo, a former England-based interlocutor of mafia finance, implicated Pippo Calò as the principal organizer of Calvi's murder. Apparently Calvi had tried to kite mafia funds to cover the collapse of his empire's keystone, the Catholic Banco Ambrosiano. According to Di Carlo, Sindona and Gelli were also possible *mandanti*—organizers of the crime (*Il Manifesto,* October 9, 10, 1996; April 10, 1997).

Summing up both the political and the financial entanglements associated with P2, the Cordova report observes that "deviated" masonry appears to be "the connective tissue of the organization of power" in Italy (quoted in Nicastro 1993: 186). The journalist Guido Ruotolo uses the word "metastasis" to make a similar point (*Il Manifesto,* April 16, 1996). Reports from the Ministry of the Interior refer to "networks of illicit *lobbying*" (using the English word). All have in mind a capillary formation that extends through virtually the entire national territory, with ties into similar formations worldwide—a sort of "transversal super-party" for people of all parties occupying high positions of power (Forgione and Mondani 1994; Commissione Parlamentare Antimafia 1993: 24). Leonardo Messina, a *pentito*, reminds us that well into the 1980s, narco-mafiosi were plugged in. Inserting themselves into the metastasis, they ended up with adjusted trials and useful financial contacts. "Naturally," he adds, "I am referring to the absolutely secret lodges, for which you would never find membership lists. It is not written anywhere that Riina is affiliated" (quoted in Nicastro 1993: 187).

CONCLUSION

The preliminary assessment of what the mafia *is*, sketched at the end of chapter 2, emphasized the need to go beyond what prosecutors have learned about its internal organization and ideology to consider its relationship with the state. Focusing on the political (and financial) *intreccio* that enabled mafiosi to expand into the new domains of urban activity following World War II, this chapter has done just that. It has also illustrated how mafiosi who feared being marginalized by these urban and modernizing trends, and who resented the implied disrespect, fueled the pace of the expansion: those left out wanted in and, using violence, got their way. In addition to being an organization that a corrupt state allowed to happen because it helped mitigate peasant insurgency, the mafia is also a predatory institution with agency and motivation of its own. Covering the same Cold War decades, chapter 4 explores the mafia's internal dynamics.

CHAPTER 4

The Cultural Production
of Violence

"In a world as complicated as the Cosa Nostra's," *pentito* Calderone has said, "even small wrongs are remembered for years and there are thousands of tangled relationships; . . . grounds for suspicion and [sinister] hypotheses are never lacking" (in Arlacchi 1993: 62). A mafioso sometimes murders a fellow *cosca* member out of fear that the other person could—and therefore might—betray him. Sometimes the victim is done in after a convivial meal, a scenario that Calderone likens to the Last Supper (see ibid.: 135). In such an atmosphere, participants in the plot have every reason to "suspect each other of treachery in the future." As Buscetta told Arlacchi, "The man who stands beside you might take you to your tomb as easily as he would take you to a party. . . . The anxiety is continuous and is born of the fact that one never knows" (Arlacchi 1994: 155).

Calderone's and Buscetta's powerful stories may well exaggerate the tensions endured by mafiosi. Having themselves committed an ultimate act of betrayal through their collaboration, they are compelled to depict the life they left behind as awash in revenge, a degeneration of the "honorable society" to which they once belonged. In most cases, such important witnesses are heavily protected by the state; disowned by the mafia, they would surely have been killed otherwise. This circumstance also contributes to the mistrust that pervades their recollections. Nor can we minimize their own intense desire for retaliation, stoked by the vendetta killings of their friends and kin. Buscetta lost two sons in the rampage, then a nephew, son-in-law, and brother in late 1982. Salvatore Contorno, like Buscetta the first to "turn," lost cousins and in-laws; Calderone lost his brother and their close friend, the would-be collaborator Di Cristina (Stille 1995: 60–61). To the extent that the magistrates who interrogate the collaborators press for details on the machinations of their enemies, the need to even the score finds ample expression in their testimony. The problem of insecurity, in other words, should not be taken out of context—the context of an institution under great and mounting external pressure, prefiguring its possible containment.

Yet, a closer look at the social and cultural aspects of the mafia reveals it to be an engine of insecurity, its order-enhancing structures and solidarity-building rituals frequently distorted by rivalries and provocations. Overarching "commissions," for example, seek to regulate the use of violence, but conflicts over the nomination of commissioners can turn violent. Similarly, although initiation rituals induct novices into a collectivist fraternity, they also express each novice's quasi-feudal relationship to a particular sponsor bent on developing his own power base. Making note of these and other contradictions, the following pages shed light on the mafia's internal dynamism, on the energy that underwrites its continued, if stress-laden tenacity in a changing world.

THE ORGANIZATION OF THE *COSCA*

According to the Central Directorate of Criminal Police (the "Criminalpol" under the Italian Ministry of the Interior), as of 1994, there were about 181 mafia families in Sicily with a total of 5,500 adherents, the great majority in the western provinces. The city of Catania on the eastern coast became a locus of mafia activity after World War II; otherwise, the eastern provinces supported very few *cosche* or none at all (Paoli 2000: 21–23). The evolution of the Commission after 1957 brought with it a new layer of organization in Palermo Province, the *mandamento*, or district, made up of three or so families. There were about fifteen such *mandamenti* during the 1980s, each with a representative on the Commission (ibid.: 59).

By convention, each family is supposed to have about 10 members; large families should be broken up into subunits, called *decine*. It is now known, however, that during the "long 1980s" the *cosca* of Corleone had a nucleus of 39 members, including prisoners and fugitives, apparently ignoring this requirement. The Corso dei Mille family in central Palermo counted 65 members plus 38 affiliates in roughly the same period. In the province as a whole, average mafia family size was 23.8. By contrast, the Catania *cosca* had 44 members plus 170 affiliates, thanks to having collectively "baptized" all of the members of a rival criminal group (ibid.: 24–25). These references to "affiliates," and to variations in size, are a clue that the *cosche* are less discrete and clearly bounded than might at first appear. Moreover, the escalation to power of the Corleonesi dramatically showed how one *cosca* could infiltrate and dominate others. Yet the *cosche* pretend to a territorial bias, each bearing the name of a rural town, small city, urban neighborhood, or suburb.

As a rule, local leaders are elected or re-elected annually by the membership. These leaders include, in the 1990s as in the nineteenth century, the *rappresentante* ("representative") or *capofamiglia* ("family head"), his vice-capo, empowered to fill in during the capo's imprisonment or other absence, two or more *capi-decina* (literally, "heads of ten") where subunits exist, and a *consigliere* (councillor), whose role is to advise and watch over the *rappresentante* (ibid.: 42). The heads of families were not supposed to be eligible for election to leadership of the Provincial Commission, but this rule was often broken. Several also doubled as the (elected) leaders of the *mandamenti*.

Presumably, it is the prerogative of each *cosca* to extort a *pizzo*, or tribute, from business activities in its territory, to impose on the territory's employers requirements that they hire particular mafia dependents, and to mediate local conflict and the return, for a fee, of locally stolen goods. Although individual members conduct these activities as private entrepreneurs, *cosca* leaders can claim a percentage of the proceeds. Mafiosi from other *cosche* who wish to be active in the territory are supposed to ask permission of these leaders. Even to purchase land or build a house in the zone of another *cosca* sometimes means supplicating its capo (see ibid.: 214n).

The mafia has no formal constitution and its members keep few written records, other than the personal address books that prosecutors love to find. The *pentiti,* however, tell of rules and regulations that are remarkably uniform from one *cosca* to another. Foremost among these is the rule of *omertà*, the first principle of what Paoli (ibid.) calls the mafia's "normative order." In addition to demanding sealed lips in relation to all authorities, *omertà* implies that "men of honor" possess the courage, valor, and capacity for violence that render them capable of avenging intrusions and insults without resort to the law. Numerous "mafia" proverbs convey the salience of keeping quiet: "to talk little is a beautiful art"; "the mouth is the betrayer of the heart"; "long steps and short tongue"; "to witness is good as long as it does not harm your neighbor"; "I know nothing, neither today nor yesterday" (see ibid.: 142). Other rules prohibit adultery, kidnapping, and involvement in prostitution and establish graded levels of permission to kill, depending upon the victim's geographical and social location.

"Men of honor" from different *cosche* who do not know each other should not discuss matters of mafia interest until they have been presented to each other by a third person who is also a "man of honor." Coded words communicate crucial information in these encounters. As explained to us in the 1960s, if mafioso A presents B to mafioso C, and says, "C, I want you to meet B. He's a friend of ours," it means C should understand that B is also a mafioso. Alternatively, A might say, "C, I want you to meet B, he's the same thing [as we are] . . *(è la stessa cosa)*." But if A says, "B is a friend of mine," it means only that. Brusca enumerates his version of the most serious rules: "Use a third person to be presented to another affiliate." "Never touch the woman of another man of honor." "Alert your capo *mandamento* before being away from your own territory." "Never do anything on your own initiative; always be prompt and at the disposition of your capo *(a disposizione)*." "If you end up in jail, no need to worry because Cosa Nostra will take care of you and your family" (Brusca, in Lodato 1999: 32–33).

As we noted in chapter 1, remarkably similar initiation rites, reminiscent of the ritual practices of other secretive societies, have characterized the local *cosche*. Brusca recalls his initiation as follows: He was taken to a remote spot in the countryside, where he expected to attend "a *schiticchiata*. That is a banquet, as they call them in Palermo." Instead, there was a large round table bearing a pistol, a dagger, and a card with the image of a saint *(santina)*. The assembled company, mafiosi from both Corleone and his home town of San Giuseppe Jato, asked him whether he could take the life of another man and commit criminal acts. "If you end up in prison," they continued, "will you be faithful and not betray . . . Cosa Nostra?" Then someone pricked his finger, marked the *santina* with his blood, and "(Totò) Riina set the image on fire and put it in my hands, covering them so I could not throw it down. And he says, 'If you betray Cosa Nostra, your flesh will burn like this *santina* is burning'" (ibid.: 32–33). "At the end of the ceremony they all kissed, raised glasses of champagne. My father [Bernardo Brusca, noted capomafioso of San Giuseppe Jato] told me that Riina is *la stessa cosa* [the 'same thing'] as himself. . . . On all such occasions there are *grandissime mangiate* [huge banquets]" (ibid.: 35).

A 1956 initiation described in *L'Ora* in 1960 was similar in most details except that the novice was blindfolded. When the cover was removed from his eyes, he found himself surrounded by a dozen men (five pairs of brothers plus another two), all with a gun or knife pointed at him! The initiate, Giuseppe Luppino, unable to follow through on a murder he was ordered to commit, "confessed" to the authorities and was killed ten days later (*L'Ora*, September 8, 1960).

There are several reasons why, for over a century, mafiosi have viewed themselves as part of an institution that transcends local boundaries, maintaining an overarching etiquette of comportment, a vocabulary, and a set of ritual performances. From their bandit origins in the nineteenth century, these figures have pursued activities that are, by their very nature, geographically deterritorialized, in particular, sheep stealing and the clandestine butchering and sale of stolen meat, the establishment of monopolies over urban produce markets, and the contraband mediation and sale of tobacco and narcotics. One might even say that, emigrants excepted, mafiosi were historically the most mobile of Sicilians, encountering each other far from home at sheep and cattle fairs, or on the road carrying grain and fruit. The landowning families who protected them had translocal networks of intermarriage and political affiliation anchored by *palazzi* in Palermo, and this, too, broadened their universe of useful connections. Finally, as chapters 2 and 3 showed, Palermo and its hinterland, or better, the area between Palermo and Trapani, constituted a hegemonic "core" of mafia development, episodically a locus of coordination.

HIERARCHY AND SOLIDARITY

Dense kinship relations flourish among "men of honor," whose (actual) families not only intermarry (both within and across *cosche*) but are characterized by a higher than usual incidence of patrilateral parallel cousin marriage (between the offspring of brothers), as well as of two brothers marrying two sisters (see Schneider and Schneider 1976: 187–88).[1] The most powerful mafia leaders typically have a father, cousin, uncle, in-law, or brother at their shoulder—an outcome of the partially kin-based recruitment system, as discussed below (see Lupo 1993: 210; Pezzino 1995: 136; Schneider and Schneider 1976: 187–88). Nevertheless, the word "family" as applied to the mafia *cosca* is metaphorical. Like the words "brotherhood" or "fraternity," it seeks to import the presumed solidarity of kinship into a fictive kin group.

Mafiosi even deploy the fictive kinship tie of godparenthood metaphorically, referring to each other as *compare,* or "godfather" (rather than *frate* or "brother"), even when they select others—officials or politicians, for example—to be the godparents of their children. Unlike a blood tie, godparenthood is contractual, yet it too conveys a strong sense of mutual obligation and good will.

In many ways, the mafia *cosche* resemble the burial societies that peasants, artisans, and working-class Sicilians traditionally organized to care for their dead. Rather than meeting the emotional and financial costs of funerals, however, their focus is on imprisonment. Taking care of members who land in jail is considered the *cosca's* foremost obligation—just compensation for misfortune suffered in the line of duty. It also gives the mafia leverage over members who might otherwise talk. Prison terms have rarely interrupted a mafioso's career, not only because lax rules and corrupt officials make it possible to conduct business from inside, but because an incarcerated man has the assurance that his *cosca* will sustain him.

In the 1960s, we speculated that the *cosca* had "no fund for mutual aid, no dues, bank account, or treasurer" (Schneider and Schneider 1976: 189–90). According to the journalist Pantaleone, mafiosi instead sequestered and ransomed outsiders on an ad hoc basis in order to cover legal aid and aid to the families of prisoners (1962: 190–92). Recent *pentiti* depositions suggest, however, that the *cosche* tapped extortion earnings to build up funds controlled and administered by the *consigliere.*[2] The depositions also reinforce the earlier view that when the need to help a prisoner arose, *cosca* members contributed from their own pockets. Anyone who held back lost prestige and authority, acquired a bad reputation, and probably jeopardized his own future should he be arrested. Mafiosi tell apocryphal stories of imprisoned affiliates seeking revenge upon their release because they felt abandoned (Brusca, in Lodato 1999: 32–33). "Prison, illness, and disgrace prove the hearts of friends" was already recorded as a mafia saying in the late 1800s (Alongi 1886: 76).

In whatever way the resources were assembled, an imprisoned man expected that his legal expenses would be met and a lifeline provided for his wife and children. In the 1960s we accompanied a mafioso's wife on her visit to the household of a man who was in prison. It was almost as if the convict's wife had just been widowed and, like a widow, was in need of food, encouragement, and solace. Support of this kind could continue for decades and even include putting up the dowry for an imprisoned mafioso's daughter; at times it was substantial enough to help convince a young recruit to "take a fall," that is, submit to conviction and imprisonment in lieu of a more senior member of his *cosca* (Pantaleone 1962: 190).

According to the recent depositions, the typical *cosca* also used its common fund to provide an income for rank-and-file soldiers who had no other way to live. Operating according to a concept of redistribution, it thereby spread the returns from extortion more or less equitably. One function of the *consigliere* was precisely that of watching the money, so that the capo would not keep too much for himself (Pezzino 1995: 284).

Leaders of the *cosche* adopted a demeanor that communicated authority and latent power—and wanted their dominion to be acknowledged through the obvious deference of others—but, like the mythic Beati Paoli, they did not advertise difference. Their dress was characteristically modest and other markers of status were also eschewed. As Calderone told Arlacchi, mafiosi should avoid bragging and showing off (Calderone, in Arlacchi 1993: 57).[3] Exceptions existed, of course, and became more numerous with the circulation of drug profits. In chapter 3 we met the silk-suited "American-style" gangster Angelo La Barbera. Drug bosses Stefano Bontade and Salvatore Inzerillo lavishly rebuilt the houses they inherited in their respective *borgate,* striving for "magnificence" (ibid.: 130; see also Lupo 1993: 185). A particularly stunning example of what money could provide was the Ciaculli estate and villa where Michele Greco regularly hosted both mafiosi and an array of contiguous notables at hunting parties and banquets. Yet the jealousies that these exceptions created proved the rule. Brusca, reflecting on his first experience as an "exile" in court-ordered obligatory residence *(soggiorno obbligato)* on the island of Linosa, recalls that he got on well with the local population of fishermen because they compared him favorably to a predecessor, Leonardo Greco, a big spender who forced everyone to admire his massive gold watch, behaving like a jerk (in dialect, *u scemu*). Brusca, by contrast, mixed with the people, wearing jeans and knit shirts. True, he spent on himself. He describes liking Lacoste, Missoni, and Fila shirts and Rolex, Cartier, and Lucien Roché watches, but says he never flaunted them (Brusca, in Lodato 1999: 40, 44).

In the same, "leveling" vein, Brusca evaluates the super-wealthy Salvo cousins. Ignazio was "highly educated and well prepared," but Nino was "more Cosa Nostra, more open, more sincere, more one who kidded around. We found ourselves better off with him, he was available" (ibid.: 60). Similarly, Riina fared well in the eyes of Brusca. "If one of us had economic problems, Riina did not ask that we say so twice before he put his hand in his pocket." If, however, someone thought to take him for a ride, whether for a few cents or for a million, "he went crazy. He is generous, but in his own way" (ibid.: 65).

Under the influence of the south-east *schieramento* (alignment), the Commission expelled both Buscetta (in 1958 and 1963) and the drug trafficker Badalamenti (in 1977) for their involvement in transatlantic syndicates in which they accumulated "excessive" amounts of wealth (Lupo 1993: 194, 207). The leaders of this more "traditional" faction also pursued what might be called a redistributive pattern of peacemaking. The *pentito* Leonardo Vitale, described below, related how Riina resolved a conflict between the *cosche* of Porta Nuova and Noce in Palermo over the right to impose kickbacks on a construction project that involved both neighborhoods. The Noce capo accepted the mediation even though it disfavored his *cosca,* agreeing with Riina that the Porta Nuova family *"deve 'assaggiare' qualcosa"* (has to taste something) (ibid.: 197).[4]

Following the *scalata,* or rise to power, of the Corleone bosses, the mafia economy ran on a roughly redistributive track into the 1980s, that is, well past the moment of maximum accumulation from drugs. Members contributed to funds that were raised on behalf of imprisoned comrades; monies gained from territorial operations were more or less dispersed downward from the bosses to the soldiers, some of whom (an increasing number, according to Paoli 2000: 196–206) had no other source of income. Even the fabulous narco-profits circulated to some extent. In the late 1970s, the Commission under Michele Greco established a "schedule of dockings" so that each coalition of traffickers would have access to shipments on a rotating basis (see Pezzino 1995: 257–59). As we know, the Corleonesi also used drug profits to capitalize small construction firms, enabling young and "hungry" mafiosi to enter the bidding games that Angelo Siino, their top business planner, regulated, apparently with an eye toward taking care of as many loyal followers as possible. The fact that accumulation and redistribution were linked processes in the mafia economy is consistent with mafia concepts of revenge and equity. Solidarity, such as it was, benefited from this linkage.

RECRUITMENT

To some extent, *cosca* organization reflects kinship relations, the status of mafioso being passed from father to son, uncle to nephew. By the same token, mafiosi often named each other as *compare* or "godfather" to their children. In families where the father, uncles, cousins, older brothers, and godfathers are *cosca* members, it is almost obligatory for up-and-coming youth to consider a criminal career. Given ever more realistic guns as toys, expected to join in neighborhood gangs, they are taught that the best way to not be pushed around is to push. Traditionally, older boys were invited to participate in hunting parties—their first experience with the use of actual firearms and the sight of blood. After that came target practice, which produced a sense of exaltation: "It made you feel like a god, a superior person with enormous powers," according to one autobiographical account (*Una Città,* April 1999).

Kinship, however, is hardly a straightforward solution to reproducing the mafia through time. A mafioso who seeks to induct several sons or nephews may seem to be planning a power grab; concern about this has led some *cosche* to set limits on the recruitment of kinsmen. Furthermore, adhering to genealogical succession alone cannot guarantee replenishing the *fegato,* or "guts," on which organized crime depends. The *cosche* must, therefore, also be open to talent. During the traditional hunting parties and target practices, older mafiosi observed their sons and nephews with an eye toward weeding out those who were unsuited. Introverts who dwelled too much on their moral qualms or did not like being given direction were considered *babbo, cretino,* ridiculous. If a youth chose to demur, he was simply excluded; if he actively rebelled, however, he risked some kind of sanction. The story of Giuseppe Impastato, a young journalist in open rebellion against the *cosca* of Cinisi in the late 1970s (see chapter 7), is poignant for the fact that his small-time mafioso father was held in contempt by the town's preeminent boss, Gaetano Badalamenti, for failing to bring him into line. A powerful film, called (in English) *One Hundred Steps,* documents this intense psychological drama.

In rural Sicily in the mid-1960s, we noticed that parents in general, and the parents of mafia families in particular, frequently commented and acted upon perceived differences of character (they used the word *carattere*) among their children. In a mafia household we knew well, both the mother and the father warmed to their younger son, who charmed adults with a quick wit, while (it seemed to us) they offered less affection to his older brother. Only the younger son, it appeared, was being groomed to follow in his father's footsteps.

The forty-four-year-old son of a mafioso—we will call him Tizio[5]— recently granted an interview to the magazine *Una Città* (April 1999).

Growing up in a *borgata* whose small buildings and surrounding orchards were succumbing to "cementification," he watched his father become embroiled in the competition over building contracts and mysteriously disappear. Recently, a *pentito* has revealed that this man was strangled by his rivals, tied up, and thrown into the sea. Tizio remembers his father as barely educated, unable to write a letter without making countless mistakes, yet modestly well off and knowing how to act in a "refined way." He frequented circles of "the Palermo that counts—professionals, politicians, administrators," among whom he promoted his real estate and construction business.

At the same time, his father had another side to him, a Mr. Hyde. Tizio recalls feeling uneasy at the excessive gestures of respect, the exaggeratedly hospitable offers of wine or coffee, put to his father on the streets of the *borgata* by shady "friends." He especially disliked witnessing his father's flashes of anger while strolling with these friends, and the prickly atmosphere in the bar and billiard room where they often ended up. He has since learned that his father committed two murders with his own hands and was the *mandante* for others, that he was caught up in a chain of assassinations committed to consolidate and maintain territorial control—control he ultimately lost despite subjecting himself and his family to a life of risk. Regardless, Tizio remains grateful to his father and his many mafioso relatives for permitting him to be a different kind of person. Even before he realized it himself, they had defined him as someone who would never stomach prepotency and imposition and who should therefore be *posato*, set apart. As such he did not receive "instruction" in becoming a "man of honor" as his brothers did and was left to experience only an "immense sense of shame" when his father was jailed. In the end he joined the 1968 student movement at the University of Palermo, remaining involved even as it was absorbed into the 1980s antimafia movement.

Generally speaking, mafiosi do not "hire" outside specialists; important tasks, from carrying messages, to collecting extortion fees, to murder, are committed by "soldiers" whom they know and trust.[6] Over and above their own descendents, there are always plenty of candidates for this, casualties of the Sicilian economy's high rate of un- and underemployment. In Calderone's words, "Around every man of honor of a certain rank, there is always a circle of twenty or thirty kids—nobodies who want to become somebody. These youths are at his disposal, there to do small favors, to be put to the test" (Calderone, in Arlacchi 1993: 126). Some commit petty thefts in order to impress the bosses. Significantly, one meaning of the word *mafiusu* in Palermo slang is "young tough," a hot-blooded man with an "exaggerated sense of personal honor" (Renda 1991: 9–10).

Unrelated newcomers are at once crucial to a *cosca's* viability and a threat to its discipline and hierarchy. To cite Calderone again, attention must be paid to avoid "overloading—letting in too many . . . (potentially) unfaithful and untrustworthy young men *out of a love of power and greatness"* (in Arlacchi 1993: 126, original emphasis). And so mafiosi choose with care, applying the yardstick of "guts" and reliability in criminal enterprise. Anyone with kinship or friendship ties to the police is assumed to be undependable; so are youths deemed to be *too* hot-headed. To paraphrase Calderone, if a kid is causing a lot of trouble committing robberies and continues to do so after being warned, perhaps he should pay a price. By contrast, kids who show respect might be guided by mafiosi as to when and where to steal (ibid.). In the 1970s, a foreign ballerina and night club performer was knifed in the popular market of the Vucciria of Palermo by a young delinquent trying to steal her purse. Members of the local *cosca* strangled the young man and left him in the trunk of a car with the following sign around his neck: "This is how worms who throw mud on Sicily die" (see Grasso 2000).

Clearly, wherever the mafia is powerful, a life of crime outside of it can be dangerous. Beyond offering an ostensible escape from risk, the *cosca* holds out to restless youths the considerable rewards of status and belonging, an identity that separates them from the crowd. If, as Calderone claims, young delinquents look up to mafiosi as "rock fans look up to Madonna" (in Arlacchi 1993: 130), this is because many powerful senior bosses cultivate a charismatic personal style. In Tizio's view, no doubt colored by his antimafia identity, the least suited for joining the mafia are persons of strong character like himself who feel repulsed by its heavy indoctrination. Insecure individuals, artificially inflated by violence, fill the organization's ranks. Such persons follow the orders of older bosses "as if their mother had asked them to go and buy the bread." They are then rewarded for their deeds and, through the rite of initiation, made to feel like "true men."

The sponsor-protégé relationship, crossing generations and suffused with charisma, is important in kin recruitment, too. In 1973, investigating magistrate Aldo Rizzo ordered a psychiatric evaluation of Leonardo Vitale, imprisoned for criminal insanity after deciding to "confess" (then murdered for this violation of *omertà* in 1984). The purpose was to determine his state of mind and the credibility of his deposition, which accused many mafiosi of serious crimes. The transcript of the psychiatrists' interrogation reveals that Vitale followed his uncle, a capomafioso of Altarello, "for everything and in everything." At his uncle's behest he killed two other mafiosi and attempted to take the life of a third. When asked about his motives, he responded that he had committed the murders to show to himself and to others that he was the equal of other men, "one of the boys," capable of manhood, and not one of "them"—the women. Indeed, the killings had helped him deal with his growing concern that he might be inclined toward "pederasty," by which he meant being sexually attracted to young men. He also said, "I did it to achieve the friendship of my uncle," as if that friendship were a treasured gift (Galluzzo, Nicastro, and Vasile 1992: 96–111; see also Lupo 1993: 181).

Vitale knew that he was speaking to three court-appointed psychiatrists; moreover, one reference says little. Along with other confessions of the 1980s, however, it underscores the role in mafia formation of something like vassalage, in which the neophyte member, whether or not tied by kinship to the organization, defines himself, and is recognized by others, as the sponsor's man. In the words of justice collaborator Leonardo Messina, "There is always a person who guides you; every man of honor has around five, ten or fifteen persons near him." Messina elaborates that some novices, invited to choose their *padrino*, are too clever for their own good, going straight for the most powerful capo (Pezzino 1995: 282–83).

The sponsor, meanwhile, adds to the density of his personal following within the organization, so much so that senior mafiosi who initiate "too many" young recruits generate tension among their co-equals. Sponsors are also held responsible for the future misdeeds of their protégés. Such quasi-feudal relations of hero worship and patronage, intrinsic to the recruitment process, lurk in the background and can disrupt the solidarity of the brotherhood. Generating intensely affective dyadic bonds, they define the axes around which factions develop. Because of them, disputes over territorial authority and over critical resources are often infused with envy and apprehension, turning struggles of interest into struggles for respect and affection. Paradoxically, although the mafia sodality maintains an ethic of mutual friendship among its members, mafioso friends can end up killing one another.

MAFIOSI AND "MAFIA WOMEN"

The internal dynamics of the mafia are further complicated by the pattern of gender relations that it has fostered. Calderone reports that because most wives of mafiosi are themselves from mafia families, they have "breathed that air since their birth." What they cannot figure out for themselves, they are told by sisters, friends, and sisters-in-law. But, says Calderone, "men of honor" are guarded in what they communicate to their wives and daughters, to protect them from knowledge that could make them judicially vulnerable—in effect, to give them the protection of deniability (in Arlacchi 1993: 145ff). For example, although mafiosi typically place their assets in their wives' names, sheltering them from the claims of creditors and the confiscatory power of the state, they do not necessarily provide transparent information on how the assets were won. Whether the women are thereby innocent of criminal activity is nevertheless open to question. A mafia wife cannot be ignorant of her husband's status and may well play an active role in promoting that status by hosting his friends, running some of his affairs, and generally basking in the reflection of his prestige and the goods his money buys.[7] Her reciprocal involvement might extend to ensuring the safety and comfort of fugitives her husband feels obliged to hide. Her sons will no doubt join the company, her daughters marry into it, and she participates in preparing them for these futures (Calderone, in Arlacchi 1993: 145ff; see also Principato and Dino 1997; Siebert 1994).

The mafia, in general, looks out for its members' women, supposedly sanctioning men who fool around and watching out for the "widows" and "orphans" of prisoners. As there are high rates of marriage between the children of mafiosi, there are obvious risks for those who betray their wives and thus cuckold their brothers-in-law or father-in-law. Frequent intermarriage also promotes communication, solidarity, and cooperation among women who, even though they may live in different towns or cities, are related through mafiosi. Beyond this, mafia men are no exception to the general Sicilian norm that requires heads of families to oversee the economic security, reputation, and respectability of their closest kin.

That many mafia women are sympathetic to the cause is evident in the vehemence with which they denounce the justice collaborators, particularly those whose collaboration has led to the arrest or conviction of their close kin. When the Di Filippo brothers became *pentiti,* their sister made a public statement disowning them on behalf of herself and her parents: "We cannot open our shutters for the shame of it," she said. In the eyes of their wives, they were so *infame* (traitorous), it would have been better were they dead (see Jamieson 2000: 230–31). Another, much discussed instance involved Rita Atria, a seventeen-year-old woman from the town of Partanna in the province of Trapani who had been present at the assassination of her (mafioso) father and had later suffered her brother's murder as well. Following the lead of her brother's widow, who did not have a mafia background, she courageously decided to talk to Judge Borsellino in 1992. Declaring herself unprotected and desperate after Borsellino's death, Atria committed suicide, only to have her grave desecrated by her mother, who disowned her for collaborating.

In her book on women and the mafia (1994), Renate Siebert takes us beyond these issues to consider the gender dynamics of the *cosca*, the mafia family with a capital "F," to which women do not belong. As she observes, young men, aspiring to join the fraternity, perceive "made" mafiosi as a rarified and often charismatic elite. Although overtly homophobic, these already established members may engage in "quasi" homoerotic behaviors in recruiting particular youth. The dynamic produces the extremes of loyalty and secrecy demanded by the *cosca*, even at the expense, if necessary, of the members' respective natal and conjugal families. Women, although the guardians of these families, are no less constrained than men to internalize the priority of the metaphorical Family. They, too, must demonstrate loyalty and be secretive before the law regardless of whether—and this is the ultimate test—some of the men they know are bent on assassinating their very sons.

The culture of the *cosca* denies and denigrates femininity. Siebert considers the resulting "narcissism" of this fraternal organization to be its defining feature. Through rituals, feasts, and hunting trips, the members shore up and continuously reassert a form of masculine identity that repels affection and dependency as womanly signs of weakness. Underscoring the women's exclusion, participants in these activities are affectionate with one another. As occasions for celebrating men's intense commensalist bonding, mafia rituals create a space for adolescent, even erotic horseplay.

MALE BONDING

Indicative of male bonding are the names mafiosi give one another. Nicknaming is an old practice in Sicily, where each rural community traditionally had a limited pool of surnames and, because children were named for grandparents and local patron saints, an overworked pool of first names, too. Handy for identification, nicknames are usually unflattering and not used to people's faces (the dialect word for them is *'nciuria*, or "insult"). With modernization, nicknaming has declined, especially in the cities, except among mafiosi. Examining documents from the maxi-trial, Gambetta and Pizzini found nicknames for at least a third of the 459 men accused, their presence being more evident in the urban than in the rural *cosche* (n.d.: 9–10). Many of these mischievous appellations refer to physical appearance, such as "Big Bottle" and "Shovel Face." Others elevate with irony, like the Greco names—the "Pope," the "Engineer," the "Senator." (Michele, the Pope, was so named for carrying holy cards in his pocket and quoting from the Bible [Orlando 2001:67]). In the course of the trial, the *pentiti* not only evoked nicknames to refer to those they were accusing; they also explained the elements of character or appearance to which the names referred. For example, the nickname "Tweezers" indexed its bearer's habit of "plucking his eyebrows and cheekbones"; "Tractor" derived from skill in murdering ("he flattened everything and wherever he went the grass stopped growing"). Such "linguistically slick" choices, Gambetta and Pizzini argue, "enhance the pleasures of veiled mocking allusions as well as the relief provided by shared humour at other's expense" (Gambetta and Pizzini n.d.: 5, 14).

Besides wordplay, the *cosca* was an arena for food play, sustaining a lavish and much mythologized banqueting tradition anchored by the characteristic toasts, "blood and milk for a hundred years" (see Fentress 2000: 218). Brusca's description touches the basic elements:

La Cosa Nostra was divided into good persons and bad persons. It is made up of persons all of whom from the start have to kill, and have to know how to kill. Conscientious objectors could never belong. We were all assassins, is the premise. But we also had our good times, in our own way naturally. The *grandi banchetti, grandi schiticchiate* in the countryside were the principal occasions for socializing in Cosa Nostra. . . . Women were never admitted. We ate and we discussed. At first in little groups then everyone together at the table. Different men brought different dishes: baked pasta, meat, fish, cakes and sweets. . . . The food was cooked over a grill; pasta was cooked in big copper pots, as in the old days. We had some excellent cooks. . . . They cooked for all their comrades when they were in prison. When everything was ready we sat down and there began a game of offering food and drink; you had to accept whatever you were offered and it would be rude to refuse. We drank champagne and then coffee into the evening, with endless quips and jokes and never a silent moment. In our eyes, for example, Riina was not a bloodthirsty killer, but rather a jovial and spirited person, full of sympathy for the young men. We also talked about women. . . . The banquets almost always ended in general bacchanalia *[baldoria]*, with the men throwing around sacks of water and plates and glasses going flying. . . not one remained intact. (in Lodato 1999: 180–84)

During the 1960s, P. Schneider had occasion to witness a series of five rustic banquets, organized to celebrate a peace among competing meat wholesalers, which took place in a succession of rural towns over several months' time. Not all of the assembled guests were mafiosi. Indeed, as the numbers snowballed from banquet to banquet, they came to include ever more public officials and professionals—the mafia's interlocutors— a pattern we return to in chapter 5. All, however, were men. Men, indeed, revealed a striking ability to carry on without women by preparing each of the lavish, multi-course feasts entirely on their own. In one isolated country house, barrels of wine were placed upstairs in a room over the banquet tables, with plastic tubes and spigots descending through holes in the ceiling, ready at hand to fill the convivial glasses. Most important, as each of the extravagant meals drew to a close, the revelers settled into an hour or more of hilarious, carnivalesque entertainment that parodied the absent sex.

At the first banquet, three participants disappeared for a few minutes to emerge from a side room ringing a bell, and draped in tablecloths and other paraphernalia as mock priestly vestments (see fig. 7). With one holding a beach umbrella over the head of the "priest," and the third assisting, they sang a mass whose liturgy was authentic in rhythm and tone, but whose content was a ribald commentary on the food and wine, the people present, and the behavior of their wives and daughters. Instead of "amen" at the end of each verse, the congregation was led to chant *minchia* (a scatological term for "penis"). The mass was then followed by singing and dancing in which some of the bon vivants performed erotic imitations of women doing a strip tease. At each subsequent feast, the mass (now nicknamed the *messa minchiata*) became more elaborate, including fireworks and costumes. One participant on the last occasion dressed up in pink silk women's underwear with lace trim, a pink satin nightgown and a hooded black satin cape. Plump oranges were used to give the illusion of breasts as he cavorted about (Schneider and Schneider 1984). At the close of the banquets, as at their opening, mafiosi from different *cosche* greeted each other through the exchange of a kiss on both cheeks—the way other Sicilians do with close kin and friends. In anticipation of the parting kisses, moreover, they formed lines of guests and hosts, almost like members of opposing soccer teams at the close of a match.

The banquets, we believe, nurtured an aura of exclusivity as well as fraternal sodality among those present, insulating them in cultural and psychological space from regular ties to, and reciprocal obligations with, less-favored members of society. The fun and games, the horsing around,

Figure 7. Mafia banquet entertainer lampooning the clergy.
Photograph by Peter Schneider.

seemed the prerogative of a privileged few, the more so as they drew
prestigious guests into the company. In Calderone's words, "We are the
elite of the criminal world . . . vastly superior to common criminals . . .
worse than everybody!" (in Arlacchi 1993: 2). Young men, the novices
and would-be initiates, were thrilled to be included. Considering themselves for the moment among the intended (*'ntisu*), they perhaps felt immune from the epithets that the mafia levels at ordinary men: a "nobody

mixed with nothing," an "empty sack." Through ridiculing the rest of society—through declaring irrelevant the moral registers of family, community, and religion—mafiosi created an exalted "hothouse" effect. The result was their unique moral register, which valorized aggressive acts, up to and including extortion, intimidation, and murder. Having culturally produced an elite identity, they came to feel a greater freedom to indulge in grotesque and destructive games, according to rules and values that most people would find repugnant—that are, indeed, opposed to wider norms.[8]

A SUBCULTURE OF VIOLENCE

How do mafiosi themselves understand, explain, and legitimate taking another person's life? Before we approach this question, it is important to remember that mafia killings often involve a whole cast of characters. First, the ostensible rules dictate that whoever commands a territory has jurisdiction over what takes place within it. Second, assassinations, in contrast to lesser crimes, are supposed to receive at least the *nulla osta* if not the support of the *cupola* or Commission. Third, there is frequently a division of labor between those who order crimes (the *mandanti*) and those who commit them (the *sicari*). Finally, depending on the complexity of the operation, it may require more than one material killer, or *sicario,* with additional personnel being called in to remove traces of evidence by burning cars and causing bodies to disappear. If a bomb is used (as in the case of several of the "excellent cadavers"), a group of operatives is necessary to prepare it, inform on the target's movements, and detonate the explosive with precision.

Several *pentiti* report intense anxiety on their first "assignment" but note that this was assuaged by the fact that they were not alone. During their initiation, the assembled older company made clear to them that they could be ordered to kill an acquaintance, perhaps even a relative or someone dear; such bonds are secondary to their commitment to the fraternity. By the same token, if a neophyte were indeed ordered to commit a murder, his sponsor was often there to help, nervously staking out the area and hovering nearby until the deed was done (Calderone, in Arlacchi 1993: 135).

Until the "long 1980s," when arsenals of Kalashnikovs and car bombs proliferated, the weapon of preference was the sawed off shotgun, whose scattered shot—*lupara*—was well suited for killing wolves (the Italian for wolf is *lupo*). Shepherds protecting sheep carried such a weapon, as did peasants who hunted, bandits who rustled animals and crops, and the many layers of guards and extortionists offering protection against them. To this day the *lupara,* for which obtaining a license was never difficult, is mythologized as the classic mafia weapon, so much so that if one disappears without a trace it is referred to as a murder by *"lupara bianca"* or "white *lupara.*"

Our survey of *pentiti* statements and other first-person accounts results in the following, overlapping motive categories for mafia murders. First are the *fatti provi,* the "proven deeds," in which murder is committed to establish one's potency or capacity as a mafioso or, as the *pentito* Marsala has said,

> to prove your valor. Within a mafia family prestige is gained above all by the consummation of homicides in the sense that this is the testing ground (the *banco di prova*) on which a man of honor demonstrates his valor. In such a case, you can say he is a "valued" person *(una persona che vale).* And the more important the homicide that is committed, the greater the rise in the prestige of the mafioso who commits it. (Marsala 1985)

According to Buscetta, Pippo Calò proved that he was a brave man when he was still very young "by shooting at the man who had killed his father" (Buscetta 1984: II, 25–26). Vitale, in explaining why he had become a killer, told the investigators that it was "to make myself look good *[farmi bello]* in the eyes of the others, to be equal . . . to all, to feel that I too was a man" (in Galluzzo, Nicastro, and Vasile 1992: 101). Many are convinced that Salvatore Inzerillo, furious that the Corleonesi faction had ordered the killing of Carabiniere Captain Basile without consulting other capi, plotted the assassination of the magistrate Costa to show he too could disregard the Commission. In Buscetta's words, "The Costa murder was, by Inzerillo's own admission, nothing more than a way of demonstrating to his adversaries the strength and power of his family" (Buscetta 1984: I, 72).

Many murders, including murders committed as *fatti provi,* are instrumental, intended to eliminate inconvenient persons and, during the "long 1980s," to obstruct inconvenient measures being taken by the state. Judge Costa, for example, had been an effective adversary of Inzerillo, having courageously signed an indictment against him and other bosses. Additional victims in this category include the fifteen or more "excellent cadavers" of that terrible decade, as well as journalists like Mauro de Mauro, Mario Francese, Giuseppe Fava, and Giuseppe Impastato who had the temerity to investigate and publish links between mafia crimes and political patronage. A double instrumentality can be achieved by committing a murder in the territory of a rival, who then becomes the focus of police and public pressure. Inzerillo was "particularly alienated" when the capomafioso Giuseppe Di Cristina was killed in his territory. In addition to the corpse, he complained to Buscetta, even the car used by the killers had been abandoned there.

Some murders seem laden with symbolic intent. This is especially the case when the victim's face or genitals are mutilated to convey a *sfregio*—"a deadly insult and an act of gratuitous aggression" against a victim considered worthless, devoid of honor (Fentress 2000: 178–79). A *sfregio* can be announced even without mutilation—for example, by causing a corpse to disappear. Just as the 1982 appointment of Carabiniere General Carlo Alberto dalla Chiesa to be prefect of Palermo and coordinator of a national antimafia campaign symbolized the state's desire to present a strong public antimafia posture, so was his assassination an assertion of utter disrespect for that effort. Buscetta describes the earlier murder of Public Prosecutor Pietro Scaglione in 1971 as a murder with three objectives: to remove a troublesome prosecutor, to bring heat on two rival mafiosi who were being tried by Scaglione and who might be thought culpable, and to create the suspicion that Scaglione had collaborated with the mafia (Buscetta 1984: I, 70). Calderone further suggests that the Scaglione assassination was the mafia's way of proclaiming its return to potency after the Catanzaro trial, during which it had been quiescent (in Arlacchi 1993: 87–88).

Yet mafia killings can also defy explanation, or seem banal. Another broad category of murders occur because someone has been a "pain in the ass," the enemy of a friend, or the friend of an enemy. Buscetta offers the example of Alfio Ferlito, who was a real "thorn in the side" of Nitto Santapaola of Catania, his boss. Ferlito was also a close friend of Salvatore Inzerillo. Mafiosi from Palermo who were not in Inzerillo's faction happily did Santopaola the big favor of eliminating Ferlito (Buscetta 1984: I, 57ff). Along similar lines, Stefano Bontade scorned Stefano Giaconia. Although he had supported him to become the head of the Palermo Centro *cosca* after the debacle with the La Barberas (see chapter 3), their relationship soured when Giaconia become a co-godparent with Totò Riina, Bontade's enemy. Calderone (in Arlacchi 1993: 159–60) reports that Bontade showed up late at an important meeting called to discuss a bribe to be paid so that the ring road around Palermo would go through Ciaculli. Stepping out of his Porsche Carrera, he apologized for his lateness, saying, "I had to change a flat tire and I had to *inchiaccare* [strangle] Stefano Giaconia." Michele Greco, present at the meeting, approved, saying that Bontade had done well to get rid of this scum, after which Bontade added, "that *cornuto* [cuckold] gave me trouble right up to the end. After I killed him, we set his clothes on fire, and while they were burning there was an explosion. It was a pen-pistol caliber 22 that Giaconia carried with him." Someone present made the sarcastic comment that he was quite a man of honor, still able to shoot from the grave![9]

Although it may be interpreted as a form of braggadocio, one is struck by the apparent nonchalance with which the *pentiti* discuss homicidal techniques. Murder, it seems, became routine—in Brusca's words "a job" *(un lavoro)* like any other. Among the most gratuitously brutal of criminals, Brusca describes the "work" of killing as follows:

> I tortured persons to make them talk; I strangled those who confessed and those who remained silent; I dissolved bodies in acid; I roasted cadavers on the grates; I buried the remains by digging trenches with machines; [and] this aspect of my activity never made much of an impression on me. Tortured persons rarely reveal their secrets. . . . We used pincers on their ears or hammers on their knees, nothing more. But if it was clear that after a half-hour nothing would come out, then we killed them, using a nylon cord to strangle them. Two of us held the arms, two the feet, and one pulled the cord from behind. It took at least ten minutes, and you could tell that it was over when the victim urinated and defecated. Still you had to be sure. It would be very risky to put a body in a barrel of acid and then have a convulsion or spasm—a splash of acid would be deadly for everyone present. . . . Until the early 1980s we used a much slower more primitive system for getting rid of cadavers: roasting them on the grates. We started in the early morning and finished at sunset. It took seven or eight hours to eliminate the whole thing and a truckload of wood. . . . Then we, too, turned to acid. (in Lodato 1999:161–64)

This apparently casual attitude toward atrocity was, we believe, nurtured by the moral environment of the *cosca,* with its collective ridicule of "nobodies" and hierarchical relations stressing obedience to charismatic leaders.

CONCLUSION

Viewed from the "inside," the mafia is a secretive fraternal order whose norms and ritual practices situate its members "outside" normal society and, in their minds, "above" it. *Cosca* members engage in intense male bonding, self-consciously and demonstrably separating themselves from women. An idiosyncratic verbal and gestural lexicon, terms of address and nicknames, a symbolically laden rite of initiation, and the code of *omertà* further bolster their sense of social solidarity, as do mutual aid during crises of imprisonment and lip service to a redistributive ethic. There is also a commitment to elected leadership and short terms of office. And yet, even apart from the ecological and political-economic fault line that has continuously generated "winners" and "losers" in the Palermo region, the mafia is awash, and has long been awash, in psychological tension. Heads and vice-heads of families are easily insulted by actions staged in their territories without their knowledge or permission. Competition for loyal "soldiers" pits leaders against one another. Ambitious and rebellious protégés like Luciano Liggio threaten destabilization. Most important, although hierarchy is limited by bows to direct democracy and equity, it is expected that leaders will avenge lapses of respect. At one of the banquets described above, a heated quarrel broke out because three semi-professional soccer players, there at the invitation of the son of a capo, had the nerve to tease another capo for his style of making toasts. At stake here is a feudal style of social relations.

In effect, two models are in play. At the same time as the mafia is structured through localized fraternities, it is a reticulate social form, a continuum of membership, in which affiliation radiates downward from an inner circle of "made members" toward the *picciotti*—the younger, would-be recruits. Dyadic sets of patrons and clients are configured into vertical chains that link the lowliest *picciotto* to the *cosca* bosses through his sponsor. In contrast to the *cosca*-Commission model, in which fraternal solidarity and secrecy are foremost, we are confronted with clientelistic ties between elders and juniors, magnetic personages and impressionable novices, aggressive upstarts and others who fear or admire them. Nor are the outer limits of these relationships ever clear, extending as they do into wider social and political fields. Both models are valid; indeed, the contradiction between them contributes to the atmosphere of treachery and suspicion that the *pentiti* have described. The second model is particularly crucial, however, to broaching the problem of the mafia's relationship to "Sicilian culture," the thorny issue to which chapter 5 is devoted.

CHAPTER 5

Seeking Causes, Casting Blame

Perhaps the most difficult and intriguing question about the Sicilian mafia is how, given the gross behaviors that set it apart from normal society, it became so thoroughly intertwined with elements of that society. A first approximation hinges on an argument one often hears debated by antimafia activists: that killers on the scale of Giovanni Brusca are an outgrowth of the "long 1980s," when the mafia was distorted by trafficking in drugs. Although many concede this point, they are quick to add that the older, "traditional" mafia—the agrarian mafia even—was also capable of much brutality. The disturbingly gruesome photographs by Nicola Scafidi include, among other horrors of the 1950s, the ten-year-old boy killed by mafiosi during a shootout for control of the Ficuzza forest. His body is laid out on a slab in the morgue of Corleone with his weeping mother next to him and his high-top mud-caked shoes set out below (see fig. 8).

The question forms part of a larger discussion at the core of today's antimafia process: how to locate responsibility for the mafia, or, in other words, who to blame. This means trying to assess the relative contribution to mafia formation of, on the one hand, locally generated history and culture—"ways of being Sicilian"—and, on the other hand, "external forces" emanating from Italy and beyond. Although not mutually exclusive, these elements are weighted differently by different analysts, with consequences not only for social theory but also for the strategies and targets of intervention.

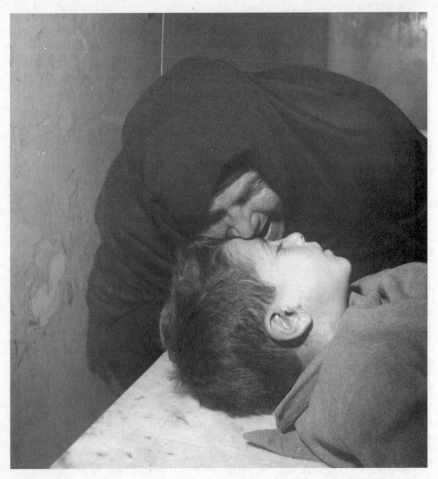

Figure 8. Boy killed by mafiosi in a 1959 shootout for control of the Ficuzza forest near Corleone, a refuge for rustled animals. Photograph by Nicole Scafidi.

If the mafia's nineteenth-century history gave rise to prejudicial stereotypes of Sicilians, this was no less so after World War II. By this time, however, the atrocities of the Holocaust had given racism a bad name, and there was a shift in emphasis from genetic inevitability to another kind of permanence based on unchanging cultural "traditions" (see Balibar 1988). During the "long 1980s," as mafia-related violence was exploding in Sicily, the American-produced CBS program "Sixty Minutes" covered the emergency with a circuitous detour through the rows of well-preserved mummies in Palermo's Capuchin catacombs, proclaiming that Sicilians are burdened with a centuries-old "passion for death." The Italian-American community of New York vehemently protested and CBS issued a formal apology, but the "death wish" metaphor persists, evidenced by frequent quoting of Prince Fabrizio Salina, the imposing protagonist of Giuseppe Tomasi di Lampedusa's novel, *The Leopard*. "In Sicily," the prince told a Piedmontese diplomat, "it doesn't matter whether one does good or evil: the sin that we Sicilians never pardon is simply that of doing" (see Rosengarten 1998: 129).

Whether they conjure up centuries of fatalism, ensconced codes of honor and vendetta, or barely masked genetic determinations, the very words "Sicilian culture" imply a set of values and practices that is here for all time, shared by all, and impervious to change. Of course, these values and practices need not be interpreted in a negative light. Much like the "Pro-Sicilia" movement of the Notarbartolo era, Cardinal Ernesto Ruffini, the first postwar archbishop of Palermo, countered prejudicial representations of Sicilians with a classic "Sicilianist" defense. The mafia, he argued, originated in the distant past to answer the needs of the landed class for order in the countryside. To obsess about organized crime in the present is to indulge the propaganda of northerners who "wish Sicily ill" (Alongi 1997: 24–28 n. 27; Stabile 1986).

The postwar decades also saw a proliferation of political-economic analyses of the mafia, which sidestep the cultural question. Reminiscent of Napoleone Colajanni, in his time almost a lone voice, they attribute causal significance to Sicily's past of domineering landlords, repressive governments, and intense social suffering, in part induced by outsiders. This mode of theorizing illuminates an aspect of the mafia that continues to be important: the institution's deep engagement with certain propertied interests, on the one hand, and with creating livelihoods for dislocated classes, on the other hand. We will ask, however, whether such analyses adequately address the mafia's entwinement not only with the Italian state but with Sicilian society, a question that bears on Sicilian responsibility.

The later sections of this chapter describe how mafiosi "condition" and "provision" elements of the society of which they are a part, creating and servicing relationships with non-mafiosi on whom they depend for cover. To many antimafia activists, mafiosi are advantaged in this regard by Sicily's long-standing system of clientelism. Interpreting this wider favor system as the integument of the mafia, these reformers advocate replacing it with a modern "civil society" and "civic culture." Their agenda requires that we confront, not evade, the cultural issues involved. Perhaps needless to say, we embrace an understanding of culture as nonessentialized, consisting of many contradictory beliefs and practices that are not shared but contested, not constant but variable through time, and, most of all, shaped by the interplay of interested social groups and institutions, working often at cross-purposes to influence or alter the hearts and minds of others.

MARXISM AND THE MAFIA

Following World War II, and in the context of the struggle for land reform, Marxist analyses of the mafia became prevalent. Giuseppe Montalbano, a Communist deputy in the regional parliament and professor of law at the University of Palermo, is a good example. In polemical opposition to the racist prejudice that "Sicilians are by their organic nature delinquents, all mafiosi or tending to be mafiosi" (Montalbano 1949: 5), he elaborated a "class analysis." Sicily's "weak" middle class and "overbearing" landed class were the cause of a system of cliques and clienteles that fostered organized crime. As a kind of occult "middle class," mafiosi secretly inserted their tentacles into every social stratum, imposing their personnel on the landed aristocracy while intimidating the peasantry. To eradicate the mafia, it would never be enough to activate the police; one had to develop the island's backward economy and restructure its oppressive class relations, first and foremost through land reform. Like most of Sicily's Communists and Socialists of the 1950s and 1960s, Montalbano defined the mafia as, effectively, the vigilante backbone of the landed class.

The argument recalled Gramsci's discussion of southern Italian history in the *Prison Notebooks* (1971: 90–102) and, before that, Colajanni's turn-of-the-century response to the Italian school of criminology, which attributed the crime rates of southerners and Sicilians to race. Colajanni's grand-nephew, Pompeo, an important left-wing politician of the 1960s, also explicitly attacked the racism of northerners for deflecting attention from the island's real problem: oppressive class relations. Yet precisely during the 1960s, the ground for a class analysis of the mafia was shifting in confusing ways. As the land reform law of 1950 began to take effect (although not along lines that had been intended), the peasant struggle dissolved into a myriad of projects for mechanizing agriculture. Labor poured out of the countryside, both to the cities of Sicily and to northern Italy and Northern Europe. There were 640,000 Sicilians earning their living from the land in 1951, 488,000 in 1961, and 316,000 in 1971—a precipitous decline. Palermo, we recall, was 41 percent larger by 1981, having added some 206,000 people.

For many Communists and left-wing intellectuals, the land reform carried the promise that the mafia, understood as the product of an obsolete agrarian class structure, would disappear. They either did not recognize its exploding urban presence or they interpreted real estate corruption and, eventually, drug trafficking as the distressing but normal accouterments of urban life under capitalism. Montalbano did not agree and published a long list of rural crimes committed during a few October days of 1962 as a challenge to the thesis that the rural mafia was in decline. As early as 1956, moreover, he delivered a speech to the regional assembly, "The Mafia Is a Plague to Extirpate," about the first mafia war on urban turf, provoked by the transfer of the wholesale produce market from Zisa to Acquasanta. What outraged Montalbano was the authorities' apparent refusal to intervene, based on an "absurd, inhuman, immoral, un-Christian, and unjust thesis that the more mafiosi kill among themselves, the better it is." Logic of this sort undermines respect for the law, he argued, while encouraging the barbarism of private vendettas. In the past such "chains of crime" had plagued rural Sicily, but now they were disrupting city life (Montalbano 1956).

In his later writings, Montalbano anticipated the much younger left-wing intellectual Mario Mineo, who argued for the existence of a *new* Sicilian bourgeoisie, parasitical and nonproductive like its agrarian forerunner, but now urban. Instead of mediating between peasants and landlords, it articulated relations with northern Italian capitalism. Assuming power at the local and regional levels of government, pursuing profits through illegal means, enabling the domination of various *cosche* over urban and rural zones and sectors, and aggressively entering new (especially urban) domains of activity, this *borghesia mafiosa* had emerged like the tip of an iceberg out of the agrarian crisis of the 1950s.[1] The consolidation of the Christian Democratic Party and especially of the institutions of the regional government, gave it the resources necessary to dominate all of Sicily, including the formerly mafia-free eastern provinces. Mineo's analysis, although largely ignored by older leftists, was a point of reference for Sicily's "New Left" intellectuals, who found that it illuminated not only illegal mafia enterprises such as extortion rackets but also legal activities (real estate and construction) penetrated by mafia bosses, capital, and methods (see Mineo 1995; Santino 1988: 204; 2000: 233–34, 249–50).

SCIASCIA: BETWEEN MARXISM AND MYSTIFICATION

In his 1961 collection of essays, *Pirandello and Sicily,* the acclaimed Sicilian novelist Leonardo Sciascia defined the mafia along Marxist lines as
an "association for crime with the aim of enriching its members and posing itself as an element of (parasitic) mediation between property and labor." We know this, he added, because we know "who it shoots"—martyred peasant leaders and left-wing intellectuals (Sciascia 1961: 165). In
the same collection of essays, Sciascia also depicted his fellow Sicilians as
suffering from insecurity. Rather than invest or use accumulated wealth
(roba), they treated it as a nonfungible treasure to be passed on at death,
almost as a patrimonial projection of the person. "The rhythm of accumulation is the rhythm of death" (ibid.: 23). Reflected in this, Sciascia argued, were the pervasive dislocations that had shaped Sicilian history
since medieval times; Sicilians anticipated, almost as a morbid obsession,
that when they died their successors would be at risk (ibid.: 22–26).

Furthermore, Sicilians suffered from an "exasperated form of indi-
vidualism" and corresponding litigiousness, again because of their history. Little *questioni rurali* having to do with property lines, rights of access, the laying out of mule tracks, easily passed from the "land survey
to the ballistic survey" (from the *perito catastale* to the *perito balistico*),
as people sought to police their space and its boundaries on their own
(ibid.: 24). Apprehension rather than avarice motivated their vigilance,
the same apprehension that was directed toward family members, above
all, wives and daughters. Just as a plot of land could be invaded by a
neighbor, the respect due to family members might be violated as well.
In one of his "mafia novels," Sciascia had a police captain muse that for
Sicilians the family is more "a dramatic juridical contract or bond
than . . . a natural association based on affection. The family is the Sicilian's State," and this makes the political state "extraneous to them,
merely a de facto entity based on force" (Sciascia 1964: 95). Accumulating family honor paralleled accumulating *roba.*

A burning question for Sciascia was why, despite the extreme misery
and oppression of Sicilian peasants and miners, class consciousness was
only weakly developed among them. In good leftist tradition, he believed
this problem correlated with the presence of the mafia. Further explanations were borrowed from Gramsci, who, in a famous essay of 1926 on
the Italian "Southern Question," described the entire south as *una dis-
gregazione sociale.* Gramsci's *Prison Notebooks* further developed this
theme: victims of injustice in the south and Sicily are depicted there as

possessing a " 'generic' hatred [which] is still 'semi-feudal' rather than
modern in character" (Gramsci 1971: 272–73). Similarly for Sciascia,
there was a *realtà Siciliana* that gave the regional Socialist movement its
own "particular development," different from the movement of workers in the north (Sciascia 1961: 13). Uprisings resembled anarchism more
than socialism, that is, "an individual revolution, an end in itself," driven
by personal "instincts." The mafia, he believed, had its origins in these
outbursts—these *vendette di classe*—origins it later betrayed.

Despite Sciascia's well-deserved reputation as a pioneering intellectual
of the antimafia movement—his novels were among the first texts to "tell
it like it is" in matters pertaining to the mafia and political corruption—
his admiration for some charismatic "men of honor" was barely con-
cealed. *Mafia Vendetta* (Il giorno della civetta) describes one such man (al-
beit with an overtone of irony) as "an exemplary father, an untiring
worker. He's got rich, certainly he has, but by his own efforts. . . . Certain
men inspire respect: for their qualities, their savoir-faire, their frankness,
their flair for cordial relations, for friendship . . . (they have above all) a
sense of justice . . . naturally, instinctively . . . which makes them inspire
respect" (Sciascia 1964: 62–63). In the same novel, the mafioso in question divides humanity into five categories: "men, half-men, pigmies, arse-
crawlers—if you'll excuse the expression—and quackers," then flatters a
police captain by calling him "a man" (ibid.: 102–3). Interviewed in 1979,
Sciascia drew attention to a *carte souvenir* that members of the Di Cristina
crime family had prepared in 1961 to honor one of their own who had
been killed. It eulogized the victim's "true man" qualities, calling him imposing, respectful, an enemy of all injustices (Sciascia 1979: 28).

Such intimations of respect for individual mafiosi are anathema to the
antimafia leaders of today. As we discuss in chapter 8, before his death
in 1989, Sciascia quarreled bitterly with them, accusing them, in effect,
of being zealous to the point of betraying their Sicilian roots. They in
turn were repulsed by his *Sicilianismo,* suggested by his 1979 reflection
that "in myself as . . . in any Sicilian, the residuals of mafia feeling are
still present and alive," so that fighting the mafia is like fighting "against
myself . . . a split, a laceration" (quoted in Paoli 1997: 66).

HISTORY-LESS HISTORIES

Robert Putnam's *Making Democracy Work: Civic Traditions in Modern
Italy* (1993) blames a wide range of southern Italian and Sicilian problems, including crime and corruption, on governments dating to the thir-

teenth century that were at once feudal, bureaucratic, and absolutist—
governments that did little but try to impose "hierarchy" over a "latent
anarchy" (Putnam 1993: 123–30). Sciascia's view was similar. The Norman period was creative; a state emerged that organized an interior
unity. There followed, however, five centuries of conflict—between pa-
pacy and empire, Christianity and Islam, Latin and Germanic cultures,
city-states and nation-states—during which this unity fell apart, with enduring consequences for Sicilians as a people (Sciascia 1961: 9–11). But
unlike Sciascia who valorized this people, Putnam sees them burdened by
a litany of woes. Lacking civil consensus, public faith, or any "spirit of
association," they are prey to inept and arbitrary justice, factionalism
and corruption, the impossibility of guaranteeing contracts or regulating
risk, and a mountain of fear and suspicion. Putnam is aware that this assessment, which he also applies to southern Italians, is reminiscent of Edward C. Banfield's *The Moral Basis of a Backward Society*. This much-
criticized 1958 book reduced all of Italian society south of Rome to the
single behavioral trope of "amoral familism."

A similarly bleak outlook underlies Diego Gambetta's widely cited
theory of mafia formation. Conjuring up a market metaphor, Gambetta
defines the mafia as "a specific economic enterprise, an industry which
produces, promotes, and sells private protection" (Gambetta 1993: 1).
As a first-order explanation, he focuses on the legislative creation of private property in early nineteenth-century Sicily, which required institutional arrangements and a regulatory apparatus that the (then Bourbon)
state was incapable of generating. This circumstance spelled widespread
uncertainty and intense conflict over the management and disposition of
resources, whether in agriculture, urban markets, or local politics. Such
were the structural conditions that made protection by force and intimidation a welcome, hence marketable, substitute for mutual trust, enabling other forms of economic exchange to develop. The advantage of
turning to mafiosi as "sellers of protection" was their capacity to control and handle information discreetly, to administer violence and intimidation, and to cultivate a reputation for power and influence. The
mafia's contacts in high places also immeasurably enhanced its ability to
provide order-enhancing services.

In Gambetta's model, the Sicilian market for "illegal" protection was
vast because protection was not forthcoming from more conventional
sources, such as private and public insurance companies, the judiciary,
and the police. Yet beneath this nineteenth-century crisis there lay a
deeper history. Envisioning Sicily, along the lines of Putnam, as an "un-

civil society," Gambetta argues that its social institutions—the family, the Church, and the community—had, over the long run, failed to cultivate mutual trust. Perhaps the Spanish conquest and rule of the island in the late sixteenth century had initiated this downward spiral (Gambetta 1987; 1993: 77–81). Whatever its origin, Sicilians entered their nineteenth-century encounter with the preeminent forces of the modern world already crippled by untrusting relations—an additional reason for their eagerness to buy illegal protection when the seas got rough.

Gambetta recognizes the mafia's latent violence: in providing protective services, it may also provoke tension and uncertainty. But he is reluctant to characterize mafiosi as extortionist. Because Sicilians are chronically unable to trust each other, protection is genuinely needed and desired. Pursuing this line of reasoning, he has engaged in an interesting polemic with sociologist Raimondo Catanzaro, who defines the mafia as a quasi-political group with intermittent financing based on extorted prestations. Unlike a bandit or a thief, the mafioso must maintain ongoing social relations with his victims, so he presents himself as a protector. As an entrepreneur of protection, however, he is the menace as well. In other words, his capacity for violence is absolutely critical, as extortion becomes regularized in exchange for guarantees of security (see Catanzaro 1992, 1993, 1994; Gambetta 1994).[2]

In the abstract, Gambetta has no quarrel with Catanzaro's interpretation: an offer can create a demand. There is no need, he admits, to hypothesize a "generic, indigenous, *sfiducia* [lack of trust]" to account for why the market for protection might reinforce itself. At the same time, however, Gambetta seems convinced that a long "prehistory" of absent trust is what got things derailed in the first instance. Mafiosi thus appear in his writing as "violent illegal protectors" (Gambetta 1993: 151) rather than "violent illegal aggressors." As noted at the outset of this chapter, there is often a tradeoff between stressing (national) politics and (local) culture in accounting for the mafia. Gambetta, with his evocation of Sicilians' "lack of trust" and his attribution of that lack to a deep and consistent history, implies a greater emphasis on culture than he would perhaps intend.

This argument, like Putnam's, is reminiscent of path dependency theories of economic development, which propose that pre-existing regional cultures shape regional histories and institutions, above all the trajectories that favor or impede such development. In some versions of this argument, the shaping culture is presented as consisting of particular patterns of kinship, residence, supra-familial cooperation, religious practices and values, but other versions are simpler, zeroing in on trust or lack thereof as in Fukuyama's "low trust" and "high trust" societies. Such terms are extremely general, making it impossible to correlate them with the myriad developmental situations characteristic of recent times. Still more to the point, they preclude our asking how particular histories and institutions—the institutionalization of the mafia, for example—contribute to building or undermining social trust (see Leonard 2001: 539–49).

Assigning a centuries-long pedigree to purportedly Sicilian attributes of character is a way to essentialize without appearing to. Franchetti pioneered the formula: in Sicily, banditry, crime, and dereliction were necessary outgrowths of hundreds of years of feudal government, oppressive landlords, peasant and urban squalor, and an absent middle class. Whether this history encompasses "hundreds of years" or three hundred or five hundred matters little; the point is that it renders the mafia inevitable, an inexorable outcome of a Sicilian "way of being" that has changed very little through time. If nothing else, antimafia activism calls into question this resolution of the mafia-culture problem, dictated by the *longue durée*. Closer to an evolutionary proposition, to what Hegel referred to as "history-less history," it freezes Sicilians in a mold of the past, implying that change must always come from outside. Offering no room for alternatives, or for movement, such histories hardly illuminate what is happening now. Unforeseen by most, including ourselves in the 1960s (although perhaps it was not unforeseeable), the continuing antimafia struggle challenges the idea of culture as constant.

THE *MERIDIANA* GROUP AND THE NEW SOUTHERN HISTORIOGRAPHY

Practitioners of the new historiography of the mafia have also had to confront the "culture question." Their answers reflect their association with a wider group of mainly southern Italian scholars who, in the 1980s, came together around the journal *Meridiana*. Affiliated with the Universities of Naples, Bari, and Catania, this group was wearily impatient with the seemingly immovable Italian discourse on "southern backwardness"—the south's failure to develop as against the north's success, and the north's dynamism as against the south's "history-less history." The time had come to move beyond these binary categories with their implied cultural determinisms and, as Piero Bevilacqua, an early leader insisted, to study the south in its own right and on its own terms

(Bevilacqua 1993; see also Davis 1998). From a *Meridiana* perspective, there is nothing to do but bracket as irrelevant the "ways of being Sicilian" that so many others have linked to the mafia's formation.

A common thread connects the *Meridiana* group to postcolonial intellectuals who have similarly had to confront outsiders' stubbornly entrenched opinion that their people's culture is a recipe for backwardness and worse. Not surprisingly, perhaps, some have taken a step reminiscent of the work of Indian historian Partha Chatterjee (1993), turning the moral tables on whose culture is inadequate. As Mariella Pandolfi has written, "Some southerners, including intellectuals, would counter the deeply ingrained Italian motif of a rupture between a hard-working north and a poor, parasitic, and mafia-ridden south by denouncing the northern region as a capitalist wasteland with a long history of starving its own workers and peasants, as well as appropriating southern resources" (1998: 285). John Davis puts it this way: "One of the most important features of the new southern historiography" has been its "more brutal assessment of the processes of capitalist development in the North" (1998: 218).

In a recent book on "southern identity," Mario Alcaro, a philosopher at the University of Calabria, goes so far as to argue for reclaiming the "southern" values of familism and hospitality as an antidote to the "northern" values of an impersonal technocracy. In his formulation, southern culture exemplifies the generous and humane practice of "the gift" as against the crass, self-serving practice of the commodity. Whereas the former reinforces community, the latter dissolves it into alienating and utilitarian relationships. Contra Putnam, the risk of an uncivil society is not in the south but in the north (Alcaro 1999).

But what about the undeniable pervasiveness of clientelism, and the obvious, if not pervasive, manifestations of organized crime in southern Italy and Sicily? For the *Meridiana* scholars, these phenomena have everything to do with the formation of the Italian nation-state and the state's orientation toward these regions since its unification in 1860. Here, they show, the nation-state "prioritized the creation of networks of political patronage at the expense of productive investment" (Davis 1998: 210). Its late nineteenth-century tariff policies favored the more "backward," latifundist sector of the regional economy over the dynamically developing sector of luxury crops and vineyards (see Giarrizzo 1983). And, as the suffrage expanded, national political leaders turned to unscrupulous mediators of the electoral process in the south—mediators who wove the *intreccio* of the mafia and politics. As purveyors "not only of protection but also of votes and social control," mafiosi were "essential partners in government" (Davis 1998: 218–19). If a wide berth was thereby given to criminality and corruption in Sicily, blame should be cast in the direction of those who made, and continued to make, the regimes of governance in Rome—not at the so-called culture of the island.

Clearly, the new historiography removes the onus from Sicilian culture as an incubator of the mafia, recruiting a new cast of culpable characters to the drama. Such a move is consistent with the thinking of contemporary antimafia activists who assign a large dose of responsibility for the "long 1980s" to the national-level political regime of Giulio Andreotti and the Christian Democratic Party. The fundamental question of responsibility is thus answered: the "moral sickness of the south" was not "an indication of an inferior level of civilization" but the consequence of a distorted involvement with the national system of power (Lupo 1990: 152). Yet activists and scholars alike recognize that some of the problematic national-level scoundrels are of Sicilian provenance, that, indeed, Italy's discursive north-south opposition "masks the deep continuity of a national structure of political power in which southerners have been significant participants" (Pandolfi 1998: 285).

MAFIA, CULTURE, AND POWER

During our first sojourn in Sicily in the 1960s, we made note of a cluster of attitudes or dispositions evident in the words and actions of those around us that we glossed as a preoccupation with honor, following the then prevalent terminology of anthropologists studying the Mediterranean littoral. The issue, it seemed, was people's sensitivity to status injury or denials of respect in which material and emotional considerations were fused. People's feelings about "things," including property and resources, merged with their feelings about people. Violations of claims to either provoked an intense sense of personal harm that was, simultaneously, "interested." The very word "interests"—*interessi*—was laden with commitment.

Concern for individual efficacy or potency and a related touchiness in interpersonal relations accompanied this pattern. Among near-equals in Villamaura, the town we studied, status inferiors sought parity, superiors feared envy, and resentment spoiled any number of cooperative endeavors. It was expected that people would closely defend their own interests and take offense at signs of encroachment by others. Self-conscious about equity, persons who improved their positions knew, or anyway believed, that they were the objects of unkind gossip or, at best, grudging admiration. Prophylactic rituals, such as distributing sweets on auspicious occasions and placing amulets on infants, were intended as antidotes to the spiritual danger of a rival's evil eye (see Schneider and Schneider 1976: 100–102).

Many of the Sicilians whom we met in those days also cared a great deal about reputation, categorizing themselves and each other as *furbo* or *fesso*. The *furbi*, or clever ones, were those who successfully defended their turf and were admired for it, whereas the *fessi* let themselves be pushed around. Even trivial slights had to be answered, lest their subject lose face. A related value was that of *fare i fatti suoi* (minding one's own business). Together these dispositions created a moral context in which third parties—those who were neither aggressors nor victims but merely bystanders to an altercation or an encroachment—felt justified in looking the other way and remaining silent.

Interwoven with these values was the extraordinary warmth and generous hospitality for which Sicilians are rightly proud and at the same time often self-critical. People saw themselves living in a world in which personal connections made the difference between getting ahead and falling behind in life. Going through life, one cultivated a series of quasi-contractual relationships—between patrons and clients, favor bestowers and favor seekers, friends and friends of friends, saints and sinners—all of them a mix of instrumentality and affect. Friends were persons whose company one enjoyed but who might, at some hypothetical point, also be "useful." Through generosity and hospitality, people invested in people, just in case. Expressions such as "he who does not accept a gift does not deserve it" *(chi non accetta non merita)* and "with friends one goes a long way" capture the subtle yet palpable power plays that render guests or recipients of favors *vincolato*—obligated for the foreseeable future, even if grudgingly. Notwithstanding the warmth and wonderful times, this potentially demanding edge to generosity added a modicum of tension to interpersonal relations.

Yet other sides to Sicilian cultural practice were evident even in 1965. People we knew in Villamaura self-consciously diffused interpersonal tensions in various ways. One was for the parties to a conflict to pronounce themselves *sciarriati*—the dialect word for "not on speaking terms"—a civil alternative to persistent quarreling or worse. Disputants also often sought and willingly accepted mediation; informal mediators of all kinds, not necessarily mafiosi, were frequently able to negotiate the terms of a settlement between estranged parties. Contrary to the impression of many that peasant politics were necessarily imbued with the sentiment of individual vendetta, in the 1960s we were greatly impressed by the adherence of thousands of peasants and artisans to a coherent left-wing ideology of class struggle that seemed to transcend their experience of personally humiliating relationships with landlords. Describing the workshops of local artisans as "little universities," peasants as well as artisans gathered in them in the evenings to hear newspapers read aloud and analyze why the "system of production" caused suffering and oppression. Armed with this perspective, they seemed to us to stand outside of, and to self-reflectively criticize, some of the attitudes outlined above. The same might also be said of the cluster of young idealists, generally from peasant and artisan families, who gathered around Danilo Dolci, the self-styled "Italian Gandhi," who, in the 1960s, led marches and hunger strikes to draw international attention to Sicilian poverty.

During the 1970s, we undertook a follow-up study of Villamaura, focusing on its "demographic transition" from a high to a very low birthrate. Because the town's different classes experienced this change in different decades, and for different reasons, we became particularly attentive to cultural variation among them. Artisans (shoemakers, tailors, seamstresses, cabinetmakers, stonemasons, blacksmiths, and so on) stood out as different. Not only were they the backbone of the local Communist Party; for reasons of their work and travel and way of life, they exhibited a particular affinity for the universalizing rational culture of the French Enlightenment, a culture that many intellectuals of the time, among them Sciascia, felt strongly attracted to but did not think their fellow Sicilians could share. In a second book, *Festival of the Poor* (1996), we analyzed in detail why it was that these artisans were enthusiastic about, and a conduit for the diffusion of, a strikingly rationalized birth control method, coitus interruptus, borrowed from France. Among other reasons, artisans enjoyed companionate marriages, in which, far from any caricatured "code of honor" with its implied pattern of patriarchy, husbands and wives were partners.

Looking back now, it seems obvious that yet other possibilities and alternatives would have been evident had we taken account of the cities. Knowing little about urban life except as occasional visitors to Palermo, we were, for example, quite ignorant of the brewing student radicalism at the university, notwithstanding our own backgrounds in the anti–Vietnam War movement in the United States. Yet, as chapter 7 clar-

ifies, some of the seeds of the late twentieth-century struggle against the
mafia were planted in 1969—the "'68" of the University of Palermo.

Our 1976 book, *Culture and Political Economy in Western Sicily*, reflects the influence of Montalbano and Sciascia, as well as several historians, Sicilian and otherwise, writing at the time about Sicily (in particular, Denis Mack Smith, Eric Hobsbawm, Francesco Renda, and
Rosario Romeo). Consistent with all of this work, whether Marxist or
liberal, it interprets the mafia as an outgrowth of capitalist and state-
making processes of the nineteenth century. The book also describes
mafiosi as "specialists" in the values and behaviors described above, especially those surrounding honor, friendship, hospitality, and wit. In setting themselves up as "men of honor," mafiosi, we suggested, were in-
tensifying the expression of Sicilian culture. It was not our intent,
however, to essentialize these values and behaviors. On the contrary, our
project in Sicily had been stimulated in part by our critical reading of
Banfield. Yet our way around this problem then seems unsatisfactory
now—to trace the foundations of the cultural codes in question ("familism" among them) to Sicily's deep history of conquests and coloniza-
tions, reinforced through continued subordination to Italy and the West
in recent times. The point was to explain the codes, or account for them,
in ways that—should anyone think them unflattering or "backward"—
exonerated Sicilians.

Such a strategy, we have come to see, denies agency to the subjects of
one's research, whose practices and values, like any other people's culture, are an inconsistent and at times conflictual mix. People in Sicily as
well as outsiders find elements in this mix to criticize and other elements
to praise. And they do not necessarily agree with each other in their evaluations, in part because different constituencies have authored values
and practices at odds with the "mainstream." This is the case not only
for the already noted cultural innovators—artisans, university students,
members of the regional Communist Party, contemporary antimafia activists—but also true for the mafiosi, who go to extraordinary lengths to
separate themselves in some respects from the rest.

By the same token, the Sicilian cultural values and practices surrounding reputation and friendship, hospitality and cleverness, have a
far wider geographical distribution than does organized crime. Whereas
the mafia emerged and was concentrated in western Sicily, such values
and practices have also been reported for eastern Sicily and southern
Italy, and in provinces having nothing to do with the Neapolitan
Camorra or the Calabrian *'Ndrangheta* (see Davis 1969, 1973). Further

inflected by local and regional histories (see Herzfeld 1980), variations of them flourished in a pan-Mediterranean universe (Gallant 2000: 375 n.60). For most of this universe, moreover, there was no necessary connection between "the cluster of attitudes and attributes often glossed as honor" and acts of violence. In certain times and places, ritualized dueling engaged elites; in other times and places, shepherds, peasants, or the urban poor confronted one another in equally rule-bound knife fights. Just as often, however, masculine efficacy was expressed through hurling insults. In a study that traces changing manifestations of honor in nineteenth-century Greece, Gallant argues that although the "credible threat of physical violence" was often implied, the concept was far more "malleable" than most allow (ibid.: 373–81).

Nevertheless, most antimafia activists believe that mafiosi have benefited from having remnants of an historical "honor culture" in their environment. This is nowhere more evident than in the mafia's remarkable ability to condition and provision others. In spinning webs of patron-client relations, mafiosi pick up on the wider cultural significance of generous hospitality and bestowals, expectations of reciprocity, and sensitivity to slight or disrespect, all of which give these relations a compelling edge. Indeed, it is because of these values and orientations that both patrons and clients think twice before dropping the ball in the favor system, the patrons because they fear their clients' enmity and disloyalty; the clients because they fear being abandoned in the future. Apart from self-help justice, no pattern of cultural practice is more anathema to the antimafia struggle than *clientelismo*—the mafia's scaffolding of social and political support.

FRIENDS, AND FRIENDS OF FRIENDS

Mafiosi, we believe, have long established an organic connection to their surroundings through two ongoing processes of association. One is the process of self-consciously *conditioning* elite interlocutors, constructing webs of mutual reciprocity that go beyond any narrow instrumentality; the corollary process involves *provisioning* ordinary folk. Because of the vast array of conditioned political connections that mafiosi enjoy, they are often better able than nominal officials of the state to assist ordinary Sicilians with jobs, access to bureaucratic offices, solutions to other problems. Neither process entails direct blackmail as a modus operandi, yet the mafia's reputation for violence surely lurks in the background, ensnaring conditioned elites and provisioned subalterns in a potentially menacing tangle of social relations. At the same time, however, mafiosi invest in making these exchanges rewarding and normal, even prestigious, such that their interlocutors and clients might think themselves fortunate to be involved.

Tizio's comment (in chapter 4) that his rustic mafioso father was up to frequenting the "circles in Palermo that count" was not idiosyncratic. In his father's day, leading mafiosi typically sought to rub shoulders with professionals, politicians, officials, and businessmen in informal settings conducive to mutual enjoyment and casual talk. In Palermo they cultivated an especially dense network of relationships with entrepreneurs and officials involved in the construction industry. With a few exceptions, it was preferred that these notables be "contiguous" rather than *cosca* members. By not belonging, they could hope to avoid any criminal liability and escape as well an endless barrage of demands from lesser initiates. Within the mafia, this arrangement enhanced the authority of individual capi who functioned as exclusive brokers between rank-and-file "soldiers" and important patrons.

Perhaps it goes without saying that lawyers, judges, police officers, bankers, doctors, and public officials can be useful to the mafia, the more so as they occupy positions of authority in key institutions. But their efficacy is ensured in the degree that they are "friendly," the point being to condition them to make decisions, or non-decisions, that enable mafiosi to thrive. Typically, a mafioso who must solve a problem involving a key institution asks himself or a close friend, *"Cu ci avemu 'dda?"*—dialect for "Who do we have there?"—meaning, whom can we rely on to lend a hand?

Vignettes told by Calderone illustrate how conditioning works. Once he and his brother, both of Catania, were asked to help the wife of a judge whose small property was about to be bisected by the Catania-Enna highway under construction. Owners of the firm that had won the contract to build this road were already friends; so the brothers went to them and "the road was shifted; [the firm] even rearranged the layout of the [judge's wife's] property." Subsequently, the judge expressed friendship toward the Calderone brothers, paying a hospital visit to their ailing father. Here then was a judge on whom one could count. The brothers continued to visit him, taking him gifts of fresh fish and black market cigarettes ("Marlboros for him and Muratti Ambassadors for his family"; Calderone, in Arlacchi 1993: 156). Meanwhile, the contractors had "loads of lawyers and judges in their pockets," including a powerful supervisory judge nicknamed Napoleon, for whom they did a great deal of work, gratis. Other judges lived rent free in an apartment complex that the contractors built. Having learned through their own connections with an officer of the Carabinieri that one of their cousins was about to be arrested, the Calderone brothers went to the owner of the contracting firm, who intervened with the judiciary to have the cousin's name struck from the list (ibid.: 156–58). Calderone notes that Salvo Lima, the Christian Democratic mayor of Palermo and Euro-deputy, also helped them solve problems, for example, when the brothers went to him for help in arranging the transfer of a policeman *"chi dava fastidio"* ("who was a bother") (ibid.: 177).

Calderone likens the mafioso to a spider as he "builds his web of friends, acquaintances, obligations" (ibid.: 20). During our first years in Sicily, the web of associations that underpinned "conditioned" relationships was less hidden than it later became, and our understanding of how it works comes partly from personal observation, as well as from the confessions of the *pentiti*. Typically, mafiosi invited local and regional notables—the mayor, the local parliamentary deputy, clerics, lawyers, bankers, and owners of land and enterprises—to their major life-cycle celebrations, above all, weddings and baptisms. They often also asked such persons to serve in the role of witness to a wedding, or godparent to a child, this being a way to establish a life-long patron-client relation with a potential interlocutor. As a rule, the invitations were not refused. Although they surely elicited varying degrees of apprehension about eventual requests for reciprocity, it was considered flattering and possibly auspicious to be asked. Significantly, mafia funerals were notorious for the large number of officials and professionals who joined the mourners. At the funeral of mafioso Giuseppe Di Cristina in Riesi, the Christian Democratic flag was hung at half-mast outside the party headquarters, bordering the procession route (Cimino 1983).

In addition to the life-cycle celebrations of the mafioso and his family, a strategic occasion for nurturing relationships with notable interlocutors was the rustic banquet, or *schiticchia*. Affairs similar to the banquets that Peter Schneider attended could be held for any number of reasons and were standard fare at the annual sheep shearings. We participated in several of these in the 1960s and 1970s at which the local priest, veterinarian, politicians, and officers of the Carabinieri joined shepherds, mafiosi, and their families in awesome feasts of stewed innards and roasted lamb or goat. Women, it should be noted, joined in these events, cooking and serving the meals. (Calderone says that women took pleasure in serving mafiosi "around big tables" [Arlacchi 1993:

148], and we have observed the same). Much as at weddings and baptisms, the wives of mafiosi interacted with the wives of notables, some of whom might already be godparents to their children.

Among the legendary sites for *schiticchie* were the properties of the mafioso cousins Ignazio and Nino Salvo, who, although denounced by the Parliamentary Antimafia Commission and forced to give up their tax collection franchise in 1982, had for a long time been supplementing their own funds with massive Italian and European Community financing to develop model cattle ranches and vineyards, tourist hotels, distilleries, and bottling plants throughout Sicily (*La Repubblica,* August 6, 1984; *Unità,* August 17, 1982). In the mid-1970s, we attended a sheep-shearing feast at a Salvo-owned vineyard near Villamaura at which a Carabiniere officer got drunk on the wine, embarrassing himself before all the invitees. These references to rural properties and rustic banquets should not give the impression that past occasions for amicable encounters between the mafia and other elites were only small-town affairs, however. The upper crust of Palermo society, proud owners of country estates that they visited periodically, included judges and other professionals. It used to be taken for granted that a magistrate would be friendly with the employees of his rural estate—the overseer, guards, and shepherds—even though they invariably belonged to the local *cosca.* Their children played with his children; they generously welcomed his guests (from Palermo, Italy, and abroad) when at dawn he brought them up to a cheese-processing hut in the mountains for a bowl of fresh ricotta; and he graciously attended their baptisms and weddings as a gesture of reciprocal good will.

It is our impression (based on the *pentito* reports) that mafiosi and notables involved in the "sack" of Palermo acquired and made extensive use of secluded country houses to hunt, target-shoot, and banquet with "friends and friends of friends" (see Calderone, in Arlacchi 1993: 116). A shooting range and club in Addaura at the northern edge of the city was one such place. Another was Michele Greco's Ciaculli estate and villa, replete with a shooting range. The comings and goings of important personages to this property generated constant gossip and a certain mystique. In February 1985, when Michele ("the Pope") and his brother, Salvatore, were fugitives, the police and Carabinieri sealed off and conducted a four-day blitz in and around Ciaculli. Rumors immediately circulated that while searching Greco's house (in vain), they had stumbled upon a network of tunnels and chambers accessible through a trap door covered by an oriental rug in the living room. According to news reports, these subterranean pathways were lined with niches for torch lights and led to a large circular gallery, evoking the Beati Paoli. Seats carved out of stone lined the circumference of the room, which was lit by additional torches, while a large, well-equipped kitchen occupied an adjacent gallery.

Shortly after this account was published with great fanfare in the *Giornale di Sicilia,* investigators learned that it was largely false, the fantasy of a journalist and the policemen responsible for the search. What existed was merely a basement room outfitted for entertaining friends. Yet the story rekindled the mystification of the mafia and the power of its charter myth. It also pointed up the moral ambiguity of breaking bread with the mafia. Such basement locales were also places where mafia leaders made weighty decisions to eliminate enemies, where they strategized to gain control of the fragile and contested Commission, and where they hid both armaments and fugitives for extended periods of time (ibid.: 129–30). How privy to all this were their guests from the world of legitimate business and politics is something that the investigating magistrates would love to know.

If Palermo's top bosses and notables were welcome guests in country settings, they gravitated, as well, toward any number of urban locales. The *pentito* Marino Mannoia tells of seeing an opening, "perhaps one of the tunnels of the Beati Paoli," behind the wall of a suburban villa belonging to the Inzerillo family, this being a place where men of all sorts gathered (Arlacchi 1995: 93). The luxurious Art Nouveau hotel, Villa Igea, was another haven. Its manager and assistant were recently convicted for allowing it to become a retreat for fugitives, a place for the bosses to hold receptions, an employer of "recommended" personnel, and a safe haven for drug traffickers (*Giornale di Sicilia,* October 20, 1999). At one of his hotels, the Zagarella, located just east of Palermo on the coast, Nino Salvo entertained powerful politicians, among them Lima, a regular weekend poker companion (Calabrò 1984; Calderone, in Arlacchi 1993: 175). In 1995 this hotel became a centerpiece in the dramatic trial of former Prime Minister Giulio Andreotti, accused of having colluded with the mafia. Not long after the trial opened in Palermo in October of that year, photographs taken in June 1979 by renowned photographer Letizia Battaglia were introduced into evidence. One of them shows Andreotti with Nino Salvo at Zagarella, both in the company of Lima and other regional DC leaders. The manager of the hotel at the time testified that Salvo had ordered the "best possible" buffet and personally conducted Andreotti on a tour of the finest rooms (Arlacchi 1995: 105; Buongiorno 1995; *Il Manifesto,* October 11, 1996).

According to Calderone's recollection, Nino Salvo and his cousin Ignazio were not only the "richest men in Sicily" but splendid hosts. Badalamenti was proud of and guarded his friendship with them. A parade of people filled their offices, seeking their favor. When the Calderone brothers sought Lima's help to arrange the transfer of the troublesome Catania police inspector, it was the Salvo cousins who intervened. "Outside of Cosa Nostra they were powerful and unreachable." But "inside we were all equals. . . . Dinners at their Palermo apartment were very refined" (Calderone, in Arlacchi 1993: 148). Brusca, though, as noted above, found Nino Salvo to be more gregarious than Ignazio—"more Cosa Nostra."

In all probability, the web of associations just sketched had only a limited potential to shield the vast expansion of illegal drug trafficking after 1970. For one thing, this commerce depended on cultivating a wider than usual network of contacts, one that reached out to international financiers and secret service operatives. In addition, the traffic provoked antimafia initiatives by elements of both the state and civil society that, however piecemeal and timid at first, rendered the celebratory occasions in secluded or exclusive locales less and less comfortable for outsiders. To understand the circumstances of conditioning during the "long 1980s" properly would require penetrating another world, the inaccessible and truly off-stage arena of the deviated masons touched on in chapter 3. Masonry, we recall, sets a person up with a vast network of dependable friends in all of the institutions.

PAYBACK

In conditioning outsiders, mafiosi are less concerned to establish quid pro quo exchanges than to cultivate "many-stranded relationships" of intertwined interest and affect (see Wolf 1966). Relationships of this sort are morally ambiguous. They draw the notable into *liking* the mafioso— into knowing about his family and their circumstances, enjoying some outrageously good times, looking forward to the next feast—despite his reputation for violence. The notable, so conditioned, becomes, then, an open-ended resource, a person who is perhaps never approached for favors but who is always approachable, *a disposizione,* as the saying goes.

An entanglement of our own in the mid-1960s can serve as an example. We had become friendly with a mafioso butcher whom we will call Vito, enjoying his family's hospitality and participating in events like sheep shearings through his mediation. During a week when we were absent from Sicily to attend a conference, he had been arrested on a charge of selling stolen lambs. Upon our return, he asked Peter Schneider to drive him to the city of Trapani, where he hoped to encounter the magistrate investigating the case. They would travel in our almost new Fiat 850, which we were soon to sell, our time in Sicily having virtually ended. Vito determined to leave at five-thirty in the morning, not because of the distance to be covered but because he would need to follow several strands of his network in order to find someone who knew someone who knew the judge.

Three different channels were pursued, connections suggested by Vito's brother who was a priest, by a mafioso butcher in a very large town who had friends in the archdiocese of Trapani, and by two horse-meat butchers in Trapani who also traded in horses, used cars, and trucks. Although at the end of the day it was not these two butchers who had produced the contact that mattered, Vito felt obligated to them for their efforts and, returning to their shop, asked them if they were interested in buying the American's car. They were, and the American agreed to the sale, even though he had already begun negotiations with another potential buyer and intuitively distrusted the men with whom he now had to deal. The sense of being trapped in a situation not of our own making and little to our liking was owed, in the end, to another sense— that of feeling obligated to Vito (see P. Schneider 2000).

Thanks to their skill in conditioning, in elevating the comfort level of officials and professionals in various sectors and institutions, mafiosi themselves constitute a resource for local populations. They, and sometimes they alone, know where to go to "fix things." Their clients are myriad: people who want jobs, who want to move up on the list of eligibles for public housing, who have a bone to pick with a neighbor, whose children are taking examinations in school and need recommendations. These large and small things are an integral part of the reciprocities that have long sustained poor people in Sicily and continue to do so today. One detects their importance from the very word that is used in approaching employers: *datori di lavoro,* "givers of work." Can they, will they, *assumere* a person? This word, which in English means "to assume," also has a religious connotation in Italian. The Assumption was when God "assumed," that is, took responsibility for, Mary, who rose, by His will, into Heaven. In provisioning the supplicant poor of Sicily with mediated access to various institutions, mafiosi pave the way for some of them to be "assumed" in this almost miraculous sense.

Here a quid pro quo does exist: the votes of the client and his or her close kin are to be cast as the mafioso dictates. Other reciprocities are open-ended but possible, so much so that, like the *popolino* whom Italo Pardo (1996) has described for Naples, most Sicilians go out of their way to avoid entanglements. Unfortunately, life is not predictable, and things happen. A friend of ours was a young teenager when her father incurred some debts and turned to a mafioso for help. Some time later, he was asked to hide a fugitive in their small apartment. At age sixteen, our friend found herself giving over her room to this unexplained and uncomfortably inexplicable stranger.

CONCLUSION

Like spiders, mafiosi have spun an ensnaring web. Through their conditioning practices, they have rendered a segment of society contiguous to, if not complicitous in, their affairs; through provisioning they have commandeered the Italian political system. In Arlacchi's words, "The almost metaphysical halo of mystery and secrecy that has always surrounded this theme is connected to extremely embarrassing facts that had to be kept hidden so as to avoid endangering careers, reputations, and the bases of legitimacy for various established powers" (Arlacchi 1993: 13). This is why antimafia activists believe they must overturn a moral-cultural as well as a political-economic "destiny."

We began this chapter with an overview of recent theorizing about the mafia; in conclusion it is striking how inadequate most theories are for addressing the culture question. Either it is ignored (by Marxists, for example), essentialized (Sicily is a generic "low trust" kind of place, period), or broached defensively ("our ways" are not only separable from organized criminality, they are morally preferable to other ways). In no case are we guided to appreciate the investments made by mafiosi in penetrating, taking advantage of, and also altering, the world around them. Yet these investments, and the world that responded to them, in part out of familiarity with wider clientelistic practices, are crucial to understanding what the antimafia process is up against.

It is a complicated matter whether persons conditioned and provisioned by the mafia should be thought of as having had a say in the matter or not. To the extent that the institution is predatory—by means of charisma and charm as well as violence—interlocutors and clients can seem innocent. Add to this the implications of the historical context: what is abhorrent to many today may have been a "normal" part of everyday life in the past. It is, finally, very human for the weaker person in a potentially menacing situation to rationalize his or her compliance by accepting the stronger person's claim to legitimacy. In this sense, argues Gouldner (1970: 290–97), "might" sometimes makes "right." All of which translates into considerable moral complexity when it comes to judging others for complicity.

If the theories covered in this chapter have little to contribute to dilemmas surrounding the relation of "Sicilian culture" to mafia formation, however, some of them—the Marxist theories—are pointedly strong on the historical development of class relations in Sicily. As will become apparent, after the 1970s, Marxism lost its analytical edge within the antimafia movement, giving way to analyses centered on cultural reform. It is a very big problem that, for all of its cultural interventions, the movement has, to date, not come close to resolving fundamental issues of employment, health, and well-being for lower-class people, for which some kind of class analysis remains salient.

CHAPTER 6

Mysteries and Poisons

Just as the "long 1980s" became a crucible of violence, it also framed an intensified police-judicial crackdown on the mafia, the highpoint of which was the maxi-trial, known colloquially as the maxi, which began in February 1986 and lasted until December 1987. During this period, sometimes called the Palermo *Primavera,* or Spring, Sicilian prosecutors indicted 475 mafiosi, trying 460 of them in a bunker courthouse specially constructed for this purpose inside the walls of the Ucciardone, the city's massive nineteenth-century Bourbon prison. Most were convicted, and, to the surprise of many, the convictions were upheld several years later, in 1992, after the final stage of appeal.

This chapter traces three themes in the vicissitudes of the criminal justice effort. The first is its marked discontinuity. Prosecutors gathered momentum from the late 1970s into the years of the maxi but then were undercut by a public opinion backlash whose purpose, they believe, was to delegitimate them. From their perspective, the attacks opened the door to a series of imbroglios that prefigured the dramatic massacres of Giovanni Falcone and Paolo Borsellino in 1992. The judiciary was revitalized in the aftermath of these terrible murders and the police action became effective again, yet the path remains bumpy, with the issue of delegitimation continuing to reverberate through the courthouses of Sicily and the nation.

Second, contributing to the discontinuity of the criminal justice effort are the intrigue and uncertainty produced by the relationship between

the mafia and politics. Given its history of conditioning powerful interlocutors, the mafia was almost always able to deflect police and judicial
investigations that ran afoul of its interests. The investigators and journalists who follow it closely speak not only of interwoven networks but
also of a covert local, regional, and national power grid. Nodes of this
grid lie hidden in the very offices of the police and judiciary of Palermo
and Rome. It is the local view that investigators who come too close to
certain "hot wires" *(fili caldi)* are asking for trouble. Typically, they find
their actions hindered for reasons that are unclear at the time; tragically,
some of them have been assassinated.

And, finally, the third theme: despite the unevenness and vulnerability of the police-judicial effort, the magistrates and police inspectors believe they have turned a corner, above all in the wake of 1992. Two
broad developments have encouraged this shift: first, the earlier emergence in 1982 of a Palermo-centered social movement, the *movimento
antimafia,* which has consistently supported the judicial effort and continues to do so; and second, the fall of the First Italian Republic in 1992.
The antimafia social movement is the focus of chapters 7–9. This chapter considers the reasons for the 1992 regime change and its implications
for the prosecution of mafiosi. We begin with a brief sketch of Italy's judicial institutions.

THE ITALIAN MAGISTRACY

The Italian judiciary, grounded in Roman law, has historically followed
an "inquisitorial" system, which is different from the "adversarial" systems of England and the United States. Appointed for life, the magistrates are qualified to serve as judge or prosecutor. Until a recent reform,
an "instructional judge" reviewed evidence gathered by the police and
prosecutors and could either acquit the accused or bind him or her over
for trial, the "instructional findings" becoming part of the trial record.
The reform has resulted in a process that is closer to the adversary procedure of Anglo-Saxon law, in which the probatory value of the evidence
is not weighed until it is presented in the courtroom.

Consistent with the inquisitorial style, trial by jury is far less common
than trial by judges in Italy. A single judge, or *pretore,* hears cases in the
lowest-level court, the *pretura,* a court that has recently been eliminated.
More serious civil cases are brought before tribunals presided over by
three judge panels, and criminal cases before courts of assizes, in which
twelve lay jurors deliberate conjointly with a judge. Cases may be ap-

pealed to appeals courts and ultimately to the Supreme Court, the *Cassazione,* which renders a final ruling on procedural correctness, ordering retrials when errors are found. A Constitutional Court, consisting of fifteen members, five elected by Parliament, five by the head of state, and five by the Supreme Court, rules on the constitutionality of parliamentary law.

Three unusual features of the Italian judiciary—the power of the magistrates' governing body, or "Superior Council," the overlap of careers between prosecutors and judges, and the seniority principle regulating these careers—have been of great importance to the antimafia prosecutions (Jamieson 2000: 126). The historical development of these features and the controversies surrounding them are considered below.

Italian judicial procedure began life in the modern nation-state as an extension of the executive, a specialized sector of public administration in which magistrates' careers were determined by the Ministry of Justice. By the twentieth century, the magistracy's expanding numbers and more serious preparation in schools of law inevitably led to professionalization, and with this a growing pressure for independence from the ministry (Guarnieri 1992). In 1909, the parliament established a Superior Council of the Magistracy (*Consiglio Superiore della Magistratura,* or CSM), which took over from the Ministry of Justice the authority to assign and reassign jurists. The pace of change was slow at first, but the new Constitution of 1946 provided for a stronger CSM, set up to recruit, promote, and discipline prosecutors and judges. Two-thirds of this body consists of members elected by the magistrates (who have inevitably formed factions across the left-right spectrum); one-third are academic jurists elected by the Parliament. (The president of the republic is the CSM's nominal president.)

In the hierarchy of magistrates, Supreme Court judges are at the top, followed by the public prosecutors *(procuratori generali della repubblica)* and the presiding judges *(presidenti)* of the large district tribunals. An important judicial center such as the Palazzo di Giustizia in Palermo houses both a prosecutor's office, or *procura,* and the courts of the tribunal. Lower down are the presidents and chief prosecutors of the courts of appeals, followed (until recently eliminated) by the *pretori* and, finally, the *uditori,* who simply hear arguments. Each level of judicial administration is internally ranked, its lower positions overlapping with the higher ones of the court below, while other specialized courts—most importantly the criminal courts of assizes (the Palermo Palazzo di Giustizia houses this court, too) occupy a mid- to high point in the schema.

Magistrates in positions near the top of the hierarchy have been, over the years, conservative with regard to opportunities for advancement, whereas those near the bottom have been "innovators" (Guarnieri 1992: 94–95). As might be expected, innovation has come through the application of political pressure, some of it linked to conflicts in the wider political arena. Though this may be an oversimplification, during the 1960s, the innovators—younger and of lower status—sought the creation of a seniority system modeled on the labor unions, promising all magistrates an orderly and predictable career (ibid.: 101). Enacted in 1966, this system was considered the best defense against political interference from the Ministry of Justice, then a stronghold of the Christian Democratic Party (Ginsborg 1990: 100–101, 146–52; Guarnieri 1992).

In the 1970s, some extra-parliamentary groups of the extreme left and the extreme right in Italy turned to terrorist violence in an effort to destabilize "the system." Members of the national magistracy and indeed the entire political and economic administrative elite became vulnerable to kidnappings, assault ("kneecappings"), and assassination. Whatever their political leanings, prosecutors and judges closed ranks against extremism, presiding over the effective suppression of leftists and rightists engaged in terrorist acts. Many of them subsequently turned their attention to organized crime (the *Camorra* and *'Ndrangheta* as well as the mafia). Then, in 1990, the chief prosecutors of the Milan Prosecutor's Office launched its earth-shaking "clean hands" *(mani pulite)* investigations of "bribesville" *(tangentopoli),* the bribery scandal over the illegal financing of the Christian Democratic and Socialist parties.

Inevitably this trajectory generated opposition to the magistracy's growing power. Perhaps, critics argued, the alternative "Anglo-Saxon" model of adversarial justice, in which defendants have many more rights, should be attempted. Called *garantismo* (in reference to the guarantee of civil liberties), this alternative critical stance has been supported over the years by a broad and diverse group of philosophers and intellectuals, jurists and defense attorneys, criminals and their interlocutors, as well as the Anglophile members of Italy's secular and liberal parties, the Radicals and the Liberals. Beginning in 1988, their campaigns bore fruit in the form of a series of referenda and parliamentary acts curbing judicial power. Ambiguous meanings surround these measures, for although they express a genuine concern about overzealousness on the part of the magistrates, an exaggerated ideology of *garantismo* can also undermine genuine efforts to prosecute and convict the authors of criminal acts.

Some critics of the magistrates further conflate "judicial activism" with what they consider a dangerous "leftist hegemony." Mere membership in a left-wing faction of the magistracy is enough for a prosecutor to be suspected of advancing left-wing political goals by judicial means (see Burnett and Mantovani 1998). Similarly, notwithstanding the distribution of antimafia prosecutors and judges across the political spectrum—indeed, notwithstanding a widespread view of Falcone and Borsellino as politically neutral—critics of the antimafia process (the *anti-antimafia*, as it were) sometimes promote the idea that the crackdown on the mafia is a Communist plot. The fact that antimafia activism in the 1950s and 1960s was indeed led by the left-wing parties lends credibility to this accusation, as does the parallel fact that, to date, a substantial majority of the persons "above suspicion" who have been accused and tried for collusion are former Christian Democrats.

THE SICILIAN MAGISTRACY AND THE ANTIMAFIA POOL

Since the 1970s, Sicilian magistrates, formerly always close to the landed aristocracy, have emerged from a more heterogeneous social base. Also better educated, they are considerably less vulnerable than their predecessors to mafia "conditioning." The story of a magistrate, whose father had been a magistrate, is emblematic of the new atmosphere. In pursuing his own career he felt compelled to distance himself from his father's rural associates, above all, the overseer of their country property. Upon graduating from law school, he was, not surprisingly, approached by this now quite elderly mafioso for assistance in dealing with a criminal charge. Not having maintained the kind of relationship characteristic of his father's day, he found it relatively easy to refuse, even when confronted with the memory of sitting on this man's knee and being jostled as a child.

Many "second-generation" magistrates in Sicily share experiences and professional networks with the national cohort that prosecuted terrorism in the 1970s. At the end of the decade, a group of them in the Palermo Prosecutor's Office, led by Falcone, Borsellino, and the more senior head of their office, Rocco Chinnici, created an informal antimafia "pool." Consolidating their individual efforts to reconstruct and document criminal histories, they cooperated in the development of investigative and prosecutorial strategies. Most important, they assumed collective responsibility for carrying mafia prosecutions forward: all the members of the pool signed prosecutorial orders, so as to avoid exposing any one of them to particular risk.

In the early years, the pool had few resources—little office space, too few telephones, no computer technology, inadequate physical protection—yet its half dozen members demonstrated an impressive esprit de corps and confidence. Their most significant innovation was the cultivation of the *pentiti*. In the past, individual police officers had informants (known as *confidenti*), but the informants were generally not willing, or expected, to testify in public (Lupo 1993: 222–23; see also Pezzino 1995: 266–70). Indeed, it sometimes resulted that police officers acted as informants *to* the mafia. When, in the 1970s, Leonardo Vitale did offer to testify to his own crimes and those of his mafia colleagues, he was declared mentally ill. The second mafia war altered this dynamic through the exaggerated violence it visited upon the "losers," provoking the pioneering collaboration of Buscetta and Contorno. Their decisions to collaborate were momentous. As Falcone wrote of Buscetta, he "furnished a great deal of information on the structure . . . and functions of Cosa Nostra, but especially gave us a global vision . . . an essential key for reading its language and codes" (Falcone 1991: 41; quoted in Pezzino 1995: 269).

THE JUSTICE COLLABORATORS AS FLASH POINTS

The strategy of encouraging *pentitismo* derived from the prosecution of terrorism, which had relied heavily on the cumulative effect of turning some of the accused into witnesses against others. In addition, Falcone was in close communication with the U.S. Justice Department, which was simultaneously pursuing the transatlantic drug-smuggling network known as the "pizza connection." The Department's Federal Witness Protection Program gave asylum to Buscetta and Contorno, protecting them from their potentially lethal enemies.[1] The U.S. program then became, like the American RICO (Racket Influenced Corrupt Organization) law, a model for tightening criminal justice in Italy. Thanks in part to this context, the number of collaborators, nationally, reached 1,200 by 1997 and has continued to grow. The 363 witnesses against Cosa Nostra in 1997 represented 6.6 percent of the presumed 5,500 organized crime figures in Sicily (see Jamieson 2000: 104–5; Paoli 1997: 159).

Given the internal dynamics of the mafia wars, many of those who became *pentiti* were already in such jeopardy that they felt they had little to lose from flaunting the mafia's code of *omertà*. By testifying they could gain a reduced sentence, a more comfortable incarceration, financial aid and other support for their immediate family, the opportunity to subject a mafioso enemy to police capture or a stiffer sentence, protection from the enemy's machinations, and sweet revenge against mafia leaders who, as *mandanti,* had set them in motion but then abandoned or betrayed them.

At first the *pentiti* were extremely reluctant to identify political notables—persons "above suspicion"—as mafia accomplices. According to Buscetta, to do so would have jeopardized the position and possibly the life of the investigating magistrate (in this case, Falcone) who was taking the deposition, not to mention his own legitimacy as a witness. After the clamorous assassinations of 1992, however, he and other collaborators did testify about highly placed persons who were collusive. As a result, each announcement of a new justice collaborator generates considerable tension not only among mafiosi but also among persons who have been conditioned by them. Not surprisingly, an ongoing criticism of the magistrates is that they place their trust in unsavory characters with reputations for violence and questionable motives for confessing.

One aspect of *pentitismo* that feeds the polemic against it is the extent to which the collaborators' testimony is manipulated. During weeks of interrogation, the investigating magistrate poses questions and transcribes the answers, translating them into Italian if they are in dialect, so as to produce a coherent document that reports the witnesses' statements. Until a recent procedural reform that allows for videotaping the interrogations, the magistrates' questions were not recorded, leading defense attorneys to accuse them of piloting the *pentito* statements. In both Naples and Palermo, prosecutors have attempted to avoid using the word *pentito* in the media, substituting "justice collaborators," or so-called *pentiti,* instead. They understand that to label the collaborators "penitent" is to attribute to them a moral authority that few can accept. At the same time, they avidly seek corroborative evidence from letters, address books, and diaries found among the possessions of mafiosi, and from wiretaps, money trails, and other police investigations. To skeptics, however, well-corroborated accounts are the more dangerous for their appearance of truth when in fact they might hide a manipulative maneuver: a *pentito* attempting to support the position of the prosecution in order to obtain his own freedom (*Il Manifesto,* October 26, 1997).[2]

Meanwhile, the *pentiti* live tremendously complicated lives, the ups and downs of which can affect the magistrates' projects. They are entitled to be represented by attorneys at the state's expense, but until the collaborator role became common, such expertise was hard to find. There is also the challenge of adjusting to a new status. On release from jail, the witness protection program relocates the collaborator in a community far from home where he does not speak the local dialect, feels culturally isolated, and cannot approach even the parish priest for fear of putting his security at risk. The local police assigned to protect him may well be indifferent or hostile. Should a *pentito* be joined by his wife and children, other things can go wrong—the allowance granted by the state is barely enough to care for them; the apartment that it rents is too small or damp; the children have difficulty staying healthy or adjusting to a new school; the wife is miserable and possibly responsive to relatives back home who see her husband's collaboration as an infamous betrayal of their former life. Although a potential target of vengeful retribution, she might return to Sicily. Occasionally the wife, sister, or mother of a collaborator publicly disowns him, ostensibly from shame but possibly also from terror.

Generally, the *pentiti* have not changed their stories even when deeply dissatisfied with their treatment by the state.[3] The issue for the magistrates in this dissatisfaction is that word of it will circulate, discouraging other witnesses from turning. And so an effort is made to meet the collaborators' demands. But this only enhances the image of the *pentito* as a manipulator, a criminal extorting the judicial process for his own ends. Not surprisingly, a few *pentiti* have returned to a life of crime. Two bosses of San Giuseppe Jato, Baldassare (Balduccio) Di Maggio and Giovanni Brusca, illustrate the drama of *pentitismo* with particular intensity.

As discussed below, Di Maggio contributed to the capture of Salvatore Riina in 1993. In retaliation, Riina's allies, led by Brusca, kidnapped Di Maggio's eleven-year-old son, held him prisoner for two years, then strangled him and dissolved his body in a vat of acid. Brusca, identified as a central participant in the 1992 massacre of Falcone, was finally arrested in 1996, following which he declared himself a *pentito*, too. He was turning, he said, because five colleagues who were supposed to assist with killing the boy had left him to carry out the deed by himself, and because his own son, in tears, was pressing him with questions about the incident (*Il Manifesto*, December 10, 1996). In the meantime Di Maggio began committing murders and other crimes in retaliation against Brusca's close associates. Remarkably, he was also the source of testimony that Giulio Andreotti, the seven-time former prime minister, and Totò Riina had been seen to greet each other with a kiss on both cheeks at a meeting in 1987. His rearrest in 1997 constituted a major complication for Andreotti's prosecutors.

In many respects, the *pentito* controversy came to a head with the state's decision (in 2000) to grant Brusca the status of justice collaborator. The divergent reactions of Falcone's surviving sisters illustrate the moral complexity of such a move. One sister, the oldest, is horrified; the other is suspending judgment until it can be learned what Brusca has to say. In 1996 we heard a leading prosecutor give a speech to schoolchildren in which he brought up the son of the *pentito* Di Maggio, whom the monstrous Brusca had strangled and dissolved in acid:

> You have to understand that the so-called *pentiti* represent a strategy for us that is irreplaceable. They were mafiosi. No doubt they extorted and killed because this is what mafiosi do, but they knew the mafia from a privileged position, from inside. They were close to the brain of the mafia. Hearing them is like a little load of explosives in a wall of stone, of marble. It creates an opening for us to excavate inside. This is why the judges are enamored of them.

PHASE I: THE POLICE-JUDICIAL CRACKDOWN

The trajectory of the police-judicial crackdown on the mafia resembles the flight of a bird in stormy weather. An upswing around 1980 peaked in the maxi-trial of 1986–87; a downswing then reached its nadir in the summer of 1992. The subsequent upswing has been erratic, its duration still uncertain. The transition from the first to the second phase, and the rough flight thereafter, have been marked by an intensification of the controversies surrounding judicial reform and *pentitismo*.

Our account begins with Giovanni Falcone, whose career bracketed the first two phases of the crackdown (see fig. 9). He was born in 1939 to a middle-class family in a neighborhood of central Palermo where the mafia was present but quiescent; Tommaso Spadaro, a boy with whom he played ping-pong in a Catholic Action recreation center, would later become a notorious mafioso smuggler and killer, but mafiosi were not a major presence in his childhood (La Licata 1993: 23, 83). After taking a degree in law at the University of Palermo and passing the examination for the magistracy, he was assigned to the Prosecutor's Office in Trapani and Marsala, and then to the bankruptcy court in Palermo. It wasn't until early 1980 that he joined the Office of Instruction of the Palermo Prosecutor's Office, coming on board at a uniquely tense moment. Cesare Terranova, a former parliamentary deputy and antimafia reformer, was to have headed this office, but he was killed on September 25, 1979. Only two months earlier, on July 21, 1979, Boris Giuliano, head of the

Figure 9. Judge Giovanni Falcone, martyred antimafia magistrate,
June 1990. Photograph by Alessandro Fucarini, Labruzzo Agenzia,
Palermo.

police investigation squad and in pursuit of heroin traffic, was assassinated. The mafia killed his successor, Captain Emanuele Basile, on May
5, 1980.[4] Taking Terranova's place was Rocco Chinnici, whose days
were numbered but who, for the moment, was Falcone's boss.

Around this time, fifty-five members of the Spatola, Inzerillo, and
Gambino alliance—the *schieramento* of northern and western
Palermo—were accused of drug trafficking and related crimes and taken
into custody, their arrest warrants signed by the head of the Palermo
Prosecutor's Office, or *procuratore capo*, Gaetano Costa.[5] When the case

was passed to the Instructional Office, Chinnici assigned it to the young Falcone, who, applying the skills he had honed unraveling bankruptcies, began to follow the money trail created by heroin deals. To the amazement of many and consternation of some, his explorations produced a picture of "the mafia of Sindona"—the network of the banking figure encountered in chapter 3. Illegal traffic, money laundering, heroin sales, and ties to masonry were all involved (La Licata 1993: 69–71). In conducting this investigation, Falcone was probably the first Sicilian magistrate to establish working relationships with colleagues from other countries, thus developing an early understanding of the drug traffic in its global dimensions. Through Belgian and French inspectors, he learned that the chemists of the "French Connection" had moved from Marseilles to Sicily, where clandestine labs for refining heroin had already been established; visiting the United States at the end of 1980, he worked with the U.S. Justice Department on "some of the biggest international law enforcement operations in history" (Stille 1995: 36). His inquiry also extended to Turkey, an important stopover on the route of morphine base that originated in Southeast Asia, and to Switzerland, where bank secrecy laws facilitated money laundering, and to Naples, where cigarette-smuggling rings were being reconfigured as heroin operations.

On August 6, 1980, just as Falcone was beginning this investigation, Costa was murdered (Salvatore Inzerillo's way of matching the audacity of the Corleonesi). The atmosphere of intimidation was thickening, yet Falcone demonstrated an impressive ability to see the big picture and determination to explore it, however handicapped by ridiculously meager investigative resources. As Stille has written, Falcone won seventy-four convictions in the Spatola case, based on his having proved "with a web of solid evidence—bank and travel records, seized heroin shipments, fingerprint and handwriting analyses, wiretapped conversations and firsthand testimony . . . that Sicily had replaced France as the principal gateway for refining and exporting heroin to the United States" (ibid.: 46).

On May 1, 1982, Carabinieri General Carlo Alberto dalla Chiesa, veteran leader of the national campaign against terrorism in the 1970s, arrived in Palermo to become the prefect and to coordinate the state's repression of organized crime. Around the same time, the young deputy chief of the police investigative squad *(Squadra Mobile)*, Antonino (Ninni) Cassarà, developed a relationship with Contorno as an informant, code-naming him, prophetically, *Fonte di Prima Luce* (Source of First Light). Cassarà used Contorno to create a map of the families of the Palermo region and a report on their increasingly conflictual relations and involvement in narcotics. He worked closely with Falcone and two months later they unleashed a dragnet roundup of 162 mafiosi wanted for drug trafficking, homicide, and crimes of *lupara bianca* (La Licata 1993: 98–100).

Among the bosses who remained at large was Salvatore Greco, nicknamed the Engineer, whom the *Giornale di Sicilia* described as the "gray eminence of the entire organization, the one who held and pulled the strings, whether the task was to guide the extermination of enemies or to decide on strategies for moving drugs" (July 14, 1982). He had been a fugitive for twenty years, living a life of luxury in Venezuela. His cousin and deputy, Michele the Pope, also escaped the dragnet, although he headed the list of those sought (which was titled "Michele Greco plus 161"). All told, the Greco clan was like a lion, the newspaper said, but sweeps of their Ciaculli territory had so far yielded only "little fish." Moreover, their chief Corleone allies, Salvatore Riina, nicknamed *la Belva* (the Beast) and Bernardo Provenzano, *u Tratturi* (the Tractor), seemed invincible. Riina was at large, and Provenzano had already established his enduring reputation as one of the mafia's most illusive fugitives.

As 1982 unfolded, the troubles multiplied. April 30 is the date of the assassination of the Sicilian Communist leader and national parliamentary deputy Pio La Torre, a leading proponent of antimafia legislation. The next to fall was General dalla Chiesa, gunned down in his automobile on the Via Carini of Palermo, together with his driver and young wife, on September 3. Given his popularity and the significance of his appointment as "super-prefect" of the antimafia forces, this event was a national scandal. In its wake, and energized by the massive outflow of sympathy and anger that the murders of La Torre and dalla Chiesa generated, the Parliament enacted the legislation that La Torre had promoted in vain before his death. The new law, known as the Rognoni–La Torre Law, granted the judiciary greater access to bank records in order to follow money trails, allowed the state to sequester and ultimately confiscate the assets of convicted mafiosi, and defined membership in the mafia as a crime independent of other possible criminal acts.[6] Under its provisions, Falcone and Chinnici issued fourteen arrest warrants for the dalla Chiesa killing with Michele Greco, still at large, again at the head of the list. That was July 9, 1983. On July 21, a car bomb massacred Rocco Chinnici, two of his bodyguards, and the concierge of his building. Like the murders of Terranova and Costa, this event was brutally unsettling, and it, too, called for an investigation.

Chinnici's replacement as head of the Instructional Office of the Palermo Prosecutor's Office was Antonino Caponetto, a distinguished Florentine magistrate. Although near retirement, he too proved to be a strong supporter of the antimafia process, and under his administration, Falcone with several other investigative magistrates—including Borsellino, Giuseppe Di Lello, and Leonardo Guarnotta—reinvigorated their work as members of the antimafia pool (Caponnetto 1992; Stille 1995: 85–90). By June 1984, Falcone was off to Brazil to arrange for Buscetta's extradition to Italy. Buscetta's extraordinary testimony produced what became known as the Buscetta Theorem, namely, "that the Cosa Nostra was a unitary and secret organization and that the events that signified its life, apparently unconnected, were not independent one from the others but were connected and responding to a single strategy," a strategy that was set by the *cupola,* or mafia Commission (La Licata 1993: 99–100). It was this proposition, coupled with Buscetta's other revelations, that enabled Falcone to issue another 366 arrest warrants by September 29. From there, he went on to prepare, together with Borsellino, the prosecutorial document for the maxi-trial: "8,607 pages in forty volumes, plus appendices of 4,000 pages, including documents and photographs, laying out evidence against 475 defendants," 460 of whom had been arrested. In Stille's words, "the maxi-indictment, the bulk of which was written by Falcone himself, is . . . a great historical saga with the sweep of a Tolstoian novel. . . . Like the great historical novel of Sicilian life, *The Leopard* by Giuseppe di Lampedusa, it is a lucid diagnosis of a diseased society" (1995: 174; see also Stajano 1986).

The last stages of preparation for the maxi-trial took place in a maximum security prison on the island of Asinara. Falcone and his fiancée, magistrate Francesca Morvillo, and her mother, together with Paolo Borsellino, and his family took refuge there in the summer of 1985 as tension increased in Palermo, occasioned by a series of catastrophes in the police *Squadra Mobile.* The murder of police inspector Beppe Montana initiated the crisis. Both Borsellino and (policeman) Cassarà had grown to admire this young man, who in 1983 had discovered Michele Greco's arsenal of pistols, machine guns, and sawed off shotguns. The following year Montana arrested Falcone's childhood ping-pong partner, Tommaso Spadaro, who was by then a major trafficker in cigarettes and drugs. More astonishing still, on July 25, 1985, Montana's men arrested eight mafia fugitives, one of whom was a business partner of Michele Greco (Greco himself would remain at large until February 20, 1986).[7] Three days later, Montana was dead, felled by four shots from a pistol. Borsellino and Cassarà were devastated. The tragedy deepened when a twenty-five-year-old man arrested as a suspect in the killing was allegedly beaten to death by enraged policemen. Three senior officers of the police were ordered transferred by the president of Italy; ten other officers were charged with responsibility for the death of the prisoner.

Then, on August 6, perhaps to avenge the death of the man in custody, Cassarà was murdered, together with his young assistant officer Roberto Antiochia. Compounding the trauma for the police and magistrates, Cassarà's trusted driver, Natale Mondo, who had been fortunate to escape the bullets, came under suspicion of helping to set up the ambush. He was later exonerated (and later still, killed by the mafia), but this and other events of the time served to unravel "the team of able investigators that had been slowly and painfully reconstructed after the assassinations of Boris Giuliano and Emanuele Basile" (Stille 1995: 170).

Falcone and other members of the pool saw the handwriting on the wall: the more the police went after the fugitives, the more the mafia would attempt to destroy the police. Despite the large number of arrests that led to the imminent maxi-trial, the mafia-in-hiding remained capable of terrible deeds—hence the preventive sequester of Falcone, Borsellino, and their families. Stille captures the irony as follows: "[It] was a telling indication of the upside-down nature of life in Sicily on the eve of the maxi-trial: mafia fugitives moved freely about Palermo while government prosecutors had to live in prison for their own protection" (ibid.: 172).

THE MAXI-TRIAL

And yet, the trial began in February 1986, and on December 16, 1987, the judges delivered their stunning guilty verdicts on 344 mafiosi. The court accepted the so-called Buscetta Theorem: the mafia was a hierarchical organization coordinated by a commission such that membership could itself be considered a crime. Among the guilty were the already-convicted Luciano Liggio of Corleone, Michele Greco ("the Pope") of Ciaculli, at last arrested, and the absent Corleone "butchers" Riina and Provenzano. The Salvo cousins, Nino and Ignazio, who "for forty years had conditioned the economic and political life" of Sicily (Caponnetto 1992: 36), were also charged. Nino died before the trial, but Ignazio was convicted despite pleading that Sicilian businessmen only survive by "(coming) to terms with the enemies of society" (quoted in Stille 1996: 189). Several defendants remained fugitive, and 114 were released for insufficient evidence. In 1984, however, Buscetta's and Contorno's testi-

Figure 10. The exmayor of Palermo, Vito Ciancimino, during his trial in Palermo, June 1990. Photograph by Alessandro Fucarini, Labruzzo Agenzia, Palermo.

monies had led to the first "third level" arrest: Corleonesi-allied former mayor and public works commissioner, Vito Ciancimino. A central player in the "sack" of Palermo, he and his son were further charged with money laundering through a Montreal bank. Following a 1990 trial, Ciancimino was sentenced to ten years for *associazione mafiosa* (see fig. 10).

Like most of the important antimafia prosecutions, the maxi-trial was staged in Palermo. Other provincial capitals of Sicily—Agrigento, Caltanissetta, Trapani, Catania—are also frequent sites for trials (indeed, any case involving a Palermo magistrate as victim must be tried in Caltanissetta). In addition, a few trials involving the mafia have been set in continental Italy. But the Palermo Palazzo di Giustizia, a massive and forbidding structure in Fascist Modern, has been the center of the storm. Here, notwithstanding the stark marble interiors and cavernous corridors that seem to dwarf all human endeavor, reducing voices and footsteps to muffled echoes, small groups of prosecutors and judges turned their offices and meeting rooms into workshops for making history. That

these beehives of activity would provoke unease and jealousy inside the
palazzo was, perhaps, inevitable, the more so if we remember that the
grid of the mafia's hidden power had penetrated the institution. In no
time at all, the place acquired a nickname: *Palazzo dei Veleni* (Palace of
Poisons).

The maxi-trial did not take place in the Palazzo di Giustizia, however,
but in a specially built bunker courthouse inside the Ucciardone. A low-
lying two-story building, painted white with bright green accents, it
seems almost cheerful by comparison. Among its amenities are a kitchen
and several small apartments to house the judges and jurors during their
sequestered deliberations. The actual courtroom is a large, semi-circular
auditorium, with "The Law Is Equal for All" carved in wood across the
dais. During the maxi, the defendants were arrayed in thirty barred cages
around the back with officers of the Carabinieri positioned before them,
while visitors sat in a second-story balcony above the cages (see fig. 11).
Between the cages and the judges' platform were rows of desks for the
attorneys and other participants.

The bunker courthouse was designed to maximize security. The Ucciardone envelops it like a fortress, with armed guards in its sentry posts
atop the gray stone walls and armored tanks driving slowly around its

Figure 11. The accused and their lawyers at the maxi-trial, December 1987.
Photograph by Alessandro Fucarini, Labruzzo Agenzia, Palermo.

perimeter. Vehicle entry was possible only through a double set of massive steel gates. Both visitors and official personnel had to traverse an elaborate security checkpoint, all under the watchful eye of heavily armed police.

The guards brought the defendants into the courtroom through a long passageway that connected the bunker with the prison. In 1987, we met the police officer in charge of these logistics, assigned to Palermo from Genoa. On the night before each session, he planned the walking groups and cage assignments based on the prisoners' declarations of intent to attend or not and on his computer modeling of their amicable and conflictual relations. As added security and compensation for this hardship assignment, he and his companion were given a comfortable apartment inside the prison, reconstructed from an old warehouse, and with it a cook, an office, a vegetable garden, and rabbits tended by the prisoners.

At the time of the maxi, all manner of officials in the criminal justice system in Palermo felt that for the very first time their eyes were being opened to the inner workings of the mafia. Beyond the depositions of the *pentiti* they were able to watch how the prisoners comported themselves and confronted one another at the trial. Several officials pointed out to us that when Luciano Liggio spoke, the other defendants in the cages grew quiet, in deference to him. We asked the Genoese officer about this in the seclusion of his apartment and were astonished to see him leap up at the mention of Liggio's name and close the window to the garden outside where some of the prisoners were working. Liggio, he explained, "could burn any one of us."

The presiding judge of the trial, Alfonso Giordano, whom we met in his office in the bunker courthouse, generously commented on the defendants' demeanor. In his view, Liggio was "surprisingly courteous," given his reputation for rudeness. One day in court he had lost his temper, but the next day he apologized. Greco, by contrast, was cold, a *tipo freddo*, Buscetta surprisingly "cultivated," although very cunning *(molto furbo)*. In Giordano's view, the high point of the trial was the confrontation between the Corleonesi ally Pippo Calò and Tomasso Buscetta; indeed, he had us view a videotape of their exchange in court. Capturing a moment of maximum tension, it showed Buscetta accusing Calò of murdering his (Buscetta's) family and Calò accusing Buscetta of infamous betrayal, *'nfamità*. Buscetta, Calò thundered, had more than one wife, and he left the country while his son was in prison so he couldn't look after his boy as a father should. As background to Calò's accusations of betrayal was Buscetta's voice, droning, "Hypocrite, hypocrite, hypocrite."

Outside the Palazzo di Giustizia and the bunker courthouse, life for the antimafia magistrates was by turns exhilarating and frustrating. Given the dangers to which they were exposed, they lived (and still live) an armored life, prisoners of the measures that are necessary to protect them. Although they did not wear masks, as did their counterparts in Colombia, they could circulate only in armor-plated vehicles driven by one of their "guerrillas" and escorted front and back by unmarked police cars with sirens screaming. Shopping for clothes, going to the cinema, swimming at the beach, and eating in popular restaurants—pleasures that people of their class take for granted—were all forgone. Meanwhile, during the maxi, Palermo as a whole took on the appearance of an armed camp as additional police, soldiers, and Carabinieri were assigned to guard its streets.

PHASE II: 1988 TO 1992

Almost before they were over, the maxi-trial in Palermo and a comparable trial of *Camorra* leaders in Naples were raising the specter of an institutional threat to civil liberties, due both to the large scale of the trials (the sheer number of defendants and charges being tried) and their reliance on *pentito* testimony. The Neapolitan magistrates, less cautious than their Palermo counterparts, had particularly fanned the flames by convicting a popular TV personality, Enzo Tortora, of collusion in *Camorra* activities, based only on the unsubstantiated testimony of one, rather unreliable, *pentito* witness. Tortora was later cleared of the charge by an appeals court, but the fact that he spent considerable time in prison (and subsequently died of cancer) made him emblematic of the call for civil liberty "guarantees" (see Jacquemet 1996: 288; Stille 1995: 203–11).

On January 10, 1987, almost a year before the maxi ended, the famed novelist Sciascia launched an unsettling missile in the form of a review of a recently published book by British historian Christopher Duggan on the fascist prefect Mori (Duggan 1986). Writing for the Milan daily, *Corriere della Sera,* Sciascia used the review as an occasion to mount an attack on what he labeled the *professionisti dell'antimafia*—the "antimafia professionals." First, he established his own antimafia credentials by quoting extensively from his early "mafia novels," *Mafia Vendetta* (Il giorno della civetta, 1960) and *To Each His Own* (A ciascuno il suo, 1966). When he first published them, he noted, it was fashionable to ignore the mafia; today it is the fashion to talk about it all the time. The current "flood of rhetoric" was preferable to the past indifference, but it contained a confused "racial resentment" regarding Sicily and Sicilians, as if Sicily could not be pardoned for its sins, even though it had also produced such luminaries as Verga, Pirandello, Guttuso (and by implication, Sciascia himself).

The review referred to the vastness and pain of the mafia problem, and the complicated ways that ordinary people are complicit with it. This is not mystification, claimed Sciascia. One can understand the mafia, but it would take more time, and a more nuanced analysis, than the antimafia *professionisti* seemed prepared to give. Most important, they were naive about the clear risks to democracy inherent in an overly aggressive approach. Mori, according to Sciascia, was authoritarian; he had a strong sense of duty and belief in the legitimacy of the state through which he justified his assumption of "virulent powers." Anyone who dissented was labeled mafioso. Now, he continued, there was a magistrate, Paolo Borsellino, who was promoted out of the line of the magistrates' own rule of seniority because he dealt with mafia crimes. Nothing better enhanced a magistrate's career than bringing a mafioso to trial; others were held back because they lacked this opportunity. The attack created a storm of shocked protest, as Borsellino was second only to Falcone in public esteem in the antimafia pool. On January 14, Sciascia retracted, telling reporters that he did not mean to impugn the judge's qualifications, only the modality of his promotion, adding, however, that the antimafia activists' reaction had proved his point.

The Tortora case and Sciascia's bombshell invited criticism of the magistracy, adding fuel to an emergent national campaign for a referendum on civil liberties, promoted by a coalition of Liberals and Radicals, together with Socialist Party leaders who had become involved in a bribery scandal in Milan. The heart of the proposed reform, which won by a substantial majority in a vote in 1988, was that judges and prosecutors should be made personally liable and subject to civil lawsuits for "errors" leading to wrongful arrest and imprisonment. The Parliament further expanded the rights of defendants, in particular by separating the functions of prosecutor and judge. Instituted in 1989, this reform meant eliminating the position of the instructional magistrate (as exemplified by Falcone), replacing it with the less powerful figure of the *giudice per indagine preliminare* (judge for preliminary inquiries, or GIP). New rules of procedure and evidence were also promulgated, moving Italian jurisprudence a little closer to the adversarial systems of Great Britain and the United States.

Perhaps in response to the shifting climate, the mafia once again showed its fangs. In 1988, Giuseppe Insalaco, former mayor of Palermo, was killed, followed by the appeals court judge, Antonio Saetta, responsible for hearing the maxi appeal. These events, together with the dismantling of the *Squadre Mobile,* framed the crisis that developed after Caponnetto, head of the Office of Instructional Magistrates, announced his retirement in January 1988. Most of the Palermo judges and prosecutors, Caponnetto among them, fully expected that Falcone, the moving force in the antimafia pool, would be appointed to head the office (which was not eliminated until 1989). Instead, the CSM rigidly followed the 1966 law that established seniority as the basis for promotion and appointed a more senior magistrate who had little experience in prosecuting organized crime.

That the decision came after heated debate and a split vote in the CSM did little to alleviate tensions in the Prosecutor's Office of Palermo. The new head of the Instructional Office, Antonino Meli, proceeded to assign cases as if there were nothing special about those involving the mafia. In effect, this eliminated the antimafia pool by encumbering its members with investigations that were peripheral to organized crime, while assigning mafia cases to magistrates who had neither the historical memory nor the appetite to pursue them. In the middle of the summer of 1988, we were among an audience in the city of Agrigento for the presentation of a book about a major mafia trial in that province. One of the speakers was Judge Borsellino, who took advantage of the occasion to denounce the "dismantling of the pool" and to accuse the state, in dramatic and chilling words, of failing to support the antimafia judicial effort.

Falcone was about to suffer a series of indignities. In 1989, the Instructional Office was eliminated as mandated by the reform. Meli retired and the other "instructional" prosecutors, including Falcone, were folded into the Prosecutor's Office under its new head, Piero Giammanco. On May 16, 1989, Contorno was arrested in Bagheria near Palermo and charged with participating in several attacks on the Corleonesi. Shortly thereafter, five letters written by an anonymous *corvo* (literally, "crow," but meaning "provocateur") circulated within the Palazzo di Giustizia, charging that Falcone, together with police inspector Gianni DeGennaro, had manipulated Contorno's secret return from protective custody in the United States so as to set him up for these misadventures in Sicily. On June 20 there was a serious attempt on Falcone's life—a bomb found in the water near a secluded beach house in Addaura where he happened to be entertaining two Swiss magistrates who were working with him on a money-laundering case. This provocation could only have matured with the clandestine help of one or more "moles" operating inside the Palazzo di Giustizia. According to one of Falcone's colleagues, he himself was, at the time, very concerned because "he knew in his gut but could not prove that there was a mole with secret service connections in the *procura.*"

Shortly after the Addaura incident, the anonymous letters were made public and Domenico Sica, the high commissioner for the fight against the mafia (a position created by Parliament after the killings of La Torre and dalla Chiesa) initiated what can only be described as a most bizarre investigation into their source. Sica accused a colleague of Falcone in the Palermo Prosecutor's Office, Antonino Di Pisa, saying that Falcone had suggested the name. Falcone immediately denied that he had named anyone to Sica, while Di Pisa vigorously denied being the *corvo.* In a strange turn, however, Di Pisa also asserted that he was in full agreement with the content of the letters. Meanwhile, Commissioner Sica improperly tricked Di Pisa into leaving his fingerprints on a glass in order to compare them to the fingerprints on one of the letters. The results were inconclusive, Di Pisa was eventually exonerated, and the identity of the *corvo* never established.

In this tension-filled context, Falcone continued his work as an associate to Giammanco, the *procuratore capo,* but his working conditions did not improve over those of his tenure in the Instructional Office under Meli. He had always been reticent to discuss in public his personal situation in the "Palazzo dei Veleni," but he did confide in several friends, including the journalists Francesco La Licata and Liana Milella, entrusting to Milella an account, published after his death, of specific demoralizing events in his relationship with Giammanco. These frustrated his work, and in 1991 he accepted a specially created investigative position in the Ministry of Justice in Rome (see Caponnetto 1992: 81–97; Falcone 1991; La Licata 1993: 121–33).

THE MURDERS OF FALCONE AND BORSELLINO

On January 31, 1992, the Supreme Court in Rome upheld the vast majority of convictions from the maxi-trial. Given the mafia's historical relationship to the regime of center and center-left parties then led by the Christian Democrat, Andreotti, this outcome was unexpected. Many of the defendants in the trial had direct or indirect ties with Salvo Lima, the former Palermo mayor, then deputy in the European Parliament, and

Andreotti's Christian Democratic point person in Sicily (see fig. 4, chapter 3). Everyone knew, moreover, that the Supreme Court traditionally assigned mafia cases to the section headed by a judge with a reputation for leniency toward mafioso defendants, Corrado Carnevale, who was also linked to Andreotti (Caselli et al. 1995).[8]

But 1992 was a time of shifting sands for "old regimes" all over Europe, and Italy was no exception. Already in the summer of 1991, dissident Christian Democrats, allied with former Communists and emergent Greens, had orchestrated a significant electoral reform through a national referendum, threatening all of the old political parties. In December of the same year, Italy signed the Maastricht Treaty, its leaders having to take seriously the stern warnings of Europe's central bankers and technocrats regarding government waste and organized crime. In northern Italy, the *mani pulite* investigations were about to explode. Neither Andreotti nor the highest court in the land could risk the outcry that overturning the Palermo sentences would surely provoke, and the maxi-trial appeal was assigned to a section of the court not headed by Carnevale.

On March 12, 1992, soon after the convictions were upheld, the mafia murdered Salvo Lima, certainly for his failure to "adjust" the maxi-trial in the manner to which the mafia was accustomed. As the *pentito* Gaspare Mutolo has since revealed, "Lima was killed because he did not uphold, or couldn't uphold, the commitments he had made in Palermo. . . . The verdict of the Supreme Court was . . . like a dose of poison for the mafiosi, who felt like wounded animals. That's why they carried out the massacres" (quoted in Jamieson 2000: 56). (Ignazio Salvo, the mafia's closest link to Lima, was killed, probably for the same reason, on September 8, 1992.)

On May 23, Judge Giovanni Falcone, his wife, Judge Francesca Morvillo, and three members of their police escort were massacred on the highway from the airport to Palermo, as their cars passed over a culvert where mafiosi had hidden 500 kilograms of explosives, packed into plastic drums and covered by a mattress. At first, neither the killers of Falcone nor their possible *mandanti* were identified, allowing the usual clouds of dust, rumors, and poisons to thicken. A remarkable anonymous letter theorizing a conspiracy between a faction of the mafia and certain leaders of the Christian Democratic Party was mailed to a seemingly arbitrary selection of thirty-nine politicians, magistrates, and journalists in Palermo. The conspirators had masterminded several assassinations, the letter claimed, that of the judge being only one piece in a much larger, and still more sinister, puzzle.[9] Then, stunning the world, on July 19, Falcone's close friend, colleague, and successor, Paolo Borsellino, together with his police bodyguards, was killed by a car bomb in front of his mother's apartment house.

In the short run, at least, the mafia's terrorism backfired. Two weeks after the Falcone massacre, a "law decree," effective immediately, then strengthened after Borsellino's demise, enlarged the definition of prosecutable crimes and established new protections for the justice collaborators. Prison for mafiosi became substantially more onerous. Only their immediate kin could visit them and then only once a month, to communicate by intercom through a dense glass wall. Mail was censored and outgoing phone calls forbidden. Falling under Article 41bis, these prison regulations were amplified by the increased dispersal of mafia bosses to distant, island jails, and by interdicting their opportunities to speak with each other wherever they were incarcerated (see Jamieson 2000: 41–48). Further demonstrating the state's resolve, seven thousand troops were sent to Sicily, given police powers, and deployed to keep watch over sensitive offices, residences, and arteries. The Parliamentary Antimafia Commission was reinvigorated, setting the stage for a series of new hearings and reports, including one on the mafia and Freemasonry. At the same time, a new institution under the Ministry of the Interior, the *Direzione Investigativa Antimafia* (Antimafia Investigative Directorate), or DIA, received full powers and vastly increased personnel to coordinate the sectors of the police, Carabinieri, and Finance Guard that specialized in organized crime.

Investigations into the Falcone massacre began immediately and with unprecedented dispatch soon pointed to the *cupola* of the Corleonesi. Police attention focused on a hillside villa overlooking the highway from which the lethal payload was detonated with a remote control device. There they found cigarette butts left on the ground by a chain-smoking killer; DNA analysis of them (carried out by the FBI laboratory in the United States) confirmed Giovanni Brusca as the culprit.

On the day of Falcone's funeral, the Parliament rejected Andreotti's candidacy for president of the republic, electing, instead, Oscar Luigi Scalfaro, who, although also a Christian Democrat, had a far more credible record of opposing crime and corruption. Events of 1991 and early 1992 had already rattled Andreotti's apparent invincibility. The *mani pulite* investigations in Milan, launched on February 17, were quickly swirling toward Bettino Craxi, the Socialist Party leader with whom Andreotti had shared the governance of Italy for over a decade. Even more ominous was the March 12 assassination of Lima, an act read by virtually all commentators as retaliation not only for Lima's, but also by implication for Andreotti's, inability to undo the maxi-trial convictions upheld by the Supreme Court. In the national election of April 5, the Christian Democrats and the Socialists, reeling from the Milan scandal and Lima's murder, had suffered losses.

Underlying this electoral result was the change in voting procedures that had been accomplished through the referendum. Sponsored by a "transversal" coalition of reformers in rebellion against their respective political parties, it ended the system of proportional representation for the national parliament.[10] A parallel reform in 1993 provided for the direct election of mayors. This shift, capped by Andreotti's defeat, spelled the end of the First Italian Republic, the national structure of power that had governed Italy from the end of World War II through the Cold War era. Falcone's murder, many believe, helped push this old regime over the edge. Although there is some debate about declaring the 1992 watershed the "birth of the Second Republic" (Ginsborg 1998), there is no question that the mafia was left scrambling to reconstitute its political shield. Soon an avalanche of new *pentiti* surfaced, several from among the Corleone faction, and some providing coveted information enabling the capture of fugitives. Giammanco resigned as *procuratore capo*, to be replaced by a magistrate from Turin, Giancarlo Caselli, who, as a member of the CSM at the time of Caponetto's retirement, had been a vociferous supporter of Falcone over Meli. Prophetically, many think, Caselli's tenure in Palermo, which ended in 1999, began just after Riina's clamorous arrest in January 1993.

Reacting ferociously to these events, in 1993 mafiosi bombed cultural and artistic targets in Rome and northern Italy. A bomb planted near the Uffizi Galleries in Florence that damaged both paintings and structure as well as other nearby architectural treasures and killed an entire family, raised immense public ire. Other attacks were thwarted or not carried out, but learned of later. The strategy, it seems, was to force the state's hand in a negotiated retreat from Article 41bis and other repressive measures. It was not these bombings, however, that reopened the door for reining in the magistrates; on the contrary, the bombs elicited great public disgust. Rather, the decision of the Palermo Prosecutor's Office to push its investigations to the third level, and specifically to prosecute Andreotti, again made the antimafia prosecutors objects of criticism.

PENTITISMO AND THE PURSUIT OF ANDREOTTI

Shortly after his arrival in Palermo, Caselli and his team charged Andreotti with "having contributed—more than occasionally—to . . . Cosa Nostra, in particular in relation to judicial processes against members of the organization" (quoted in Centro Siciliano di Documentazione . . . 1996: 17; see also Caselli et al. 1995). In a separate action in Perugia, Andreotti was also accused of having ordered the mafia-executed murder of a journalist in 1979. Both trials, which ended in acquittal for want of sufficient proof in 1999, in turn provided fodder for renewed attempts to delegitimate the magistrates. Leading the charge was *Forza Italia,* a national political force that emerged after the political sea change of 1992. The media magnate, Silvio Berlusconi, whose holding company Fininvest acquired a near monopoly on private television networks in Italy, created the party and its candidate list in 1994 and was elected to the prime ministership that year. Its leaders have been especially critical of magistrates with left-wing political sympathies, among them Caselli, whom they accuse of promoting a Communist agenda through judicial activism. Berlusconi has himself been the target of prosecution for a variety of economic crimes, based in part on *pentito* testimony, and is a strong supporter of legislation to further curtail *pentitismo.* In the spring of 2000, he reassumed the prime ministership by a narrow margin.

Under pressure from critics like Berlusconi, in 1997 Parliament revised Article 513, completely disallowing a collaborator's statement as evidence in court should he later decide to change or retract the statement, a modification that the Supreme Court has upheld and even applied retroactively.[11] Subsequently, three collaborators, apparently in exchange for the offer of a "pardon" from certain mafia leaders, and out of fear that their immediate families were in danger, decided to abandon their agreement to testify. To critics of the magistrates, Article 513 in this case served the useful purpose of flushing three allegedly false *pentiti* out of the criminal justice stream—a further nail in the coffin of *pentitismo.* The magistrates, however, blame the new legislation for giving mafiosi the power to offer "amnesty" to particular *pentiti* whose testimony they want to change. Piero Grasso, Caselli's successor in 1999, believes that "513 threatens to annul everything that the magistrates have accomplished," for now the *pentiti* will surely "raise their price." Justice, according to another magistrate, "has become a hostage"; the collaborator can "turn the faucet on and off according to his arbitrary will" (*Il Manifesto,* August 19, 1997).

The conclusion of the Andreotti trial and its aftermath conveys the complexity of these issues. In 1999, the prosecutors Roberto Scarpinato and Guido Lo Forte presented their summary of the case against the former prime minister. After over two hundred court sessions, they asked for a sentence of fifteen years—the maximum penalty. The star *pentiti* in the case, Marino Mannoia, who had told of Andreotti's direct personal encounters with Stefano Bontade in the 1970s, and Balduccio Di Maggio, who testified to the famous Riina-Andreotti kiss, were, the prosecutors argued, vindicated by evidence that had been found to corroborate both. Yet, as we know, Di Maggio had been rearrested two years earlier. In an apparent effort to reinstate himself as credible, he claimed that certain unnamed persons were pressuring him to retract his testimony. Caselli used his brief press conference following the prosecution's summary first to thank Scarpinato and Lo Forte and second to reassure the public that an investigation into the pressures on Di Maggio was going forward. Indeed, he proposed, this investigation could shed light on other, as yet ambiguous aspects of the case, in particular, why Andreotti's bodyguards remained steadfastly silent about his travels in Sicily and why other witnesses had refused to testify regarding his acquaintance with the Salvos. Notwithstanding, the three-judge panel decided against conviction.

FUGITIVES AND POISONS

In many ways, a Pirandellian epistemology reigns in Palermo, where much critical knowledge is inaccessible and things are seldom what they seem. Hence the press's reference to the "Palace of Poisons," its nicknaming the mafia *la piovra* (the octopus), its characterizing the city as "choked by a *polverone* [dust cloud]." To some investigators, it is a mistake to indulge in such mystifying metaphors. Falcone, in particular, insisted that "we must not transform (the mafia) into a monster. . . . We must recognize that it resembles ourselves" (quoted in Jamieson 2000: 2). Yet, looking back over the saga of the police-judicial crackdown, one cannot help but appreciate the pervasive sense that Palermo is a city of intrigue and mystery, that there are persons and organizations pulling strings behind the scenes, maneuvering obscure and violent events but escaping responsibility for them. Although theoretically knowable, these forces are experienced as occult because it would be too dangerous to know them.

There are four significant kinds of occult force. First are the *latitanti*, fugitive capi who have been able to evade arrest for two decades while still living somewhere in Sicily. Second are the mafia's interlocutors, "third-level" persons above suspicion whose super-refined minds (menti raffinatissime) are thought to have willed the execution of this or that "excellent cadaver." Third are the "crows" (corvi), who write anonymous letters, together with the gossipmongers, who impugn the reputations of leading magistrates and police inspectors. And fourth are the dangerous mafia spies, the "moles" (talpe) in these magistrates' and inspectors' very precincts.

Because they were the victors of the second "mafia war"—and because so many of the losers were either killed or jailed, or "turned" to become pentiti—the most resilient fugitives in recent times are from the Corleonesi faction. Their notoriety began in Ciaculli, in 1982, when the first big police dragnet failed to snare the preeminent Greco cousins, Salvatore ("Chicchiteddu," or "Little Bird") and Michele ("the Pope"). Salvatore the "Engineer" (the "gray eminence . . . who held and pulled the strings") was away in Venezuela, one of relatively few fugitives to live abroad. The following summer, Michele was indicted for the killing of dalla Chiesa, along with his brother Salvatore (the "Senator") and the Corleone killers Riina and Provenzano, all of them fugitives. Remaining at large despite the indictment, what role did these personages play in the car bomb massacre of Chinnici, Falcone's boss? As it turned out, a Lebanese drug trafficker allied with Michele Greco "had warned the police that a Palermo magistrate would be blown up in response to the arrest warrants in the dalla Chiesa case" (Stille 1995: 82). A related question was, of course, why no one had acted on this warning (La Repubblica, July 29, 1983).

Many antimafia activists claim that the state could capture its most wanted fugitives if it were to commit sufficient energy and resources to the effort; only in the immediate aftermath of the 1963 massacre of Ciaculli did significant numbers of mafiosi disperse to other continents. Yet these illusive figures seem to have lived a charmed life, escaping one police blitz after another, notwithstanding the use of armored cars, dogs, and helicopters. It is hard to imagine that they do not have privileged sources of information within the police and judiciary. A high official of the Carabinieri who was involved in the capture of Liggio in 1974 insisted, in an interview, that beyond internal treachery, the police are constantly thrown off the trail by anonymous phone calls, by mafiosi placing their victims in the territories of their rivals so as to misdirect investigations, by tips that are deliberately disinforming. There is also the

threat of murder. We recall that Beppe Montana, one of the most creative police inspectors on the trail of important mafiosi and their arsenals, was killed three days after arresting eight fugitives. Greco himself
was finally apprehended at the time of the maxi-trial, having been in hiding for four years. But this arrest was marred (as was Liggio's) by intense
rivalry between the police, the Carabinieri, and the Finance Guard, with
the police feeling offended that the Carabinieri received credit for the
capture. Ironically Greco, at last behind bars, pleaded victimization by
"occult powers"—specifically, the American "Black Hand," which was
maneuvering the *pentiti* and seeking to bewitch him (*La Repubblica,* November 19, 1988, December 9, 1988).

The capture of Michele Greco heightened people's awareness that key
players in the Corleonesi alliance were still at large. It is now known that
Totò Riina "ordered" the murders of Falcone and Borsellino while in
hiding, yet neither he nor Provenzano, his closest associate, had been
seen for over twenty years (Stille 1995: 201, but see 50). The police knew
that Riina married Antonietta Bagarella in a church in Palermo in 1974
(Father Coppola, a priest who was later tried for collusion, performed
the ceremony) and that she was the sister of Calogero and Leoluca
Bagarella, important Corleone bosses. Their four children were born in
hospitals and "registered dutifully under their real names" (Stille 1995:
201). Clearly, as Stille has written, Riina was "living right under the
noses of investigators in Palermo, presumably with the protection and
complicity of many, many people" (ibid.). During the "long 1980s," the
number of similarly illusive figures was over two hundred.

Finding refuge means cashing in on past investments in provisioning
and conditioning. Both fellow mafiosi and non-mafiosi are willing to
host or help the fugitive because they feel obligated to him or to a mutual friend. Perhaps they are also intimidated by his reputation for violence and dare not refuse, although the wise mafioso is reluctant to be
harbored by frightened hosts, lest their anxiety result in stupid errors. To
be hosted and protected—medicated, too, if the fugitive has health problems—is to incur a future obligation. Brusca reports becoming furious
when he learned through a *pentito's* testimony that Riina had wanted
him dead for violating the agreements of a drug operation. This was an
ugly betrayal given that, early in the second mafia war, Brusca's father
had not only allied his *cosca* of San Giuseppe Jato with the Corleonesi
faction, he had gone out of his way—even risking his life—to collect Riina from his hiding place in Palermo and bring him up to the mountains
for a change of scenery (in Lodato 1999: 12–14).

On January 15, 1993, activist friends in Palermo telephoned us in New York to announce they were opening a bottle of champagne to celebrate the arrest of Totò Riina, captured—thanks, in part, to the collaboration of Baldassare Di Maggio—in the neighborhood of Palermo, Uditore, where he had been rumored to be living in recent years. The next high point of antimafia police activity was Brusca's capture in May 1996 (see fig. 12). Aided by the crescendo of *pentito* testimony to which some Corleonesi were by then contributing, the investigators zeroed in on a beachfront community near Agrigento. Unable to identify the particular house that Brusca was using, but having tapped his cellular telephone, they cleverly listened to his conversations while an officer drove a noisy motorcycle through the nearby streets. When the sound of the motorcycle in the background of the intercepted phone conversations reached its peak volume, it in effect pinpointed the sanctuary, allowing them to take their prey before he could slip away. Brusca's captors escorted him back to Palermo as if he were a trophy, honking their horns and waving their rifles as they entered the city. This triumphal moment, appearing on television and in the press, was so intense that the following day, high-ranking police officers expressed embarrassment over the unprofessional spirit of vendetta it had revealed.

Figure 12. Giovanni Brusca on the day of his arrest. Photograph by Alessandro Fucarini, Labruzzo Agenzia, Palermo.

It is still not clear how the authorities were able to locate Riina, though. Two *pentiti* now charge that Di Maggio's lead was a cover for the fact that the perennial fugitive, Bernardo Provenzano, had betrayed his former associate (*Giornale di Sicilia,* May 29, 1999; Brusca, in Lodato 1999). Riina was arrested while driving near his house of refuge. Within hours of his capture, before it could be canvassed by the authorities, the house was mysteriously emptied of its contents and repainted (see Jamieson 2000: 233). As a final irony, the press reported in June 2000 that the owner of the repainted apartment, the person who paid Riina's electric bill, was the engineer son of the Communist intellectual and antimafia strategist of the postwar decades, Giuseppe Montalbano—so far above suspicion as to be the perfect cover (*La Repubblica,* June 2, 2000). The ultimate enigma is whether Provenzano has become the "gray eminence pulling the mafia's strings" and, if so, from where. All known photographs of him are more than two decades old.[12]

SINISTER HYPOTHESES

Because people believe in *mandanti occulti*—hidden elites who order mafia killings from behind the scenes—every important assassination prompts grotesque speculation: which of the possible third-level interlocutors wanted that person out of the way and is secretly toasting his elimination? Sinister hypotheses are fed by rumor, by leaks of investigations, and by the diaries and personal papers found among the possessions of martyred victims. Although he could not attach names to his suspicions, Gaetano Costa left papers suggesting that he suspected hidden elements, some of them mafiosi but others not, behind many events he could not understand: people who had disappeared, businesses that were subject to extortion, the traffic in drugs, the system for allocating public works contracts, the choice of locales for school buildings, the urban plan of Palermo, the outcome of various competitions for jobs, the outcome of elections, and the arrogant comportment of certain officials (*L'Ora,* December 6, 1982). Judge Chinnici's diary (1983), leaked to the press following his murder, named a Palermo prosecutor and the Salvo cousins' defense attorney as persons to suspect should he eventually be harmed.

Chinnici further identified others in the Palermo Prosecutor's Office who, he believed, were collusive with the mafia or cowardly in the face of pressures to derail the antimafia investigations. From the Chinnici diary one also learns that, on the eve of his assassination, Piersanti

Mattarella, president of the Region of Sicily, had been looking into a web of collusion surrounding public works contracts for street lighting and maintenance, garbage collection, and other municipal services. These contracts are the focus of one of the most troubling diaries—the personal papers left by Giuseppe Insalaco, the murdered Christian Democrat who had been mayor of Palermo for a few brief months in 1984, during which he tried, but failed, to initiate reforms. Identified as standing in the way of reform were several politicians, mainly fellow party members, including Salvo Lima and Giulio Andreotti. Insalaco also referred to the Knights of the Holy Sepulcher, an elite Catholic alternative to Freemasonry. Was it an accident, Insalaco wondered, that two illusive figures, Count Arturo Cassina, the most privileged of the construction impresarios in Palermo, and Bruno Contrada, agent of the police and secret services, also belonged to this fraternity; that, indeed, Cassina was its head?

Having been advised by Chinnici to keep a diary, Falcone began to write sketchy notes toward the end of 1990. As noted above, he made a copy available to a trusted journalist, not for publication but to keep just in case, knowing that dalla Chiesa's private papers had disappeared from his office safe on the night that he was murdered. Although brief, Falcone's document confirms his frustration over having been marginalized in the Prosecutor's Office of Giammanco, to the point that he felt thwarted in pursuing his investigations into certain hot wires: the NATO Operation Stay-Behind, Gladio (see chapter 3), drug trafficking, and the mafia corruption of public works (see Stille 1995: 329–31).

To this day, speculation as to the "real" motive for Falcone's death touches the world of the construction industry. Angelo Siino, Riina's "minister of public works" and a recent *pentito*, has drawn attention to the Ravenna-based Ferruzzi Group headed by Raul Gardini, a target of the *mani pulite* investigations who suicided in 1993. Ferruzzi's Sicilian subsidiary, Calcestruzzi, was an exceptional beneficiary of public works contracts in Palermo, perhaps in exchange for favors to the Corleonesi. (Siino testified in 1997 that Gardini met with representatives of the Brusca family several times.) Shortly before leaving Palermo for Rome, Falcone ordered a Carabinieri report on Palermo public works. The report was completed but never followed up by Giammanco, and it was leaked to the mafia, presumably by someone within the Prosecutor's Office. One can easily hypothesize that the mafia's knowledge of Falcone's efforts regarding the Ferruzzi relationship hastened his assassination (see Jamieson 2000: 213–14).

Recent testimony by Brusca points to the possibility that, following the assassination of Falcone, "pieces of the state" entertained negotiating with Riina in the name of preventing further bloodshed, but that Borsellino was adamantly opposed—hence the decision, made by Riina, to kill him, too (*La Repubblica,* September 29, 2001). However, other motives have also been advanced. Working feverishly after the death of his colleague (and with similar obstacles thrown in his path), Borsellino broke new ground with the help of new *pentiti,* in particular Leonardo Messina, who told of Riina's system for distributing contracts, administered by Siino, and Gaspare Mutolo, who reported that Contrada had engaged in collusive transactions with the mafia. (Borsellino was also taking testimony from Rita Atria, the young woman from a mafia family who suicided after his death.) Jamieson, outlining the suspicions regarding public works contracts and the death of Falcone, eerily continues,

> After the [Falcone] attack, Paolo Borsellino decided to reopen the Mafia-public works enquiry in strictest secrecy . . . without the knowledge of the chief prosecutor Giammanco, who had shelved it 18 months before. In the course of 1999 there was mounting evidence that Borsellino's decision to pursue this investigation was a precipitating factor in *Cosa Nostra*'s decision to murder him. Otherwise it is hard to imagine why the organization would have invited further repression. (2000: 213–14)

It is surely significant that Palermo's construction industry and allocation of contracts for public works is so often at the center of assassination narratives. So is extreme right-wing involvement, although this is usually trumped by the construction industry story. The murder in 1979 of Michele Reina, a Christian Democratic leader with construction industry connections, was initially charged to right-wing terrorists, only to be reexamined, based on the testimony of eight *pentiti,* in relation to a different kind of *mandante*—the politician Ciancimino. According to a Supreme Court decision of July 1999, the motive was to protect the construction interests of the Corleonesi (*Giornale di Sicilia,* March 9, 2000). Similarly, investigators into the killing of Mattarella initially pursued a theory, advanced by Mattarella's widow among others, that a neo-fascist terrorist, Giusva Fioravanti, had lent a hand in exchange for help from Cosa Nostra in eliminating an enemy of his. In the end, the same court attributed the murder to the *cupola* alone—because of outrage over Mattarella's attempt to "moralize" public works.[13]

Honest investigators disagree over the credibility of various scenarios. Moreover, sometimes caution is the best defense against pursuing false or planted leads—traps of disinformation set on purpose to land a magistrate in difficulty. In 1989, Falcone prosecuted a *pentito* for falsely asserting that Salvo Lima had been the *mandante* in the Mattarella murder. Falcone's decision to challenge the accusation against Lima upset the antimafia mayor, Leoluca Orlando, who charged, in what became a notorious polemic, that the magistrate possessed incriminating evidence that he failed to act upon.

In the early years, Falcone used the term "third-level" to refer to the highest level of mafia crime—the assassinations of the excellent cadavers—as if no person beyond the *cupola* were involved.[14] As we have seen, the *pentiti* of those early years, Buscetta and Contorno, likewise would not testify to the existence of a wider circle of complicity. And yet, already at the time of the maxi-trial, other prosecutors were convinced that such external interlocutors must bear great responsibility for the mafia emergency in Palermo. Although always cautious—in the opinion of some, too cautious—Falcone eventually moved a few degrees closer to this point of view—and then he was killed.

During the "long 1980s," assassinations of highly placed persons were often preceded by a pattern of progressive isolation. The relevant ministry withheld material and moral support, local authorities turned a deaf ear to the victim's complaints about this, and the press and informal gossip circles spread erroneous rumors that the official in question was overzealous in carrying out his duties and/or guilty of some procedural error or ethical fault. Potential victims were also often accused of misusing their office to promote their own careers (becoming professional "mafiosi of the antimafia"). Thus Chinnici was warned by his superior that the young Falcone was "ruining the Palermo economy with his investigations" and should stop "acting like a sheriff" (Chinnici 1983: 64). The anonymous letters of the *corvo* accusing Falcone of manipulating Contorno began to circulate only days before the attempt on his life near his beach house. By the time the bomb or bullets struck, the victim had already been marked and rendered vulnerable, as if to blunt some of the predictable public outrage over the enormity of the crime (see dalla Chiesa 1984). These practices fed the atmosphere of rumor and innuendo, ambiguity and mystery, that came to pervade the antimafia process in Palermo. Fortunately, they are not the whole story. For the "long 1980s" also produced a broadly based antimafia social movement, which, among many other things, has advocated for the magistracy at critical, difficult junctures, calling for the promotion of "clean" judges and the removal of judges who are compromised. Every antimafia prosecutor is aware of the difference this has made.

CHAPTER 7

The Antimafia Movement

Caught in the cross-fire of the civil liberties campaign, criticized for politicizing their investigations, and shaken by the anonymous acts of the moles among their colleagues, the police and magistrates needed the support of mobilized citizens and citizens' organizations. Emerging as a predominantly urban social movement after the killing of dalla Chiesa in September 1982, by the mid-1980s, such a social force had achieved a political presence in its center of greatest strength, Palermo. Here Leoluca Orlando, a charismatic antimafia politician (of Christian Democratic provenance) served as mayor from 1985 until 1990, and again from 1993 until December 2000. With a rhetorical flourish, Orlando likes to describe the antimafia process as a cart with two wheels, one the wheel of social, cultural, and political reform, the other the wheel of police and judicial repression. Only if both move in unison does the cart go forward; if one wheel moves while the other stands still, the cart spins in a circle without advancing.

Extremely sensitive to such violent provocations as the excellent cadavers, the antimafia movement has manifested periods of high mobilization and periods of latency, its initial enthusiasm muted by the same ideological backlash that unsettled the magistrates. The multiple organizations and associations comprising the movement are not always able to communicate effectively, let alone share meanings or sustain an overarching consistency of purpose. Of course, many social movements disintegrate into factionalism, often, it is thought, on the downswing of a

protest cycle, when the constituent organizations must intensify their distinctive ways of framing the issues in order to compete for followers (see
Diani 1995). Even when such fragmentation is absent, tension emanates
from the many fault lines within and between movement groups. One
salient fault line for antimafia activists—as for many social movements
throughout the world in the 1980s and 1990s—is traceable to the ideologically driven polarization of politics during the Cold War. For Italy,
this meant a division between "Catholics" and "Communists," that is,
persons whose political socialization was rooted in the historic relationship between the Roman Catholic Church and the Christian Democratic
Party, regardless of the intensity of their religious commitment, and persons who grew up with the secular left, even though they may have been
practicing Catholics. The resulting "red-white" dialectic was nowhere
more consequential than in Sicily, where, in the decades after World
War II, most antimafia activists were leftists, whereas most Christian Democrats had to live with the appearance, if not the reality, of mafia conditioning.

Without belaboring the scholarly debates regarding "new" social
movements,[1] today's antimafia movement clearly belongs to this type,
having parted ways with the politics of class struggle characteristic of the
postwar era. In part the transition reflects the emergence of new social
groups and generations. Antimafia activists of the 1950s and 1960s, participants in the struggle of peasants for land, tended to be male, small-
town, and not well schooled, in contrast to the more or less gender-
integrated, urban, and educated middle-class core of the movement
today. This is not to say the core is homogeneous. Some activists come
from comfortable and long-established professional families, the kind of
family that is likely to have lived in Palermo for several generations, its
various nuclei occupying the same family building, their large and comfortable apartments repositories of heirlooms and antiques. A few, most
notably Orlando, hail from the landed elite. Others are of more plebian
origin, their peasant or laboring parents not having gone beyond elementary school and their living situations quite modest. Nevertheless,
the most engaged activists, women as well as men, have been in their for-
ties or younger and have held degrees from the University of Palermo,
where they participated in student politics during the 1960s. The backgrounds of the activist clergy frequently include exposure to the curric-
ular reforms inspired by Vatican Council II in the same period. On the
whole, antimafia leaders constitute a politically experienced intelli-
gentsia, persons with careers or aspirations for careers in social work,

teaching, law, government, journalism, health care, and the clergy (see Ramella and Trigilia 1997). Dense networks cut across these professions and occupations. It is our impression, in fact, that school ties are salient building blocks of antimafia organization.

Today's antimafia movement is not a *de novo* phenomenon unencumbered by political baggage from the past. As we will see, although a majority of activists think of themselves as left of center, some do not and a substantial number have Christian Democratic or, more broadly, Catholic backgrounds. Perhaps needless to say, activists have had to invest considerable time, energy, and patience in building trust between the left-wing heirs of the peasant struggle and these new recruits. Terrible events demanding a broad response have contributed to this process of accommodation, as has a prior, if submerged, history of Catholic radicalism, on the one hand, and, on the other hand, of Communist compromises and defections. In the following pages we review these histories for the light they shed on the antimafia conflicts of the 1980s and beyond.

CATHOLICS AND COMMUNISTS: TO 1968

Given Italy's strategic importance to both the United States and the Soviet Union during the Cold War, it is not surprising that it nurtured two mutually antagonistic political subcultures, one associated with the Communist Party and the Communist and Socialist unions; the other with the Christian Democratic Party, Catholic unions, and the Roman Catholic Church. According to Mancini, this "wide and apparently bottomless cleavage" was "unparalleled in Europe with the possible exception of France" (2000: 122–23). Persons in the "red" subculture were disinclined to pursue alliances or build political projects with persons in the "white" subculture, and vice-versa. In Sicily, where perhaps fifty Communist and Socialist leaders of the peasants' agitation for land were martyred by the mafia, the dialectic was considerably more than rhetorical.

Etched in the collective memory of the Sicilian left are several specific cases in which gross miscarriages of justice enabled perpetrators to escape being apprehended or convicted. In 1944, the Sicilian Communist leader and former partisan Girolamo Li Causi was wounded along with ten or so peasants while speaking before a crowd in Villalba, the rural town of Don Calogero Vizzini. The attack was carried out by Vizzini's men, but he was never arrested, thanks to a series of imbroglios (later exposed by Pantaleone 1962; see Sabetti 1984 for a contrary interpretation). Other frequently cited examples are those of Accursio Miraglia, secretary of the Chamber of Labor in Sciacca, who was killed in 1946, and Placido Rizzotto, the union leader who met the same end in Corleone. In both of these cases, the alleged murderers were brought to trial but acquitted for lack of proof. (Rizzotto's killer, Luciano Liggio, was later jailed for other crimes.) Recently, these acquittals have been revisited through initiatives of the antimafia movement.[2]

The May Day massacre of 1947 at Portella della Ginestra, orchestrated by the rogue bandit Salvatore Giuliano (chapter 3), was another notorious event in this history. Two years later, legal scholar Giuseppe Montalbano, representing the "people's bloc" in the regional assembly, accused members of the noble Tasca family and their allies of being "criminal delinquents," manipulating Giuliano, first for separatist, and then for anticommunist ends. It was time, he argued, for the national Parliament to set up a commission of inquiry into the mafia. His opponents insisted that such a commission would cast a "racist shadow" on the people of Sicily (see Montalbano 1964a).

Following the Ciaculli massacre of 1963 (chapter 3), a Parliamentary Antimafia Commission was established with representation from all of the political parties, but it disappointed its (mainly) Communist advocates. Two of these, the Sicilian deputies Pio La Torre and Cesare Terranova, revisited the Portella shooting in their "minority report" of 1976. Giuliano, they argued, had intentionally attacked a "nerve center of the Province of Palermo where the CGIL (the Communist-allied General Italian Chamber of Labor) and the parties of the Left were particularly well developed." Arming him were "forces linked to the agrarian bloc . . . (and also to foreign [read United States] centers)" whose purpose was to drive a wedge between the nascent Christian Democratic Party and the left, both regionally and nationally. It was no accident, they admonished, that in the weeks following the shooting, several nearby towns (San Giuseppe Jato, San Cipirello, Partinico, Monreale, and others) were the scenes of attacks on the seats of the Communist and Socialist parties and of the CGIL in which numerous peasants were killed or wounded. The result was a climate of terror in the province that lasted until the elections of 1948, during which a leftward momentum, led by the "people's bloc," was checked and reversed in all of the affected communities (quoted in Alongi 1997: 112–13 n. 7; see also Commissione Parlamentare d'Inchiesta 1976; Santino 2000: 148ff).

At the same time that the Sicilian left commemorated its martyrs, the postwar archbishop of Palermo, Ernesto Cardinal Ruffini, revitalized the "Sicilianist" defense. He accepted electoral arrangements between the mafia and the Christian Democratic Party on the grounds that they enhanced the Church's mission to fend off Marxist atheism. The "sack of Palermo" that evolved from these relations was, in his view, a sign of the city's well-being and progress, not a cause for alarm. Following Ciaculli, an official in the Vatican, undoubtedly on behalf of Paul VI, wrote to Ruffini suggesting that he make a pastoral statement against the mafia, given that a leader of Sicily's tiny but (to the Vatican) influential Waldensian congregation had just done so. Ruffini responded by saying that the very idea of an association between the mafia and religion was a lie spread by the Communists to accuse the DC of having mafia support (Alongi 1997: 24–25). In a pastoral letter on Palm Sunday of the following year, Ruffini became the first Sicilian bishop to include the word "mafia" in an official document, only to declare it off limits for future use (ibid.: 25–26 n. 27). To this day he is associated with the slogan, "The mafia exists only in the minds of those who wish Sicily ill."

The highest officer of the Sicilian Church, Ruffini contributed substantially to the formation of the DC's tainted electoral machine. In the name of anticommunism, the bishops and their parish priests supported the Christian Democrats, urging parishioners to do the same, and ignoring the mafia's manipulation of those parishioners' votes. Ruffini died in 1967 and was replaced in 1970 by Salvatore Pappalardo (son of a Carabiniere officer from eastern Sicily), whose anticommunism was considerably more attenuated.[3] Even so, the Church had taken such a combative stance that antimafia activists had difficulty endorsing Pappalardo, except briefly in 1982–83, after he delivered a notably antimafia homily at the funeral of General dalla Chiesa.

THE SUBMERGED HISTORIES OF THE "YEARS OF LEAD"

In Italy, the years 1968–79 are sometimes referred to as the "years of lead" *(anni di piombo)* for the armed violence of the Red Brigades on the left, and neofascist squads on the right. In the course of them, many student radicals turned against the Communist Party, finding it "out of date," lacking in revolutionary imagination, and sadly intimidated by the example of counterrevolutionary regimes in Greece and Chile. Mobilizing workers in the industrial cities of the north, inspired by Lenin and by a militant left agenda, they also formed extraparliamentary groups such as *Democrazia Proletaria* (Proletarian Democracy) and *Lotta Continua* (Continuous Struggle). Parallel groups emerged to counter them on the far right. Meanwhile, the Communist Party's electoral strength was growing in relation to the Christian Democrats, with the PCI reaching 34.4 percent of the vote (its all-time high) in the national elections of 1976, as against 38.7 percent for the DC.

Given this impressive showing, both the Communists, led by Enrico Berlinguer, and a reform current of the Christian Democrats, led by Aldo Moro, explored the possibility of an "historic compromise" between the two dominant parties. In exchange for contributing to multi-party "center-left" voting majorities in Parliament, the Communists would receive one or two ministerial positions. This initiative, coming on top of the Communist Party's mounting electoral success, constituted a crisis for the more radical students. Although many of them moved toward institutionalized politics, some became terrorists. Still others, disillusioned, withdrew from collective action into cult-like or atomized styles of protest enhanced by drugs (whose supply was becoming abundant, thanks to the contemporaneous entry of the mafia into heroin trafficking). Yet another large group went on to address newly recognized injustices suffered, in particular, by women and the environment (Diani 1995; Lumley 1990; Melucci 1989; 1996: 258–83; Tarrow 1989).

The "lead years" came to a head in 1978 with the kidnapping of Aldo Moro by the Red Brigades. The anti-Moro (and anticommunist) DC faction led by Andreotti declined to negotiate with the terrorists for Moro's release, provoking the suspicion, still at large today, that it had in some manner been complicit in his sequester. The historic compromise having failed, the Andreotti faction went on to dominate national politics throughout the "long 1980s," more or less in alliance with the rightward-turning Socialists (Gilbert 1995; McCarthy 1995: 124–30).

In Sicily during this period, some Catholic university students joined Moro's reformist current of the Christian Democratic Party, which, on the regional level, was led by Piersanti Mattarella (assassinated in 1980). Others, taking heart from Vatican II, went further, questioning the Church's association with the DC and its practice of dictating people's voting behavior (see Barrese 1973: 180). A network of dissident priests even debated whether voting Communist could be compatible with the Gospel. Such dissident Catholics found sustenance in two or three points of reference in Palermo, among them the Redemptorist Order, whose handful of priests occupied an eighteenth-century convent in the neighborhood of Uditore. Here a half-acre of citrus groves, miraculously untouched by the 1960s invasion of multistory apartments in the zone, offered an oasis for quiet reflection. Nino Fasullo, a gentle and soft-spoken but determined Redemptorist seeking a meaningful encounter with the

lay world, transformed the order's bulletin into the outstanding journal
Segno. Its editorial staff and contributors include lay as well as religious
social critics, many of them leaders of the antimafia movement (the martyred judge Chinnici was among the founders).

Another point of reference was the Centro Studi Pedro Arrupe, which
the Jesuits founded in the late 1960s. Although anticommunist, the center
nevertheless promoted a critical engagement with Marxist philosophy and
advocated political autonomy from the DC, fearful that young people,
alienated by the party's politics, might also distance themselves from the
Church (Alongi 1997: 145). Young radical lay Catholics participated in its
seminars and discussion groups, hearing such figures as Danilo Dolci, the
Gandhi-inspired pacifist from northern Italy who had become a champion
of Sicilian peasants, and Tulio Vinay, the Waldensian minister. In addition,
they became an effective pressure group promoting socially conscious legislation in the Regional Assembly, such as a 1980 law decentralizing
Sicily's cities into *quartieri* or districts, each with its own elected council
(see Alongi 1997: 153–62). When the established political parties, including the DC, continued to manipulate Palermo's twenty-five new district
councils for their own ends, the lay Catholics close to the Centro Aruppe
formed a "civic list," independent of all the parties, called *Città per
l'Uomo* (City for Humanity), launching a journal of the same name in
1982. All of these developments advanced the transformation of Sicily's
left-wing Catholics from staunch anticommunists to antimafia activists—
from viewing atheism as the all time enemy of the Sicilian Church to viewing organized crime and corruption as morally worse (ibid.: 165).

Transformations on the "red" side of the "red-white" cleavage were
unfolding in tandem. During the 1960s and 1970s, the universities of
Palermo and Catania grew rapidly, as national reform made higher education more accessible. No less than in Milan, radical students in Sicily
participated in *Democrazia Proletaria, Lotta Continua,* and other ultra-
left groups. They lent support to the local shipyard workers being organized by the CGIL and agitated for decent housing and medical care
on behalf of poor people. As elsewhere in Italy, their action coalesced
outside of, and to some degree in opposition to, the Communist Party.

A particular focus of criticism was that, in the Sicilian context, the historic compromise meant going to bed with Ciancimino and Lima. Indeed, to the despair of the student radicals, it appeared that the Communist leadership had failed to apprehend the threat of the expanding
urban mafia, even as Sicilian mafiosi were becoming the world's principal traffickers in heroin. In part the old guard was stymied by its Marx-

ist conviction that, as the vigilante arm of the landed gentry, the mafia was incapable of surviving the land reform, except as a variant of everyday delinquency, endemic to urban capitalism.[4] Older leftists were also shielded by their past reputation as the only really committed antimafia force on the island. To really understand what happened to the Sicilian Communist Party and leadership during the historic compromise, however, it is necessary to look at the construction industry.

FOR THE SAKE OF JOBS

Writing about organized crime in New York City, Robert Kelly focuses on the construction industry, which, he argues, is best characterized as an economic sector because it consists of numerous branches (commercial, highway, industrial, pipelines, housing, monuments), is divided between public works and private projects, and employs a broad mix of skilled and unskilled workers (Kelly 1999: 76–77). Addressing the question of why the sector is highly permeable to corruption and racketeering, Kelly makes the following useful observation:

> The construction industry is fragile because it is so atypical. Construction work more than most other types of industrial work depends on weather, coordination and integration of dozens of subcontractors, specialized crafts, and groups of laborers. Site clearance, demolition, and excavation must be done; concrete poured; superstructures raised; plumbing installed; carpentry and electrical work carried out; telephone wiring and elevator installation completed —all in a predetermined order and often unchangeable sequence. . . . A racketeer with influence or control over supplies, union officials, or building inspectors can exacerbate or reduce the fragility; the racketeer thus has many opportunities to extract money from the industry's participants. At the same time, the contractors who themselves are often victims or potential victims of gangsters do not hesitate to exploit those gangsters for their own greedy designs or to ensure some degree of stability in an otherwise capricious work environment. Consequently, it is not unusual for a builder/contractor to seek out racketeers who can eliminate competition, quiet labor unrest, or skirt the maze of regulations that fills the construction landscape. (ibid.: 90–91)

The Palermo experience points to another ingredient, as well. Heavily capitalized construction firms from northern Italy and Germany bid on contracts in Sicily, and some construction components are modular, transportable from place to place (see Linder 1994). Yet, by its very nature, the building business is grounded—dependent for profit and promise on local contractors and subcontractors, on local materials, and on the local and regional administration of laws governing transportation, public housing, zoning, contract bidding, taxation, credit, and finance. This, plus the industry's dependence on local labor, or labor that has migrated into the area, constitutes a rich terrain for mediating political relationships—for industry representatives and friends to deliver the votes of construction workers and suppliers to compliant municipal and regional politicians, in turn prepared to look the other way when the "maze of regulations" is violated. The question before us is how this system, which revolved around the DC administrations of Lima and Ciancimino, came to contaminate the Communist Party as well.

In the 1960s and 1970s, Palermo was bursting with newcomers, many of whom found employment in the building trades, which all of the unions, including the Communist union, competed to organize. Most employees of the region's largest construction companies—in particular, four large Catania-based firms whose owners had received honorific knighthoods from the state and were known, therefore, as the Knights of Labor (Cavalieri del Lavoro)—were represented by the Communist union, the CGIL. The union defined these companies as "progressive" and cooperated with their owners in the maintenance of labor peace. The subsequent indictments of these owners for collusion with the mafia is among the scandals that student radicals of the time foresaw. Furthermore, in the 1970s, the Communists organized several cooperative building firms, known as "red cooperatives," which benefited from the politics of parceling out public works contracts to competing firms in proportion to the electoral success of the parties with which they were affiliated. Dependent on rigged bidding, this practice was of course illegal, as were the rigged auctions through which the red co-ops, along with many other firms, obtained subcontracts from the largest companies.

In the 1980s, both external and internal critics of the Communist Party and union were becoming a vocal presence in the antimafia movement. Significantly, no one we talked to thought that the leaders profited, personally, from corruption; rather, they were seen as motivated by the need to create employment for a rapidly expanding peasant-to-worker constituency and by their desire to be involved in the provision of public housing. Yet the criticism stung, putting older generation leftists on the defensive. Until the late 1970s, the Sicilian Communist Party nurtured a political culture premised on a model of society in which dramatically unequal social classes confronted one another across discrete boundaries. According to the resulting morality of struggle, solidarity within the class on the bottom took precedence over individually negotiated ties of patronage between members of this class and their class superiors, ties that were heavily stigmatized. Inevitably, Communist Party stalwarts resented the exposure of clientelistic practices in the red co-ops and union; after all, the workers' votes were already assured through party discipline. At the same time, they expressed nostalgia for a simpler time, when it was clear who held the moral high ground with regard to the mafia.

Defenders of the left's antimafia credentials like to remind their critics that until the late 1970s, the Communist Party bankrolled the daily *L'Ora,* founded by the Sicilianist Florios in the 1890s but now famous for exposing the scandals behind savage construction. Under editor Vittorio Nisticò, reporters such as Orazio Barese and Marcello Cimino wrote stories on the city's delay in approving an urban plan, on its failure to guarantee adequate space for services and recreation amid the spreading concrete jungle, on specific instances of corruption involving DC officials in City Hall and mafioso contractors and suppliers who were their friends. Defenders are also quick to insist that the damage done by the CGIL and the red co-ops pales in comparison to the "sack of Palermo" organized by the mafia-sponsored contractors allied with the Christian Democrats. In self-defense, one PCI leader, referred to as a "Communist boss" by his detractors, once stated (in widely quoted words), "Well, we cannot analyze the blood of everyone we do business with" (see Alongi 1997: 102–3). In 1984, the Italian Communist deputies in the European Parliament voted against discussing Euro-deputy Salvo Lima's ties with the mafia, reluctant, apparently, to rock the boat of the Palermo construction industry. The ties in question had been exposed by the 1976 report of the Antimafia Commission and brought to the attention of the Parliament by a dossier entitled "A Friend at Strasbourg," prepared by Umberto Santino's Center for Documentation, described below.

While the Sicilian Communists were softening their position on the mafia, radicals to their left were hardening theirs, a contrast illustrated by the story of Giuseppe Impastato, a young journalist and new left militant from Cinisi, the town of capomafioso Gaetano Badalamenti. By controlling the location, construction, and operation of the Palermo airport at nearby Punta Raisi, Badalamenti had gotten a precocious start in the transatlantic heroin traffic. Impastato's father, Luigi, a lower-ranking mafioso, was a close friend of Badalamenti; other members of his family and their friends belonged to Badalamenti's Cinisi *cosca.* It seems likely that Giuseppe would have been destined for a similar career had he not broken with his family and been politicized on the left as a university student in the late 1960s (Santino 2000: 235).

As a neophyte journalist in Cinisi, Giuseppe Impastato founded his own radio station, Radio AUT, and with irony and humor began to expose the airport planners for having accommodated the mafia-linked economic and real estate interests of local landowners at the expense of public safety. (The facility was opened in 1960 on a narrow plain between the mountains and the sea that is poorly adapted to air traffic.) He also criticized the design of the highway serving the airport as unnecessarily curvaceous and costly, for the same reason. Impastato went further to wage an open war against the mafia of Cinisi and against the town authorities for advancing speculative and abusive construction along the nearby waterfront. Specifically, mafia-allied contractors were misusing public funds targeted for tourist development; they were illegally excavating construction materials from virtually all of the surrounding hillsides; and they were encumbering a beautiful coastline with an overbuilt jumble of houses. Impastato denounced this in his satirical broadcasts.

In May 1978 his body was found, blown up alongside the railroad track near Cinisi. It could appear as if, in the manner of an ultra-left terrorist, he had been about to dynamite the track and had detonated the bomb in error, or had committed suicide in the attempt (Impastato 1986; Santino 2000: 255; Vitale 1995). His student friends doubted these official hypotheses, however, and began their own investigation. When they found traces of blood some distance from the bombsite, they urged the police to consider that Impastato had been murdered, but it took more than twenty years, and the eventual testimony of a *pentito,* to indict and convict Badalamenti and the material executors of the crime.

Soon after the murder, Impastato's friends and political companions began publishing "counter-information" about his death, and on May 9, 1979, the first anniversary of the killing, they went to Cinisi to stage what they called "the first national demonstration against the mafia in Italian history," out of which grew a dramatic publication, *Mafia Oggi* (1981). This magazine, richly illustrated with riveting photographs taken by Letizia Battaglia and Franco Zecchin (press photographers and chroniclers of the mafia's grisly violence for *L'Ora*), was offered as a contribution to another initiative of the Regional Assembly, Act 51, dedicated to promoting "a civil and democratic consciousness against mafia criminality" through education and cultural activities (see chapter 11).

In 1977, in a parallel development in Palermo, Umberto Santino and Anna Puglisi, activist intellectuals, founded a Sicilian Center for Documentation on the Mafia. Rapidly accumulating an archive and library, they too pursued the events surrounding Impastato's death and in 1980 named the center for him; their purpose was to acknowledge his particular martyrdom, having come from a mafia family, as well as his brilliance in analyzing and confronting the mafia (see Santino 2000: 235–38). With support from scholar-subscribers and by dint of much personal sacrifice, Santino and Puglisi subsequently rented the apartment adjacent to their residence as an office and meeting place for the Centro Impastato, rendering it a continuing presence in the antimafia process as well as an unparalleled resource for scholars.

SAN SAVERIO IN ALBERGHERIA

Sociologist Mario Diani has studied how, in the 1980s, clusters of activists with ostensibly opposite political identities began to work together in some Italian cities (1995). His case is the environmentalist movement of Milan, made up of conservationists opposed to the degradation of natural and artistic resources at the hands of "mass" industrialization, and Marxist "political ecologists" struggling to improve working, health, and safety conditions for industrial laborers. Attempting to understand the mutual, if sometimes fragile tolerance of these two clusters for each other, Diani cites the waning of Cold War tensions, and with them Italy's red-white dualism, well before 1989; the transformation of the Italian economy from an emphasis on large-scale industry to small-scale industry and service sector expansion; and the associated emergence of a well-educated "new middle class" whose members influenced the styles of protest of both conservationist and political ecology organizations. Especially significant, he thinks, was the socialization of many of the political ecologists in the "new politics" experiments of the previous decade, the 1970s. Disenchanted with intractable quarrels, they had then learned to eschew ideological exclusiveness and compromise with progressive Catholics (see also Melucci 1996: 274). By the same token, the conservationists moved leftward, joining with political ecologists in specific local arenas, for example, to oppose the construction of nuclear power plants.

In Sicily, nuclear power plants were not an issue, but nuclear arms were, as youthful protesters of Catholic and Communist background came together in the 1970s to agitate against the installation of a NATO missile base in the rural town of Comiso, a protest led by Pio La Torre. Allied in grassroots organizations and through volunteer work, protestors also tackled crises of poverty and housing in Palermo, which still showed the effects of the 1943 bombing, compounded by earthquake damage from 1968. In concert, grassroots organizers of secular and Catholic persuasion mobilized squatters to occupy unused spaces, form settlements, and demonstrate in the hope (almost never fulfilled) that the city would provide utilities and transportation.[5]

The rectory of the San Saverio Church in Albergheria was a beacon for this kind of activity. A small nucleus of priests from towns to the east of Palermo with a history of mafia violence—Casteldaccia, Bagheria, Altavilla—had become interested in the neighborhood's destitute families living in crumbling, bomb-damaged structures. One of the concerned priests, Francesco Stabile, became a regular contributor to the journal *Segno*. Another, the Redemptorist Don Cosimo Scordato, was assigned to be rector of San Saverio, where he created a model social center. Lay radical members of the Giuseppe Impastato Center for Documentation, engaged with the same issues, gave their wholehearted support.

By 1985, Scordato had made the tiny San Saverio Church into a focus of antimafia activity. The church itself, a baroque jewel with spiraled columns flanking its entrance, was cleaned and restored, the piazza in front of it cleared of parked cars and lined with potted trees and benches. A large mural was painted on a wall facing the piazza. Mimicking the scenes of feudal combat that were traditionally painted on Sicilian carts, it pictures people at work (a knight in armor laying bricks!) over the slogan, "Reconstruct the City." An ice cream bar and a restaurant employing local youths blossomed nearby. The restaurant occupies the ground-floor warehouse of an ancient building, but the formerly decrepit space has been made attractive by exposing its old sandstone vaulting and rustic tile floors. On our first visit in 1987, Scordato showed us pictures of its wretched condition before the renovation and confided his vision that someday foreigners would visit the quarter and eat in the restaurant as part of a package tour. He was already writing a history of the *quartiere* for tourists and training youthful reformed purse snatchers to act as tour guides.

Under Scordato's energetic leadership, a small square a few blocks from the church was also cleaned up, planted with shrubs, and lined with a wooden fence. On a large rock placed in the center, a plaque was erected commemorating the death of a little girl, Maria, a victim of parental abuse. Scordato hoped this neighborhood tragedy would focus people's attention on the evils of violence, evils that he regularly preached against in church. Most important, with the help of local artisans, including an exprisoner in semi-liberty, he engineered the recuperation of an abandoned religious refuge (the Opera Pia Reclusori Femminili), turning it into a headquarters for the social center. Its two stories of rooms and interior courtyard have housed numerous initiatives, financed by all levels of government, including the European Union. Among the initiatives are a health clinic for women and children, an after-school program aimed at returning "adolescents of the streets" to school, apprenticeship programs teaching artisan skills to men and women, and programs, including summer camping trips, to shelter small children from the influence of local gangs. Elderly residents began meeting at the center under an initiative set up for them, while its spacious ground floor and courtyard served to organize an all-absorbing summertime "Olympic" festival in 1986, 1987, and 1988, described below. The programs depend heavily on volunteers. In 1988, about 50 persons, around 35 of whom were paid a modest wage, took care of some 170 children and a number of families. Many of the volunteers, above all the paid ones, were recruited from the neighborhood, others from a nearby university dormitory, still others as conscientious objectors, assigned to perform socially useful activities in lieu of military service.

A remarkable aspect of the Centro Sociale San Saverio—an aspect that has furthered alliances between the secular and the religious left— is its avowedly apolitical and nonconfessional stance. Formally chartered in 1986, it explicitly defined itself as autonomous of all political parties and the Church hierarchy as well. The actual church of San Saverio became a place for debate and discussion of the problems of housing and employment faced by the people of the neighborhood. Knowledgeable lay activists such as Umberto Santino and Danilo Dolci were invited to speak. Although the church pews faced the altar for Sunday mass, Scordato invited a secular definition of the sanctuary by turning them toward the right for public meetings and toward the left for dramas and concerts. In an interview with us in 1987, he explained that when someone is sick, "we listen to anyone with a prescription." Augusto Cavadi, a high school philosophy teacher, an advocate of liberation theology, and a close collaborator of both Scordato and Santino, subsequently wrote that it was an "eloquent sign of the times to find Catholics and Marxists side by side, both repenting the dogmatic ideological choices that kept them apart ten or twenty years earlier" (Cavadi 1989: 156).

THE ANTIMAFIA MOVEMENT TAKES SHAPE

Most antimafia activists would date the emergence of the new antimafia movement to the massacre of the popular Prefect dalla Chiesa and his wife, Emanuela Setti Carraro, on September 3, 1982. To the historian Francesco Renda, this was the first of two great "waves of emotion," the second of which came in 1992 after the killings of Falcone and Borsellino (Renda 1993). Not only did both waves produce significant new legislation in support of the antimafia prosecutors; both also turned citizens into demonstrators and protagonists of a cause. National political leaders attending dalla Chiesa's funeral encountered a hostile crowd—grieving, angry, and in some cases voicing their "suspicions that the politicians were complicit in what had happened" (Alongi 1997: 15, 17 n. 11).

Dramatically, Cardinal Pappalardo delivered a stinging homily, broadcast and published in the national media, in which he proposed as a metaphor for Palermo the ancient city of Sagunto, destroyed by its enemies while Rome (that is, the political class) stood idly by. In 1981, following the killings of Terranova and Mattarella, Pappalardo had already referred to "an *intreccio* . . . between common delinquency, operating in the open, and occult maneuvers; . . . between the executors and the *mandanti* of crimes; between the prepotent men of the neighborhoods and *borgate* and mafiosi with a wider range and dominion" (Stabile 1989: 115). Now, it seemed, he was throwing down the gauntlet. Nino Alongi, author of a book on the antimafia movement and a leader of Città per l'Uomo, writes that "within a few minutes the Church seemed to recuperate from decades of silence and complicity," so much so that the old taboo against speaking about the mafia disappeared forever (Alongi 1997: 15–16).

Within a few months, however, Pappalardo had retreated from his outspoken zeal. Some people suggest that this "reentry" was prompted by his experience in 1983, when not a single prisoner showed up to attend his traditional Easter mass in the Ucciardone. Members of the radical clergy debate among themselves whether the Christian Democratic establishment had not already reined him in before this menacing act. At any event, the radical clerics were dismayed to see him lose his critical edge; it reminded them of their disappointment when the Pope visited Palermo two months after the dalla Chiesa murder but did not publicly utter the remarks about the mafia that were part of his prepared talk—because of exigencies of time, he later said (see ibid.: 31–32).

Following the dalla Chiesa assassination, the general's son, Nando, a sociologist at the Bocconi University in Milan, and his brother-in-law, Alessandro Cestelli, a biologist at the University of Palermo, put together a committee that created a traveling exhibition on the mafia to raise money in northern Italy for a monument to the "fallen in the struggle" (Acuto et al. 1983). Funds accumulated primarily in Milan (Nando dalla Chiesa's city), augmented by funds from the regional government, were sufficient to engage shipyard workers to construct a tall steel structure near the port commemorating the mafia's victims. On the first anniversary of dalla Chiesa's murder, the committee also organized a candlelight procession in which an estimated thirty thousand citizens participated. Meanwhile, a Sicilian lawyer of Communist background, Alfredo Galasso, began considering how the general's survivors, Nando dalla Chiesa and his sister, might constitute themselves as a protagonist "civil party" in the eventual prosecution of the assassins.[6]

These and related initiatives convinced Nando dalla Chiesa that a new antimafia movement had been born. In an academic article (1983), he emphasized its differences from the antimafia movement of the past. The new agitation gravitated around schools and universities, teachers and students, and involved the development of educational initiatives promoting civil society and democracy. The arenas of struggle were to be study groups, symposia, roundtables, conferences, and book presentations, at which those present would raise their consciousness about morality in politics, decrying the corruption of the entire party system, the *partitocrazia*. Superseding the categorically antistate discourse of the old left ("the state is mafioso"), and the related theory of the mafia as the "fruit of (agrarian) capitalism or underdevelopment," the new movement would include clean and honest representatives of the state (of which his father was a prime example) and religious groups, liberal bourgeois groups, and small merchants and shopkeepers, as well as the traditional left. Obviously, several of these groups derived from the political tradition of Christian Democracy (dalla Chiesa 1983: 51). Nothing better symbolized the new, ecumenical direction than their presence at the innovative candlelight procession, at which not a single party banner, poster, slogan, or official representation was exhibited. The then mayor, Elda Pucci, nonetheless accused the organizers of being "the Communist cell" of the university's science faculty (ibid.: 42, 52).

In a later essay with Pino Arlacchi, dalla Chiesa further described the new movement as "considerably more ethical and civil than political," an expression of aspirations for liberty against the vestiges of an arbitrary feudalism (1987: 129–31). Attuned to "profound cultural issues" (ibid.: 52), its participants would escape the ideological polarization of the older generation of activists. As such they resembled other "new social movements" founded on universal values—movements for peace and against weapons of mass destruction, for environmental protection and against nuclear power, and (although dalla Chiesa does not mention it directly), the movement for women's rights. At the time of his father's death, Nando dalla Chiesa was a member of the Italian Communist Party, but he subsequently gave up his membership. In an interview with us in 1988, he recalled being moved by the condolences he received from Catholics and expressed impatience with the continued skepticism of some Communists regarding Catholics' antimafia credentials. His primary identification, he told us, was with the Circolo Società Civile of Milan, an "apolitical" organization that he had helped found in 1985, presciently anticipating the "bribesville" *(tangentopoli)* scandal.

A series of euphoric moments characterized by the coming together of former ideological opponents marked the early years of the Palermo-centered antimafia movement. In 1984, prodded by the Centro Impastato, representatives of some nineteen associations, political parties, and unions, ranging from the Communist Party and CGIL to ACLI, a Catholic worker group close to the Christian Democrats, formed a *Coordinamento Antimafia* (Antimafia Coordinating Committee). A majority of its members were Communists or former Communists, as was the eventual leader, Carmine Mancuso, a police officer whose father, Lenin Mancuso, also a policeman, was assassinated along with magistrate Terranova in 1979. Numbering thirty or so persons, they met at first in Mancuso's apartment, then in the Togliatti Section of the Communist Party, which happened to be in the apartment building of another activist. But this made them appear to be "the long arm of the Communist Party," as Mancuso later put it, so they shifted to neutral spaces in sports clubs and cultural centers, including the Centro Impastato. They also scuttled the parliament-like structure of their earliest meetings because, they said, the effort to represent party and union constituencies had produced a "tower of Babel." To confirm this break with the past, in February 1986 an inner circle of nine (six of whom were of Communist background) went before a notary to charter the *Coordinamento Antimafia* as an organization of "independent citizens."

Guided by this small nucleus, at the center of which was Mancuso and a woman of similar PCI background, Angela Locanto, the *Coordinamento Antimafia* set itself the task of promoting an antimafia consciousness among citizens by organizing research projects, seminars, roundtables, debates, conventions, and film screenings. In 1986, it took over planning for the September 3 commemoration of dalla Chiesa's murder. Most visibly, during this and the following years, it staged a film or forum event in honor of the slain members of the *Squadra Mobile*—Beppe Montana, Nini Cassarà, and Roberto Antiochia—whose deaths in 1985 had so destabilized the antimafia magistrates. Projects that would publicly embarrass complicit politicians of the DC did not get off the ground, however; for members of the ACLI constituency, this was going too far (see Santino 2000: 254–57).

The 1987 *Squadra Mobile* commemoration, held on July 28 at the Jolly Hotel in Palermo, drew on speakers from Bologna, Venice, Milan, and Catania, who addressed the "mysteries of Italy." Several called for a nationwide petition demanding the release of documents exposing secrets of state, including documents that had been archived by the Parliamentary Antimafia Commission. Americans had their Watergate and Irangate; now it was time for Italy.[7] The massacre in the Bologna railroad station and the known links between mafiosi and representatives of right-wing terrorism, the secret services, and the super-secret masonic lodge, P2, all came up. As the mafia was not just a problem of Sicilian delinquency but of the Italian "system of power," attempts to combat it only in the "pastures of Palermo" were doomed to fail. One speaker recalled the graffito that appeared in Palermo after the dalla Chiesa killing: "Here died the hope of honest Sicilians." It should have said, he proposed, "Here lies the birth of good Italians."

The *Coordinamento Antimafia* also initiated a journal, *Antimafia*, with articles on organized crime and drugs in Italy and other countries. Significantly, this and the other projects engaged the support of Leoluca Orlando, made mayor of Palermo in 1985 during a crisis in the Christian Democratic Party. His membership in that party, past experience as a city commissioner, and above all his descent from a family of *civile* and noble landowners in Prizzi, a town not far from Corleone, would seem to belie any claim to an antimafia commitment. Yet it appeared that Orlando was different. Before pursuing a law degree at the University of Palermo, he had attended the city's elite Jesuit high school, the Gonzaga, and studied in Heidelberg, meeting student radicals there. A cosmopolitan, fluent in both English and German, he became a close friend and legal counsel to Mattarella and was devastated by this DC reformer's assassination.

At the Centro Studi Aruppe, two Jesuit intellectuals, a northerner, Bartolomeo Sorge, and Ennio Pintacuda from Orlando's hometown of

Prizzi, elaborated a political theory of Christian Democracy as a "third way," between the right and the left (see Sorge 1989). Although Sorge eventually quarreled with Pintacuda and abandoned Palermo, and although Pintacuda and Orlando eventually went their separate ways, both were initially important in the mayor's political formation. In speeches and interviews of the time (see Perriera 1988), Orlando described the left-right spectrum of party identities as a residue of past conflicts that must yield to the noncollectivist values of individual merit and commitment. It is the person and not the label that counts. Ideological badges reminded him of "tribalism"—the debilitating claims of lineages on the body politic as if it were a "camp of tents" with nothing going on between them. In another of his favorite metaphors, he likened the typical party identity to a nesting Russian doll or Chinese box in which removing the surface layer only reveals more surface layers, down to the core, which is equally superficial.

Orlando's rejection of party "tribalism" was accompanied by a series of magnanimous gestures that set the tone for the "Palermo *Primavera*"— a period of three or four years beginning in 1985, marked not only by the maxi-trial but by a euphoric mood in and around city hall. He took out a membership in the *Coordinamento Antimafia* (there were about three hundred members in the late 1980s) and offered the city hall's council chamber for *Coordinamento*-sponsored events. Such generosity from a Christian Democrat toward an organization led by two (about to become former) Communists (one of whom had named his son Lenin after his father, Lenin) was met with much enthusiasm.

In 1985, the mayor's supporters consisted of City Council members representing the five political parties of the center-left—the Christian Democrats, Socialists, Republicans, Social Democrats, and Liberals—each of which was entitled to a seat or seats on the sixteen-member five-party administration, or *giunta*. The Communists on the council also sustained him, but without participating in the *giunta*. Then, in 1988, he creatively resolved a crisis in his government by bringing social movement people not representing any party onto the *giunta,* and in 1989 by adding two Communists as well.

The crisis grew out of the national parliamentary election of June 1987, in which the Socialists, running on a platform stressing due process, won an unexpected 16.4 percent of the Palermo vote while the Christian Democrats, although hanging on to 35 percent, did poorly compared to past elections. The young reform-minded Communist leader Michele Figurelli reported at the time that in the popular quarters and *borgate* of Palermo, formerly "reservoirs" of DC influence, only the Socialist message of "radio Ucciardone" had gotten through. In these neighborhoods, he lamented, people were long accustomed to being approached on the street, or through their kin, with advice from local mafiosi as to how they should vote. The Socialists, even if they were not distributing pasta and bread, as was claimed by many in the antimafia movement, knew who to see to make this system work (see Alongi 1997: 197–98 n. 35).

As it turned out, in the neighborhoods of Palermo where the mafia was strongest, the Socialist vote went up around 10 percent. Mafiosi, worried about the Christian Democrats' ability to protect them from the consequences of the maxi-trial, had apparently told their voters to send the party a message: in the Greco-dominated suburb of Ciaculli, the PSI vote climbed from 5.6 to 23.5 percent, while the DC vote fell from 62.1 to 38.8 (Jamieson 2000: 4). Orlando, furious, joined Figurelli in accusing the Socialists of dipping into the mafia's electoral cauldron.

The Socialists defended themselves with the argument that their campaign for a "just justice" had wide appeal, especially among voters who were burdened by "problems with the judiciary." They also resigned from the *giunta*, believing that the mayor would have to call a new municipal election. Instead, Orlando replaced them with Letizia Battaglia, representing Palermo's fledgling Greens; Giorgio Gabrielli, elected on the Jesuit-sponsored *Città per l'Uomo* ticket that, as already noted, stands for "apolitical" civic reform with a Catholic left orientation; and Aldo Rizzo, a former magistrate, elected as an independent on the Communist Party list and appointed vice-mayor. The nicknames that blossomed to refer to the new administration are an index of how unusual it was: the "anomalous *giunta*," the "Sicilian fruitcake" *(cassata Siciliana)*, the "the Jesuit pastiche." The subsequent invitation to the two Communists, Marina Marconi and Emilio Arcuri, hardly seemed shocking after such heresy, notwithstanding that Arcuri, a medical doctor, had been a student militant in one of the ultra-left, extra-parliamentary parties in the 1970s.

Clearly, for such an administration to form, the antimafia left had to accept Orlando as a leader, even though he remained a Christian Democrat. In numerous discussion groups and meetings, the argument was made that the anomalous *giunta* was not the same as the negatively viewed "transversal alliances" that Italians refer to as *trasformismo*. In contrast to "transformist" practices, which occur "off stage" and only favor politicians, the fully public *giunta* would work for the entire city.

Widely supported by the various groups of the civil society, that is by the
"honest Palermo," it would open city hall to the citizens, allowing them
to become "responsible participants in the history of the city." The slogan, "Palermo, city of Europe," became a leitmotif of the experiment
(Alongi 1997: 211–12).

SIGNS OF SPRING

In many respects the Palermo *Primavera* was defined by events that transpired in the elegant sixteenth--century municipal *palazzo,* opened by
Orlando to the citizenry. The impressive council chamber, the Sala delle
Lapidi, dignified by dark oak paneling, its walls lined with marble
plaques and founding-father portraits in gilded frames, became the site
of seminars, debates, and cultural encounters, almost all of them including Orlando among the speakers (ibid.: 218). There was, for example, the packed December 1988 presentation of a special issue of *Antimafia,* to which Orlando contributed alongside Diego Novelli, the
former Communist mayor of Turin. Another room, newly restored, was
offered as a meeting place to grassroots activists, including members of
the Centro Impastato and the Centro San Saverio.[8] Nino Rocca, an advocate of liberation theology involved in both of these organizations,
pressed for still more space. He had dreamed of becoming a lay mis-
sionary in Africa or Latin America but in the meanwhile had found "a
piece of Senegal" in Palermo (*L'Ora,* April 22, 1988).

Constituting themselves as a "Citizen's Committee of Information
and Participation" under the acronym CO.CI.PA, Rocca and his followers began analyzing and debating the issues coming before the City
Council. CO.CI.PA went on to monitor not only the council's agenda
but the *giunta* and the budget as well. Meanwhile, the independent members of the City Council, not affiliated with any party, also found a special meeting place in the municipal building and anointed themselves the
Cartello.

During this period, the city of Palermo supported a number of interesting initiatives, sponsoring or cosponsoring and at times funding them.
One was a two-day international conference on "The Struggle against
Drugs" in June 1988, covering international trafficking, prevention,
therapies, and foreign experiences. Palermo had needle parks by this
time and the first well-publicized deaths from heroin overdosing. As a
symptom of the mafia drug commerce, newly remodeled banks with
names not easily recognized were sprouting like mushrooms, while new

indices of extravagant consumption—fur coats, discotheques, and luxury cars—conveyed a sense that drug money was around. The construction boom was again in full swing, having abated for a while after the world financial crisis of the mid-1970s, and building projects were known to be capitalized by narco-dollars. Orlando's speech at the conference positioned Palermo in the forefront of fighting these problems. In the mayor's view, the "capital of the mafia" was about to become the "capital of the antimafia"—a slogan he continues to use.

The city also undertook to install commemorative plaques and monuments and to rename streets and piazzas, so that the antimafia's victims and martyrs might be inscribed in its public memory (see fig. 13). Three initiatives of the Orlando administration were especially important: to "liberate" public works contracts from mafia-allied Sicilian firms by insisting on sealed bids and bringing in northern Italian and European firms instead; to engage a team of architects headed by P. L. Cervellati of Bologna as master planners for Palermo's future, withdrawing the contract from architects and urbanists at the University of Palermo; and to streamline the administration of city services (garbage collection, water and gas supply, and transportation). These decisions, all highly controversial, were in some cases made by small groups of "Orlandiani" in the middle of the night, encouraged by the certain knowledge that European Union financing for mega-projects, including the restoration of the historic center, was contingent on suppressing corruption in letting public contracts.

The engagement of Cervellati, considered in more depth in chapter 10, is exemplary. Based on the fact that Palermo lacked a legally mandated urban plan, Orlando declared an emergency in April 1989, enabling the (anomalous) *giunta* to appropriate the City Council's power to oversee planning. Arcuri, who had just joined the *giunta* as a Communist, was an important player in this decision (Alongi 1997: 221), which he later characterized in an interview as "taking off like a steam engine." Perhaps needless to say, major enemies were made in this and the previous year's move against local contractors, particularly among the city's construction unions. In Arcuri's view, only the teachers were supportive.

During our visits to Palermo in the summers of 1987, 1988, and 1989, and for a week in December 1988, we could sense (but hardly understand) the many strange and contradictory events on the police-judicial front. At the same time, the wider world seemed to turn inside out, as Mikhail Gorbachev met with Ronald Reagan, "democracy movements"

Figure 13. Children in front of the plaque commemorating the assassination of General dalla Chiesa on the eleventh anniversary of his killing, September 3, 1993. Photograph by Alessandro Fucarini, Labruzzo Agenzia, Palermo.

erupted in Eastern Europe, and the Berlin Wall came down. But no matter the distraction of these international dramas or the dust cloud hanging over Palermo perpetuating its mysteries, the city was exciting, probably in the way that Berlin, Prague, and Budapest were exciting in those very years. Old regimes were nearing their end; new ones about to be born. Two examples might convey this spirit of optimism.

The Orlando administration created a new department of "Parks and Livability" and appointed Green movement activist and photographer Letizia Battaglia to be its commissioner. Many have commented on her extraordinary energy and good-humored but gutsy engagement with the city (see, for example, Stille 1999). During the day she surveyed parks and public spaces, and on some nights she followed the trucks of the sanitation workers, long reputed for spending more time off the job than on it. Sometimes she would personally engage the errant city workers; at other times she urged the police to enforce the work rules. In her travels, she intercepted children throwing cans on the street when they could have been putting them in containers, encouraged trattoria owners to move tables outside for tourists, and complained to unlicensed vendors about their clutter. Clearly one person could not reverse the effects of decades of corrupt urban administration single-handedly, but her escapades made a visible difference and attracted much public attention. Even the *Giornale di Sicilia,* generally reticent when it came to antimafia, published stories about her beach cleanups and tree plantings. In Alongi's words, Battaglia "knew no procedures or rules, but . . . paradoxically this served as a stimulus to her commitment and willingness to take risks. She was ever on the run, recuperating 'green spaces' compromised by the neglect of past administrations." Citizens, so accustomed to bureaucratic torpor, were waking up (Alongi 1997: 224).

Another source of optimism was the energy that flowed from a handful of social centers in poor neighborhoods where activist priests, helped by lay as well as Catholic volunteers, got children to burn their toy guns in great bonfires and organized them to enjoy unprecedented excursions and sports meets. In 1987, we followed a summer festival at Cosimo Scordato's San Saverio Social Center, aimed at children aged six to thirteen. The children were not lectured to or monitored; instead, their energies were channeled by volunteers trained to integrate moral lessons with art, sports, and theater (Terranova 1993–94).[9] The center itself is testimony to this nondidactic approach, decorated from floor to ceiling in nearly every room by colorful children's art with antimafia content:

slogans and symbols disparage guns, violence, drugs, and crime while praising peace.

In 1987, the year we witnessed the festival, 60 children participated in the center's activities; in 1988, there were 170. The increase reflected the previous year's TV coverage of the centerpiece event, mock Olympic Games that, interspersed with displays of art work, songs, puppet shows, and dramatic performances, some of them in Sicilian dialect, went on for four days. Twelve teams of about sixteen children each, close in age but of mixed gender, competed in the various races, each being managed by two to three counselors who helped develop a team spirit, aided by color-coded banners and tee shirts. The counselors said the games were to have fun, not to win; there would be cups for cooperation, not victory. Scordato, meanwhile, spoke to all of the teams about the spirit of the *quartiere* (in the long run he envisioned staging games with teams from other parts of the city), and from time to time, cheers were orchestrated for all of the teams together.

Observers were thin on the ground; windows and balconies were shuttered. A handful of mocking older teens circled on motorbikes, occasionally interfering. A few older men stood at the end of the street where the relays were held, and there were men among the counselors as well as a man taking pictures, but the majority of the spectators were women—the children's mothers. For a change, it was women and children who dominated the public spaces. Toward the end of the fourth day, Father Scordato mobilized a group of children to help with the cleanup—just in time for the arrival of the commissioner of parks and livability, Battaglia. She was with fellow photographer Zecchin and a City Council member from *Democrazia Proletaria,* Alberto Mangano. Battaglia's participation was a tour de force. The children all knew her from her TV appearances, as did the adults. Distributing her kisses far and wide, she took pictures, some of "just the *feminuccie*" (the girls), affectionately calling one of the boys *cornuteddu*—little cuckold.

Although the games' finale coincided with the onset of the annual festival of Santa Rosalia, Palermo's patron saint, Orlando also appeared, accompanied by two bodyguards. An incredible scene ensued as children crowded around him, competing for a touch or a kiss. Presiding over the distribution of the trophy cups, he thanked the *"bambini* of Albergheria, who were setting an example for the entire city" (see fig. 14). Were any of them named Rosalia, he asked? They were owed special congratulations on this, the day of the saint. Among the cups was the gold cup for discipline, but by the time its winning team was announced, the as-

Figure 14. Antimafia mayor, Leoluca Orlando (hands folded), with Cosimo Scordato, prepares to award victory cups, the largest being the "cup for discipline," to participants in the "Olympic Games," summer 1987. Photograph by Jane Schneider.

sembled children had dissolved into chaos, their competitive urges and end-of-day antics drowning out the counselors' cries for quiet. Scordato, in a typically magnanimous gesture, invited everyone to the bar for ice cream.

At the festival's end, the volunteers met in the Centro to conduct a post-mortem discussion of their skills at defusing conflict. Praise was offered to a young man from the neighborhood who, the year before, had manhandled some of his charges but whose comportment this year was "perfect." The assembled group also analyzed two quarrels, one in which the counselor had gently calmed an agitated youth by walking him away from the fray, the other in which the counselor had reacted angrily to an eight-year-old boy's taunting insults. It was reiterated that the counselors were not only to break up scuffles but to have the combatants shake hands. On this occasion as on others, the Christian prescription to turn the other cheek was held up as a "civilizing" lesson that, despite centuries of an ecclesiastical presence in Sicily, the island's popular classes, "incompletely evangelized," had yet to learn.

THE OTHER SIDE OF EUPHORIA

In 1987, there seemed to us little evidence of tension in the antimafia movement; on the contrary, much was made of the mutually supportive roles of the *Coordinamento Antimafia,* Orlando, and the neighborhood social centers. But political trouble was brewing and would become more intense. Rhetorically, at least, those around the *Coordinamento Antimafia* and Orlando stood for the idea that antimafia practice required making a clean break *(spaccatura)* with all persons suspected of collusion (of being "contiguous") with the mafia. The moral and cultural reforms they envisioned placed those considered to be compromised outside the bounds of civil society. Restructuring is not a "question of ideology," one *Coordinamento Antimafia* member told us, adopting the polarizing vocabulary of inclusion and exclusion: it is a question of "acceptable and unacceptable people." Unfortunately, however, given the mafia's penetration of social institutions, thousands of well-meaning people could be said to fall below the bar. Many who identified with the left particularly resented the implication that they might be among the impure; after all, the Communist Party was once "alone to combat mafiosi, physically and politically, in the countryside, in the factories, in the work sites and in the piazzas" (Di Lello 1994: 150–52; quoted in Alongi 1997: 98). Nevertheless, younger, rebellious Communist Party members, not satisfied by this legend, adhered to the call for *spaccatura* and resigned from the party. Carmine Mancuso and Angela Locanto, for example, declared the PCI "too bland" on antimafia and did not renew their memberships. Both criticized the regional Communist leadership for undermining the electoral chances of the antimafia lawyer, Alfredo Galasso, provoking him to leave the party as well.[10] Galasso gravitated toward Orlando, as did Arcuri, both transcending their former identities as leftists. Ironically, Orlando, who represented what was historically the most tainted of all the parties, the Christian Democrats, now claimed to be the standard bearer of the antimafia cause.

Outside the fold were the Socialists, accused of fishing for votes in the mafia districts of Palermo and cynically embracing Sciascia's attack on the magistrates and the clamor for civil liberties. The September 3 candlelight procession to commemorate dalla Chiesa, once a galvanizing occasion, became controversial as those surrounding Orlando began to suspect that it was being infiltrated by groups and individuals of "uncertain commitment." In 1988, Orlando and Mancuso boycotted it to organize a demonstration that excluded the Socialists. The boycotted procession was poorly attended and dispirited, more like an evening *passeggiata* producing multiple private conversations than a collective rite of commemoration. Walking with persons on the left, we were privy to the following kinds of commentary: "Antimafia has been appropriated by the Catholics"; "No one respects our history any more"; "It's as if, either you pursue antimafia their way or they define you as collusive"; "To overturn all the parties and unions in the name of a citizens' movement is to put democracy at risk." Mancuso added fuel to this fire by the aggressive way he responded to Sciascia, apparently without consulting the broad base of the *Coordinamento,* accusing him, in naming Borsellino, of deploying "one of the mafia's most sophisticated forms of warning" (quoted in Alongi 1997: 215 n. 16). Many *Coordinamento* members considered the remark defamatory—like calling the author a mafioso—and a few dropped out, complaining of a dangerous symbiosis between "Stalinism" and old-fashioned "Catholic integralism" among the leaders (ibid.; see also Campisi 1994: 82–83).

Also in 1988 but on a different front, the *spaccatura* approach to antimafia provoked increasing criticism from the grassroots organizations for which the urgent needs of the poorest citizens were as great a concern as moral and political reform. Specifically, the coalition around the Centro Impastato, the Social Center of San Saverio, and CO.CI.PA, sought a larger portion of the city's and region's financial resources earmarked by law for educational, cultural, and social service interventions. Because the Orlando administration had lost interest in their priorities, these grassroots activists believed, City Hall was falling behind on its payments to the volunteers of the Centro San Saverio. CO.CI.PA's review of the municipal budget, from within the municipal building itself, led to the accusation that Orlando had become too ideological—more interested in words than acts—and was purposely withholding contributions to the neighborhood centers. The most severe critics argued that the funds were unavailable because a new structure of clientelism was diverting them.

A related polemic surrounded three women from mafia families whose close male kin had been killed by the mafia and who wanted to participate, notwithstanding the risk, as *parte civile* in the maxi-trial. The committee that raised money to support the legal costs of such participation spurned these women on the grounds that only servants of the state were eligible. As a token of their break with the "culture of *omertà,*" one of the women, Michela Buscemi, joined the Association of Women against the Mafia. One of her brothers had been killed in 1976;

the other was subsequently "tortured, strangled, and thrown into the sea with lead weights on his legs" (Jamieson 2000: 130).

The association, together with the Centro Impastato, undertook to raise money on these women's behalf. The Centro further believed that women like Buscemi were qualified for assistance under a national law, passed at the time of the antiterrorist campaign, which provided funds for the relatives of victims of antistate violence, including fees for the education of their children. Relatives from mafia families could be needy—more needy, indeed, than the kin of the "excellent cadavers." Moreover, it was crucial to support any steps they might take to separate themselves from their former lives—steps that others might follow (Puglisi 1990; Santino 2000: 297–98). Advocacy on their behalf resonated with the grassroots communities that the Centro Impastato identified with, although not with Michela's family or the *Coordinamento Antimafia*. To the latter, it was unconscionable that the relatives of mafiosi should receive state aid.

In the fall of 1988, the labor unions reacted to Orlando's "revolutionary" call for a clean break with local contractors and construction firms in favor of outside companies. They called him a dangerous exhibitionist, operating more like a prefect than a mayor. Already in January 1986, a small group of demonstrators had appeared at the Four Corners of the historic center, carrying signs that read, "*Vogliamo la mafia*" (We want the mafia), "*Ciancimino come Sindaco*" (Ciancimino for mayor), and "*Con la mafia si lavora, senza no!*" (With the mafia we work, without it, no!). In December 1988, the Catholic and Social Democratic unions (the CISL and the UIL) called a strike of municipal employees (health and cemetery workers, traffic police, and record keepers were all affected), largely to embarrass the Orlando administration. A clamorous event, the thirteen-day strike "got out of hand," to quote one union leader, when some participants staged a mock funeral procession in which they carried two coffins, one labeled Orlando and the other Rizzo (the vice-mayor). In an improvised speech, a CSIL member declared, "If struggling for the workers signifies being mafiosi, then *viva la mafia!*" (quoted in Alongi 1997: 231). The CGIL, although not involved, did not speak up—a dramatic indication that the "red threads" of antimafia protest, unraveling since the 1970s, now seemed beyond repair.

Over and above the differences of perspective on funding priorities and mafia victims of mafia violence, there developed a dramatic clash between the grassroots organizers on the one hand, and Orlando and the *Coordinamento Antimafia* on the other, over the relationship of the an-

timafia movement to the working poor. Reluctant to sacrifice good relations with institutions that controlled the jobs their people needed,
Scordato, Rocca, Santino, and their allies believed that segments of the
unions were or could be relatively untarnished by mafia involvement.
And they did not disagree with the unions' argument that splitting with
local contractors would only give an opening to German and northern
Italian multinationals, poised to take over the Sicilian economy. Orlando, they believed, should not have declined an invitation to attend a
union-organized conference on alternative ways of fighting the mafia.
This, and his sloganeering words that "the mafia has the face of the institutions," were provocations.

To Orlando and the leaders of the *Coordinamento Antimafia,*
Scordato and the others displayed extreme political naiveté for not
loudly denouncing the union demonstrations in public. Perhaps they
were manipulated by "reactionary forces"—in particular, the *garantista*
Socialists and Socialist union, the CSIL. Peter Schneider attended an extremely heated meeting between CO.CI.PA and the *Coordinamento Antimafia* directors on December 16, 1988, called by the former to assess
this accusation and to reassure everyone that "the other Palermo"
wanted progress. Those present with ties to San Saverio used the occasion to protest the delayed payments to the center's volunteers. A CSIL
leader pleaded that the menacing "funeral procession" had been a spontaneous act of the rank and file for which he was sorry but that the issues facing Palermo's working people were nonetheless grave. The unsympathetic audience was about to agree on a joint declaration calling
for rotation of the heads of department in the municipal administration,
the immediate payment of the earmarked funds to San Saverio, and condemnation of the strike, when a quarrel broke out over a *Coordinamento Antimafia* proposal to amend the third resolution by calling for
the union leaders to resign. Two of the grassroots organizers, fearing that
this would drive a permanent wedge between the antimafia movement
and the unions, ended up accusing the *Coordinamento Antimafia* of being "fascists." An ensuing correspondence over this insult revealed that
the Palermo *Primavera* was coming to an end.

THE FORMATION OF AN ANTIMAFIA PARTY: *LA RETE*

Shortly after April 1989, when Orlando brought two (then) Communists, Arcuri and Marconi, onto his *giunta,* he received a clear warning
from the national and regional leadership of the Christian Democratic

Party that this "six-color" *(esacolore)* arrangement would be short-lived. Running as DC candidate for the European Parliament (a position one can hold simultaneously with an elected office in one's home country), he lost to the incumbent, Salvo Lima, even though Lima was by then under investigation for mafia collusion. In an open letter to the press, Città per l'Uomo expressed concern that the European Parliament would become a "cemetery of elephants," of "old and discredited notables," but Lima won anyway, if by a smaller margin than before (Alongi 1997: 236–37).

For many in the antimafia movement, it was an ominous sign that Lima's reelection coincided with the attempted assassination of Falcone (June 18, 1989) and the initiation of the diabolical "season of poisons" in the *Palazzo* of Justice. Meanwhile Andreotti recaptured the presidency of the Council of Ministers in Rome. Visiting Palermo together with Lima in January 1990, he was asked his impression of Orlando's *giunta:* "Experiments are a beautiful thing," he answered, "but I'm not sure if a city with as many problems as Palermo is an ideal place for them" (quoted in ibid.: 249). It was an opening for Andreotti's followers on the City Council to shift their allegiance from Orlando's anomalous government to the Socialists, who were waiting in the wings, causing his government to fall (although not until after it approved the engagement of Cervellati to develop the plan for the historic center).

Public demonstrations of support for Orlando poured in, including a letter, signed by 751 citizens, published in the *Giornale di Sicilia.* Then, a group of younger, reform-minded activists who were becoming leaders in the regional Communist Party proposed an interesting idea: Orlando should head an independent electoral list called *Insieme per Palermo* (Together for Palermo), which would include candidates from all the antimafia constituencies. In one of the many dramatic turning points in the antimafia process, Orlando rejected this proposal, saying he would stay on the Christian Democratic list because his electoral popularity would allow him to continue to reform the party from within. He had, he argued, already proven that he could marginalize Lima's allies ("the mafia of the *Palazzo*" he called them) in City Hall.

His strategy failed. When the regional DC leaders drew up the electoral list for the municipal election of Palermo, they put Orlando, the outgoing mayor, at the top, but the number two position went to one of Lima's closest acolytes, Domenico Di Benedetto. Orlando's extraordinary charisma, amplified by support from the Centro Aruppe and the *Coordinamento,* both of which campaigned for him, ensured the election of *all* of the Christian Democrats on the list, and the DC won close to 50 percent of the vote. In its best showing in twenty years, the party also increased its council seats from thirty-two to forty-two out of eighty, an absolute majority. The Socialists also gained, with 12.6 percent of the vote. Allying with the Christian Democrats, they promptly replaced Orlando with Di Benedetto as mayor. Far from having overthrown the Andreotti forces in Sicily, Orlando had strengthened their hand and weakened that of his allies. The big losers were the *Città per l'Uomo*, the Greens, and above all the Communist Party, which dropped by half; *Insieme per Palermo* received less than 8 percent of the vote (see ibid.: 261 n. 37).

The debacle drove Orlando from the DC to form his own political party, the single-issue national antimafia party, the Network *(La Rete)*. It was a party that, not surprisingly, attracted a number of former Communists—Carmine Mancuso and Angela Locanto, Alfredo Galasso and Nando dalla Chiesa, and (a particular blow to the left) Emilio Arcuri, among others. Meanwhile, at the national level, the Communist Party went through the turmoil of reinventing itself for a new, post–Cold War era, changing its name to the Democratic Party of the Left (the PDS) and later to the Democrats of the Left (the DS). In Palermo, new faces, some of them local and others from the north, continued to displace the older generation of party leaders and with them the expectations of the historic compromise. Locally and regionally, the PDS/DS of the 1990s resembled Orlando's *La Rete* in many ways. Indeed, notwithstanding their leftist identity, the new leaders seem hardly more patient than the people around Orlando with the sorts of compromises that construction workers make in order to stay employed.

CONCLUSION

The antimafia movement of today has departed substantially from its precursor of the postwar years, when landless peasants were considered the foremost victims of mafia violence. Antimafia leaders of those days singled out the Italian Communist Party, prime advocate of land reform on behalf of these poorest peasants, as a clean political party. In contrast, they castigated the governing Christian Democratic Party as the fount of corruption. In the 1980s, the tables were ever so slightly turned. The Christian Democratic Party, although bearing the taint of pervasive corruption, was recognized to have harbored an emergent, reformist wing. Conversely, the Communist Party began to be accused of hypocrisy and corruption, even though it was still held up as the "least compromised." In any case, the time had passed when intellectuals could locate the mafia in the class structure of agrarian Sicily and imagine its demise as the vindication of landless against propertied classes in the countryside. Except among the grassroots activists, and particularly in the work of Umberto Santino, a comparable "class analysis" does not exist among antimafia activists today.

Yet, as the remaining chapters will show, the process of antimafia is deeply inflected by class inequality. The crisis surrounding the 1987 election and the explosive meeting over the municipal workers' strike already made this clear. Committed to the fundamentalist practice of *spaccatura*, Orlando and the *Coordinamento* accused the Socialists and the unions of playing the mafia's game, but the grassroots organizers knew that poor people in neighborhoods "at risk" have real and legitimate concerns to which the unions and the Socialists were speaking. Reminiscent of the old left, these grassroots organizers saw themselves speaking *for* Palermo's "at risk" neighborhoods, whereas the moral and cultural reformers were merely speaking *to* them. In certain other respects the two broad groupings were similar. Each contained within it a close alliance between persons with a Catholic and persons with a Communist background, while the grassroots organizers were no more eager than the reformers to legitimate clientelism or revive the discredited rhetoric of "class struggle." The silencing of the language of class, not the disappearance of class issues, may be the most significant marker of the "new" social movements of the post–Cold War world.

CHAPTER 8

Backlash and Renewal

The efforts of law enforcement to suppress the mafia and the antimafia social movement both fell upon rough times in the second half of the 1980s. To pursue Orlando's metaphor of the Sicilian cart, sticks were thrown into the spokes of both wheels. In part the difficulties arose from internal tensions—the jealousies and treachery within the *Squadra Mobile* and courthouse, and the factionalism that divided the grassroots activists from the people around Orlando and the *Coordinamento Antimafia*. In part they were the consequence of great uncertainty, exacerbated by the sure knowledge that, despite the slower pace of mafia killings, the most dangerous fugitives remained at large. The third ingredient was the dissipation of the "Palermo Spring," experienced by activists as a return to "normalcy," or waning of commitment *(impegno)*—in short, the demobilization of the social movement. Accelerating the demobilization, and greatly benefiting from it, was a counter-antimafia backlash aimed not only at the magistrates and the police but also at the movement intellectuals and the mayor, indeed, at the antimafia process as a whole.

In effect, the backlash constitutes an effort to recapture and control public discourse about the mafia, which, during the maxi-trial and the *Primavera*, was monopolized by the reformers. The mafia was surely aware of, and took comfort in, this turnaround, but it was not the instigator. For although mafiosi support new laws extending civil liberties and are not shy about letting those close to them know their voting preferences, they are hardly themselves the producers of a lot of talk. One doesn't find them giving public speeches, granting interviews to the press, writing articles or letters to the editor, being asked on television to interpret the past or future. Even the *pentiti* are reticent in this regard. The response of mafiosi to police-judicial repression and the antimafia movement has taken forms more consonant with their history and ambitions: symbolically communicative acts of brutal violence.

It is also misleading to attribute the backlash only to "mafia sympathizers," as some of the more radical antimafia activists frequently do. Rather, backlash discourse is generated out of the vast gray area between the mafia and the forces that oppose it, the swath of society that is riddled with "provisioned" and "conditioned" relationships, given that such relationships were "normal" in the past. This chapter reviews the main arguments of the counter-antimafia discourse, identifying some of the key contributors as of the late 1980s. It then examines how, in the wake of the massacres of Falcone and Borsellino, the antimafia movement was renewed. Like the continued forward movement on the criminal justice front, however, this restored momentum is fragile. The chapter concludes with a brief reference to the most serious challenge—the potential for *political* promoters of the backlash ideology to galvanize the discontents of the popular classes.

COUNTER-ANTIMAFIA DISCOURSE: PRINCIPAL TERMS AND ARGUMENTS

A central argument of the backlash against the antimafia process is *garantismo,* which criticizes the magistrates for violating civil liberties and endangering rights to fair and equal treatment before the law. Often the argument warns of political ambition: these judges are using the law either to promote a left-wing agenda, or to promote themselves (out of the line of seniority, for example). Similar criticism has been directed at antimafia movement activists, accused of being self-interested careerists overly eager to marginalize those who do not agree with them. That antimafia activists are younger than those with "normal" clientelistic relations, and that many of them are women, reinforces the perception that they are of a new generation that is personally and politically ambitious.

A critical term in the backlash discourse is the verb *strumentalizzare*— to instrumentalize. Mafia *pentiti* are said to *strumentalizzare,* or exploit, the judicial process, while close kin and friends of the mafia's victims have been accused of manipulating public opinion, publicizing their grief and outrage to draw undue attention to what should have been a private affair—the loss of a loved one. Of course, to many in the antimafia struggle, this implied questioning of their sincerity is galling.

Counter-antimafia discourse also sounds a Sicilianist chord (an odd accompaniment to the rationalizing, universalistic, civil liberties values of *garantismo*). The argument implies that the antimafia movement is a foreign import that allows outsiders to disparage and ridicule Sicilians. The Monument to the Victims of the Mafia, erected after the death of dalla Chiesa, can be said to symbolize this problem. Located in the middle of a large traffic circle near the port, it is difficult to approach on foot and does not apparently refer to any Sicilian motif. Three steel plates, placed at oblique angles to one another, rise high in the air puncturing the horizon (see fig. 15). At the base are the words, "To the Victims of the Mafia," and around it is an "English lawn." Planting lawns in public spaces is an imported idea; in the hot and arid Sicilian summers, they remain green only with constant watering, which has not been forthcoming. When asked about the monument, many Palermo citizens openly express their dislike of it; indeed, we have heard it mistakenly called "the monument *to* the mafia." Even some antimafia activists complain that it is too abstract and removed from local experience to be meaningful.

The maxi-trial was a dramatic occasion for outsiders to express their misunderstanding of Sicily and condescension toward Sicilians. Widely covered on national as well as regional television, it elicited a great deal of commentary on the dialect, body language, and dress of the men on trial. Outsiders and educated Sicilians alike found much in these men's demeanor and speech to ridicule (see Jacquemet 1996 on the *Camorra* trial in Naples). Criminal justice specialists in Rome talked about "sending down" additional personnel because, although there were plenty of honest Sicilians, one could not trust them to defy the inevitable pressures of their families and friends. The Genoese prison official described in chapter 6 seemed amused that in Sicily, the close kin of imprisoned mafiosi showed up regularly at the gates of the Ucciardone, laden with packages. According to the officer, his second in command, a "tender" Palermitan, was so enmeshed in possibly compromising kinship networks that he, the Genoese, had to play "tough cop."

The counter-antimafia obsession with "negative influences coming down from the north" (see Priulla 1989: 75) resonates even among antimafia activists. Anyone who harbors nostalgia for a rural childhood or affection for less-educated kin whose Italian is awkward or absent is

Figure 15. Monument to the Victims of the Mafia surrounded by an "English Lawn." Photograph by Jane Schneider.

likely to be touched by it. A high school teacher involved in the move-ment told us how saddened he was by his students' derision of the dialect phrases he introduced in class. In his view, the desire to be modern had caused too many teachers, himself among them, to lose their regional identity. And yet, to say that antimafia reformers are an affront to the regional culture is to evoke the earlier and unwelcome defensiveness of Notarbartolo's enemies and more recently of Cardinal Ruffini. Wanting to dissociate himself from the strident "pro-Sicilia" discourse of "anti-antimafia," yet critical of the modernizing thrust of the antimafia move-ment, our teacher friend was at a loss for politically correct words.

Another commonly heard strand of the counter-antimafia backlash argues that the antimafia movement threatens the local economy, above all, the construction industry. Perhaps, it is suggested, this is because the movement has been "instrumentalized" by a rump Communist Party, which is hostile to private enterprise of any sort. Perhaps it is simply the result of an excessively hard-nosed attitude toward what everyone knows is the strong "organic permeability" of construction firms to mafia corruption (see Santino 1989: 36). Pointedly, a taxi driver taking us past the bunker courthouse in 1987 complained that the maxi-trial was bad for working people. "Those inside [the defendants] brought work. Now everything is at a standstill," he said, wryly adding, however, that "a brake on them was necessary as there were just too many *amaz-zattini* [little murders]." When the Orlando administration abandoned local contractors in favor of northern Italian firms, it set off a torrent of criticism. In the words of one skeptic, "To paint all the local contractors as mafiosi is to fire up a witch-hunt," almost as if the very word for contract, *appalto,* implied not a "pot of honey" but an "incubus."

All of the backlash arguments are morally ambiguous. Pleas to defend due process against "excessive" judicial power, and Sicilians against those who would humiliate them, are, on the face of it, entirely legitimate. More than this, they capture the sentiments of people who, not belonging to the mafia, feel wrongfully accused by the antimafia of having furthered its violent aims. One of the arguments—the one that draws a causal arrow from cleaning up the construction industry to capital flight and loss of jobs—is truly potent. Below and in later chapters, we will explore its disturbing effects when used by politicians mobilizing votes in Palermo's poorest neighborhoods.

SCIASCIA AS CATALYST

Throughout the 1980s, no one better crystallized the counter-antimafia backlash than Leonardo Sciascia, whose role as preeminent skeptic dated to the dalla Chiesa assassination in 1982. Prior to his death, the general had complained, first privately and then publicly, that neither the state nor the Palermo authorities were adequately supporting his mission. A little over three months after he was killed, Nando dalla Chiesa, his son, wrote an article for *La Repubblica* (19 December 1982) accusing his fellow intellectuals, especially Sicilian intellectuals, of promoting a *pax mafiosa,* failing to attend to the political, legal, economic, and moral implications of a system that could tolerate such monstrous crimes. Sciascia shocked everyone by attacking dalla Chiesa—father and son—in an article in *L'Espresso* (February 20, 1983) headlined, "Even Generals Make Mistakes; and Even the Dead Can Be Wrong." General dalla Chiesa was ingenuous, he said, for failing to understand that the mafia, having been transformed into a criminal multinational with terrorist characteristics, had entered a new relationship with state power. Confronting this shadowy world, imagining it could be reined in by police action, would only lead to the abuse of power (see Ambroise 1989). Nando dalla Chiesa in turn accused Sciascia of playing the mafia's game *(fare il gioco della mafia)* by making the general out to be an aspiring dictator. Sciascia, he argued, had reduced his (Nando's) accusations against the silence of the intellectuals to "the fruit of anti-Sicilianism." No wonder members of the corrupt political class in Palermo—Salvo Lima among them—had cited Sciascia with approval (dalla Chiesa 1984, appendix).

The next blow was the already noted *Corriere della Sera* review of Duggan's book on Mori, the fascist prefect, in January 1987. Besides challenging the promotion "out of line" of Borsellino, the review lashed out at "a mayor" who was beginning to exhibit himself on TV and make appearances in the schools, as an antimafioso. This mayor spends so much time in self-display, said Sciascia, that he neglects the city's problems. People outside his administration may be able to criticize him, but insiders who raise questions can expect to be removed, or at least smeared as "mafioso." Although Sciascia insisted this was just a hypothetical example, it was clearly aimed at Orlando.

There were many reasons to be unsettled by Sciascia's animosity toward the leading antimafia intellectuals and leaders, but the most compelling was his own left-wing, antimafia background. Born in 1921, Sciascia grew up in Racalmuto, in the sulfur-mining zone of south central Sicily, where the exploitation of mineworkers by domineering bosses was legion. For a while an elementary school teacher, he never lost his empathy for Sicily's poor. As we have seen, he believed the mafia was close to power—the power of the baronial class of mine owners and *latifondisti,* and of their offshoots and allies who served as parliamentary deputies and high officials of the state. Indeed, the villains of his mystery novels are not so much mafiosi as the *onorevoli* and *manutengoli* who use the mafia for their own ends. Some of the plots were modeled on or likely to evoke real instances of murderous collusion and took much courage to publish. Specifically, the assassination in *The Day of the Owl* had an analog in the killing of the labor leader Miraglia, in the town of Sciacca. The novel's epilogue alludes to the political pressures that prevented the author from ending this story as he wished.

To Sciascia, a literary person, contemporary antimafia intellectuals were "assault sociologists" whose presumption that the mafia could be defeated was naive. For although the novelist had written brilliantly about the "third level" of conspiracy and collusion, he had done so without naming names. On the contrary, the heroes of his early novels who attempted to get to the bottom (or, as it were, the top) of things were drawn as naive characters, almost asking to be made victims.[1] Collusion is indirect, Sciascia insisted. Members of the dominant class rarely need to order a murder or menacing act; their reputation of being allied with mafiosi is sufficient to have these things materialize. Nor do their alliances, articulated through networks of friends of friends, pose an obvious moral problem. In this sense, the mafia is invincible, a matter of destiny (1961: 178–79; see also see Padovani 1979: viii–ix).

Ill and living in northern Italy, Sciascia died on November 20, 1989. By that time, he had synthesized in a coherent public statement many people's apprehensions about where repression of the mafia might lead and their sense that those conducting it disrespected Sicilian ways. Significantly, no one could say he was proto-mafioso; on the contrary, critics like Carmine Mancuso who called him *filo-mafioso* lost credibility for extremism bordering on libel. Nevertheless, many commentators, among them Eugenio Scalfari, the editor of *La Repubblica,* later held him partially responsible for the heightened tensions afflicting the Palermo Prosecutor's Office. Conversations about Sciascia's statements, defined by some as a "betrayal" but by others as an "act of courage," filled the Palermo air for the next few years. Evaluating him and his actions became a litmus test of where one stood, ideologically, and in doing so, constituents of the "silent majority" found each other and their voice. From this point forward, it became plausible to simultaneously disclaim any sympathy for the mafia and yet criticize the magistrates in public.

THE PRESS

Sciascia was not alone, to quote one activist, in "controlling the faucets of public opinion." The *Giornale di Sicilia,* Palermo's main daily newspaper and the paper of record for all of Sicily, also contributed to the chorus of cynics that he seemed to orchestrate. On the surface, the paper lacked Sciascia's credentials as a battle-tested voice of the antimafia; quite the contrary, its owner, the Ardizzone family, was (and still is) known for its ties to Freemasonry and, many would say, its historical tolerance for the Palermo *cosche* (e.g. Lodato 1999: 181–84). But, like everything else in Sicily, the paper's stance is more complicated than this and requires a brief review.

By 1979, the daily consumption of Sicilian newspapers was thirty for every thousand inhabitants compared with a national average of ninety-three per thousand, yet the professionalization of journalism, like that of the magistracy, had been advancing since the 1950s (Nicastro 2000: 43). In Palermo, *L'Ora,* the afternoon paper supported by the Italian Communist Party, set a high standard. Attracting an ambitious and lively staff of leftist intellectuals and writers (Sciascia included), it reported on and analyzed the agrarian mafia, producing a major inquiry in 1958. After the newspaper published a hard look at the emergent career of Corleonesi boss Luciano Liggio, its offices were bombed. Covering the "sack" of Palermo in the 1970s (see chapter 7), it inaugurated what one writer remembers as "a glorious, and often tragic, page of Sicilian journalism that won respect and admiration outside of Sicily" (ibid.: 44). The result was serious competition for the much more staid morning paper, the *Giornale di Sicilia,* moderate in outlook and close to the Christian Democrats. Looking back, journalists point to this competition as one reason why the *Giornale* gave free rein to a remarkable investigative reporter, Mario Francese, who followed mafia trials and crimes until the mafia killed him in 1978 (ibid.: 49).

Francese's story has just been retold in a commemorative volume published by Gelka in Palermo. A talented and prodigious fieldworker in the "brigand corridor" outside of Palermo, he wrote about Liggio's scandalous escape from prison, about the large-scale organization of animal rustling, about the kidnappings of important personages, about the murders of Colonel Giuseppe Russo and Giuseppe Di Cristina (opening rounds of the second mafia war). A series of articles exposing corruption and bloody bidding wars in the post-earthquake construction of the Garcia Dam serving western Sicily was published after his death. These stories illustrate his understanding, before it was clear to almost anyone, that the Corleone mafia had launched a strategy of aggression that far transcended Corleone and would seriously rattle "the mafia of the velvet gloves" in Palermo (see Fiume 2000).

As of this writing, the investigation into Francese's murder is still ongoing. The most compelling hypothesis is that he was eliminated for what he wrote, but the question is, by whom. Looking back, it is evident that he concentrated disproportionately on the emergent Corleonesi, not only tracing their penetration of arenas beyond Corleone but also covering their home base. Indeed, he was the only journalist ever to interview Antonietta Bagarella, Riina's wife, having written about her wedding and the collusive priest who performed the ceremony. As historian Giovanna Fiume suggests, the Corleonesi might well have imagined that he was put up to his investigations by their enemies in the "losing faction," as key figures among them—Bontade and the Salvos—were known to have friendship networks that extended into the *Giornale di Sicilia.* Quite possibly they prompted the newspaper to go after Liggio, Riina, and the Grecos; this interpretation is at least consistent with the fact that, shortly before the demise of Francese, menacing fires were visited on other members of the paper's staff (ibid.: 39).[2]

In the late 1970s, *L'Ora* fell on hard times. As an afternoon paper, it was more vulnerable to the competition of television than the *Giornale di Sicilia*. More to the point, in 1976, in conjunction with the so-called historic compromise, the Communist Party withdrew its support from the paper to concentrate on its principal national daily, *L'Unità*.[3] By 1980, the *Giornale di Sicilia* was taking advantage of *L'Ora*'s weakened position and demoralized staff to raid it for four of its younger and most professional reporters—three Palermitans, Roberto Ciuni, Francesco La Licata, and Daniele Billiteri, and a journalist from eastern Sicily, Franco Nicastro. These newcomers formed a crime bureau and, in the tradition of Francese, wrote stories that were much more than gory descriptions of victims' bodies lying in pools of blood. As the second mafia war unfolded, the point was to analyze what the murders meant in terms of the mafia's grand *schieramenti,* or factions, the outlines of which were just becoming visible. Similar to the antimafia pool of the judiciary, the crime reporters shared sources and supported and substituted for one another. They were, of course, at risk. The memories of journalist Mauro de Mauro, kidnapped in 1970 and never found, of radio journalist Impastato, and most recently of Mario Francese were fresh in their minds.

In 1983, around the time of Pappalardo's "re-entry," a "reappropriation" occurred at the *Giornale di Sicilia*—almost as if, some people say, the Lima current of the DC sat down and said, "We are taking this paper back." At any event, the owner, Ardizzone, became the director; the managing editor was replaced by a more conservative Palermitan, Giovanni Pepi, and the aggressive reporters were either marginalized or fired. Nicastro left for employment in the regional government and the national press service, ANSA. Billiteri became the night editor, and La Licata was fired, ostensibly for giving an exclusive on the *pentito* Vincenzo Sinagra to the national magazine, *L'Espresso,* claiming that Ardizzone had turned it down because it did not match his political position. Fellow reporters protested his dismissal, even staging a sympathy strike, but to no avail. Adding to the journalists' sense of defeat, in 1984 the mafia assassinated Giueseppe Fava, founder and director of Catania's outspoken antimafia monthly, *I Siciliani,* whose pages regularly denounced Sicily's biggest Catania-based construction firms, owned by the famous *Cavalieri del Lavoro* (Lodato 1999: 265).

By the mid-1980s, the *Giornale di Sicilia* was once again, in the words of its critics, "a Sicilian newspaper created for Sicilians." Its main readership, these critics pointed out, consisted of employees in the offices of the state, regional, and municipal bureaucracies—the multitudes who held their positions through patronage and who so counted on the security they enjoyed that they were nicknamed the *venti-setteisti,* a reference to the fact that in officialdom, paychecks are distributed on the twenty-seventh of each month. Believing themselves superior to common laborers, they were the sine qua non of the "vast gray area"—the silent and cynical majority galvanized by Sciascia. In the eyes of such persons, the newspaper's purpose was not to challenge the status quo but rather to conserve the rituals of the day. Indeed, the delivery of the morning paper revealed every office's hierarchy: persons in top positions found it waiting for them on their desks; those in the middle bought their own; and those on the bottom borrowed the papers of the others. In the words of a journalist friend, the professionalized *Giornale di Sicilia* with its analyses of the mafia wars "had thrown this whole system of certainty, this complex of sentiments . . . into crisis."

By the time of the maxi and the Palermo *Primavera,* the *Giornale di Sicilia* constituted a veritable fountain of backlash argumentation. All of the elements were there: *garantismo* (the *pentiti* are rascals and relying on their testimony threatens civil liberties); the defense of Sicily against those who would criminalize the region; the depiction of the antimafia movement as an ambitious and politically motivated threat to the local economy; and the resistance to making waves. Moreover, as people were reeling from the shock of Sciascia's attack on Borsellino, the paper listed the names and addresses of the founding members of the *Coordinamento Antimafia,* together with details about their lives, a move interpreted by many as intended to intimidate the activists and expose them to the risk of reprisal. Reciprocally, at the July 28, 1987, *Coordinamento*-sponsored commemoration of the deaths of the police in the *Squadra Mobile,* many disparaging remarks were made (to loud applause) about the newspaper. Some called it "the newspaper of the mafia" and Ardizzone "the mafia owner of a mafia newspaper." A nickname that stuck was *La Voce di Ciaculli.*

As if to confirm these stereotypes, the *Giornale di Sicilia* sniped at the antimafia movement in various subtle ways. It was disrespectful of the relatives of victims. It generously gave space to citizens' letters that expressed by innuendo that the magistrates' noisy escorts were out of all proportion to the dangers they faced, that they engaged these armored, siren-equipped cars for reasons of prestige, that their "exaggerated" need for protection from bomb attacks was subtracting needed parking spaces and lowering property values in the neighborhoods where they lived. Through interviews, features, and editorials, the paper pushed the idea that the traditional mafia was honorable and the modern mafia a degeneration into "pure delinquency" (like every other country's delinquency) because of drugs. And it ran stories about the terrible conditions in the prisons.

With apparent determination, the *Giornale di Sicilia* of the late 1980s also reached out to Sicilianists by diligently reporting the slurs of outsiders. For example, an entire story was devoted to an Emilian minister who, upon seeing two Sicilian politicians in Rome greet each other with the customary kiss rather than a handshake, was heard to remark, "Look at the Sicilian mafiosi!" (March 7, 1985). Coverage was also forthcoming on a northern European tourist agency planning what it called "heart in your mouth *lupara* tours" of Palermo, in which visitors would be taken to the sites of the most sensational assassinations (July 9, 1985). Such examples of prejudice reminded readers of the many humiliations they had experienced while traveling, or working and living, in northern Italy, or at the hands of northern Italians in the south. Perhaps most egregiously, the paper revealed its Sicilianist bent by publishing the Beati Paoli as a full-color serialized cartoon strip. By this time, however, antimafia activists were turning elsewhere for their news, above all to the national newspaper, *La Repubblica*, which expanded its reporting on Sicily. On May 8, 1992, two weeks before Falcone was assassinated, *L'Ora* suspended publication, leaving *La Repubblica* as the only competition.

1992 CATASTROPHE AND RENEWAL

To many Sicilians outside as well as inside the antimafia struggle, Judge Giovanni Falcone was "one of ours"; he symbolized "our fight." His brutal death on May 23, 1992, described as a scene from the apocalypse by one eyewitness (see Stille 1995: 354), silenced the "counter-antimafia." A different tone and different conversations seized Palermo as fury and despair erupted with greater intensity than after the death of dalla Chiesa. Thousands filed past the coffins of the victims, which were placed, to quote Stille, "in the huge, cavernous marble lobby of the . . . Palace of Justice, the scene of [his] greatest triumphs and bitterest defeats." As dignitaries approached, coins and insults were thrown at them in a gesture of total disrespect: "Murderers! Clowns! Accomplices. Go home! Go back to your bribes!" (Stille 1995: 355–56). The funeral ser-

vice, held in the same church as dalla Chiesa's, drew a crowd too immense to fit inside. From under the umbrellas on the crowded piazza
came an outpouring of emotion that equaled the pouring rain.

As if to confirm that a sea change had occurred, a consortium of the
national trade unions—the CGIL, the CSIL, and the UIL—quickly announced a demonstration of solidarity with Sicily for June 27, at which
workers from all over Italy would descend en masse to Palermo to
protest the massacre. The proposal helped to erase the local unions' embarrassment over the debacle of 1988, when Socialist and Catholic
workers carried mock coffins designated for Orlando and Rizzo. In
Palermo, enraged and determined activists began meeting to consider
what local and regional actions might be taken. Within days, the local
chapter of the Italian Recreational and Cultural Association, or ARCI
(*Associazione Ricreativa Culturale Italiana*), assumed a coordinating
role. A point of reference for young, reform-oriented leftists, this group
invited to its sparsely furnished meeting room in the historic center a di-
versity of activists wanting to generate a commemorative event or
events.

Doing so would not be easy, for the rift of 1988 ran deep and had not
been repaired. The grassroots organizers in San Saverio, for example,
had come to believe that the antimafia movement was moribund. The
residents of the popular quarters, they said, were hardly present in the
line filing past Falcone's coffin in the courthouse and in the crowd outside of his funeral. From their perspective, this indifference was attributable to Orlando's failure to channel popular sentiment, focusing rather
on who was "mafioso" and who was "pure." If anything, the emphasis
on *spaccatura* had deepened with the formation of the new political
party, *La Rete,* which Pintacuda, its political and moral theorist, con-
ceptualized as a "revolutionary front." Gradualism, the logic of partial
reforms, the weaker idea of a "front of the honest," were equivocations
that had to be denounced, even if this meant alienating poor people (see
Alongi 1997: 301).

To add to the tension, the Social Center of San Saverio had, in the interim, launched a daring project to rehabilitate youthful offenders—to
"capture" some of the worst cases, as they put it. Under this program,
boys were released early from the juvenile detention facility, Malaspina,
on condition that they submit to a center-sponsored work routine,
closely supervised by volunteers as well as staff. The project seemed
naively idealistic to some, for example, the physician responsible for the
health clinic attached to the center, who questioned its wisdom, causing

another rift (see Terranova 1993–94). Certainly it further increased the distance between the strand of antimafia engaged with poor neighborhoods of Palermo where delinquency flourished and the strand that advocated excluding from the fold anyone tainted by crime.

Ever controversial, Orlando had gone on prime-time television shortly after giving up his mayoralty in early 1990 to accuse the antimafia magistrates, including Falcone, of failing to prosecute political criminals (specifically Lima) on whom they allegedly already had evidence in their files.[4] In September of the following year, Galasso and Mancuso rekindled the charge in a letter to the Superior Council of the Magistrates. Although some antimafia magistrates at the time would have been more aggressive than Falcone in pressing the *pentiti* on the issue of political collusion, even they considered this criticism less than constructive. Planning for events to commemorate the first month anniversary of Falcone's murder in which space would be given to Orlando was instantly controversial; indeed, many activists debated with themselves and each other whether they could, in good conscience, attend. His tears would be crocodile tears, they said, just like the false tears of those who had considered the judge "too ambitious."

Clearly, the solidarity that followed the killing of dalla Chiesa was not about to be reborn. Nevertheless, by June 12, after several testy meetings, a fractious coalition of twenty to forty activists, ranging from *La Rete* enthusiasts to Nino Rocca of CO.CI.PA, had formed a new *coordinamento*, infelicitously labeled the Cartel (the old *Coordinamento* was disqualified for being too close to the political party of Orlando). Moreover, they had reached a consensus (actually a near consensus, as the Centro Impastato sought to keep at least a symbolic distance from *La Rete* by not participating on the same subcommittees) around two ideas: an antimafia assembly addressing the new phase of the struggle opened up by Falcone's murder, and the formation of a human chain on June 23, the one-month anniversary of the killing. The Centro Impastato was the source of the first idea, which, its affiliates argued, responded to the urgent need for analysis. The second, an innovative borrowing from the global repertoire of activism, was suggested by Palermo's Association for Peace, led by Nino lo Bello. Initially greeted with a lukewarm response, the human chain was soon recognized to be a necessary "expressive" complement to the "analytical" assembly, which some feared would be tedious and fail to capture the city's raw emotions. Eventually the chain idea ignited the planners' imaginations: It could begin at the courthouse and end where? At the Ucciardone prison? No, at Falcone's apartment

Figure 16. A segment of the Falcone Tree, summer 1992. Photograph by Jane Schneider.

house, five kilometers to the north, on a street named for another martyr in the struggle against the mafia, the Via Notarbartolo. Here the sad remnant of a once magnificent magnolia tree, amputated to accommodate the volume of the building (Santino 2000: 291), had already become a shrine, its base smothered with flowers and wreathes, its trunk with appended poetry and artwork (see fig. 16).

On the day after Falcone's funeral, the residents of an apartment building situated near the municipal square in the historic center came up with another demonstratively theatrical, and original, way to express their grief and rage. The building is a "family building," one of those apartment houses that has been home to an extended kinship group for over a generation. In this case, the family was an anchor of the old left in Palermo. In one of the apartments, overflowing with books, lived Marcello Cimino—intellectual, journalist for *L'Ora,* and distinguished director of Palermo's Gramsci Institute. His wife, Giuliana Saladino, was also an intellectual activist and author. On the floor below was Giuliana's sister, Gabriella Saladino, an artist and sculptor, while across the hall lived Giuliana's daughter, Marta Cimino, a social worker, and her family. The idea that was generated by this cluster of relatives, each with a long history of political engagement, was to paint slogans on bed sheets—*"Basta!"* (Enough!), "Palermo Asks for Justice!", "Falcone, you are with us!"—and hang the sheets from their respective balconies for all to see (see fig. 17).

As Marta Cimino later wrote in a press release, to display the sheets was easy; every household had them ready to hand. And yet it was also

Figure 17. The first sheets protesting the massacre of Judge Falcone, appearing on the balconies of the Palazzo Bono in central Palermo, May 27, 1992. Photograph by Alessandro Fucarini, Labruzzo Agenzia, Palermo.

daunting, for to do so one had to "come out from anonymity." She hoped this "very small start" in transcending "our usual modesty and embarrassment [would] change the face of the city." The spontaneous gesture resonated with two rather contradictory dimensions of woman-hood in Sicily: the traditional role of embroidered bed linens in every re-spectable bride's trousseau, symbolizing not only her family's status but her sexual purity; and the emergence in Palermo of feminist groups with the courage to make public statements.

The idea of the sheets as a medium of communication was compelling. Indeed, within a few days they began to multiply, appearing on balconies throughout the city. Capturing the immediate attention of others, it led to the formation of a cohesive group of about twenty women and six men, for the most part professionals and intellectuals, numbers that could have grown considerably had the original core wanted to expand. Calling themselves the Committee of the Sheets *(Comitato dei Lenzuoli)*, they immediately set about planning their contributions to the first month's commemoration of Falcone's assassination. For example, they organized television spots through contacts that some of them had with the media. They supported the concept of the human chain for June 23, and decided to sell tee shirts and bumper stickers for it. One of two slo-gans would be emblazoned on them, "Basta!" or "Mafiosi, on Your Knees," the latter inspired by the emotional funeral oration of twenty-three-year-old Rosaria Schifani, the widow of one of Falcone's murdered bodyguards: "Men of the mafia, I will forgive you, but you must get down on your knees!"

Some members of the committee were delegated to approach the as-sociation of merchants and shopkeepers, requesting that stores be closed on June 23 and commemorative notices affixed to their windows. Other members wrote to the archbishop, Cardinal Pappalardo, to request that on June 23, all of the church bells be rung at 5:58, the exact time that the martyred magistrate expired, that the procession for Santa Rosalia deviate course during her saint's day celebration on July 14, so as to stop before the Palazzo di Giustizia; and that the customary fireworks be sus-pended during the festival nights. The latter request was made with the full knowledge that fireworks, like horse races, lend excitement to Sicil-ian festivals and, although reputed to be "mafia business," are greatly loved.[5]

Various state authorities were also approached: the national highway authority to leave the gigantic crater on the highway until the assassins were found and convicted, diverting traffic around it; the University of

Palermo to memorialize Falcone at the opening of the school year; the postal service to issue a commemorative stamp. The committee further disseminated one of Falcone's many quotable comments about the anti-mafia struggle, incorporated into posters and bookmarks: "People come and go but ideas remain. Their moral tensions remain. They continue to walk on the legs of others. . . . Everyone must do their part, small or grand as it may be, to continue to create conditions for a more humane life in this Palermo." Most important, they began urging citizens to hang message-laden sheets from their balconies on the twenty-third of every month, and to telegraph their concerns to the President of the Republic. In the end they hoped that these efforts would belie another of Falcone's observations—that the people of Palermo are "waiting at the window to see who would win the bullfight" (quoted in Stille 1995: 356).

As might be expected, not all of the initiatives worked out, but Pappalardo did announce that, because of the "situation of suffering in which our city lives," the fireworks for Santa Rosalia would give way to a silent demonstration—a candlelight procession—"as a sign of hope and commitment that each of us will do our part." And as June 23 approached, committee members doubled their efforts, designating three locations where people could come together and paint on sheets: the "Falcone tree," as the magnolia-cum-shrine had come to be called; a piazza (Ungheria) in the modern downtown; and the piazza in front of the Social Center San Saverio. As individuals, they persuaded friends and relatives to "come out from anonymity" and paint a sheet. We accompanied one member of the *Lenzuoli* into the most comfortable and bourgeois section of Palermo north as she won over several of her women friends, otherwise reticent to make so public a statement. Giuliana Saladino, meanwhile, developed a correspondence with sympathetic observers in cities throughout Italy, some of whom organized parallel "Committees of the Sheets."

The human chain exceeded its planners' expectations. With an estimated ten thousand participating, it easily covered the five kilometers from the courthouse to Falcone's home, a moving symbol that the "other Palermo" wanted "the mafia on its knees," as many of their tee shirts said.[6] Hundreds of images of women and children and (in fewer numbers) men holding hands, made more dramatic by the confluence of these tee shirts, flooded into the press and TV. So close did the occasion come to generating a sense of solidarity that the grassroots organizers of San Saverio regretted afterward that they had not taken the children of Albergheria with them. Merely telling them afterward that "old men

with rough skin, berets, and canes"—that is, "people of their class"—
had participated in the event hardly seemed convincing, nor could one
show them Nino Lo Bello's video of it without risking an outburst of
ridicule.

At the Falcone tree, at the end of the day, an open microphone was
offered to citizens who wished to step forward with remembrances or
poetry; by design there was no formal roster of speakers. Some of the volunteered words made people uncomfortable, in particular a woman who
advocated prayers for mafiosi and their eventual pardon. Such an ecumenical position was anathema to Orlando and Pintacuda, who, standing near the microphone, wanted to step in. The organizers, however, announced that the day was "for the citizens" and declared it at an end.

CONTINUED MOBILIZATION

Two days later, on June 25, the Orlando forces had their day in court
when *La Rete,* together with *Antimafia,* the journal of the *Coordinamento,* sponsored a conference in the courtyard of the municipal library.
This event was well attended: perhaps nine hundred people sitting and
standing. Nando dalla Chiesa set the tone by re-evoking the "end of the
Primavera": the fall 1988 *garantista* campaign, followed by the strike
and mock funeral procession to embarrass Orlando. He also referred to
Sciascia's attack on the *professionisti* of the antimafia, his father among
them. Ironically, Sciascia's "words for democracy" had been used to
"kill democracy," he said. Orlando, recalling Borsellino's ominous
warning, in the summer of 1988, that the "pool" of the Palermo Prosecutor's Office was being dismantled, also blamed Sciascia, saying that he
had "opened the door" to the flood of citizens' complaints about escorts
and sirens. This dramatically set the stage for the late arrival of
Borsellino, who received a standing ovation. That he was living under
enormous tension was more than evident—in his creased brow, measured words, and chain smoking on the podium. (Falcone had once told
friends who advised him to quit smoking, "Look, I'm not going to die of
cancer!")

In his speech, Borsellino confirmed as authentic the pages of Falcone's
diary printed in *Sole 24 Ore,* pages that revealed little except on the subject of the chief prosecutor, Pietro Giammanco. Falcone had supported
Giammanco's promotion to general prosecutor in 1990, despite his
known ties to the Lima current of the DC, but had felt like "a bear in a
cage" working under him. Borsellino pronounced his agreement with

Caponetto and Orlando that Falcone had started to die with Sciascia's attack on the magistrates, almost as if Sciascia shared responsibility for the massacre. Falcone's miserable conflict with Meli following Caponetto's resignation as head of the Office of Instruction also came up. Caponetto would never have retired early, Borsellino insisted, except that he was old and tired and genuinely believed that Falcone would replace him. Instead, the younger magistrate was immediately "taken for a ride by some Judas," which was why he, Borsellino, had had to speak out on that night in Agrigento.

In a fiery speech, antimafia lawyer Alfredo Galasso attacked fellow Sicilian Corrado Carnevale, the Supreme Court judge whose practice of reversing mafia convictions had earned him the nickname "Sentence Killer" (see chapter 6, note 8). Additional elites, already indicted or under investigation, were also castigated—in particular, the Knights of Labor in Catania; the tax collector, Ignazio Salvo; Palermo's former mayor and commissioner of public works, Vito Ciancimino; and the regional DC leaders, Mario D'Aquisto and Calogero Mannino. To huge applause, Galasso said he wished he had pulled Falcone out of the Palace of Poisons years ago.

The following day, June 26, was the Cartel-sponsored assembly, held in the university's Faculty of Economy and Commerce. Twenty hours of preparation lay behind this gathering, which meant nearly twenty hours of at times divisive arguments over the lineup of speakers and the topics they would cover. The role of the grassroots social centers in the antimafia struggle was a topic added during these debates. When the day arrived, over forty authorities—intellectuals, magistrates, political leaders, and activists, some from outside of Sicily—lectured to a disappointing audience of around three hundred, many of whom arrived late, absorbed themselves in small group or cell phone conversations, and left before the end. Locanto and Mancuso were there for a while, but otherwise *La Rete* was hardly represented; the most commanding speakers were, rather, magistrates and politicians of the left.

Several made reference to the *quartieri popolari*: to the urgency of penetrating and educating these reservoirs of the mafia; to the imperative for activists to "dirty their hands with the people"; to the unfairness and inefficacy of turning needed social services over to volunteers. Santino, in his speech, called for (among other measures such as putting more resources behind the search for fugitives and eliminating the immunity from prosecution of parliamentary deputies) "liberating the thousands of Palermo who were not in the human chain." Yet the grassroots organizers seemed disillusioned in the end, seconding Nino Rocca's closing speech that declared the day a failure. "It smells of too little," he said, a "model of encounter for the grand bourgeoisie" that the people stay away from. Forty organizations made up the Cartel, but fewer than a hundred people were there to hear his admonition.

Then came June 27, the day that brought over seventy thousand union affiliates to Palermo from all over Italy. Arriving by plane, train, and ship, they assembled behind colorful banners and flags at designated points, forming four great rivers of marchers that then converged on Piazza Castelnuovo, in the heart of the modern city. Sections of the UIL and CSIL were visible in the crowds, but the CGIL seemed to dominate and with it the color red. Newspapers, indeed, reported that the occasion evoked the heady days of the 1960s and 1970s. At the very least, it did seem to redeem the unions for having allowed, and then failed to sanction, the disastrous *"Viva la mafia"* strike of 1988.

Between the human chain on June 23, the assemblies and conventions, and the massive union demonstration, Palermo appeared once again mobilized. Government officials could not fail to notice that "honest citizens" were firmly behind the antimafia magistrates, whose lives they saw as endangered not only by the mafia but by the complicity or foot-dragging of the counter-antimafia political class. In the midst of the union demonstration, a cluster of people led by a group of *Lenzuoli* chanted for the removal of Giammanco from the head of the Prosecutor's Office and Carnavale from the Supreme Court. It is impossible to evaluate, however, the impact of these events on subsequent government action, for less than a month hence, on July 19, the car bomb exploded that took the life of Borsellino and his bodyguards. The magistrate's gruesome demise within weeks of Falcone's was terrifying. The funeral was private but following the open funeral of the bodyguards, held in the cathedral, national officials, including the President of the Republic Scalfaro, "had to be rescued from [a] mob" of citizens screaming insults at them (Stille 1995: 373).

Palermo remained in turmoil, with demonstrations and assemblies throughout the summer. Activists discovered a disarming photograph of Falcone and Borsellino, smiling over a confidence they appeared to have exchanged, and this, coupled with Falcone's famous quotation about "ideas walking on the legs of others," was reproduced on hundreds of posters, banners, and bookmarks distributed throughout the city. The Committee of the Sheets now promoted the display of sheets on private balconies from the nineteenth to the twenty-third of each month, thus marking the martyrdom of Borsellino as well as Falcone. Fellow citizens were further urged to welcome the newly arrived young soldiers by "inviting them for a pizza, an ice cream, or a home-cooked meal, on their days off." Over the coming months, committee members also kept up a constant correspondence with like-minded groups elsewhere in Sicily and in Italy, and with Italian government officials. Among their letters was one to Giorgio Bocca, a well-known journalist for *La Repubblica*, thanking him for his reporting but objecting to his use of a capital "M" in the word "mafia." "We in Palermo consider [the mafia] an ignoble thing to be devalued. It does not deserve the honor of a capital letter."

On January 17, 1993, Saladino wrote a letter to the new head of the Prosecutor's Office, Caselli, whose arrival two days earlier had coincided, as she pointed out, with the auspicious capture of Totò Riina. (Bruno Contrada was arrested shortly before, on December 24, 1992.) "We welcome you to Palermo," the letter said, then went on to lament that the *mani pulite* exposure of bribery scandals in northern Italy had not yet reached Sicily. "You will find many poisons in the courthouse, but also honest, decisive, prepared people who will support you, as they supported Falcone and Borsellino." As Caselli opened the case against Andreotti, the Committee of the Sheets weighed in with letters, petitions, and a sit-in in front of the Palace of Justice—all in support of the magistrates who were investigating his "presumed collusion with the mafia." The Association of Women against the Mafia went on a hunger strike to show their support for the "forces of order."

"PALERMO YEAR ONE"

These demonstrative initiatives were a prelude to the next phase of the antimafia process, which is best characterized as warding off another return to "normalcy" through energetically building and reinforcing what activists call "civil society." Bearing a close affinity to middle-class ways of organizing social life, this concept usually refers to the social space between families and the state, and to the voluntary associations with which middle-class groups typically fill this space. By contrast, the lower classes, unless they have stable employment and are able to organize effective unions, are imagined to generate another kind of scaffolding, based on clientelistic relationships.

It has been our observation that, from the 1980s to the 1990s, the "civil society" concept underwent a change of meaning in Palermo. During the 1980s, it offered a conveniently neutral set of values under which activists with antagonistic Cold War histories could coalesce around new issues, a point illustrated by Nando dalla Chiesa's 1983 analysis of the contrasts between the emergent antimafia movement and the labor and peasant movements of the past (see chapter 7). Two strands of antimafia then coexisted. Grassroots activists, inspired by models of community organizing from the 1960s and 1970s, imagined that the urban lower classes were capable, as peasants had been before them, of "autonomous" collective action, of struggling to obtain the equivalent of land, namely, jobs and decent housing. That this struggle would be antimafia in spirit did not preclude its attracting participants from poor mafia families—people like Michela Buscemi. In contrast, the moral reformers trusted no one with mafia ties and put their faith in outreach and "cultural reeducation." For them the lower classes would receive and absorb, rather than self-organize. Notwithstanding the tense altercation between the grassroots advocates and the Orlando administration, both professed to the common goal of building civil society.

In the 1990s, this balance of power shifted, marginalizing the grassroots leaders. Thanks to the 1993 electoral reform providing for the direct election of mayors, Orlando, reelected in a landslide, enjoyed a much stronger platform from which to govern. He and many others increasingly defined civil society in terms of a nemesis—the corrupt and clientelistic favor system. A new umbrella organization formed in the spring of 1993 to plan the one-year commemoration of the massacres of Falcone and Borsellino, also marked the shift. Displacing the so-called Cartel, a coalition of groups weighted toward the secular left, the new organization mobilized progressive Catholics and environmentalists, many involved in volunteer work in the popular quarters and in cleaning up beaches and public gardens. Nino Lo Bello, the Peace Association activist who had promoted the idea of the human chain, became the first head. The chosen name, *Palermo Anno Uno* (Palermo Year One), or *PAU,* depicts Palermo as a city about to be reborn. Significantly, to many of the grassroots organizers, it also occludes the antimafia struggles that preceded "year one"—above all the left-inspired struggles of the 1960s through 1980s.

In the years since 1993, *Palermo Anno Uno* has sought to supplement candlelight processions and sheets hung from balconies with "capillary" interventions. Some fifty associations coming together under its auspices have lent support to municipal efforts to rehabilitate the historic center, expand green spaces in the city and beyond, recycle abandoned properties for community use, and enrich antimafia projects in the city's schools. As Lo Bello's letter to Caselli of October 8, 1994, explains: "We want you to know that the *società civile* of Palermo, the one born after the massacres of 1992, has not gone home," but is working like "an army of ants . . . to *strappare* [rip away] the consensus [enjoyed by] the mafia."[7]

CONCLUSION

In promising to break up the mafia's consensus, Lo Bello was acknowledging the still powerful presence of the opinion makers of the "counter-antimafia." Silenced by the dramatic events of 1992, these naysayers had not gone away; on the contrary, many of them would find a home in the new political party of Silvio Berlusconi, *Forza Italia*. Together with its coalition partner, the *Alleanza Nazionale* party, FI has done exceptionally well in Sicily, starting with the March 1994 parliamentary election. Chapter 12 takes up the attractiveness of this party to the popular neighborhoods of Palermo, places where "capillary action" is, alas, difficult. In chapter 9, we look at how the committed moral reformers of the 1990s challenged clientelism in their own, middle-class groups.

CHAPTER 9

Civil Society Groundwork

To describe how mafiosi condition and provision the society around them, we borrowed Calderone's metaphor of spiders spinning their webs. From an antimafia perspective, the operative metaphor for rendering society more "civil" is "capillary action." In an effort to chart such action, the present chapter begins with an overview of the core antimafia values, then examines how antimafia reformers attempt to realize these values in the micro-practices of their own everyday lives.

"PROGRESSIVE COSMOPOLITANISM"

Calling for democracy and transparency, antimafia reformers broadly embrace what Richard Maddox (n.d.) has called "progressive cosmopolitanism"—a loose set of universalizing values that include gender equality, human rights, and respect for the environment. Among the reformers, women have been visible and vocal participants from the outset, frequently outnumbering men at demonstrations and events. In 1982, women close to the Communist Party joined Giovanna Terranova in the Association of Sicilian Women against the Mafia. Women direct at least four publishing houses in Palermo, including Gelka and the feminist press, La Luna, both of which have printed important antimafia texts. Significantly, feminists brought organizing skills and the social energy of their friendships to meetings over antimafia strategy and tactics, the Committee of the Sheets being a salient example (see Cascio 1989).

Many antimafia activists endorse and seek to implement the value of gender equality. Among movement constituents, both men and women are educated at roughly comparable levels; there are many activist couples in which both are working professionals. Some of the most committed (and courageous) younger magistrates in the antimafia judiciary are women, while in 1993, in the first wave of municipal elections after the reform allowing for the direct election of mayors, twenty rural towns in Sicily elected women mayors, a higher percentage than in any other region of Italy. Presiding over some of the "hottest" communities in western Sicily, these mayors have endured death threats, found their car tires slashed, and been menaced in other ways. Amazingly, most were re-elected in 1997, as were the male antimafia mayors. Most of the activists we met are tolerant of premarital cohabitation among young people, tolerant of divorce and homosexuality, and most telling, they are critical of the patriarchal arrangements that with some justification they believe are still entrenched in Palermo's popular quarters.

Antimafia activists are also considerably "greener" than these popular quarters, contributing a disproportionate number of volunteers to one or another of Palermo's (competing) environmental groups. Like the former Commissioner for "Livability," Letizia Battaglia, they have energetically criticized the paucity of parks and gardens in the city and the encroachments on them of offensive garbage, "abusive" vending, and illegally constructed apartment houses. By contrast, many in the working classes would willingly put up with more "cementification" if it would staunch the erosion of employment opportunities.

The core value of antimafia ideology—the value that receives the most attention—is the value of good citizenship, the cornerstone of a vibrant civil society. Promoting it means, first and foremost, attacking *clientelismo,* and with it the attitude that "a friend is better than a legal right." Montalbano's 1960s analysis of this problem clearly states what activists in the movement believe they are up against now. "In Sicily," he wrote, "one does things not because they are just or not, legal or not, but because a friend has asked it." Moreover, not only are the favors "manifestations of prestige or power because they are obligations to a friend"; clientelism requires *dis*favoring persons who happen to be the friends of one's enemies. A "civil" relationship between the citizen and the state is thereby abrogated. Rather than being able to vindicate their rights, citizens end up submitting to the "habitus" of the local notables, enduring a long and humiliating mediation in which they may be asked, perhaps by a mafioso, to trade their votes for favors (Montalbano 1964b).

These themes were recapitulated in a pamphlet prepared and distributed by the Committee of the Sheets in 1992, "Nine Uncomfortable Guidelines for the Citizen Who Would Combat the Mafia." According to these guidelines, citizens should learn to claim their rights vis-à-vis the state, not beg for them as favors. They should educate their children in democracy and respect for the law. Workplace suspicions of bribery, corruption, extortion, favoritism, and the waste of public money should be reported to legally constituted authorities. So should irregularities in the delivery and billing of medical, legal, and other services, as well as other illegal acts. Before, after, and during elections, citizens should refuse any exchange of favors for votes. "Nothing will change if we continue to vote for parties that have governed us for many decades, allowing the mafia to poison public life, consigning pieces of the state to the mafia's hand." Related values, expressed in a religious idiom, characterize reform Catholicism in Palermo, which counterpoises the gospel of love to what is perceived as its "opposite"—the vendetta complex. The journal *Segno* is an important forum for promoting the evangelical perspective on conflict, frequently publishing documents from around the world on the themes of Christian peace, justice, and forgiveness.

ANTIMAFIA CONSCIOUSNESS RAISING

In considering the capillary action through which the values sketched above are brought to bear on everyday life, it is necessary to envision antimafia reformers in the full round of home and play as well as work. For people of their social standing—broadly speaking, the middle classes—Palermo is a compartmentalized city. People spend time with their own kind as defined by family, old school ties, professional connections, and workplace affinities. A few, generally of higher status, participate in the life of the *circoli* that, many say, is a legacy of the historic *snobbismo* of the aristocracy. Cliquish groups find each other in clubs dedicated to sport, culture, or politics. We were able to observe numerous informal gatherings of friends, kin, and colleagues—occasionally in such clubs but most often in the antechambers of political meetings, over dinners in restaurants or at people's homes, in the course of volunteering at social centers, and on summer outings.

Antimafia discourse warns against the return of a past normality when respectable citizens had no compunctions about including mafiosi, or friends of mafiosi, in their social networks. But actually breaking off ties with such persons, making them feel socially unacceptable, is mired in complications. Where does the world of mafiosi leave off and the world of "clean citizens" begin? What about the vast gray area between these moral poles? We heard one discussion in which a person who grew up in Ciaculli claimed to be at a big disadvantage compared to persons growing up in Palermo north. The Grecos were always cordial, he remembered, making it hard to realize that "we all live with an enemy in our house and we have to throw him out."

The dilemmas encountered require a rich vocabulary for ranking the category of people who, although not "made members" of the mafia, are suspected of collusion in its activities. Expressions that occur frequently are *in odore di mafia* (literally, smelling of mafia) and *chiacchierato* or *in chiacchiera di mafia* (a subject of mafia gossip). Especially revealing are the arguments and debates over specific ambiguous persons, for they illustrate how difficult it is to draw an unequivocal line. Gossip enables the evaluation of these borderline cases.

Three kinds of ambiguous case are common: persons killed or harmed by the mafia who, however, may also have been collusive, compromising their moral status as victim; persons under investigation for collusion, perhaps even convicted of collusion, for whom many well-meaning antimafia activists believe there are legitimate excuses; and persons who are consistently *chiacchierati* who nevertheless seem to have escaped the magistrates' shadow. With regard to ambiguous victims, we have already noted the controversy surrounding the mafia widows (see chapter 7). That their loved ones were murdered by mafiosi places them in the same condition as the wives of murdered magistrates—women who have continued to enjoy public sympathy and a public presence. And yet, as Umberto Santino and Anna Puglisi discovered in attempting to support three such women, few antimafia activists are prepared to imagine that mafia kin can be without guilt, especially if they do not exude bourgeois respectability.

Another obvious instance of ambiguous victimhood concerns merchants and businessmen who regularly pay the *pizzo*. Do they enter this transaction out of fear that, as Gambetta (1993) emphasizes, other forms of protection are unavailable? Or do they willingly pay up because their business benefits from mafia involvement? Only in the first instance can one define them as victims, yet it is hard to know which is the case. Such discriminatory reasoning also applies to businessmen receiving usurious loans who, although victimized, refuse to identify their contact or to cooperate with a police investigation. Perhaps they are traumatized by terror, perhaps collaborators in a criminal scheme, perhaps both.

Complicated debates take place around persons long suspected of collusion who become victims of mafia assassination. The *Coordinamento Antimafia* of the 1980s argued intensely over the status of Michele Reina, head of the DC for Palermo Province who was murdered in 1979, knowing that he had participated in the allocation of public works contracts. Was he killed for attempting to reform this system or for his failure to meet the expectations of certain mafiosi? Subsequent investigations pointed toward the latter. In 1999 the Supreme Court definitively convicted all the members of the *cupola* for three "excellent" homicides—Michele Reina, Piersanti Mattarella, and Pio La Torre (chapter 6). In the case of Reina, the motive was that he had dared to compete with the Corleonesi for building contracts.

Among ambiguous victims, few have been more controversial than Salvo Lima. When he was killed, Andreotti and the head of the national DC, Forlani, came to Palermo to participate publicly in his funeral, held in the same church as dalla Chiesa's (and soon Falcone's). In his eulogy, Cardinal Pappalardo said, "The horrible crime of which *Onorevole* Salvo Lima was the victim strikes, as well, the entire city of Palermo . . . making it, too, a victim" (quoted in Alongi 1997: 314 n. 38).[1] But right there, at the funeral, other messages were communicated, not least because neither Cossiga, the president of the republic, nor De Mita, another DC leader, were present. Asked in an interview whether Lima belonged or not to the roster of "excellent cadavers," Andreotti replied, "It is an old and ugly habit, that of discriminating among the dead." The first to suffer from this "partial, hidden, and subtle criminalization," he added, was Michele Reina (*Panorama*, March 14, 1992).

The headlines of the *Giornale di Sicilia* echoed Andreotti's irritation: "That campaign of hatred *(odio),*" said one. The stories emphasized Lima's break with Ciancimino and openness to the Communist Party, even as his relationships were known to have been "not always clear" (March 13, 1992). One hopes, said an editorial, that people will now "re-evaluate and cease referring to him as the 'head *[vertice]* of the mafia' " (ibid.). A few days later, the paper reported that Cossiga, notwithstanding his absence from the funeral, had confirmed that the murder of Lima "is of the same nature as that of Mattarella, La Torre, and dalla Chiesa," a comment that infuriated the widow of La Torre and others among his followers, according to whom Lima was a mafioso, even if this had not been proven in court (ibid., March 19, 1992).

Following the massacre of Falcone, the Committee of the Sheets designated a subcommittee to prepare a television spot whose content generated unanticipated controversy among an otherwise harmonious group. Not only was Lima's name on the list of fifty-one "victims of mafia assassinations" scrolled before the eyes of viewers; because the list was in chronological order, his name appeared adjacent to the names of Falcone, his wife, and their bodyguards. The intensity of the exchange over the inclusion of Lima and his position on the list prompted the members of the subcommittee to write to the committee defending their decision. A simple list of names, they pleaded, dramatized the mafia's "strategy of blood from which we want to escape" (*Comitato . . .* Archive). But the controversy surrounding the spot continued. At the June 26 assembly of the *Cartello,* Nunzia Agostino, the sister of an assassinated policeman, said her anger had deepened upon seeing it. How could Lima's name be there and not her brother's?

Two other personages over whom activists have disagreed are still alive—Francesco Musotto, the president of the province of Palermo, and Bruno Contrada, the head of the investigative squad and high officer in the secret services. Musotto's brother had generously offered the use of their jointly owned country house to the notorious mafioso fugitive and brother-in-law of Riina, Leoluca Bagarella. Contrada had come under suspicion ever since Buscetta warned Falcone, in 1984, that he (Contrada) was thought to protect certain bosses, tipping them off about possible police raids. Falcone indeed suspected Contrada of informing the mafia of his intention to invite visiting Swiss prosecutors to his summer house in Addaura on the afternoon of June 19, 1989, when an attempt was made on his life (see Stille 1995: 285–86). The *pentito* Gaspare Mutolo, who unbuttoned to Borsellino after Falcone was killed, also impugned Contrada's honesty, as did Giuseppe Marchese, another collaborator. Marchese, indeed, alleged that the notoriously successful fugitive Totò Riina was among the bosses whom Contrada had warned (ibid.: 370, 386–87).

Contrada was arrested on December 24, 1994, Musotto in 1995. Both were tried and eventually acquitted. Along the way, each evoked sympathy among *some* in the antimafia movement, on the grounds that there is more to the story than meets the eye. Musotto, his sympathizers argue, had long been estranged from the brother in question and is credible when he protests that he had no knowledge of Bagarella's use of the house. Contrada's defenders describe him as a skilled undercover agent whose "apparently" collusive relationships derived from his methodical cultivation of police informers. Both continue to have their detractors, however, and the controversy surrounding them continues. This is in marked, and perhaps ironic contrast, to the evaluations of a handful of powerful economic actors—lawyers and businessmen above suspicion, believed to belong to super-secret lodges of the Freemasons or the Knights of the Holy Sepulcher—who have never been prosecuted but who are *chiacchierati* by just about everyone.

If the process of classification breeds disagreements, so too do discussions about remedies. At meetings and small gatherings in 1992, we heard antimafia activists argue over proposals to organize boycotts of particular merchants. Should they refuse to buy meat from certain butchers or a car from certain dealers? Apart from the question whether merchants who pay protection money should be thought of as collusive or not, there were problems of identification. In cities, some argued, names tell you nothing; imputing guilt by name or by hearsay is a sure way for the antimafia process to degenerate into a witch hunt. Several activists did, however, give up purchasing cigarettes on the black market. Another debate was whether to initiate a letter-writing campaign against a media figure whose name had come up in Calderone's confession. What would it mean if the executives of the national television network fired this comedian who was tainted by the mafia, given that the executives themselves might figure in the vast scheme of payoffs between politicians and industry that the *mani pulite* magistrates were exposing in northern Italy?

Occasionally, participants in these debates were themselves impaled on the horns of a dilemma. For example, two antimafia leaders were investigated by the police for alleged improprieties in ordering books for the library that employed them. Although eventually cleared of any wrongdoing, they were caught for several years in the maws of the slow-moving judicial system, their faith in "judicial activism" almost (but not quite) shaken.

Often, the consciousness raisers seemed compelled to return to their own behavior. Don't we (Palermitani) violate the law every time we break traffic and parking rules? Why does no one ever question the extralegal but convenient "parking attendants" who arrange parking for a fee in the crowded heart of the city? Because motorists' inconsiderate manners come up so often as a metaphor for poor citizenship, one sometimes has the impression that in the activists' minds, traffic and the mafia are related. At other times, though, the same activists are quick to cite Falcone's warning that "if everything is mafia, then nothing is mafia."

PROFESSIONS UNDER STRESS

Another way to explore the moral and psychological dilemmas of anti-mafia consciousness raising is to imagine the situation from the perspective of particular careers or walks of life. We have already touched on Palermo's magistrates and journalists; we enter the worlds of architects and city planners in chapter 10 and of schoolteachers in chapter 11. The present discussion covers some of the challenges faced by lawyers, doctors, and priests seeking to moralize their respective professions.

To the frustration of many antimafia professionals, there seem to be no "clean" institutions in Sicily, including trade unions and political parties, no obvious points of reference to anchor their struggle and deepen its social base. Rather, within each office or bureaucracy, hospital or diocese, they must discover and enlarge that subset of persons whose behaviors appear uncorrupted by entanglements not only with the mafia but with its protectors and friends. To the extent that they subscribe to a program of *spaccatura,* they advocate blowing the whistle on corruption, refusing to transact gifts for favors, neither accepting nor seeking recommendations. Unfortunately, each behavior is a prescription for alienating friends and colleagues and becoming embroiled in unpleasant conflicts at work.

Lawyers pose a particularly thorny problem. Mafiosi surely have a right to an aggressive legal defense, but some of the attorneys who represent them are drawn into unprofessional compromises, smuggling contraband in and out of prison, delivering messages, enabling the continuance of their clients' illegal affairs. The mafioso Antonino Madonia's account book, sequestered on his arrest, contained an entry that said *"stallaggio avvocati"* (stabling and feeding lawyers). Lawyers for the mafia are well paid; indeed, mafiosi complain about the high cost of their lawyers' fees, although they view the cost as inevitable, something they dare not question for fear of "spreading panic in a category on which the lives of prisoners so heavily depend" (Brusca in Lodato 1999: 78). One antimafia magistrate told us of a defense lawyer who bragged that, thanks to the maxi-trial, he had made enough money to build himself a house by the sea. With Calderone's post-maxi revelations came more money—enough to build another house in the mountains. By contrast, in the early 1990s, no more than three or four defense lawyers in all of Palermo—Alfredo Galasso was prominent among them—represented relatives of mafia victims in criminal cases. The same small group signed petitions publicly declaring themselves to be against the mafia. Together with the lawyers who defended the *pentiti* (an even smaller number), they sacrificed both income and clients for their commitment.

Most antimafia activists see doctors as less "political"—less potentially corruptible—than lawyers, and give them less attention in discussing "what is to be done." Activists who are themselves doctors, however, are among the most anguished of the movement's participants. Palermo has three large public hospitals in which corruption has been legion. One, the Ospedale Civico, was administered until his retirement in 1993 by the brother of Salvo Lima, Giuseppe (Beppe) Lima. He seems to have made the institution, with its 4,300 employees and substantial budget (Gulisano 1996: 30) into a swollen patronage operation—Beppe's fiefdom, one doctor called it—in which everything, from new staff appointments to the supply of goods and services, transpired in exchange for votes and other favors. Physicians employed there report a recent past in which essential medical supplies were chronically unavailable at the same time as useless, redundant, or defective equipment clogged the basement storerooms. The hospital was legally denounced for having allowed one hundred ambulances, newly purchased by the city, to sit unused for four years (see Folena 1993: 8). The reason, of course, was that medical products were ordered to favor certain contractors, who were in turn enmeshed in Salvo Lima's political machine.

In 1996, the Catania-based monthly *I Siciliani* published the names (obtained from the Parliamentary Antimafia Commission) of over 2,400 members of the main masonic lodges of Palermo, dating to 1947. Part of a series on Freemasonry, the names were accompanied by analytical articles, pointing, among other things, to the large number of Palermo doctors, surgeons, and medical personnel (some 250 in all) belonging to secret societies to which mafiosi and persons *in chiacchiera di mafia* also belonged. Masonic connections of this type seemed to underlie the most lucrative career paths. Pietro Calacione, head of both the technical office of the Ospedale Civico and the P2-linked Centro Sociologico Italiano (see chapter 3), had just been indicted for receiving kickbacks from the hospital's contractors and suppliers (Gulisano 1996: 30).

But this problem pales before the collusion of doctors who falsify test results or medical records to help mafiosi evade tough sentences.[2] In 1982, Dr. Paolo Giaccone, a professor of forensic medicine at the University of Palermo, was assassinated outside his office, allegedly for failing to honor the request "that he 'fix' the scientific report" of a mafioso's fingerprints so as to facilitate his defense (see Stille 1995: 64, 166–67). Doctors have also helped fugitives keep their cover or, in the worst-case scenario, caused inconvenient witnesses to disappear. In 1993, Pietro Folena, then regional secretary of the PDS, described the Sicilian health care system as suspended between deals *(affari),* the mafia, and (deviated) Freemasonry. Here was "fertile terrain," he argued, for illegal arrangements to metastasize, even to the point of covering the tracks of Riina. Had not his wife, Ninetta Bagarella, given birth in hospitals, no questions asked about her husband who was, at the time, among the "most wanted"?

According to the prison official we interviewed during the maxi-trial, prisoners, kept four to six in a cell, were expected to defend themselves by any means, including feigning illness. In Jamieson's words, "Tommaso Buscetta, held in Palermo's Ucciardone prison from 1973 to 1977, spent his entire imprisonment in the hospital wing, where he was able to receive friends, family and lawyers and telephone all over the world" (2000: 25). Here is Brusca's account of being moved to the infirmary during his first term in that prison in 1982:

> There I found other "men of honor." . . . I encountered all the Inzerillos, who had ended up inside following the arrest warrant of the *procuratore capo* of Palermo, Gaetano Costa. All of the Spatolas. . . . In the "fourth section" (of the prison), the infirmary was composed of enormous rooms that housed ten or twelve persons. I have always thought that the prison was the university of encounters. In that period, it was not difficult for "men of honor" to pretend sickness. (Brusca, in Lodato 1999: 37)

Antimafia doctors working in institutions where their colleagues participate in such deceptions, and in corrupt purchasing and contracting practices, complain bitterly about the burden of denouncing them. We need only imagine ourselves in their shoes to appreciate that whistle blowing in a hospital is considerably more stressful than boycotting a suspected butcher. In the mid-1980s, a group of doctors at the Civico denounced Beppe Lima for having permitted a wing of the hospital to be rebuilt without relocating the patients. Lima, however, was later able to intimidate one of the physicians who withdrew his support for the complaint. This had the effect of silencing the others, one of whom then employed a bodyguard. Mysterious mail, such as a Christmas greeting with the words, "We still think of you," further dampened their protest. Only after the *Primavera,* when a group of reformist doctors engaged a section of the CGIL as a surrogate to denounce wrongdoing, did the situation improve. Today Beppe Lima is deceased and there are several doctor-masons in jail.

The priesthood presents another range of complexities. Once in 1920 and again in 1952, a Sicilian bishop made public statements to the effect that killers and their *mandanti* should be excommunicated (Stabile interview 1987), but these were exceptions to the rule. Priests in those days took their problems to the mafia and vice-versa. The committees that raised money for patron saints' festivals typically included mafiosi as well as members of the confraternity that organized the festival. Priests and bishops were not beyond colluding with local contractors over the construction and repair of ecclesiastical buildings, and priests performed services for mafiosi in hiding.

After Cardinal Pappalardo replaced Cardinal Ruffini as archbishop of Palermo, expectations began to change; Pappalardo, at least, did not reprimand priests who refused to perform the sacraments for mafiosi. He did not, however, make public statements endorsing such "acts of conscience," leaving them in the realm of individual responsibility. In chapter 7 we followed the archbishop from his "Palermo is Sagunto" eulogy at dalla Chiesa's funeral to his mass in the Ucciardone the following Easter, when not a single prisoner showed up. Activist priests were enormously disappointed by his subsequent caution, viewing him as a diplomat and not a hero. Indeed, he pronounced himself fearful of being seen as a demagogue, declaring, in a press conference a week before the opening of the maxi-trial, that Palermo was not Sagunto after all. Yet reform-minded clerics argue that people need the support of the Church in order to change; they want their "revolution" to be blessed. That being a Christian is incompatible with having a "mafioso mentality," that *omertà* is a sin, should be pronounced at the top, perhaps via a Church convention or pastoral letter leading to clear guidelines for the bishops and priests, who would then go along. If a single priest refuses to preside at the funeral of a mafioso, his gesture lacks symbolic weight, he feels isolated, and the family involved simply goes to another parish.

In the early 1990s a courageous priest, Pino Puglisi, took over the parish in Brancaccio, the neighborhood bordering Ciaculli that is considered among the most "difficult" from an antimafia perspective. Following the model of San Saverio, he set up a social center focusing on young people and refused to be manipulated by builders who wanted the contract to restore his church. For his efforts he was menaced, and then murdered on September 15, 1993. Following this tragic event, the bishops of Sicily, supported by the Pope, spoke out on the incompatibility of the mafia with the Gospel, its participation in evil, and the need to combat it through evangelism. They did not, however, respond to petitions requesting that they directly involve themselves in commemorating Father Puglisi or bringing his assassins to justice (Santino 2000: 307–8, 314).

Throughout Sicily, it remains the rare priest who, even in the absence of intimidation, takes truly bold steps. Mafiosi are embedded in kin networks just as everyone else; their life-cycle ceremonies—marriages, baptisms, last rites—involve whole families, not just individuals with blood on their hands. Priests encounter the problem of "mafia victims of the mafia" in a particularly poignant way, a nuance that movement activists appreciate. Applauding those who would deny last rites to an individual killer, they hesitate as the circle widens—for example, in the case of a priest refusing to preside over the first communion of a mafioso's daughter. In 1996, the bishop of Agrigento issued a circular asking priests to scrutinize the persons whom their parishioners were proposing as godparents to their children; mafia-tainted candidates should be disqualified. But this was a highly unusual action, prompted by the murder of a very young magistrate in the province (Rosario Livatino), whom the bishop was proposing as a candidate for beatification.

Many priests who want to be antimafia in the end pursue the easier route advocated by the Italian Episcopal Conference in 1992, which is to encourage mafiosi to "repent within themselves" and "prove their sincerity" before being admitted to the sacraments (Jamieson 2000: 139).[3] The idea that even mafiosi can be forgiven—that they are themselves victims of a pathological situation who need the healing love of Jesus—is complicated, however. To quote from a 1987 speech by the mother of slain policeman, Roberto Antiochia, "The blood in the streets of Palermo is becoming a river," "The Italian state has not yet paid," and "We want justice from a state that allows criminals to murder others." "Our lost blood cries for vendetta." To hold out the possibility of pardoning mafiosi, reintegrating them in society as if genuine *pentitismo* were possible, comes across as a shallow or facile solution to anyone whose pain is deeply felt (see Santino 2000: 315).

Since Falcone's murder, the ground has shifted somewhat; politicians no longer walk behind the coffins at the funerals of mafiosi as if, in the words of one activist priest, "the President of the Republic had died." Their old excuses—"he was just a friend," "his brother was a member of the City Council"—are totally without credibility. By the same token, resorting to a mafioso to resolve a problem, although it may still happen, can no longer take place in ignorance of the moral compromises involved. On the very day that Falcone was assassinated, the mafioso Nino Madonia was married in prison. A rumor soon circulated that mafia leaders (perhaps the fugitive, Totò Riina) were boasting that the mafia had given Falcone's death to Madonia as a wedding present. Furious activists sought reassurance that the couple was married by the chaplain of the Ucciardone, a man merely doing his job, not by some accommodating priest brought in from outside. A few years later, a major figure in the Sicilian church, the bishop of Monreale, was indicted and tried for receiving kickbacks from construction companies doing restoration work on the magnificent Monreale cathedral.

University professors also have a difficult row to hoe,[4] especially if they choose to contest the long established system of recommendations, in which influential persons (including mafiosi) attempt to gain a preference for certain applicants for positions, and certain students in the grading of examinations. By the late 1980s, written examinations at the University of Palermo had become less contaminated, thanks to computer grading, but the oral examinations continued to be a sore point for reformers. "The system continues," said one, "because this is the ship in which the politicians navigate." In an earlier time, recommendations were so normal as to escape the stigma of corruption, but now they are viewed as humiliating, even disgusting.[5] Yet students continue to feel the need of them. It is interesting that both students and faculty members active in the antimafia movement say that the students from the provinces are more likely than the students from Palermo city to seek the crutch of a recommendation.

Conversations among academics often also touch on the corruption of the university itself. Like the hospitals and the churches, this institution is perceived as making decisions and allocating resources to favor particular interests and contractors. In the mid-1980s, for example, reform-oriented biology professors learned that certain pieces of laboratory equipment had been purchased at a price 40 percent higher than necessary. As they prepared to complain, the laboratory director intervened: "Look, we got the equipment you requested. What difference does it make to you how much it cost?" Like hospital patients, students have passively accepted institutional compromises—in their case, closed libraries, cramped classrooms, missing books, absent teachers. Or have they? Thanks to the spreading consciousness of moral and political reform, in 1995 a national student strike aimed at addressing such problems was launched from Palermo.

These vignettes of the professions at best scratch the surface of the complicated lives of individuals with an antimafia consciousness. A final note might be added about their relationship to the press. As noted in chapter 8, the antimafia middle class turned away from the *Giornale di Sicilia* toward, for the most part, *La Reppublica*. The opposition daily *L'Ora* was also attractive to some in this group, but it suffered hard times in the 1980s and folded in 1992. In the late 1990s, competition to the *Giornale* intensified: *La Repubblica* introduced a Palermo page and two new papers arrived at the newsstands. No doubt in response, the *Giornale di Sicilia* has softened its harsh critique of the antimafia movement and magistrates, fearful, some believe, of losing even more readers. No longer publishing the cartoon strip of the Beati Paoli, it now devotes substantial space to the sorts of antimafia projects we will be discussing in the next two chapters. Even so, antimafia activists remain upset over not having had a daily forum for the reliable exchange of information of significance to the movement. This lament, of course, refers to a time before e-mail and the Web were much used in Palermo—a circumstance that no longer pertains.

BUREAUCRATS, ENTREPRENEURS, AND WORKING CLASSES

In all of the professions, resistance to corruption has had to confront the long-standing hegemony of what Mineo called the "mafia *borghesia*"— the overlapping set of political-economic coalitions, reinforced through secretive fraternal gatherings, that include not only professional, government, and business elites but also the capi of the important *cosche*. This nexus has exerted a greater influence over the domains of public service and entrepreneurship than over the professions, however, and these domains have produced correspondingly fewer reformers. Indeed, through the 1990s, both were characterized by the dramatic martyrdom of isolated individuals who were completely alone in their crusades.

Many, including ourselves, believe that the Orlando administration had an impact among public servants in the city government. In several offices that serve the public one notices employees, the *burocrati*, treating their positions as jobs rather than sinecures—a contrast with the past that is evident in promptness, shorter breaks, a willingness to solve rather than shelve problems, and helpful answers to telephone queries. Yet transparency remains elusive in the offices of the regional government. Debates continue, for example, over the relationship between Giovanni Bonsignore's rigid commitment to legality as a functionary of the regional agricultural commission and his murder in May 1990 (see Bonsignore 1994). For a particularly intractable office, consider the regional branch of the national forest service. Very few wooded acres have survived many centuries of deforestation in Sicily, but those that have are ideal places for hiding rustled animals, fugitives, and munitions. Strong suspicions by a few forest service employees that their colleagues turn a blind eye to this have come to naught. The most cynical activists point to the persistence of the web of masonic organizations through which top bureaucrats find covert ways to divert the path of reform. According to *I Siciliani,* in 1996 about fifty officials of the regional government belonged to compromised lodges (Gulisano 1996).

Entrepreneurs wanting to confront the system of the *pizzo* and the usurious loan-sharking practices of mafiosi find themselves surrounded by a business community that will not, or cannot, listen. Before them, moreover, is the lesson of clothing manufacturer Libero Grassi, who was killed in 1991 after publicly denouncing the mafia for extortion. In Grassi's view, "Being intimidated and being collusive are the same thing"; some pay up out of fear that they or their business could be harmed, but others enjoy boasting "about having important strings to pull." For more than five years Grassi had been threatened for his refusal to pay—his business robbed, his dog nearly killed, his factory torched—but the more he denounced what was happening, the more his colleagues abandoned him, accusing him of attracting negative publicity to all the businesses of Palermo (see Jamieson 2000: 35–37). To quote Santino, Palermo's merchants and entrepreneurs are caught in "a sedimented culture of subjugation and complicity" (2000: 284).

Meanwhile, the city's working classes, more or less concentrated in the popular quarters of the old city and in several of the *borgate,* or suburbs, have acquired a reputation for immunity, if not antipathy, to civil society reforms. It is not simply that the important mafia *cosche* of Palermo are located in these places, or even that, as impoverished, they have spawned their share of micro-criminality. It is rather that, although morally compelling on the surface, the antimafia values of gender equality, environmentalism, and, for religious activists, Christian love, are in tension with popular everyday experience, and none more so than the values of "meritocracy"—good citizenship and the rule of law. Antimafia discourse refers to poor neighborhoods as "at risk" *(a rischio),* or "other" *(altro),* immersed in a patriarchal and clientelistic culture, almost as if they belonged to a different world. Reformers who volunteer time at their social centers see themselves offering women an institutional escape, a sympathetic sounding board for complaints about men's aggression and spendthrift ways. It is their goal, as well, to "subtract" youth from the "vendetta complex" and disrupt the favor system with teachings on citizens' rights. But these behavioral complexes carry a different meaning for people whose livelihoods are insecure and who, as well, are likely to embrace the cultural assumptions and practices of folk Catholicism. Well rooted in the neighborhoods "at risk," this variant of Christianity scorns the gospel of loving your enemy.

The folk Catholic repertoire includes healers with magical powers who, in curing, divine social causes for illness or misfortune—offenses to indignant saints, for example—and recommend ways to make amends. Rather than trust that merit will be rewarded, people plead with these saints to whom they feel close in a way that parallels their negotiations with terrestrial patrons.[6] In a popular quarter like Albergheria, the saints are an everyday presence, their images peering out from niches and shrines in the crumbling walls of buildings, eagerly awaiting offerings of flowers, displeased if the votive candles, lit in their honor, are snuffed out—in short, ready to bargain. We are not far from the folklorist Salamone-Marino's account of the Sicilian peasant who made regular votive offerings to Saint Benedict but, upon suffering some misfortune, would blow the word "Benedict" into his cap, throw it on the ground, and stomp on it. "Now we will see if you bring justice!" he declared to his saint (see Sciascia 1965: 20–21). In the same vein, although now transformed as tourist attractions, popular genres of folk drama—the traditional puppet plays and epic narratives sung by traveling minstrels—tell tales of bloody revenge against deserving enemies.

Working-class culture is not homogeneous, however. Poor neighborhoods are also home to rank-and-file union members and Communists whose political identity was historically antimafia. Notwithstanding the "historic compromise," some of this tradition remains. There are, as well, a few Pentecostal churches with small followings in poor neighborhoods. In a 1980s study, anthropologist Salvatore Cucchiari compared Pentecostal healers with traditional diviners, finding that while the latter attribute misfortune or illness to an envious, malicious relative or other social relation, the former seek causality in the cosmic context of individual sin and divine forgiveness (Cucchiari 1988: 427). Pentecostal sanctification also "has profound anti-patriarchal potentialities," so much so that "men and women measure themselves by the same standards" (ibid.: 435). In the end, Palermo's working classes are a challenge to the capillary action of antimafia reform not so much because they hold contradictory values as because these values speak to the precariousness of their lives.

LIVELIHOODS AT RISK

It might be asked, by way of illustrating this argument, when Palermo last had a viable economy. Perhaps not since the historic exodus of peasants from agriculture in the 1960s, which dramatized the inability of urban industries to absorb them. In 1970s Palermo, 22 percent of the labor force had manufacturing jobs, and in firms that employed an average of 5.3 employees, compared with 41.6 percent in Milan, where average firm size was 13.4 (Chubb 1982: 41). A handful of publicly subsidized large plants existed. The largest of these, the shipbuilding yards, had nearly 4,000 employees during World War II, when government contracts were plentiful, but they were subsequently reduced to dry dock repairs. Similarly, Palermo lost contracts to manufacture railroad cars and equipment after the war, in part because of a national policy to disinvest in railroads (Barbadoro 1966: 83–84). Such losses were hardly compensated by the city's food processing and associated chemical industries, which had also declined, still less by its host of small marginal firms in clothing, shoes, furniture, and auto repair (Chubb 1982: 41).

Enter the construction industry and the industries supplying construction materials, which together account for a greatly disproportionate share of the Palermo economy—33 percent of the industrial work force in the 1970s, compared with 10 percent in Milan. Made up of myriad firms employing twenty-five to thirty workers or fewer, this sector also provided the city's "major source of wealth," the more so as national government moneys became available for public housing (ibid.: 131). As late as 1999, a glossy brochure put out by City Hall to attract investment capital indicated that 48.2 percent of the 14,201 firms registered with the Palermo Chamber of Commerce were in the construction sector, more than all other forms of manufacturing activity combined.

The regime shift of 1992 and the unfolding of the "clean hands" anti-corruption campaign in northern Italy were accompanied by a national economic crisis, recognizable through rising unemployment, unsettling inflation, and a devalued lira. In contrast to the past, it was now the European monetary system and not the Italian Central Bank that pointed the way forward. And it did so in terms of the neoliberal principles of fiscal conservatism, cutbacks to the pension and welfare systems, encouragement of flexibility in labor markets, and the termination of the *Cassa per il Mezzogiorno,* or Development Fund for the South, caricatured as having squandered valuable resources. Palermo's poorest citizens would now be less wanted and cared for by the state. A report in the financial section of *La Repubblica* (June 21, 1999) correlates rising unemployment in the south and Sicily with the consequent declining level of public investment, which fell from 4.3 percent of GNP in 1980 to 1.3 percent in 1998.

A concurrent slowdown in new construction meant growing worker redundancy for much of Palermo. Because estimates of unemployment are based on persons registered at local unemployment offices, they exclude the many who have become discouraged and have dropped out of the labor force. At the same time, however, participation in the informal economy is not reported in the official statistics. Between these two lacunae, there are no accurate measures of unemployment. The estimates are nevertheless disturbing. *The Economist* (June 26, 1993) reported teenage joblessness at 50.4 percent for southern Italian boys, and 68.2 percent for girls, compared with 15.1 percent and 27 percent, respectively, in the north. In the course of our research, we heard the figure "from 25 to 40 percent unemployed" for Palermo overall, the "official" rate having climbed from 25.5 to 35 percent between 1981 and 1991 (the last census). In its "dossier" for the year 2000 ranking all the provinces of Italy on various economic and quality of life indicators, the newspaper *Il Sole-24 Ore* assigned the province of Palermo the rank of 100 out of 103 on the employment scale, stating that 28 percent of the workforce was in search of work (December 11, 2000). With 48 percent of its businesses failing for every 1,000 registered, Palermo Province ranked 96 out of 103 on business health.

To refer to Palermo's less privileged groups as "the" working class is misleading. Identified with blue collar rather than white collar jobs, they are often under- or unemployed. At the same time, many are thoroughly immersed in very small-scale, often off-the-books, entrepreneurial activities (see Pardo 1996). This is why we have adopted the expression "popular classes" *(il popolo)* or, alternatively, "working *classes,*" both of which convey a more open-ended and varied understanding of work. Whatever their label, it seems clear that if the *popolo* "prostitute themselves through the subtle channels of clientelism," there are good reasons (Vitale 1989: 94). Poor people depend on the mediation of others to obtain health insurance, housing, diplomas, licenses, opportunities, and jobs. Moreover, they seek these benefits for family members and friends as well as themselves. Secular and religious patronage systems sustain their livelihoods at the same time as they are suffused with reciprocal obligations—ideas about the right distribution of life's rewards and principles of equity. Both material and moral risks inhere in cutting loose from this system, even if it has been the integument of the mafia. For many in the popular classes, *spaccatura* not only seems demanding; it is an affront to common sense.

CONCLUSION

The capillary action of the antimafia process is less overt and visible than are processions and demonstrations, painted sheets and human chains. A form of "consciousness raising" with the attendant rearrangement of social relations, such action is nevertheless pivotal. Intellectuals, professionals, and others who engage in it have not only been nourished by social movement experience; they keep the movement going, greeting each demobilization with shared expressions of regret and mutual accountability, retarding the return to "normalcy." Most important, capillary action feeds the projects that advance the antimafia cause. Some of these projects are political, channeling both discourse and votes toward "clean" parties and candidates. Others are more broadly transformative, in a social and cultural sense. The large-scale projects for urban renewal and school reform, described in the next two chapters, would have been unimaginable without the support of dedicated citizens volunteering their time and broadcasting their enthusiasm. That these projects have also encountered obstacles in, especially, Palermo's poorest neighborhoods in no way diminishes these citizens' contribution.

CHAPTER 10

Recuperating the
Built Environment

Nothing better illustrates the hopes of the antimafia movement than its commitment to the recuperation of Palermo city, undoing the "savage" expansion of the periphery and shameful neglect of the historic core. From the first burst of activism in the early 1980s, the city's renewal has been a movement priority, both an emblem of the desired cultural changes and a test of the extent to which they are progressing. The recuperation of historical architecture in the old city center and the development of a wider urban plan anchor the rhetoric of "reversible destiny," pointing at once to physical and symbolic transformation.

Between the two world wars, modern architecture and urban planning were professionalized in Italy as the fascist regime, deeply engaged in social engineering, patronized architects and planners, harnessing them to the task of remaking, managing, and "civilizing" society. Bold strategies of expropriation, zoning regulation, confiscation, and the redefinition of eminent domain went forward; private as well as public investors in large and ambitious projects worried little about the rights of anyone in the way (Booth 1997: 152–74; von Henneberg 1996). Although today's antimafia professionals work under the very different conditions of a parliamentary democracy, some of the dynamics affecting their vision and its implementation are similar to the dynamics of ordering the urban environment in those long ago days. In particular, today's planners continue to view architecture and planning as instruments to reshape society, "a pedagogical project" (von Henneberg 1996: 98).

Through the built form, the tenets of modern civilization—the values of
civil society—are to be not only taught but "carved in stone."

PLANNING OPPORTUNITIES AND THEIR LIMITATIONS

Private speculation overwhelmed urban planning in post–World War II
Palermo, confronting the city's growing population with an absurd
deficit of low-cost housing as luxury apartments went begging. Not even
the 1968 earthquake could disrupt this pattern, however much it exposed the crumbling health of both people and buildings in the already
bomb-damaged historic center. Funds from the *Cassa per il Mezzogiorno,* intended to cover earthquake relief, demolition, and rehabilitation, flowed toward speculative investments in the periphery while designated contractors were allowed to auction off rehabilitated properties
to private buyers (Chubb 1982: 151–54). In 1973 the City Council reacted, seeking to reassert a public interest in "the historical-artistic patrimony of the *Centro Storico* [historic center] and . . . the preservation
of its existing socioeconomic fabric through provision of public housing" (ibid.: 155). Sadly, however, the DC administration, paralyzed by
clientelism and internal disputes, squandered a substantial public investment for related public works—roughly $108 million from the re-
gional government and the national public housing authority, ICAP, followed by an additional $500 million. "Incredibly," writes Chubb, "with
such extensive financial resources available . . . at the beginning of 1981
not a single project had yet been initiated" (ibid.: 156).

By an ironic twist, the resulting *scempio,* or "sack," of Palermo rendered its hollowed out core a planner's dream. Many buildings are
empty, partially empty, or occupied by squatters. These include persons,
often new immigrants, who pay no rent because owners want no responsibility for the condition of their buildings. Notwithstanding the
ravages of vandals and weather, these structures excite the visionary urbanist to imagine new uses for the available space. Because many of the
empty buildings are city-owned following their condemnation, planners
need not engage the cumbersome instruments of rezoning and expropriation to effect dramatic change.

Whether the Rognoni–La Torre Law constitutes a further advantage
is another question. Passed in 1982 shortly after the murder of dalla
Chiesa and modified in the 1990s, it obligates the state to sequester and
confiscate the assets of convicted mafiosi that were acquired through illicit activity and to recycle these assets into functions deemed "socially

useful."[1] Such a plan was enough, many believe, to motivate the assassination of Senator La Torre. Yet the law is a far cry from other historical instances when the confiscatory power of the state propelled deep social change, for example, the expropriation in Sicily in 1867 of ecclesiastical properties, whose sale at auction contributed to the consolidation of the new *civile* class and with it the rural mafia. As illustrated below, implementing the law is fraught with uncertainty.

Once a mafioso has been indicted, agents of the Ministry of Finance immediately move to sequester his assets, yet the transition from sequester to confiscation is hardly straightforward. In the summer of 1999, we visited the *Ufficio Compartamentale del Territorio* (Office of Confiscations), located off a dingy and creaking elevator in the ministry's regional headquarters. Admitted to a large room with files of paper piled high on several tables, we encountered four people huddled around a computer. Typical of the new culture of bureaucracy in Palermo, they were open with us, notwithstanding the fact that we had arrived unannounced (at first they thought we wanted to acquire a confiscated property). As we later learned, communications technology had just been installed in this office, and in the absence of technical support, the staff was uncertain about entering and retrieving data. Meanwhile the bulging files, an ocean of paper, threatened to drown them.

Each file had a mafioso's name handwritten across the top and contained the paperwork pertaining to his sequestered properties. In many of the three hundred or so cases, a multiplicity of assets was at stake— a "portfolio" of apartments or apartment buildings, land parcels, businesses, and stocks. Keeping track of them meant determining for each property whether or not it had been purchased with ill-gotten money, the value placed on it by the Finance Ministry's technical office, and the progress, or lack thereof, in rendering the asset "free" for subsequent use. According to the law, "free" means emptied of current tenants or users.

As many as twelve years might pass between the act of sequester and the final confiscation. Just for starters, mafiosi mislead the authorities by signing over what they own to others—often their wives. The Finance Guard, the ministry's police branch, may have difficulty locating sequestered residences, let alone assessing their value. An unwelcome presence in many neighborhoods, its agents encounter local *omertà*. Consider, too, the protests mounted by the employees of affected businesses. In one case, the tenants of a store, upon learning that they had to relocate because their landlord was a front for Totò Riina, wrote to the president of Italy: "We are victims [who] must lose our clientele built up piece by piece over twenty years, lay off two employees, and give up an activity that our son and our partner's son expected to inherit" (*Giornale di Sicilia,* August 25, 1999).

Active firms are run by court-appointed administrators until their eventual disposition, most probably to a workers' cooperative. Although by law, anyone with a criminal record is to be purged in the interim, this does not usually happen. Instead the administrators, in the interest of the firm's viability, alter as little as possible. When one of the four large Catania construction firms was seized, the workers struck, declaring the action a threat to their well-being. The businesses and real estate holdings of the most important mafiosi—say, the Salvo cousins—will only be confiscated, if at all, after years of litigation. In Italy as a whole, assets worth $3.4 billion were seized from organized crime figures between 1990 and 1997, compared with only $240 million that were actually confiscated (Jamieson 2000: 113). The list of properties actually confiscated in Palermo as of April 1999 totaled 213, the majority of them small apartments and plots of land. Perhaps, some argue, it would be better to sell the mafia's assets at auction, despite the risk that mafiosi would be among the bidders.

Once a property has at last been confiscated, the Ministry of Finance announces its availability to eligible institutions: the municipality where the assets are located and the forces of order—the police, the Carabinieri, and the Finance Guard, itself. The latter are eager to acquire suitable apartments in which to house their personnel, but the city of Palermo, already swamped by a glut of empty apartments, is more likely to offer residential spaces to voluntary associations for meetings or recreation. More to the point, these properties are not necessarily desirable. During the decade or so that elapses between sequester and confiscation, apartments easily fall into disrepair, making them a burden to their eventual owners even though the state is entitled to use any income they generate for basic maintenance. Because being a mafioso does not guarantee solvency, particularly in light of lawyers' fees and bad gambles in real estate or drug deals, many of the assets are also encumbered with debt. Most important, the parcels of land and apartments are frequently tenanted, more than likely with relatives or clients of the mafioso. Although the state is obliged to help all legal tenants of an affected building find another residence, the tenants, given sixty days' notice, often balk. Would anyone choose to live in or use an apartment formerly owned by a "man of honor" if relatives of his had been evicted, or if they lived downstairs? Similar obstacles surround the recycling of rural properties, which, if they are embedded in a suburb, can be turned over by the city to volunteer groups running sports programs, drug treatment centers, bocci courts, "pocket gardens," or programs for exprisoners, organized into cooperatives.

Between deterioration, debts, and the threat of retaliation, the state is already accumulating properties that no one wants. As of 1999, the city of Palermo had rejected about a third of the real estate offered to it by the Finance Ministry—a rejection rate so high that the prefect complained, after which a few more properties were taken on as a "moral obligation." At the time of our interviews, however, the assets of a major construction impresario—some thirty to forty buildings in an affluent section of Palermo north—were awaiting an expected confiscation order from the Supreme Court. Several had been built for scholastic use, others as office buildings, with the city as the prime tenant for many years. Were Palermo to acquire these buildings outright, it would mean a substantial savings of rent in the municipal budget. Here, informants felt, the La Torre Law might really make a difference.

RECUPERATING THE HISTORIC CENTER

When the Rognoni–La Torre Law was passed in 1982, it captured the hopes of antimafia activists, who viewed it as evidence, finally, of the state's commitment to profound social change. Particularly to activists on the left, the provisions that enabled prosecutors to follow the money and confiscate property seemed imbued with revolutionary potential. Given the relative insignificance of the confiscations to date, its effects lie in the future. Easier to gauge are the plans, funded by the city, regional, national, and European levels of government, to address the problems of the historic center and wider metropolitan area. As of December 1999, Sicily as a whole expected approximately $12 billion from the EU for infrastructure and services during the first seven years of the twenty-first century (*Giornale di Sicilia,* December 3, 1999).

To our surprise, we discovered that planning for the recuperation of the historic center predated the first Orlando administration and the Palermo *Primavera*. Indeed, although the vision of Palermo as a mini New York prevailed throughout the *scempio*, the Prague model was also there, just below the surface. Palermo is, after all, an Italian city, and Italy—sometimes characterized as "postmodern before there was postmodernism"—was, from the 1950s, a source point for influential schools

of historic preservation and the revival of the city as a "theater of memory" (Ellin 1996). Acknowledging this legacy, Palermo hosted a European conference on "reconstructing the city" in opposition to industri-
alized architecture in 1978 (Le Corbusier was by then redefined as a
"destroying angel"; see ibid.: 15–20). Under the pressure of events, and
notwithstanding its reputation for corruption, in 1979 the (DC) city administration created a commission of four architect-planners representing the electorally successful political parties. Eventually nicknamed the
Quattro Saggi (Four Wise Men), their task was to develop a project for
the restoration of the historic center. Giuseppe Samonà, a Palermitan by
birth but for most of his career a leader of the Venetian school of architecture, was asked to be the head. Samonà was a Communist, but at age
eighty, the Christian Democrats who appointed him gambled that he
would be inactive, producing only meager results. The other appointees
were Samonà's former student Giancarlo De Carlo, also representing
the Communist Party, Umberto Di Cristina for the PSI, and Annamaria
Sciarra Borzì for the DC. As it turned out, even Samonà was surprised
by the capacity of his natal city, so beautiful and yet so damaged, to galvanize his interest and passion. Collaborating with both De Carlo and
his son, who taught architecture at the University of Palermo, he engaged
a large number of local architects, engineers, students, and faculty in the
production of a plan for revitalizing the old center. It was their hope to
"find a role and a significance for architecture (and urban planning) that
connected with an idea of general transformation" (Ajroldi, Cannone,
and De Simone 1994: 10–11).

The collected correspondence between Samonà and De Carlo suggests
that they labored in an irritating and sometimes desperate political context. By November 1981, De Carlo, fed up, wrote that he was accumulating "many good reasons for not continuing to occupy myself with
Palermo." He was convinced, he said, that the city administrators believed (and hoped) that the work of the "Four Wise Men" would amount
to absolutely nothing. "Whatever we do," De Carlo wrote, "will be
swallowed up . . . and made irrelevant by the tremendous force of immobility that pervades the city." Samonà, however, countered his colleague's wish to bail out with two arguments: the intense fascination of
"this ancient city," and "the good will and enthusiasm of at least seventy
percent of our collaborators" (ibid.: 189–90).

A plan was completed in 1982. Although approved by the municipal
administration in 1983, it was only general and "directive"—not sufficiently detailed to be operational. Samonà died shortly after the plan was

submitted. The Orlando administration, taking power in 1985, assigned the task of rendering an operational plan to an interdepartmental team of university faculty and students. Delays at this level confirmed the new mayor's suspicion that the planning process was contaminated by the old corrupt relations between politics and the construction industry. After all, two of the commissioners were affiliated with political parties, the DC and the Socialists, in which mafia influence was legion. Moreover, all of the commissioners had been appointed by the administration that had presided over the *scempio*. Perhaps most telling, the University of Palermo was itself much compromised by real estate and construction maneuvers made during the building boom and by the scandalous neglect of its own historic buildings. Orlando's impatience culminated in the late night meeting of June 1987 where the municipal *giunta* supplanted the authority of the City Council and voted to engage another team of architects and planners, authorizing them to operationalize the Samonà plan. This time, *all* of the players were outsiders, "none of them Sicilian, to prevent conflicts of interest," he later wrote (2001: 126). Pierluigi Cervellati, the chief architect of the restoration of Bologna's historic center, was called in to be the coordinator, along with Leonardo Benevolo, Italo Insolera, and a Spaniard, Sola Morales, who later dropped out. Meanwhile, announcements were made that henceforth, priority would go to northern Italian and continental firms in all contract bidding.

Cervellati, of course, had his own ideas, which superseded those of Samonà. Consistent with his renovation of Bologna, he envisioned a pristine, historicist recreation of Palermo, guided by maps and land registries from the 1870s and following the logic of "integral conservation." This means providing for not only the renovation of existing structures but the reconstruction of fully or partially destroyed buildings. Where documentation—for example, in the form of old photographs—exists, reconstruction is to be "philological," replicating what can be known. An absence of documentation is not a license to innovate, however; in this case, the plan mandates a "typological" reconstruction. Samonà's approach, open to experiments in contemporary architecture, was more flexible (see Trombino 1998). According to its vision, ruins would be cleared away to open up more piazzas and gardens and there would be international design competitions for new buildings to bridge empty spaces. An example of the differing approaches was a debate over the Palazzo Bonagia, a bombed out ruin on the Via Alloro whose breathtaking divided stone staircase, set off by Baroque balustrades and arches, remained intact. In Samonà's version, the staircase was to be preserved as the theatrical accouterment to a fanciful modern building, whereas Cervellati proposed reconstructing the entire palazzo.

Committed to fostering an urban discipline, Cervellati would empower the municipality's Technical Office to decide on the street-level uses of buildings. In contrast, Samonà's plan recommended observing and validating the patterns of use that spontaneously emerged. In the Cervellati approach, intrusive modern buildings, deemed out of place amid the venerable *palazzi,* would be demolished, among them a public school. Samonà would at most have eliminated a nineteenth-century palm grove that impedes the sight-line to the medieval Norman palace. Cervellati's words are telling: "The . . . streets and blocks, the physical consistency of the buildings, the destinations of use and the habits of those who live there"—all fall under the strategy of conservation (Cervellati 1996: 121–22). Such rigor is consistent with the practice of *spaccatura*—a clean break—aiming, as it does, to bring back a distant past while erasing as many scars of the postwar period as possible. Orlando and his associates appreciated this, believing that it placed a firm brake on the destructive course of the *scempio*. In a 1996 interview Emilio Arcuri, by then the commissioner for the historic center, explained to us that Palermo needs a "conservative," even "rigid," urban plan, preferably implemented by northern Italians, so as to avoid recreating the atmosphere of clientelism. With Samonà's ideas, he said, there was the risk of a synergism between fanciful new buildings and disgusting old relations of money, power, and the mafia.

Arcuri believed that, except for the schoolteachers, "the entire city was against us" after the late night meeting. Although reluctant to criminalize all of the hostile citizens, he depicted them as detesting rules, even though rules are essential. Indeed, our conversation was punctuated by a disapproving glance toward his office window, through which we could see, in the street below, an unlicensed street vendor hawking *stighioli*—the salty and heavily peppered roasted innards that Palermitans enjoy. Declaring the scene both "abusive" and "typical," he portrayed himself and the mayor as "men of state battling inside of a revolution." And this without mentioning the young men who raise race horses clandestinely in some of the popular quarters, harness them to surreys at five or six o'clock on Sunday mornings, and race them on a nearby boulevard before a small crowd of bettors.

The professionals and students who made up the Samonà–De Carlo team feel that Orlando's *spaccatura* orientation unnecessarily closed off avenues of alliance between a broad range of antimafia forces, tarring too many good-willed persons with the brush of collusion. To them it was also short-sighted to stigmatize the university, as it is the most significant property holder and source of tenants in the entire historic center, after the Church and the military. Because the late night transfer of responsibility from the university to Cervellati occurred during the Palermo *Primavera,* however, the professionals who were thereby marginalized have been reluctant to speak out, fearing that to do so would be to "offer arguments to the mafia." Only in private do they lament the "extremist sectarianism" of the Orlando group, claiming it to be bad politics.

The Cervellati plan was prepared expeditiously, in 1989, but in 1990 Orlando entered into his disastrous tangle with the DC and was forced to resign the mayoralty, leading to three years (1990–93) in which the antimafia forces lost their momentum in City Hall. Even so, the plan was approved in 1991 at the municipal level and in 1993 at the regional level. In presenting it to public audiences, Cervellati insinuated that opponents were seeking to favor the infiltration of mafia interests in the restoration effort. Even if they were not, he argued, this would be the effect of their opposition (see Trombino 1998: 343). Municipal and regional officials were further pressured to approve the plan by widespread demonstrations and sit-ins on the part of various citizen groups—above all Greens and shopkeepers—and by the collapse of several buildings in the *centro storico,* one of which killed two persons (see Cannarozzo 1998).

FROM DECAY TO A WORK IN PROGRESS

In 1993, Orlando was reelected mayor on the *Rete* ticket. Following the regional government's approval of the Cervellati plan, his administration set up a special department for the *centro storico,* headed by Arcuri (now the vice-mayor). In addition to restoring monumental buildings for public use, it is charged with purchasing and refurbishing heavily damaged buildings as residences (Pirrera 1996: 107–10). The office also maintains city-owned properties in the historic center, green spaces, and spaces designated for parking. Funds from the state, region, city, private sources, and the European Union are funneled through it (ibid.: 110–12).[2]

The most dramatic proposals in the Cervellati plan have to do with restoring the Palermo waterfront. The multi-lane highway that now divides the *centro* from the coast is to be sunken below grade, an archaeological park created at the site of an ancient fortification, and long stretches of beachfront turned into pedestrian walkways. In preparation for the United Nations Convention on Organized Crime, the city broke up the Luna Park, dispersing its various entertainments to several new (and of course controversial) locations. The vista to the sea finally opened, grass-covered parkland and walkways appeared, lined with inviting benches. But ground has yet to be broken for reconfiguring the highway and amplifying underground parking.

In 1993, Palermo initiated projects for the restoration of six historic buildings and monuments. By spring 1999, 206 churches, monasteries, and palaces were wrapped in protective nets and scaffolding. The Department of the Historic Center had also launched projects to repave streets in the original stone, install new lighting, restore fencing, and engage in emergency maintenance, spending five times more in 1996 than in the three-year period 1990–93. In 1997, the outlay increased again (*Informa Palermo* 1999; *Città di Palermo* 1998). In official publications and on numerous public occasions, the city's political leaders have proudly drawn attention to a roster of transformations: the rehabilitated monuments and buildings around the Piazza Marina and its garden; a former convent turned into a middle school; another former convent become the headquarters of the Department of the Historic Center; a fifteenth-century *palazzo* reincarnated as the new Civic Gallery of Modern Art. They also tout the many historic neighborhoods where rubble and garbage have been removed and greenery introduced.

No longer a decaying jumble of masonry, central Palermo became a work in progress in the 1990s, as symbolized by the appearance of outdoor restaurants in theatrically suggestive (and formerly abandoned) piazzas. Middle-class people from Palermo north, many of them motivated by the antimafia spirit to explore their city's architectural patrimony, dine in them and relate the experience to others. Parking in the narrow, winding streets can be tenuous and it is wise to leave handbags at home. In some of the piazzas, poor children stare down at the open-air diners from surrounding balconies while teens on motorbikes hang out along the periphery. But notwithstanding these signs of an uneasy transformation, a sense of renewal and adventure prevails. In 1995, the city closed the ancient Corso Vittorio Emanuele (the *Cassaro*) to traffic on long summer weekends, encouraging its redefinition as a mall for strolling and shopping. Other experiments with pedestrianization have produced more aggravation than enthusiasm, but the *Cassaro* closing works, thanks, in part, to the participation of youth from the middle-class neighborhoods who have not, as yet, given their entire loyalty to the new McDonald's in Piazza Castelnuovo, the gateway to Palermo north.[3]

Two restorations have completely captured the public imagination: a vast sixteenth-century church, Santa Maria dello Spasimo, embedded in the heavily fortified wall that the Spanish viceroys erected near the Botanical Garden, and the Teatro Massimo opera house. Situated near the bombed out Piazza Magione, where both Falcone and Borsellino grew up, the Spasimo is a source of positive energy for the recuperation of one of the old city's most degraded, yet symbolically charged, neighborhoods. Here the city authorities discovered, almost by accident in 1986, that a miserable hospital housing the elderly indigent and insane since the nineteenth century had, as an adjoining wing, the ruined walls of an enormous sanctuary. Condemning and closing the hospital, a portion of which was crumbling, they mobilized regional funds, volunteers, and a specially created cooperative of exconvicts to remove rubble, research the history of the complex, and begin renovations. It was the time of the first Orlando administration, the energetic interventions of Letizia Battaglia and the Palermo *Primavera,* so hundreds of people were eager to lend a hand.

Several surprises ensued. The sanctuary turned out to be a thrilling architectural space with high pointed arches, beautiful umbrella-ribbed vaulting, Catalan Gothic carvings at the bases of graceful columns and pillars, and a shapely tree, growing where the pulpit had been (the roof over the nave having long since disappeared). Architectural historians reported that over the last five centuries the building has had a number of incarnations. The first inhabitants, an order of Olivetani, were forced out in 1573, when the structure was incorporated into a massive pentagonal fortification. Subsequently it became a theater, a grain warehouse, an armory for munitions, and finally a deposit for embellishments salvaged from churches bombed in World War II (see La Duca 1975: 27–29).

In its latest incarnation, the Spasimo is a favorite venue for warm weather cultural events, the Orlando administration having invested in enhanced lighting, parking, and security in the area. After an inaugural concert by Sicilian composer and cellist Giovanni Sollima on July 25, 1995, workmen, almost on a dare, began removing plaster from the courtyard of the hospital to find, underneath, the arches, pillars, and capitals of a sixteenth-century cloister. It is difficult to exaggerate the excitement that the entire complex has generated or the role it plays in the antimafia process. To quote Franceso Giambrone, the commissioner of culture in the mid-1990s, "Today both the Spasimo and the city are different . . . and these are two facts . . . of definitive achievement crossing a line of no return" (quoted in La Fisca and Palazzo 1996: 9).

The Teatro Massimo, the second example of a symbolically freighted restoration, is in some ways the opposite of the Spasimo. Far from losing its urban presence under curtained layers of subsequent construction, or by sinking into oblivion, Europe's third largest opera house continued to sit majestically on its site, where the Via Maqueda comes to an end and Palermo north begins. Closed in 1974 for renovations mandated by the fire code, for twenty-three years it never reopened, a supremely visible and daily reminder that Palermo was a city where building inspectors and contractors took the state's money and avoided doing the work. When the Fenice opera house in Venice burned to the ground in February 1996, the Massimo was still in a state of partial repair, its grand walls of golden sandstone surrounded by an ugly corrugated barricade and its interior known to be suffering from a badly leaking roof. Cynics in Palermo immediately predicted that the newly burned Fenice would be rebuilt and reopened before the Massimo.

The shame of the Massimo rankled, and after the Fenice fire Arcuri and Giambrone went into high gear to ensure the theater's reopening by May 16, 1997, the centenary of its inauguration. Two concerts were held that night, and although restoration work was not complete, by the following April it was possible to initiate a season of opera with Luciano Pavarotti in *Aida*. Unlike the Spasimo, whose rebirth is intimately tied to that of an entire popular quarter and which has become a gathering place for a very wide swath of civil society, the Massimo's surrounds and audiences are, for the most part, celebrity-centered and upper middle-class. Moreover, some antimafia critics, accusing the city administrators of hastening the theater's reopening so as to coincide with Orlando's re-election campaign, imagine that compromises were made in the speed-up effort. Nevertheless, had the eyesore of a fence not come down and the imposing doors swung open, the Massimo would stand as a "monument to corruption"—a powerful visual contradiction to civil society.

THE DREAM OF REPOPULATION

Thanks above all to the Massimo and the Spasimo, as well as to the two hundred other renovations, central Palermo once again supports a night life. But the planners also envision its repopulation, its restoration as a viable and vibrant residential area. The center is of course still home to many people. Yet its 23,000 residents in 1996 were fewer than the 50,000 of 1974 and many fewer than the 200,000 who lived there at the end of the war (Chubb 1982: 152; Lo Dato 2000: 16; Lo Piccolo 1996:

70). No reliable figures exist by which to estimate the number of documented and undocumented immigrants from Africa, Asia, and Eastern Europe who occupy some of the empty spaces; Palermo as a whole was thought to have *around* 10,000 in the late 1990s, down from 19,000 earlier in the decade because of migration northward (Booth and Cole 1999: 192–93).[4]

Here and there a noble or gentry family continues to inhabit some of the dozens of rooms of an inherited *palazzo*, seeking funds from tourists and state programs to keep walls and ceilings from falling in on them. Pouring their own personal savings into the conservation of majolica floors, hand-painted silk wallpaper, Murano chandeliers, and coral-studded chapels, they dwell amid ballrooms, dining rooms, and salons whose scale and grandeur mock the intimacy of everyday modern life. (The eighteenth-century chandelier in the ballroom of the still-inhabited Palazzo Alliata, with ninety-nine arms, was until recently the largest in Europe.) In the winter months, the only warm spot is the circle of plush chairs around the hearth.[5] Meanwhile, other undivided *palazzi* are in the hands of absentee owners who are considerably less involved. In a press conference, Arcuri expressed his impatience with them for lacking a "culture of maintenance," irresponsibly depending on the city to secure their buildings against further deterioration (*Giornale di Sicilia,* December 3, 1999).

The plan for the *centro storico* anticipates the "return" of fifty thousand residents, who, according to officials in the Department of the Historic Center, are expected to be middle-class. There has been a corresponding cessation of new investment in centrally located public housing. At the same time, these officials are aware of the class and racial polarizations that have characterized restoration projects in many other cities, including Bologna, where, despite the best efforts of the planner, Cervellati, the center is now as costly as it is gorgeous (Légé 1993). Palermo's gentrification, they admonish, should not be allowed to threaten poor people already living in the center, including the recent immigrants who now inhabit the most degraded spaces. If anything, many believe that central Palermo presents an opposite risk, that it will continue to be home mainly to an impoverished and indigent *popolo,* a handful of eccentric aristocrats, and successive waves of transients.

There are many obstacles to resettlement, one of which is surely racism. A bus driver we interviewed near his home in an outlying *borgata* is reluctant to return to the center, where he still owns an apartment, because of stories he has heard from fellow drivers who cover the center routes at night when "only immigrants" ride the busses. "If just a few had come," he said, "integration would have been possible. It's the difference between the rain and a storm." The wealthy owner-occupant of a grand *palazzo* told us of a friend who had decided against restoring his family's grand home and moving back because there were too few white people living near it. Yet, in part because immigrant housing has been so readily available in Palermo—also because many immigrants eventually move north—the city has so far manifested considerably less racial tension than other cities of Italy and Europe (see Cole 1997). The wealthy interviewee and his wife were quick to defend their neighbors. Whereas others considered their street noise a "nuisance," they preferred to "understand it" as the inevitable consequence of living in apartments without buzzers and having to shout from the street to be let in.

The grand *palazzi* constitute another obstacle to repopulation. According to the Cervellati plan, there are nearly 350 such buildings in the four quarters of the historic center, most of them divided up and/or condemned, a few of them still intact. The plan envisions adaptive reuse of their interior spaces, for example, as offices, child care centers, and cultural facilities, so long as these do not disturb the "original" layout of the "noble" floors. Yet some of the rooms on these floors are large enough to hold entire apartments. The conservative restoration of such spaces poses huge functional and economic challenges, not the least of which is creating real estate that has a market value.

Most of the *palazzi* are not the responsibility of a single owner. Irretrievably fragmented, they have been carved up by multiple owners, many of them absentee, who hold title to the individual apartments, as well as the myriad street-level spaces—former stables and storerooms. Some of these owners are affluent, but most lack both educational and financial resources. The Cervellati plan offers precise guidelines regarding a range of interventions, from simple maintenance, to demolition, to restoration, to restructuring. In the case of nearly destroyed buildings, it poses the alternatives of building to conform to earlier documents and photographs or, if these are nonexistent, to a "type." Yet, to apply for the available grants and loans to make these changes happen is daunting: experts must be called in to draw detailed plans and compile lists of materials, colors, and finishes to be used. The application packet also requires narratives and photographs detailing past and present conditions, as well as descriptions of how the project will articulate with adjacent apartments and buildings. Multiple copies of supporting documents attesting to family size, income, and other requirements have to be vetted

by lawyers, stamped by notaries, and postmarked by certain deadlines—
and are turned back if not in good order (Cervellati 1996: 161–66)—all
of which is not to mention the rules of eligibility, complicated, until very
recently, by the planners' commitment to staving off speculative investment lest the door be opened to persons in *odore di mafia.*

For example, financial contributions are earmarked for persons who
are not "construction entrepreneurs"; owners can apply for one project,
only; and "absolute priority" is given to current residents. Nonresidents,
if awarded funds to restore an apartment, are obliged to live in it for ten
years following the completion of the work, abide by a rent cap if they
rent it instead, or repay the contribution (Cervellati 1996: 158–61). This
bias in favor of resident-owners renovating single dwellings takes little
account of the parceling out, filling in, and cobbling together that has so
affected the small and grand *palazzi* of central Palermo for over a century. Boundaries of ownership vary from floor to floor within single ed-
ifices, creating unpredictable, even fanciful, "trees" of responsibility that
are difficult to understand or analyze (Cannarozzo 1996: 40–41; Lo Piccolo 1996). In such circumstances, it makes little sense for the owners
of single apartments to upgrade, however cheaply they can acquire the
money to do so. In the words of one critic, "the recuperation of an
apartment, when the entire building is in decay, from the foundation to
the roof . . . is clearly not practicable" (Cannarozzo 1998: 176). Owners of small properties, many of them absentee, have so far viewed
restoration as neither feasible nor worthwhile (Leone 1998: 354).
"Piecemeal interventions of little consequence" are, alas, the result
(Cannarozzo 1998: 176).

We know of a small four-story *palazzino* that was condemned and
emptied after the 1968 earthquake, with the city purchasing two of the
four apartments. Structural cracks dating to the Allied bombs had
widened to the point of endangering the inhabitants. Under the Samonà
plan, the building was to be leveled for a parking lot, but the Cervellati
plan calls for its restoration. Inspired by this, the owner of the remaining apartments approached the city with the idea of jointly applying for
financial aid to restore the entire building. Impeding any plan is the fact
that this building, precarious as it is, props up an adjacent apartment
house, which, although still inhabited, is also cracking. How could a
restoration begin without removing the densely criss-crossed beams that
lace these decrepit structures together at the level of their third and
fourth floors? And who will organize their various, mainly absentee,
owners to participate?

In conversations with people about the long-term prospects for the *centro storico,* topics like absentee ownership, buildings that collapse, squatters, illegal landlords who collect rents from apartments they do not own, the use of empty and unclaimed space for raising horses and concealing hot goods, come up, as does the fact that no person is an island when it comes to making decisions about where, and how, to live. On one of our walks, we met an elderly man in front of a sixteenth-century *palazzo* facing the beautiful Oratorio of Santa Cita, recently restored by the city. He owned an apartment in the *palazzo* and was eager to see it renovated but was cynical about the prospects because, even though the owners of most of the other apartments were his relatives, they could not agree on a plan. Hours upon hours of meetings had resulted in some of his kinfolk becoming more, not less, intransigent about committing their own funds.

The tendency for kin to live in close proximity to one another contributes to immobility in the outlying neighborhoods, too, but for a different reason. Notwithstanding the forced resettlement of many Palermitans after the earthquake, by now their disrupted kin-clusters have been rewoven. For some family members to return to the historic center and others to remain in the periphery would mean hours of commuting in miserable traffic just to stay in touch.

And so, the submission of applications for grants and loans got off to a slow beginning. From 1994 until March 1998, the city considered 549 applications and accepted 309, mainly for single apartments, rooftops, or parts of condominia (*Città di Palermo* 1998: 13–18). Such low numbers hardly represented "a new regime" (Leone 1998: 346). Yet momentum was gathering, especially for young people. In the summer of 1999, we calculated that 36 percent of all real estate listings for two-room apartments, attractive to middle-class singles and newlyweds, were in the historic neighborhoods, as were 23 percent of all listings for three-room apartments. At the other end of the scale, 25 percent of apartments larger than seven rooms had historic center addresses. Middle-sized apartments, most suitable for middle-class families, were far less plentiful.

Critics of the Cervellati plan argue that it does not sufficiently appreciate the vast differences between historic Palermo and historic Bologna. Whereas Bologna was home to a large and diverse range of "middle classes"—artisans, merchants, professionals—who built themselves decent, if modest houses over many centuries, Palermo's built environment expresses a polarized class structure. Few intermediate buildings bridge

the gap between the exaggerated major architecture of the church and nobility and the continuously fragmenting spaces of the poor (Cannarozzo
1998: 176). In his concern "to withstand a hoard of speculators," Cervellati may also have discouraged the very people upon whom repopulation
depends (ibid.: 176–77). A better approach would be to promote private
restorations, help people jump through the hoops of applying for loans
and grants, and intervene to organize multiple nonresident owners for
projects that are collective. In evaluating applications, say the critics,
preference should shift to whole buildings, even if the applicants intend,
in the end, to rent them rather than live in them. In fact, the Office of the
Historic Center has recently moved in just these directions.

Typical of the antimafia process, leaders are damned if they do and
damned if they don't. An equally damning criticism circulating among
activists is that the department has already caved in to past practice. By
focusing so much attention on the Spasimo project and the adjacent Piazza Magione, it created an island of promise for investors who now include individuals and cooperatives with ties to the city government.
Contractors *in odore di mafia* are rumored to be involved; even if the
contractors are clean, they have surely had to subcontract to tainted
smaller firms. People on all sides of these debates hope that the recuperated historic center will, in the end, be more than a theatrical 250
hectares, full of remembrances of the past but empty of everyday life.
In such a scenario, *palermitani* would offer up their patrimony to
tourists, to enjoy it themselves only on weekends. The trajectory is still
in the balance.

THE MORASS OF THE MASTER PLAN

While Cervellati and his partners were engaged in developing a plan for
the historic center, the Orlando administration charged them with producing an urban plan—a *Piano Regolatore Generale,* or PRG—for the
city as a whole. No such plan had existed since the "mafioso PRG" of
1962. According to law, if the new PRG developed by Cervellati was not
approved with dispatch, the 1962 plan would continue to set the parameters for urban development.

Cervellati's plan divides Palermo into eight subcities called *circo-
scrizioni,* each with its own nucleus for offices and shopping and its own
identity, reinforced by local buildings, gardens, and monuments of architectural interest. Following the administrative elections of November
1997, the coordination of libraries, cultural activities, sports, and social

services was devolved to these new entities. Continued administrative decentralization, plus the projected construction of surface and underground parking lots connecting to new trams and busses, is expected to ameliorate some of the city's traffic problems. Envisioned is an eventual change in the habits of Palermo's citizens, who, as things stand now, prefer their cars to public transportation and, except for the ritualized evening *passeggiata,* are not fond of walking. Indeed, walking is difficult in the city, not least because the exploding number of cars has led drivers to park them on the sidewalks as well as in the streets. In the spirit of imagining new cultural practices surrounding transportation, the PRG also provides for three hundred kilometers of bicycle paths along the coast.[6]

The most important difference between the 1962 plan and the new PRG is the latter's assumption that Palermo is overbuilt, will not grow in citizenry, and must therefore consolidate and curate what it has. Not only does a portion of the cement already laid down stand empty; more spaces will open up through the ongoing recuperation of the *centro storico.* Sealing the argument is a staggering datum: national standards of urbanism dictate that a city of Palermo's size (700,000 inhabitants) should have 12,600,000 cubic meters devoted to "services"—schools, parking, public amenities, parks, and gardens—or approximately 18 cubic meters per person. In Palermo, such services are allotted only 2,485,000 cubic meters, or 3.55 cubic meters per person.[7] The PRG proposal for closing this gap is to consider outlying parkland—the *Favorita* with its 135 hectares, the basin of the Oreto River with its 164 hectares, and Monte Pellegrino, the circus tent promontory that frames Palermo's harbor, with its 771 hectares—as part of the formula, inflating the cubic meters of "service space" per person to 15.5. These, and any other green expanses, including all agricultural lands still in the city limits, should be defined as no longer potentially buildable under any circumstances. The residual agrarian properties need not be expropriated; they can continue to be cultivated by private owners. But the PRG interdicts these owners from selling them for development. In other words, the plan would put a halt to the driving force of its 1962 predecessor—the subdivision and cementification of what was formerly green (Cervellati 1995).

Two zones of expansion in the city's outskirts are flash points for this dramatic shift in public policy: Pizzo Sella and Ciaculli. Pizzo Sella, or "Saddle Point," is the south-facing slope of Monte Gallo, a prominent mountain along the coast, visible to the north from all of Palermo. One night in 1978 the Building Commission surreptitiously granted 314 per-

mits to build small "villas" or single-family homes at high elevations on
this site, even though it was officially zoned for "agriculture." A local
construction company called Sicilcalce, allied with none other than
Michele Greco, did the building, then sold the villas to Calcestruzzi, the
Ravenna company of Raul Gardini, represented in Sicily by mafiosi (see
fig. 18).[8] Many innocent, as well as not so innocent, people became the
owners, little imagining that between 1993 and 1998 investigators
would learn that Pizzo Sella was a laundromat for drug profits (*Giornale
di Sicilia,* January 30, 2000).

From the outset, antimafia activists called for the villas' demolition.
Constructed on steep and treeless terrain, they are considered to have ruined the panorama of Monte Gallo. Like the Massimo before it was renovated, they constitute a daily visual reminder of corruption and illegal-
ity. Lengthy court battles, fiercely supported by the *Coordinamento
Antimafia,* in which Pizzo Sella was often referred to as the "hill of dishonor" and the houses on it the "Michele Greco houses," culminated in
November 1999 with seventeen parties to the transactions, public officials among them, receiving sentences totaling thirty years. The court
also levied fines and an order that all of the villas be demolished. Bulldozers have already leveled a few of them, their owners, if they bought

Figure 18. The "hill of dishonor" with abusive "houses of Michele Greco."
Photograph by Alessandro Fucarini, Labruzzo Agenzia, Palermo.

in good faith, counseled to constitute themselves as a "civil party" and
seek restitution in the courts from those responsible. Instead, they have
joined to sue the city for what they call "justice that is unjust." What
does it mean, one owner asked the press, to call this "the 'hill of dishonor' when I, more green than the Greens, have honored it by planting
pines that now reach six meters?" (*Giornale di Sicilia,* January 30,
2000).

Had the PRG of Cervellati been in place at the time, Pizzo Sella would
never have been violated. Nor would the many orchards and vineyards
that rise up along the foothills of the Conca d'Oro to the west and south.
Bringing them back to their verdant past is of course no longer feasible,
but the plan does explicitly define some six hundred to eight hundred
hectares near the hamlet of Ciaculli, an area historically controlled by
mafiosi, as an "agricultural park." On land confiscated from the Grecos,
small farmers are to cultivate mandarin oranges for international markets and make the landscape accessible for passive recreation. According to a technical report commissioned by the City Council, the purpose
of this proposed "peri-urban agricultural park" is to "rehabilitate" the
relationship between the city and the countryside, provide work for
farmers, improve the quality of their products, promote consciousness of
Palermo's environmental patrimony, valorize the landscape, enhance
biodiversity, and enable recreation (*Modello di gestione agricola* 1997).
In preparation, the European Union's "Programme Life 94" underwrote
an association of commercial promoters and a cooperative of one hundred cultivators. Additional support came from the Agricultural School
of the University of Palermo, which initiated a biodiversity museum in a
restored farm building where past and present vegetation of the Conca
d'Oro began to be exhibited. Meanwhile, the city promised to subsidize
the water for irrigation and pay for tour guides. Looking ahead, advocates envisioned removing the territory of Ciaculli from the mafia and
saving it from cement (but see below).

Among its other significant provisions, the Cervellati PRG proposes
to restore the waterfront, turning Palermo back toward the sea. (We
have already noted how this would be accomplished in the historic center: submerge the waterfront highway under parkland.) Sports facilities,
marinas, and a new secondary port are proposed for the shoreline to the
south; recuperation and historic preservation for the northern industrial,
fishing, and resort communities of Acquasanta, Arenella, Addaura, and
Mondello. Of special interest is the PRG's attention to large-scale buildings throughout the metropolitan area whose purposes have run their

course. These include some of the real estate owned by the three largest institutional actors—the Church, the military, and the university—as well as the now defunct Lolli railroad station, a chemicals factory in Arenella, the old Ducrot furniture plant in Zisa, an immense residential mental hospital with its surrounding campus, and the former slaughterhouse. In each case, an imaginative new use or uses is suggested, with the goal of making the property in question a pole of attraction for the decentralized "submunicipality" in which it is located. Tourist shops, artists' studios, exhibition spaces, concert halls, antique markets, and galleries are mentioned. Thirteen of the Ducrot manufacturing sheds in the Zisa neighborhood have already been turned over to such uses, generating stable employment for 130 persons.[9] Most remarkably, the plan takes up the case of the Ucciardone, which has recently been superseded by the huge new Pagliarelli prison complex located on the ring road (see fig. 19). Hard to demolish, this nineteenth-century fortress ought to remain as a monument, it is suggested—possibly a "monument-memorial to itself." Noting that, over the "long 1980s" there was a greater media presence at the Ucciardone than at the Cathedral, Cervellati proposes with tongue in cheek that it could become a "museum of the mafia" (Cervellati 1995: 52).

Figure 19. The "Hotel of the Mafia"—the Ucciardone prison. Photograph by Jane Schneider.

To the environmentalist constituencies of the antimafia movement, the 1995 PRG encapsulates the most progressive concepts of urban planning—decentralization, conservation of nature, "sustainable development," quality of life, and values of neighborhood and community. In Cervellati's words, "If we block expansion, we can dedicate energy and resources to 'constructing' the 'already constructed' . . . to curating the riches we already have." One might even imagine demolishing a few things "because they are offensive to a civic asset"—to a panorama, for example (1995: 68–70). Others, including antimafia activists whose formation has been more red than green, see the plan as utopian, an unrealistic and arbitrary attempt to impose values, subdivisions, and transportation practices that are alien to local life. The "eight cities" notion, for example, dictates boundaries "arrived at by extemporaneous criteria," at times in violation of existing *quartieri* (Cannarozzo 1998: 168). Over the years, around fifty historical *borgate* have been incorporated into Palermo without diluting the identity of their respective residents. Indeed, minor dialect differences continue to be associated with these different neighborhoods as does the tendency for those who live in them to use the expression *scendere in città* (go down to the city) when headed for the center. That they would be amenable to identifying with a much larger *circoscrizione,* or to viewing the "eight Palermos" as equivalent "cities," seems unlikely.

The fiercest polemics reflect uncertainty about the role to be played by the construction industry in the new Palermo—the industry that has defined the city, its urbanscape as well as its economy, since World War II. Over and above the Orlando policy of *spaccatura,* according to which public contracts are to go to northern Italian and foreign contractors, there is now a law requiring any companies bidding jobs to present a certificate from the Prefecture that they are not presently under investigation or indictment. After the emergency of 1992, the city also set up a "committee for securing public order" to discuss and act on reports of the police and Carabinieri engaged in on-site monitoring of construction projects. The parties to a project must sign "protocols" of commitment to transparency and legality. At the same time, "constructing the already constructed," restoring what is there while not moving on, means shedding a substantial number of construction jobs.

In marked contrast to the quick adoption under public pressure of the plan for the historic center, approval of the new PRG has not been forthcoming. Hastily prepared with the intention of allowing planners to respond to public debate, the initial draft had to be redrawn to a closer scale and was superficial in places. Once in motion, the public process yielded many more corrections and objections than anticipated. Most serious, the planners felt compelled to reject most of the specific requests from "interested citizens" on the grounds that they violated the plan's "no-growth" intent. According to critics, numerous rejected variances were then incorporated into the plan before the mayoral election of November 1997, without the planners' knowledge.

Shortly after Orlando's re-election, the fledgling museum in Ciaculli mysteriously caught fire, after which the city did not renew the contract with the ten or so members of the cooperative it had engaged for "socially useful" work. Around the same time, an unknown person or persons killed the dogs belonging to the cooperative's leader. Again the city retreated, failing to support this leader as co-op members began drifting into relationships with an alternative local "boss." Perhaps, critics fear, the city leaders are not happy to have the Grecos as antagonists.

For reasons that are "unclear," the PRG was not delivered to the various involved parties—offices of the regional government as well as the City Council—in a timely way. Advocates of the plan on the council accused the Orlando administration of no longer being "transparent"; the administration, for its part, blamed an "occult regime," desirous of continuing to overbuild the hillsides, for pulling strings with regional authorities behind the scenes (*La Repubblica,* December 17, 2000). As of this writing, final approval remains uncertain, with the possibility that the city will revert to the permissive (even if recently amended) 1962 plan, causing Cervellati and Benevolo to distance themselves from the planning process. In the alarmist words of a spokesperson for the *Rifondazione Comunista* (a militant offshoot of the former Communist Party), "the mafia is again ready to sack the territory" (*Giornale di Sicilia,* January 23, 2000).

Meanwhile, a new initiative has unfolded, sponsored by the Ministry of Public Works in Rome and called Operation PRUSST (Territorial Programs for Urban Renewal and Sustainable Development). Based on public-private partnerships, with the private element constituting at least a third of the investment, its goal is to promote tourist and commercial development—hotels, movie complexes, shopping and recreational centers, parking lots, and so on—where possible cleaning up polluted rivers and abandoned industrial sites. Critics detect an eventual challenge to all the protected areas of the PRG. The remaining small industrial firms in Palermo also seem vulnerable, their owners tempted to give up on manufacturing, lay off workers, and sell the land for new ventures. But supporters, including Orlando and Arcuri, look forward to the honest administration of PRUSST funds, with contracts subject to the prefect's review, and the revival of construction jobs. From their perspective, the Palermo of today has decisively transcended the crises of inertia, incapacity, and paralysis born of the entrenched corruption that overwhelmed it in the past.

CONCLUSION

As would be true of any work in progress, contradictions abound in Palermo's recuperation. Although the Rognoni–La Torre law has so far produced rather piecemeal effects, the symbolic value of confiscating the mafia's assets is considerable, not least for energizing the clearance of Pizzo Sella. Similarly, the recuperation of the historic center offers a mixed picture. The city is bringing churches and palaces, stone-paved streets and piazzas back to life after decades in which they languished. So far an initiative to build a complex of "smart-wired" municipal buildings on what is now a "Mediterranean fairground" north of the Ucciardone has been defeated, ensuring greater municipal occupancy of renovated *palazzi* in the center, and thereby more clients for the center's new amenities. Restaurants, bars, shops, and several new or refurbished hotels have begun to attract foreign visitors. A few restorations—in particular the Spasimo, the Massimo, and the refurbished Ducrot factory pavilions—are the talk of the town. Because the corner has yet to be turned on creating viable neighborhoods, however, what the historic center will become in the twenty-first century is not yet clear. Some predict an eventual gentrification, others an open-air museum. Already a few noble families have followed in the steps of other aristocracies, meeting the expenses of their ancient homes by opening them to "cultural tourists."

There is, of course, an irony in restoring the grand *palazzi*, which, as the city's historians well know, owed their former magnificence to revenues that ruthless nobles exacted from miserable peasants. Perhaps the antimafia enthusiasm for historic preservation fails to resonate, or resonates only partially, with *palermitani* of the popular classes. Not only are many of them the descendants of these very peasants; their histories include the fragmentation and recobbling of the interior spaces of the palaces, the appropriation of their courtyards for storerooms and dumps and motorcycle parks, and the enjoyment of Sundays with their children at the (embarrassing) Luna Park. More poignant still, the history of the popular classes of Palermo is thoroughly enmeshed in an industry whose employers and unions are blamed for the *scempio*. Celebrating the end of growth, antimafia rhetoric excludes the building trades from the city's imagined future. Construction workers, it seems, are excluded, too. As a stimulus to employment, historic preservation pales before the building boom and in any case places a premium on highly specialized artisan skills that are not widely possessed. To many in the working classes, this reality, and the planners' no-growth approach to the rest of the city, constitute *explanations* for unemployment.

CHAPTER 11

"Cultural Re-education"

From the first phase of the police-judicial crackdown on the mafia, the schools, in particular, were viewed as a vital point of intervention. Both dalla Chiesa and Chinnici pinned their hopes for a reborn Sicily on the as yet unformed generations; Caselli tirelessly spoke to school assemblies—about the role of the *pentiti,* for example (see fig. 20). Beyond this, educators have made a considerable investment in guiding children to discover their rights as citizens. By such means, the world capital of the mafia is struggling to become the world capital of the antimafia, its past of moral degradation, and violence, giving way to democratic and civic sensibilities. This chapter looks at school programs to "educate for legality" in relation to urban geography, examining their effects—their potentialities and limitations—in neighborhoods that receive, more than they produce, antimafia ideology.

ANTIMAFIA EDUCATION: "EVEN THE SCHOOL BUILDINGS"

The Cervellati plan of 1995 cited 25,000 units built as apartments or houses in Palermo that were rented for purposes other than habitation—a figure much higher than elsewhere in Italy and the reason for amplified congestion in ostensibly residential neighborhoods. Over 10 percent of the housing stock, it alleges, was used for other purposes, mainly administration, at the same time as public buildings stood empty (1995: 53–57).

The distortion affected schools with particular intensity. Already in

Figure 20. Giancarlo Caselli, head of the Palermo Prosecutor's Office, with schoolchildren, March 1999. Photograph by Alessandro Fucarini, Labruzzo Agenzia, Palermo.

1971, the report of the Parliamentary Antimafia Commission showed that, compared to Italy as a whole, Sicilian classrooms were severely overcrowded, necessitating double and even triple turns, especially in the elementary schools, where twenty thousand pupils were affected. The reason, however, was not an absence of funds, but political corruption. Indeed, the commission demonstrated a striking correlation between mafia "infestation" and the underutilization or misappropriation of resources available for new school construction. Whereas in Italy, nearly half the scholastic buildings for which public funds had been allocated in the late 1960s were already under contract, in Sicily the percentage was 16.8 (*Commissione Parlamentare* 1972: 115–18).

To explain this, we have only to remember the circumstances of the *scempio*. Contractors like Francesco Vassallo, the most egregious example, exploited their increasingly close relationship with Ciancimino, the assessor for public works, and Lima, the mayor, to overbuild private housing. By 1958, Vassallo, although lacking collateral, had garnered over a million dollars in credit from the Cassa di Risparmio, the head of the bank joining him in several deals (Chubb 1982: 136). Built on public land and exceeding the permissible volume, his buildings contributed to the oversaturated private housing market and a decision by the city to rent vacant apartment buildings, or parts of those buildings, for offices and schools. A beneficiary of this policy, Vassallo received rents totaling $316,000 from the municipal authorities in 1969, plus another $350,000 from the province, for schools alone (ibid.: 137).

Of course, the rented spaces in residential apartment buildings were inappropriate for classrooms, subjecting children to unsanitary and hazardous as well as overcrowded conditions. Following the 1968 earthquake, however, the practice of renting classrooms from the owners of private housing stock (which the commission called the "rental industry") intensified. At the time of the Antimafia Commission report, 110 privately owned buildings or floors of buildings were serving as schools (*Commissione Parlamentare* 1972: 66–71). As the then mayor of Palermo was attacking the commission for exaggerating the mafia phenomenon, which was, he claimed, "nonexistent" (ibid.: 71), a dozen or so principals of high schools and technical schools in the city and surrounding communities were preparing, on behalf of "thousands of teachers," an eloquent letter on the "crisis" of education in Sicily, which they sent to the minister of public instruction in March 1971. How might the schools contribute to the development of a democratic society if they could not even guarantee the physical and mental health of the students, let alone adequate conditions for learning?

New school construction was a priority of Orlando's antimafia administration, which claimed to be making "the most significant intervention in scholastic construction in the history of the city" (*Gruppo Realtà* 1990: 53). In the summer of 1992, we visited two schools of the old type. One, a middle-class high school, occupied a Vassallo-built highrise, the top floors of which were accessible only by stairs and a small elevator. Not only were its classrooms configured in an awkward way; the provisional fire escape exited into an interior courtyard full of parked cars. There were no facilities for recreation or assemblies, and the plumbing was totally inadequate to its task.

The other, a middle school serving children of the working classes, was worse. Also situated in a residential building, it shared one of its four dirty and run-down floors, as well as its dismal and unpatrolled stairwell and dysfunctional elevator, with a brothel. The elevator, visible through a mesh cage, was covered with litter. The plumbing in the bathrooms was unreliable. A warren of tiny, yellow-green rooms off a narrow twisting hallway, poorly lit and poorly insulated, functioned as classrooms. The gym and auditorium, such as they were, shared a small room two floors below. By 1995, both of these schools had moved to new, modern structures, which, although far from ideal, are so much more school-like as to inspire confidence, even enthusiasm, among pupils, teachers, and parents.

1980, ACT 51

The principals' 1971 letter to the minister of education was just the beginning of agitation for reform. At the end of the decade, a group coordinated by the principal of the Antonino Ugo Middle School in Palermo galvanized the regional government's Department of Cultural Affairs and Public Instruction to press for legislation promoting "education for legality." Regional Act 51 was passed in 1980, soon to be copied in the regions of Campania (Naples) and Calabria. All three laws provide public funds for antimafia projects in elementary, middle, and high schools and for related research at the university level. Suggested projects for encouraging a civic and democratic consciousness in students include acquiring bibliographic, documentary, and audiovisual material on organized crime, creating special sections on crime and related topics in the school libraries, opening the schools to parents and neighbors, hosting or hiring collaborators and consultants, and producing written, audiovisual, dramatic, and other materials with anticrime content (Cipolla 1988: 139–43; Casarrubea and Blandano 1991: 151–53).

Many promoters of Act 51 were disappointed by its lack of teeth: the school projects are not mandated but voluntary; educators have to submit detailed proposals for particular initiatives, then await approval and financing before they can begin. Nor does the law obligate the educational bureaucracies of the region and city to promote or coordinate the activities (ibid.: 153). According to a survey in 1988–89, only 12.5 percent of eligible schools had applied for funds under the act. More to the point, the number of proposals increased from 182 in 1980–81 to 331 in 1986–87, the years of the maxi-trial, but then fell off—a rhythm that was consistent with the late 1980s retreat of the antimafia movement as a whole. The majority of teachers, unsympathetic to including the subject of the mafia in the curriculum and to making it the focus of extracurricular activities, resented having their reservations construed as *filo-mafioso*. In the context of retreat and backlash, they put the committed minority on the defensive. As we have seen, a similar isolation befell other activists around the same time (see Cipolla 1989: 132; Montemagno 1990; Stabile 1989).

Serious attempts to utilize Act 51 funds came disproportionately from the middle schools. In part this reflects the greater openness of schools at this level, whose constituents are neither little children in need of a lot of guidance nor young men and women in the late stages of preparation for specialized educational or career choices. The middle schools were also the object of a major educational reform, promoted throughout Italy in 1962 by working-class organizations and the left-wing political parties. The reform unified, in a single institutional context, the formerly separate tracks of technical and professional education—utilitarian and humanistic instruction—thus overcoming a historic stratifying division in Italian education (which still pertains at the secondary level; see Barbagli 1982). As a result of the reform, and a growing demand for schooling in Sicily, the middle schools were in effect reinvented, often with an infusion of younger teachers and administrators sympathetic to educational democratization, who were hired by the state rather than locally, as in the past. It is no accident, in other words, that the Antonino Ugo Middle School would have coordinated the pressure for Act 51. Its principal at the time was Vito Mercadante, a veteran reformer of the 1960s.[1]

DIDACTIC MATERIALS FOR A NEW PEDAGOGY

Over the last twenty years, and especially since 1992, Sicilian children have experienced a profound change in the way that organized crime is represented—at school, in the media, and in public life (if not necessarily at home). Following the assassinations of Falcone and Borsellino, the Parliamentary Antimafia Commission and national Parliament prepared and financed additional resources toward "educating for legality." At the same time, antimafia intellectuals, researchers, and teachers have created new materials for teaching history, inserting into the curriculum such subjects as the nineteenth-century origins of the mafia, the mystifying ideology of "honor" that mafiosi propagate about themselves, the development of the international narcotics traffic, and the mafiosi who have turned state's witness and what they have to say (see Cavadi 1994; Cipolla 1988; Crisantino 1994). Comprehensive bibliographies have been developed for teachers who want to deepen their knowledge, and there exists, as well, a manual, "To Teach What the Mafia Is: 6 Didactic Units for the Upper Middle and Lower High School" (Giammarinaro 1989).

Consistent with the theme of "educating for legality," the new materials emphasize principles of citizenship, contrasting them to the clientelism that is thought to be chronic among Sicilians. Rather than getting through life with the assistance of powerful patrons, students should learn what their civil rights are and be prepared to exercise them on their own. They should no longer count on the system of recommendations that pervades all levels of education in Sicily (see Schneider and Schneider 1976: 216–20), instead welcoming evaluations of their performance based on merit. Another cornerstone of the new pedagogy addresses cultural practices that encourage a misplaced respect for the mafia. Authored by lay and clerical antimafia activists as well as by public school teachers (see Alajmo 1993; Santino 1994), materials in this vein cite litigiousness, taking offense, harboring grudges, and vindicating wrongs as typically Sicilian attitudes that evoke the mafia's valorization of revenge and *omertà* (see Cavadi 1994). Children should learn, it is argued, to conduct themselves in a "sportsmanlike way," to shake the hands of their opponents at the conclusion of a match, to make peace with their enemies after a quarrel, and to be tolerant of the views of others, so that talking things through becomes an alternative to fighting. Antimafia educators wish they could convince the young boys in their classes to give up their many physical contests and shows of strength.

More demanding still, educators for legality propose that, when others break the rules or engage in violence, the boys and girls should report the fact to the appropriate authorities. Indeed, the new pedagogy advocates open, trusting communications between the generations. This is counterintuitive to young people, however, especially if they have been socialized to a kind of *omertà,* encouraged to mind their own business and avoid entanglements. In one of the middle schools of Palermo, we observed a group of elected class leaders called together by the principal to discuss a problem of vandalism in the boy's bathroom. Although not exhorting the leaders (who, interestingly, were mainly girls) to inform on their fellow students—a request that would certainly have failed—the principal nevertheless got them to explore the idea of posting monitors, "for the sake of all the male students in the school."

Educating for "legality," citizenship, and democracy is a gendered project in the Sicilian context. Many of the producers of the new materials are women, as are the majority of teachers at the elementary and middle school levels. Whether women or men, antimafia teachers question the long-standing Sicilian practice of defining the male head of household as a *padre padrone,* entitled to keep his wife and children, above all his daughters, in submissive roles. How can democratic values be advanced if half of society is treated as second-class? Teachers express this concern when they encourage their female students to speak up, or chastise the boys for being rude to girls. Sports programs similarly send a message about women's value by integrating the teams and ensuring that girls participate in the games. According to Augusto Cavadi, a philosophy teacher in a middle-class high school, the *maschilismo* of the mafia is not brutal; "the woman, if legally married and . . . inserted into the family, has her dignity, is respected . . . is not publicly betrayed." But this dignity is predicated on her fidelity and on the mafia's contempt for homosexuals. It is crucial, he argues, to "subvert this *maschilismo* even when it is purely paternalistic" and to encourage a "feminine" pedagogy (which is not necessarily "feminist") (ibid.: 94).

SCHOOLCHILDREN EXPRESS THEMSELVES

The explosive killings of Falcone and Borsellino, coinciding as they did with the end of the scholastic year, reinforced what was becoming a pattern in Sicily: year-end ceremonial events around antimafia themes. Guided by their teachers, schoolchildren prepare vibrant, and often poignant, poster art and photo exhibitions protesting violence and narcotics; they perform concerts and plays with pro-democracy and pro-peace content for parents and invited guests; they write and recite poems, and submit poetry for contests and publications; and they walk behind their school banners in the marches and "human chains" that *Palermo Anno Uno* sponsors each year in honor of the slain victims. On the marches the children chant, *"Palermo è nostra, non è di Cosa Nostra"* (Palermo belongs to us, not Cosa Nostra). In 1992, we watched the children of one middle school (the run-down school that shared its space with a brothel) dramatize the writings of Bertold Brecht. The occasion was especially moving and interesting because of the guiding teacher's conviction that, although Sicilian is spoken in most of the pupils' homes, they are more than capable of performing in Italian and should not be relegated, as some of her colleagues had argued, to putting on quaint folkloric dramas in dialect. At another equally poor school in 1999, a student-made CD-ROM was on display about the River Oreto, which, in the course of its run from the mountains to the sea, becomes an open sewer in the city. Based on class expeditions, the children lectured us not only on this urban tragedy but on how the headwaters of the river are newly vulnerable to pollution because of real estate development of the "old savage kind."

In 1993, the *Comitato Vivi Villa Trabia* (a committee set up by a group of environmentalists to restore the grounds of an unused villa as a public park) mobilized two middle schools and two elementary schools, along with an assortment of peace, women's, and antimafia groups, to symbolically "occupy" the villa's gardens (Cipolla 1995). Schoolchildren have also lent their energy to cleaning up beaches and are the principal source of the messages that are appended to the "Falcone Tree." But without doubt their most significant contribution to the antimafia process involves a program called "Palermo Opens Its Doors; the School Adopts a Monument," modeled after a similar initiative in Naples.

Begun in 1995 under the auspices of PAU and with the support of the city's architects and planners, the Adopt a Monument program was subsequently taken over by the municipal Department of Public Instruction. Each school identifies, studies, and takes steps to recuperate a particular historic building, garden, or monument in its territory. Most of the sites had been abandoned, vandalized, or closed to the public for decades, often as the result of political corruption involving mafiosi. The schools, in some cases, have to negotiate with absentee owners for access and invest the labor of teachers, students, and parents to sweep and clean. During year-long courses, children learn about the history of their monument, including the history of its degradation, incorporating what they discover into narratives and poems, photographs and drawings, exhibits and skits. By 1999, the students in several schools were producing monument-related CD-ROMs and videos.

In collaboration with PAU, the city has organized a series of itineraries inviting citizens to visit the chosen sites. An accompanying guidebook, published by PAU, contains a brief description of each site and its adopting school, as well as numerous photographs and maps—essential because many of the sites are out-of-the-way and unknown. The schoolchildren serve as tour guides, explaining the exhibits and presenting their prepared narratives and skits. A great deal of excitement surrounds this project. Living in Palermo in the spring of 1996, we had the experience of being stopped on the street by groups of children who, recognizing us as foreigners, coaxed us to join their tour. Then, and again in 1999, we were present during the week of May 23, when all of the monuments were open and the multiple itineraries combined. On these occasions, Alitalia and several local hotels discounted rates for foreign and national visitors who came for the grand tour.

Visiting the monuments, we often found ourselves in the company of

parents and neighbors of an adopting school who were either seeing a local treasure for the first time or revisiting a place they had known in their
youth but had forgotten. Their astonishment was as palpable as ours
upon entering, for example, churches that had been closed for decades.
Youthful guides met us at the door, some competing to capture our attention with their rehearsed explanations, others hanging back in shy-
ness, succumbing to cascades of giggles. Where important paintings or
stucco work had been removed by vandals—the most notorious case is
Caravaggio's *Nativity* of 1609, stolen from the Oratorio of San Lorenzo
in 1969 and never retrieved—the guides pointed this out, showing us old
photographs or drawings of the lost art. Where the churches had crypts
and catacombs, they illuminated our descent with candles and, in the
candle-lit corridors and niches below, gave us history lessons laced with
references to the "fantastic" Beati Paoli.

Apart from churches, we and hundreds of citizens discovered or re-
discovered a host of unusual places—a medieval Arab palace called the
Cuba, for one. Smaller than the Zisa and crumbling, its lovely gray stone
walls with subtly recessed arches had long been encapsulated among the
barracks of a Carabinieri base. Thanks to the Adopt a Monument program, the Carabinieri provided access and this magical ruin is now open
to the public. Other revelations were a medieval *cubula,* or "little cube,"
the size of a kiosk and overrun by an untended citrus grove, buildings associated with the former tuna fisheries of the Florio family, a monastery
and cloister that had become an art school and then a mechanic's shop
before being abandoned in the 1970s. This minimal list of hidden treasures cannot help but include the old Communal Archive, invisible because, although a stone's throw from the Four Corners, it is enveloped
by a labyrinth of narrow streets given over to a lively commerce in artisanal household wares. The architect Damiani Almejda, who designed it
in 1881, took as his inspiration the Jewish synagogue on the same site
that had been destroyed when the Jews were expelled from Palermo (as
from Spain) in 1492.

At the outset, 79 schools participated; by 1998 there were 13 itineraries covering 113 recuperated monuments. Twenty-five thousand students from 150 elementary, middle, and high schools took part in the
year 2000 (Lo Dato 2000: 13). According to Alessandra Siragusa, commissioner of public instruction in the Orlando administration, roughly
60 percent of the first round of monuments have been restored and are
open to the public, with another 20 percent in the process of rehabilitation. In Siragusa's words, there are no events that have "more pro-

foundly changed Palermo." Siragusa is herself an energetic contributor and aware of the many volunteered hours involved, as well as the cooperation of other city agencies—sanitation, transportation, and policing.

POOR SCHOOLS AND THE ADOPT A MONUMENT PROGRAM

According to Italian law, children are supposed to attend public schools in the territories where they live, but this is not always enforced. At the same time, a new (national) law differentiates schools into "autonomous" and "dependent" types, depending on enrollments. This has intensified what was already becoming a pattern in Palermo—the tendency for schools in the city's north end, where family size (as noted below) is lower than the average, to aggressively compete for the best pupils from other districts—pupils whose "parents follow them." Considered "selective," these schools loom as a challenge to the public schools in poor neighborhoods, whose principals and teachers fear that their brightest students might be snatched away. Compounding the problem was the surprising announcement, in 1999, that the national minister of education, Luigi Berlinguer, backed the concept of public support for private schools and of schools competitively turning out a product that can be measured by national standards. This, too, could leave the poorer public schools without moorings. The Adopt a Monument program unfolded in the context of this potential stratification of public schooling.

Schools in poor neighborhoods are more likely than the Palermo north schools to have boys and girls from mafia families among their pupils. Not surprisingly, such students can be enthusiastic participants in the initial display of their school's adopted monument but not show up for its second unveiling during the week of May 23, which is intensely associated with antimafia symbolism. Many teachers worry that in all of its aspects, the new curriculum risks making students from mafia backgrounds objects of ridicule and ostracism, a complexity that affects mainly the poorer schools.[2]

In 1996, the inclusion of the Maredolce Castle in the Adopt a Monument itinerary introduced another discordant note. Brancaccio, the working-class neighborhood that surrounds this Arab fortress, lacked all the countervailing institutions—sports facilities, mothers' groups, social centers. Father Puglisi, the parish priest, was working to create such amenities when the mafia killed him in 1993. Meanwhile the medieval castle had become home to some twenty families who transformed its rambling rooms surrounding an interior courtyard into a kind of village. Each family had its own whitewashed doorway in the castle wall, as well as a place to park their car or motorcycle. Contradicting this evolution, at one end of the castle a Norman chapel embedded in the Arab structure was being restored by the regional commission for historic preservation. This was to be the first step in an ambitious plan to rehabilitate the whole. Of course the resident families resented the restoration plan, not to mention the schoolchildren and teachers who had adopted the castle as their monument. During the weekend that Maredolce was on the Adopt a Monument itinerary, and again during the week of May 23, Brancaccio youths on motorcycles asserted their possessiveness over this "turf," circling the school group (from the nearby Quasimodo Middle School) and visitors until the police were called in.

Maredolce was one of the monuments removed from the circuit between 1996 and 1999. A *Giornale di Sicilia* article of June 1999 aptly demonstrates the difficulties it posed. Announcing that the castle was "finally" scheduled for restoration after three years of a tortuous process of expropriation, the article celebrated this reweaving of a "territory of memory" and revival of the building's "dignity" while ridiculing those who lived there. At last, the invasive stalls and animals—even "the long underwear of the grandfathers hanging from the castle windows"—will be gone, the paper proclaimed. "Now the gauntlet has been thrown down to people who have no idea of the castle's value as one of the richest monuments of the city." In other words, Maredolce is an "elegant building, as long as you don't notice its inhabitants" (*Giornale di Sicilia*, June 22, 1999).

Despite the contrast of schools serving different social classes in the monuments program, it is our impression that the children involved are drawn to a common endeavor. In 1999, poor schools no less than rich schools presented their monuments with the help of electronic equipment, notwithstanding having fewer parents with cars and leisure time to transport exhibits, props, and computers to the site. Moreover, the program seemed to galvanize students' energy and imagination across a broad range of schools, provoking them to think through issues for themselves. A guide to the Zisa in 1996 spontaneously told visitors that the screens behind which women sat while watching the court entertainment in the Arab-Norman Middle Ages were "unfair to women." Her partner, a boy, added that such separations were "a kind of racism, I guess." Both of these students were from a poor school. Nor did students from poor schools treat the grand *palazzi* as meaningless to their history. According to a group that adopted the extraordinary Palazzo Aiutamicristo in 1999, the nobility of those days "engaged important architects and built huge houses because they were rich, and because they wanted to beautify the city." To really encounter the limits of the antimafia process, it is necessary to look more closely at how schools in the "at risk" neighborhoods—neighborhoods like Brancaccio—relate not to their monuments but to their other surroundings.

NEIGHBORHOODS "AT RISK"

In the course of our research, we became acquainted with two peripheral neighborhoods that support large public housing projects, Falsomiele and ZEN II, and with two older popular neighborhoods that had emerged from the earlier expansion of the city into orchard territory, Uditore and Noce. In addition we lived in Albergheria, a popular quarter of the historic center, in 1996 (and for a summer in 1989).

Palermo's most criticized public housing development is called ZEN. The exotic connotation of this label derives from media stories publicizing its horrors rather than its actual meaning as an acronym for "northward expansion zone" *(Zona Espansione Nord)*.[3] ZEN II was built during the second wave of this expansion, following the completion of ZEN I. Designed with the best of intentions by avant-garde urbanists in the 1970s, it was unfortunately turned over to crooked contractors, then allowed to stand empty and without infrastructure or services. Eventually squatters' organizations invaded the buildings, tapping into electrical lines and water mains to make the empty apartments habitable and in some cases taking over blocks of apartments for the purpose of extorting an entry fee from other would-be settlers. As kin and friends of the pioneers arrived, a vibrant if precarious informal economy developed, in which ground-floor spaces intended as stores and artisans' workshops were turned into garages (some to hide stolen cars, car parts, radios, and tires). The entrance doors to apartment blocks were reinforced with steel bars so as to keep the police from breaking in. Residents also refrained from putting any identification on their doors—no nameplates, buzzers, or numbers—for the same reason. On the brighter side, they successfully pressured the city to collect the accumulating garbage. Today ZEN II has a dedicated priest who runs a number of services from a social center similar to San Saverio. The neighborhood streets have no names, only numbers, and the apartment blocks are uniformly bleak, indistinguishable from one another by their exteriors, but the anonymity thus conveyed is striking only to outsiders. Residents know exactly who is where and when, notwithstanding the continued presence of transients among the squatters (see Pino 1988).

Compared to ZEN II, Falsomiele seemed to us more alienated and depressing. Occupied through city-sponsored relocations after the earthquake, its uniform housing blocks lack the history of a squatters' invasion, with its associated pattern of strong kinship ties attracting additional residents. One of the most moving year-end displays in the middle schools we visited in 1999 was a collection of photographs taken by students at the Luigi Pirandello Middle School depicting life in Falsomiele. Both the pictures and their accompanying text stressed the lack of a social fabric: without a "downtown" or a real piazza, there were hardly any stores. There was no place for youth to gather and at best an uninsulated Quonset hut to shelter old men during their afternoon card games. The entire community was separated from the adjacent *borgate* by the six-lane ring road that was impossible to cross on foot. In 1999, a woman in ZEN II proudly told us of having organized a group of women (six at first but expanding to thirty) "to fight City Hall." They had constructed barricades of garbage containers across the local bus route and sequestered some bus drivers (treating them well, she assured us), in order to force a response to their woes during a winter flood. By contrast, the women we met in Falsomiele wished they lived somewhere else.

Noce is different again. Like its neighbor Zisa, it supported a wide range of artisan activities in the past. Some of the factories that produced textiles and furniture for Palermo's Art Nouveau tradition are located in this zone, as are a few small *palazzini* built in the Venetian Gothic style, then in vogue. The rest of the housing stock, generally older than in Falsomiele and ZEN II, was constructed by private parties; residents have been there for decades and sometimes generations. Noce also harbors a community of Jehovah's Witnesses.

Uditore, the bordering neighborhood to the west, is somewhat greener and lower in density. A classic example of a *borgata* and orchards transformed into urban space, it went through these changes without erasing all that was there before. Remnants of fruit trees remain in the interstices of high-rise apartments; the apartments are neither as high nor as bulky as in other parts of the city; and the neighborhood's central piazza looks very much like the "main square" of a rural town. Of all the neighborhoods we came to know, this one also manifested the strongest local presence of kinship networks. Related families, many with roots in the former orchard economy, occupy apartments in the same or nearby buildings. Reputed to be one of Palermo's most "secure" neighborhoods, it boasts low levels of everyday thievery and vandalism.

Each of these neighborhoods has, or has had, a mafia presence, but to different degrees. ZEN II and Falsomiele, being newly formed, support a lot of street-level delinquency but no significant *cosca.* Instead they gravitate toward the *cosche* of their neighbors—Resuttana and Partanna for ZEN II, Brancaccio and Ciaculli for Falsomiele. Historically, Noce was under the shadow of the "losing" families of the Bontade and Inzerillo; Uditore was home to the *cosca* of Giuseppe Inzerillo. Like neighboring Passo di Rigano, controlled by Inzerillo's son Salvatore, this neighborhood saw a lot of action during the second mafia war. Recall that in 1978 the Corleonesi murdered Salvatore Inzerillo's friend, Giuseppe di Cristina, in front of a bus stop in Passo di Rigano, and that eventually Riina made Uditore his Palermo home. It was here, indeed, that he was captured in 1993.

Living in Albergheria, we were daily observers of its contradictions. A source of great pleasure is the vibrant outdoor market of Ballarò with its apparently peaceful integration of African and Asian immigrants and their foods; sources of dismay or concern are unemployed men's pervasive drinking in local taverns, called *bettole,* and the ever-present need to be wary of pickpockets and purse snatchers. The informal economy seems alive and well on the local streets, with their obvious presence of illegal as well as legal lotteries, and of a great deal of errand running on the part of local youth. Off the streets, wives and mothers must cope with apartments that are crumbling and poorly plumbed, in some cases having to draw water from public fountains, and with illnesses for which the publicly available health care services are woefully inadequate. Mothers we knew worried a lot about keeping their boys out of trouble.

In 1989, a small group of conscientious objectors assigned to the Social Center of San Saverio conducted a survey of Albergheria. Interviewing fifty-six households, of which thirty-four were in "precarious condition" and eleven had no telephone,[4] they discovered that women's improved access to birth control pills and abortions meant that they felt less dominated than in the past—less compelled to respect men, especially unemployed men, *tout court.* Even so, the interviewers found these men to be heavily involved in male peer groups outside the home and demanding when they returned at night, especially if they had been drinking. And they documented several cases of teenage girls having left households they found abusive, either because of a domineering father or a mother who burdened them with the care of younger siblings and a load of household chores. Taken in by boyfriends, perhaps eloping with them, many became pregnant. This manifestation of patriarchy distorted by unemployment—the *ragazza madre* (girl-mother)—was evident in all of the poor neighborhoods we studied.

In 1997, ISTAT, the National Institute of Statistics, initiated a project in conjunction with the city to teach middle school children about the demography and sociology underlying the census and how to create statistics about their surroundings. The project divided the city into the eight districts of the Cervellati Plan, selecting one school in each to prepare the materials. Even though these districts group together several diverse neighborhoods, broad comparisons are possible. Palermo north has, on the average, an older population with a lower birthrate, higher educational attainment, higher number of rooms per inhabitant, and higher proportion of the workforce in self-employed and professional occupations when compared to the other districts. The data show that in the 1991 census unemployment rates ranged from 21 percent in Palermo north, to 38 percent in Noce, Zisa, and Uditore, to 40.5 percent in Falsomiele and surrounds, to 49 percent in the historic center. The children who prepared the drawings and charts, bar graphs and pies, for these studies saw in graphic terms roughly where their neighborhood stood.

"AT RISK" NEIGHBORHOODS AND MICRO-CRIMINALITY

In Palermo, as in many other cities, unemployment generates an underground of micro-criminality that partakes of what we might call "subsistence work" (see Dombrowski 2001). Kids "go out to steal" *(vanno a rubare),* bringing home their booty to supplement family incomes cobbled together from several inadequate elements: unemployment compensation, health benefits, migration remittances, occasional earnings from the mother's or daughters' domestic service, the husband's casual labor, or contraband cigarette or drug sales. In many cases they are encouraged, even directed, by their mothers, who are desperate for cash to add to the household budget.

Petty theft in the city at large is the core activity of youth subsistence work: purse snatching, pickpocketing, stealing construction materials, cannibalizing abandoned buildings, stealing cars and dismantling them for parts. Although the predators may carry knives, they are rarely armed with guns, and breaking and entering is also unusual. The most serious assaults occur when purse snatchers pull women to the ground while stealing their purses.[5] Generally, the predators move in small groups of three or four, in which one youth is a lookout, another drives the getaway motorbike, and a third is lined up to receive and hide the booty. A skill that contributes to the division of labor in pickpocketing and purse snatching is that of distracting not only the victim but also potential witnesses with a sideshow of some sort. Over and above these coalitions, the "subsistence workers" need more or less stable relationships with fences and, possibly, with the owners of depositories and abandoned buildings where hot goods can be stored or recycled.[6]

During the 1970s, the explosive growth of a market for illegal narcotics in Europe and the United States both enhanced and transformed subsistence work in Palermo, as the city (briefly) became a strategic crossroads of the international drug trade. The effect of this trade was notable in ZEN I, which sheltered an important retail market for heroin and other drugs, not least because of its apparent anonymity and close proximity to the ring road. Its piazza accessible by only one main avenue, couriers easily observed both the arriving customers and the movements of the police. In a 1988 book, Marina Pino gathered together the stories of ZEN women—mothers, housewives, even a grandmother—who became organizers of retail drug dealing. Either widows or married to unemployed men, these women had outside suppliers who furnished them with the drug and the ingredients to dilute it. Recruiting close friends or relatives, and possibly an addict-"taster," they made up the *bustine,* or packets, around their kitchen tables. To avoid having too much incriminating evidence on hand, they also decentralized some of this work to other trusted persons.

And they mobilized their own sons for particular roles: the youngest, say the ten to twelve year olds, were lookouts, schooled in how to whistle a warning, while the older teens served as "mediators." Typically, a boy would meet an incoming car, take the money from the driver, run to his mother's balcony, where he whistled in code, and place the money in the basket she lowered by a rope (Sicilian women typically transact with street vendors, mailmen, bill collectors in this way). Once the basket was pulled up and lowered again, he would take the drugs she placed in it back to the waiting vehicle. Mothers were famously clever at hiding the cash they accumulated. From their perspective, moreover, the possibility of being caught and punished posed a less serious danger than the possibility that one or more of their children would become addicted. In addition to the cost of a habit in money and poor health, addiction subtracted a reliable worker from the household enterprise.[7]

For some residents of ZEN, drug sales yielded enough profit for the participants to meet more than their subsistence needs: boys flung themselves enthusiastically into a new consumer culture, coveting silk shirts and motor bikes. Their mothers, yearning for a modern home, invested in "American kitchens" equipped with the latest appliances, ceramic tiles to cover rough concrete floors and walls, and new furniture upholstered in leather and finished in shiny veneers. Many husbands, although unemployed, had skills in the construction trades and joined their wives' projects for home improvement. Indeed, husbands with different skills exchanged labor on each other's apartments. One of the most deceptive aspects of ZEN I and II is that the dingy faces of the buildings can conceal rather glamorous interiors.

Because petty thieves and drug dealers benefit from the cover of their kin and friends, policing is difficult. Neighborhood opposition to the police is correspondingly strong. Locals invent unflattering nicknames to label them, invest in ever more creative styles of subterfuge, and regale each other with tales of having headed off this or that investigation at the pass. The youthful "subsistence workers" do, however, risk getting caught and serving time in a juvenile detention center or, if they are over eighteen, in jail. This risk, and the broader context of their criminalization, encourage the formation of ganglike structures among youth, both as a source of mutual aid during episodes of imprisonment and because recruitment to more organized criminal groups goes on in jail.

Delinquent subsistence work and organized crime are different yet related phenomena. Mafiosi both discipline youth offenders, sometimes with spectacular punishments, and recruit from their ranks. A teacher in Malaspina, Palermo's juvenile detention center, in the late 1980s discovered that the boys in his class simultaneously feared and respected the mafia, which they saw as providing a model for life. Some of them reported having been recruited to do errands for mafiosi. One set a car on fire for 50,000 lire; another opened the locked gate of a storefront in anticipation of a robbery for no compensation at all (Grimaldi 1987: 112–17, 134–36). That youthful offenders systematically receive lighter sentences and may even escape conviction is presumably a reason why mafiosi seek them out.

The mafia's strategic use of people deemed immune to arrest extended to the women of ZEN, who were approached to become couriers in the transatlantic shipment of heroin. Unlikely to be searched at the customs gates, they could also carry dollars back to Italy. One woman is reported to have leapt at the offer because it arrived on the very day she also received an astronomical (and unexpected) electric bill. In her view, the chance to earn money as a courier was like a gift from providence; it never occurred to her to turn it down (Pino 1988: 28).

Subsistence workers are understandably cynical about the antimafia movement, which they see as a charade. According to the Malaspina teacher, they are resigned to living under an inefficient state of which they are contemptuous and which, they believe, keeps their city divided between a "good" half for the rich people and a violent half for them (see Grimaldi 1987). This outlook in turn anchors an antischool culture in some Palermo neighborhoods, where truants consider youths who stay in school to be *fessi,* or "wimps," and publicly subvert the schools' outreach programs.[8]

THE MAKINGS OF AN ANTISCHOOL CULTURE

Youth "subsistence workers" range in age from ten to nineteen. Most are boys, although girls might participate as lookouts or distracters. In either case, their life on the streets is strongly associated with dropping out of school. Truancy and dropping out loom as major problems in Palermo's "at risk" neighborhoods. In middle schools for the city as a whole in 1991–92, 1.6 percent of the students "evaded" enrollment, another 1.4 percent enrolled then left, 1.5 percent were suspended, and 13 percent flunked out, resulting in a "dispersion" rate of 16.8 percent. By 1996–97, this rate had fallen to 13.9 percent, reflecting national legislation on "student rights" that restricted the conditions for expelling students and shifted the power to do so from the principal to a committee made up of teachers and parents. Innovative policies to reduce absenteeism such as sending student committees to an absent student's home also made a difference (Provveditorato agli studi 1996–97).

In the past, when teachers pressured principals to throw out unruly students, the principals usually went along, not wanting to undermine staff morale. The committee process is less automatic, but a source of controversy among teachers. Some approve; others see it as an obstacle to purging their classrooms of troublemakers. Students, meanwhile, are aware of the committees—know that parents and teachers participate in discussions of who should be included and who excluded from the school. Acts of vandalism are sometimes interpreted not only as signaling a poor relationship between the school and its territory but as a response to the fact that a particular student was suspended.

Responding to our interest in these issues, a teacher shared with us an essay written by two middle school girls from a secondary city outside of Palermo. Taking the form of a letter to the Carabinieri, it recounts how they were caught in a petty theft and had a terrible time at the hands of the authorities. "We have studied our history lessons," the letter declares, citing the way the newly unified Italian state deployed its military police to instill respect for officially sanctioned violence. "[After 1860] you intervened to impose payments of tribute and to arrest those who escaped the draft. The people did not love you." According to the essay, the police of today are no better. A pervasive presence, whether on TV or careening through the streets, sirens blaring, they are better at repressive than at preventive acts.

Meanwhile, the letter goes on, no one seeks to understand why youths steal. Sometimes it is for lack of work and the money that enables them to have what others have. Sometimes it is because "we find ourselves in a group gone wrong." The causes, though, are not important; what matters is "our coming out of it"—something that cannot happen "unless you, the Carabinieri, become allies in our struggle." And the school, too. "We are not always successful in remaining quiet in class, which is too much for us in many ways." And then, most remarkably, the girls note their awareness that parents and teachers have been meeting to discuss whether or not to expel them. "Some of the parents of our companions . . . want the school to be liberated of us"; some of the teachers "have given us failing grades to punish us, and now spend their time with the program for the better students." Yet "we are girls who are aware that we've made mistakes and want to recuperate—in our families, in school, and above all in life. . . . We are not bad."

The citywide figures on school attendance look bleaker in the poorest neighborhoods, where as many as 40 percent of school-age children may not be in school.[9] For boys in these neighborhoods, street life is often more interesting and certainly more lucrative than studying. Perhaps they work for their families in lieu of an unemployed or jailed father, selling fruit or cigarettes on the street, loading and unloading hot ovens in bakeries, transporting heavy packages and running errands. Girls are "dispersed" for a different reason. The persistent patriarchalism of the popular classes leads parents to want to keep their daughters at home once they reach their teenage years, protecting them from the attention of boys while harnessing their labor for household chores. The consequence is that girls easily fall for early elopement or marriage and early childbearing—all a way, however illusory, of escaping a servant's role in their parents' home. When dispersed students return to school, and some do, the adjustment is compounded by the age difference between them and their classmates, as well as by the fact that they may already be parents.

No wonder, then, that teachers in the neighborhoods "at risk" feel as though they are working in "frontier zones." Nor do their problems evaporate inside the walls of the school. Here, everyday challenges include occasional menacing acts by students, the jailing or murder of a student's father or brother, a student beaten by an abusive father, the entry of a student's mother into prostitution, a teenage female student's hidden marriage or pregnancy, a family's inability to buy school books, having gone into debt to pay for a First Communion. In light of such difficulties, the principals view staff solidarity as essential and attempt to hire, or form, teams of teachers who will collaborate with one another. Sometimes, the principals themselves are menaced, their tires slashed or their car stolen while parked in front of the school. In 1999, the principal of a middle school in our sample had a rock thrown through her office window, as well as her car vandalized in the neighborhood where she lived (because, she believes, she refused to pass a child on an oral exam). Antimafia activists in the school system and beyond interpret such acts as confirmation that certain territories are "solidly controlled by the enemies of civility and democracy" and that those who are seeking to reform them deserve "our strongest and most affectionate solidarity" (Comitato dei Lenzuoli 1992–99).

"CULTURAL RE-EDUCATION" AND THE URBAN ECONOMY

In 1996 we interviewed thirty sets of parents with at least one child, and possibly more, in the middle schools of Falsomiele, Noce, Uditore, and ZEN II, as well as three families who frequented the social center in Albergheria. Generally speaking, the families were identified for us, even introduced to us, by staff members of these institutions, meaning that the interviewees had been exposed to the antimafia process. Most of the interviews were with two parents; some were with the mother or father alone. Although a few took place in a schoolroom, in most cases the interviewees hosted us in their homes. For each couple, we reconstructed the family history of one of them, using their paternal or maternal genealogy as a way to talk about change over time.

The family histories dramatize the extent to which Palermo's working people come from rural communities—some of them immediately surrounding the city, others farther afield, still others swallowed up by urban sprawl. That thousands of peasants sought urban employment following the land reform is reflected in this pattern. Not surprisingly, recommendations and personal contacts have been decisive in finding urban employment. In many families, a string of brothers and cousins were hired by the same employer: the post office, the railroad, a restaurant, a bar, a contractor. Regardless of the neighborhood, the interviews also revealed the overwhelming impact of the construction industry in the livelihoods of postwar popular-class families. In more than half the families we met, the men worked, or had worked, in trades associated with building, either as wage earners or small-scale contractors, or a combination of both. Moreover, a majority of families had given expression to their "evolving" urban identity through the handiwork of the man or men of the household. In the boom years, construction workers of all kinds remodeled, expanded, or totally rebuilt their own and their relatives' apartments (ignoring the building codes as necessary). Interviewees proudly showed us rooftop terraces turned into extra rooms, reconstructed archways and windows, extensive floor and wall tiling. Some told of tapping into gas and electrical lines before these services were provided by the city.

Each couple or individual was also asked to reflect on a series of issues related to the changes in Palermo of the last ten years. We refrained from asking pointed questions about the mafia and the antimafia, focusing instead on broader topics—their view of the school's curriculum and programs, the Italianization of the Sicilian dialect, changing gender relations among youth, and the economic situation. Naturally, we found variation. For example, some parents were wildly enthusiastic about the Adopt a Monument program, having participated in it with their child. A few had followed one or more of the itineraries, or knew from the television and newspapers about monuments newly opened to the public. Others though were entirely out of the loop. Of the various topics, the state of the economy elicited the greatest passion, often because of people's immediate experience: the man of the household was unemployed, his brother was, his close friends were, a storekeeper friend or relative had had to close his shop. Many expressed the feeling of being at the end of an era in which life had become less precarious and at the beginning of an era of great insecurity. Several of the households we visited already showed the effects of doubling up. Young people were either postponing marriage because they lacked employment or, having married, were living with one of their parents for lack of affordable housing. Both outcomes violated local norms, on the one hand of youthful marriage and on the other of neo-local residence (because, after all, "daughters-in-law and mothers-in-law should never be under one roof").

Most of the interviewees attributed the crisis to the abrupt slowdown of construction, which they associated with the antimafia prosecutions or, to quote one, "hysteria about legality." Several said, without our prompting, "The mafia gave us work, and now the antimafia has taken this work away."[10] According to one man, thanks to the politicians and the mafia, "there used to be a lifting crane every twenty meters well into the 1980s, but now the cranes have vanished because all of their owners are in jail." An ironworker experiencing a three-quarters reduction in his work claimed it was the same for any craftsman (woodworker, tile layer, plumber, electrician) connected to the building trades. The halt in construction, in the view of still others, had a giant domino effect, construction being the first link in a long economic chain. The chain now broken, even fishmongers suffered, as customers could no longer afford to dine at restaurants that purchase fish. In other words, "If the masons don't work, neither does anyone else."

Other arguments filtered in. One woman expressed anger over the TV images of Sicily that draw attention to the mafia, claiming that the new emphasis on legality only fostered negative propaganda. Another said she "did not believe in this notion that the man should help the woman when he comes home." Two women volunteered stories of a terrible childhood. One, "Concetta," had a father who sold salt on the street and a mother who worked as a domestic. Both counted on her to mind her eleven younger siblings, prepare meals, and wash the laundry in a tub near the public fountain, there being no water at home. The father lavished all his affection on the youngest brothers; the mother, yelling, slapped her into completing a round of chores before going to school each day. So at sixteen she eloped with a young man whose only work was putting up lights for festivals. With no income, they had to live with his mother, who also treated her badly, leading to a painful separation after two sons were born. At the time of the interview, Concetta worked eight hours a day caring for an elderly person in order to make ends meet. She was extremely anxious about her two sons, the eldest of whom had stayed with his father, and she still woke up crying from dreams about her mother's relentless criticism of everything she did.

The father of a second woman, "Francesca," beat her mother and her as well. Totally irresponsible, he had contributed nothing to her trousseau—her hope chest of embroidered linens—leaving her to take in the laundry of a priest so as to finance it on her own. Again the washing was done at a public fountain, this time in the dark of night to avoid being seen. If it rained, she used one arm to hold an umbrella over her head. The father, disrespectful as always, did not attend her wedding (to a marginally employed bricklayer), leaving the priest to give her away.

Never home, Francesca's violent father ended up living with another woman by whom he had a daughter. Compounding Francesca's rage, the new family occupied the apartment on the floor below her. The building itself was a shambles, a formerly rural two-story structure engulfed by high-rise development. Intense bitterness welled up from Francesca, both for the shameful condition of this building and because her stepsister pretended to be an heir to it. She and her husband were also angry with the Orlando administration—"for only caring about the historic center and throwing people out of work."

When asked, most interviewees did not perceive the educational system as antithetical to, or undermining of, the Sicilian dialect, and all of them placed a high priority on their children learning Italian. For some this meant straining to speak Italian at home in front of them; others thought going to this length was "unnatural" and ridiculous. Several claimed that the dialect was dying of its own accord. In "their day," they pointed out, the Sicilian vocabulary was rich enough for an elite poetry tradition; now it was becoming the slang of street kids. Fortunately, many thought, the schools now teach Sicilian as an auxiliary subject; without this, children would have to keep asking their parents what certain words meant.

The most interesting reflections addressed the antimafia attempt to suppress and even criminalize clientelistic behavior. It used to be possible, several interviewees noted, citing examples from their own families, to *fare entrare qualcuno*—arrange someone's employment by means of a recommendation. "This is our mentality," they claimed, but now, if you want to help someone, you might go to jail. Ugly as it is, one woman intoned, "We can't even help our own children any more!" The moral complexities of the antimafia process are well-captured by her worry that if her children failed to get a job, they would blame her. One can view the old (and normal) practices of "clientelism" as corrupting—an obstacle to the maturation of what Suad Joseph has called the "separative selves" of rights-bearing, individual citizens. Or, conversely, one can appreciate in these practices the "connectivity" that obligates kin and friends to look out for each other in a continually shifting and insecure world (see Joseph 1993).

Interviewees were skeptical that the new legality is even working. Several pointed to an increase of street-level delinquency, a problem they attributed to unemployment, not organized crime. "They have beaten up the mafia and now, with the enterprises finished, crime is on the rise." After all, "people have children, they have to eat, they have houses they have to pay for." Some thought that the magistrates place too much faith in the *pentiti*, prosecuting innocents as a result. If someone uses your phone, one woman told us, and that someone turns out to be suspect, you yourself can be put away for six years.

Among the thirty-three families, five stood out as exceptions to this pattern of questioning or resenting the antimafia process. Instead, their positions expressed admiration for the magistrates, appreciation for the "sacrifices" they were making, and condemnation of patron-client relations. One such person, an ironworker, had long since retreated into occasional employment to avoid paying the *pizzo* to a local boss, joining a Jehovah's Witness church around the same time. Another, a bus driver, had grown up in the Communist Party and was actively trying to reform the bus drivers' unit of the CGIL. "It is true, the mafia gave work," he told us, "but only because of a false situation." He is especially angry with politicians who exploit this issue. In a third case, the head of the family was an employee of the telephone company who also grew up with the Communist Party. He spoke eloquently on how such a background helped impoverished people stay "clean," at the same time burdening them with a "double fatigue" in accounting for themselves: "When I say I don't know the mafiosi of my neighborhood, people think I am just a victim of *omertà*," he complained.

Communism shaped the past political identity of the fourth and fifth exceptions, too. The fourth, an electrician and union organizer, accused the mafia of "running construction projects where people work the way slaves did in America. Yes, the mafia gives work, but it is slavery!" The fifth, a hospital clerk, was thrilled to relate that his maternal grandfather, a shopkeeper in Corleone, had been a friend of the martyred union leader Placido Rizzotto, assassinated by Luciano Liggio. His wife reported that her father had been forced to dissolve his small construction firm when she was a girl, following altercations with "men who came to our house and threatened him."

Although a minority, the five exceptions constitute a reminder that even the most forbidding neighborhoods, from an antimafia perspective, are heterogeneous with regard to residents' experiences. Each outpost of "legality," whether a school or church or social center, is a magnet for some who, together with their kin and friends, readily attach themselves to the projects at hand, befriend the staff and volunteers, and compensate for the indifference and sometimes outright hostility of their neighbors. Yet beyond a certain point, the antimafia outreach cannot speak to the most pressing concerns of the majority. Specifically, the reformers' opposition to reinvigorating the construction industry makes them seem insensitive to the problem of jobs. As we have seen, antimafia activism is substantially feminist and green. No undertaking is more abhorrent, in these respects, than the hyper-masculine building trades, which have buried every tree in sight under a load of cement. Together with their allies in the mafia and politics, contractors and builders have produced the congestion, the aesthetic and moral horror, that needs to be cleaned up. Working people, even those who have participated in good faith in the antimafia programs of the schools and social centers, feel betrayed, not only by the erosion of decent jobs, but also by this denigration of their work. What is more—and especially frustrating—they cannot rebel because "those [antimafia leaders] who are taking away our jobs say that the mafia makes them do it," and who can be for the mafia? "But aren't *they* the mafia?" these people ask. "They are letting us die of hunger."

Except for the grassroots organizers, leaders of the antimafia movement, whether from the left or the center of the political spectrum, are often prompted by responses like these to criminalize the popular classes. Conversely, among our interviewees were several who voted for Orlando as mayor in 1993 but refused to support his candidates in the national election of 1996 on the grounds that the new legality and constrictive urban planning were a threat to them and their families. "We are not against justice," said one, "but this is not just." If the wheels of justice "cut the flow of mafia money without replacing it with other money, this only adds to the misery of the people."

PALERMO AS A GLOBAL MODEL

In June 1999, Civitas, an international nongovernmental organization concerned with civic education against crime and corruption, sponsored a four-day conference in Palermo, "Educating for Legality." Delegations of educators came from all over the world. In addition to Sandra Feldman, president of the American Federation of Teachers, and Pino Arlacchi, then United Nations under secretary general for drug control and crime prevention, speakers included Baltasar Garzon Real, the Spanish magistrate who pressed human rights charges against Pinochet; Otto Schily, German minister of the interior; and Wole Soyinka, Nobel

Prize–winning Nigerian writer. Several key figures in the antimafia establishment of Palermo also participated: Mayor Orlando, Education Commissioner Siragusa, and Cardinal Pappalardo.

Hillary Rodham Clinton opened the conference as keynote speaker, addressing an overflow audience from the stage of the Teatro Massimo. The first lady began her speech with a series of compliments on the restoration of the theater, the recuperation of the city, and "the people of Palermo and their civil society." Looking about, we did, indeed, feel surrounded by civility—well-dressed middle-class citizens, perhaps two thirds of them women, there to celebrate and nurture the city's return to order after a time of chaos and violence. Order, Hillary Clinton suggested, rests on a "three-legged stool," one leg the government, a second the economy, and a third the civil society. By the latter she meant the social space outside of economy and government from which citizens generate initiatives for moral, cultural, and political reform.

Two things transpired in the days following the Clinton speech that throw into question her uncomplicated representation of Palermo. First, we encountered several grassroots activists who had not been invited to the conference, let alone its plenary session in the Massimo. They commented with irony on a piece of gossip already in circulation—namely, that the mayor, speaking before an international audience, had described Sicily's historic struggle against the mafia as if he and his party, *La Rete,* were the only significant players. Not included in his narrative were associations like the Centro San Saverio and the Centro Impastato—vital elements of the "real" civil society, from their point of view. The second experience was to join a Civitas delegation of teachers from Cairo on a visit to Brancaccio. Greeting our bus were some forty to fifty elementary and middle school children who took us on a guided tour of a nineteenth-century washhouse their schools had adopted. Subsequently they performed folk songs for us in the parish church. Apart from the mothers of the schoolchildren, few residents of the neighborhood attended these showcase events. On the contrary, shutters were closed, most balconies empty, and the piazza in front of the church unoccupied except for a group of teenage boys on motorcycles.

Nothing happened to disturb the Egyptian visitors, but within two days of their visit, Brancaccio was in the *Giornale di Sicilia* for an ugly manifestation of *anti-antimafia* sentiment. Someone set fire to a motorcycle in a vacant lot, part of a former almond orchard that was slated to become a sports field for the local youth. There had been a benefit rock concert in the Teatro Massimo two nights after Hillary Clinton's plenary to raise funds for the lot's transformation. Now all the trees and vegetation were gone, incinerated by the fire. The local priest (brave successor to the martyred Father Puglisi), a leader of the sports field initiative, told reporters he was declaring an "SOS" because "the mafia has come back on the scene, more arrogant than ever" (*Giornale di Sicilia,* June 23, 1999).[11] Like other antimafia activists in Brancaccio, the priest was alarmed by the lack of a neighborhood center where young people might congregate. Civil society, such persons argue, "requires facts on the ground" as well as words (*Giornale di Sicilia,* June 19, 1999).

Even so, a spotlight continues to shine on the mafia's former capital, as illustrated by the United Nations Convention of December 2000. On this occasion, Kofi Annan depicted a civil society (or civilization) in global combat with criminals, drug dealers, and other "forces of evil"; the president of Poland called for a "global war" of "civilization and order" against "violence and lawlessness." There could have been no better opening for the Orlando administration to position Palermo at the vanguard of the good. "We once exported the disease," the mayor told the delegates during the opening ceremony; "now we export the therapy."[12] Nor was this hard to believe. The city lavishly hosted its guests, some two thousand delegates from 115 countries, cordoning off many miles of roadway to enable their circulation, and lining the venues of the multiple events—debates on the convention and protocols, simultaneous symposia, a performance of Beethoven's Ninth Symphony conducted by Zubin Mehta—with thousands of cyclamens and poinsettias. Green lawns were rolled out across the newly liberated waterfront and, to the amazement of everyone, over the Piazza Magione, the once bombed out wasteland near where Falcone and Borsellino grew up. So beautiful was the city, one almost overlooked the thousands of police, Carabinieri, soldiers, and guards (ten thousand, according to the press) deployed at every strategic angle, arms at the ready.

Of very great interest was the relationship between culture and economy presented to the world on this occasion by those who would package the Palermo experience as a model. Their frequently repeated narrative emphasized how, in the early postwar years, Italy had followed the prescription of the left for fighting the mafia: develop the underdeveloped south through massive capital investment. This, however, had made the problem worse. Money ended up in the wrong hands, and above all in the coffers of the corrupt politicians, who used it to wreak havoc. Now, a different approach has been tried and this one appears to be working:

create a "culture of lawfulness" in anticipation of building "an economy of legality." In this vein, Orlando defined the antimafia movement as a "cultural revolution . . . a permanent education process aimed at spreading a culture of lawfulness fundamentally inspired by ethical values" (Orlando 2000: 4–5). Any analysis of Palermo's economic realities—how people make a living—was thereby postponed, obscuring how, alongside the remarkable antimafia momentum of the 1990s, there developed a kind of hiatus in which the popular classes, the city's poor, found themselves suspended *between* economies—the old political-economy of the mafia and corruption and the economy of neoliberal capitalist investment that is promised but not yet realized.

Perhaps a brighter picture is on the horizon. During the Civitas conference, Penn Kemble, then acting director of the United States Information Agency, was reassuring. To his surprise, he said, Palermo was full of pleasant rather than stressed and fearful faces. It had created a model for the "reconquest of democracy" that could be exported to other places. Acknowledging that if people lack material benefits the mafia might come back, he offered this panacea: "international finance" will make capital flow in response to the new (political and cultural) climate. Capital must "be able to make profits, certainly, but above all it must find conditions of security and trust." He could see no reason, he said, "why American investors would not want to contribute to the economic growth of Palermo" (*Giornale di Sicilia,* June 15, 1999). Roy Godson, Georgetown University political scientist and director of another participating organization, the National Strategy Information Center in Washington, D.C., further assured the people of Palermo that their good example in "educating for legality" would translate into broader benefits. "Your city represents a model in the world for the struggle against the 'octopus.' . . . Naturally, much remains to be done but the mentality is changing." Palermo's best resource, he added, "which is certainly a great richness, is called tourism" (ibid.).[13] Happily, the 98,369 foreign tourists hosted by Palermo in 1993 climbed to 220,263 in 1999, and continues to grow (Lo Dato 2000: 18).

But competing for tourists can be a chimera, as development specialists are quick to point out, the more so in a place where many amenities have been ruined and must be reconstituted. So other alternatives must also be considered—for example, the Dublin trajectory, which emphasizes education to enhance the qualifications of the labor force, attracting jobs related to information processing. Opening this frontier are the several Italian and foreign companies currently expected to create "call centers" in Palermo (ibid.). Here the situation in the schools becomes relevant. Quite apart from the current high level of school "dispersion"— truants and dropouts—some parents, as well as many teachers and principals, fear that the public schools might be losing status, that those among the student body in the poorest schools who can make the necessary sacrifices will jump ship for a better public institution, that there will be a decline in funding levels at the "abandoned" schools, with negative consequences for keeping up with informational skills. In short, some envision the whole panoply of ills that currently accompanies educational stratification around the world.

In October 2000, Moody's Investor Service gave the city of Palermo an Aa3 rating—the same rating as Italy and San Francisco. In the words of Orlando, "Sicilian society today finds itself in a position to realize the fruit—from an economic point of view—of the cultural changes that have marked these last few years."[14] According to the service, national and European Union financing will continue to support improvements in transportation, schools, infrastructure, and historic preservation, with tourism and perhaps information processing defined as sectors for growth. Moody's warns, however, that "despite these positive signals, the city's weak local economy is still of some concern as GDP per capita remains low and, at 29 percent, the unemployment rate remains high" (Moody's Communique 2000: 64). Sadly, for children growing up in families that contribute to this high rate, the educational projects of the antimafia forces are not enough to disqualify criminal activity as a viable basis for subsistence and source of prestige (see fig. 21).

CONCLUSION

Clearly, not all Palermitans share in, or feel part of, what world leaders fighting organized crime consider civil society. Nor, as we have seen in this chapter, do the educational efforts to propagate this concept go on without encountering discouraging limits and setbacks. Should Palermo have a mafia-free future, perhaps it will be at the cost of a profound alienation of its least privileged citizens, stigmatized by the others as "mafiosi" or "protectors of mafiosi" and policed accordingly. Yet we have to ask what the school projects mean for the thousands of children who, unless they are truant or expelled, continue to absorb and participate in them. According to one middle school principal, "The outside world trumps the message of the school." But another principal, who is

Figure 21. Poised with toy gun, young boy observes visitors to the Palermo cathedral during the UN signing conference, December 2000. Photograph by Jane Schneider.

more optimistic, drew a different conclusion: "Our children," he said, "are 'bilingual.' They live in two worlds and are really good at switching from one to the other." Down the road, if the city's economy gets on its feet, it will make a difference that many "at risk" children have learned this "second language."

CHAPTER 12

Reversible Destiny

Four elements underlie the possibility that a mafia-infused Sicilian "destiny" could be reversed. First, the mafia is not derived from any "deep" history—some would say "culture"—of Sicily, but rather had its origins in nineteenth-century processes of state and market formation. Second, the modernization of Sicily after World War II brought with it an expanding urban and educated middle class, some constituencies of which have supported an antimafia social movement, a revitalized police-judicial campaign against organized crime, and a reform government in Palermo, the regional capital. Third, the leaders of these developments are engaged in a serious effort to change how ordinary people think about and relate to the mafia. Their impact is especially evident in the recuperation of the city's historic center and the "re-education" of schoolchildren. And fourth, the 1992 collapse of the Italian First Republic left mafiosi, at least temporarily, without their political referents. Political institutions of the post–Cold War era, from Italy's "Second Republic" to the European Union and the United Nations, seem bent on criminalizing drug trafficking and condemning corrupt authorities, both formerly tolerated, or incompletely prosecuted, in the name of anticommunism.

Taken together, these elements suggest that citizens' groups can confront and challenge organized crime, criminal traffics, and state-authorized but illegal violence, at least insofar as wider structures of power are on their side. Unfortunately, very recent elections in both the national and Sicilian regional governments raise questions about how long a political environment favoring reform can last. What follows is a kind of stocktaking with regard to the antimafia process, concentrating on two domains—criminal justice and politics. In each case, we attempt to convey the tension between hope and concern that, we believe, characterizes Palermo today. This tension frames the conclusion, which considers what the Palermo experience might mean for the rest of the world.

THE CRIMINAL JUSTICE "WHEEL"

The mafia still exists in Palermo. What is more, its deployment of money into international financial circuits, involvement in Eastern Europe and Russia, and expanding role in people smuggling, are cause for alarm and continued vigilance (Paoli 2001: 171). Locally, however, there are ways to put a bright face on a series of bad affairs, and these, it seems to us, suggest that the criminal justice effort remains intact even though overall morale and energy are somewhat dissipated. A few examples illustrate how apparently ominous developments can be interpreted in a positive light—positive enough to ensure a continued momentum.

The first concerns *pentitismo*. After constituting the single most important breakthrough in the prosecution of the mafia, by the late 1990s, the justice collaborators, or *pentiti*, were becoming a huge management burden. Given that each one is capable of reconstructing fifteen to twenty years of mafia history, investigators feel overwhelmed—"like going fishing with a bomb instead of a line and sinker," one prosecutor told us. "How could we ever prosecute all the fish that come floating up?" The very logistics of finding courtrooms, assembling the accused from different prisons, trying some mafiosi for multiple crimes (200 times for Riina!), are daunting challenges, calling for new procedures.

More than this, the nearly four hundred *pentiti* of today inevitably include a certain number who are unreliable, inconsistent, or prone to return to criminal activity. At the same time, the mafia has altered its stance in relation to *pentitismo*, no longer categorically punishing the collaborators and their families but, apparently, negotiating with them instead. Some prosecutors believe that the mafia now offers "amnesty" to *pentiti* who would disavow their prior confessions.[1] Article 513, the new law on justice collaborators, encourages this by precluding that affidavits be used as evidence if they are retracted. Quite possibly, some of the new *pentiti* work *for* the mafia, proffering *dis*information so as to misdirect *(depistare)* an investigation. Yet, there is a way to put these changes in historical perspective, to see the "season of the *pentiti*" as coming to an end. The prosecutorial arm of the Palermo Prosecutor's Office has increased fivefold since the late 1980s, while the poisonous rumors that once destabilized its operations are no longer pervasive. The next steps will likely proceed according to different methods, among them new investigative techniques and surveillance technologies that are not as dependent on *pentito* collaboration.

The outcome of the Andreotti prosecution, initiated after Caselli took over the Prosecutor's Office in 1993 and provisionally concluded in the fall of 1999 with a verdict of "not guilty for lack of sufficient proof," is likewise subject to varying interpretations. (Technically the case is still in the appeals stage.) By the late 1990s, trying the former head of state had become controversial even among antimafia magistrates. Such a high-profile endeavor meant draining resources and energies from other investigations that had to be delayed, and there were differences of opinion regarding the severity of the charges against him. To accuse Andreotti of being a close political ally of Salvo Lima, and through this relationship to have lent aid and comfort to the *cosche* of Palermo, was one thing; to insist on his having participated directly in a mafia conspiracy raised the bar of sufficient proof considerably. In hindsight, many think, this judicial strategy entailed too much risk, coming to hinge, precariously, on one *pentito's* hearsay testimony about an encounter between Riina and Andreotti in which a kiss as well as a handshake had been exchanged. When that *pentito* subsequently misbehaved and had to be rearrested, the damage to the case was heavy. Other *pentito* testimony of off-the-record trips to Sicily and participation in a hunting party with the mafia of Catania, even though corroborated by additional evidence, was apparently not sufficient to convince the judges of his guilt (Caselli et al. 1995).

Although acquitted of charges of collusion, the former prime minister was nevertheless found to have lied when he denied any relationship with or knowledge of the Salvo cousins.[2] His relations with Salvo Lima and Vito Ciancimino, as well as with the banker Michele Sindona, were also confirmed, as were the political gains he derived from these relations. In other words, one can interpret the Andreotti verdict in a way that does not declare him innocent of political responsibility or conclude that all is lost for high-level prosecutions in the future. That the case was brought at all is in itself a remarkable change from what Falcone had imagined to be possible only a decade earlier. More than this, the absolution of criminal involvement that would have been Andreotti's greater reward was not forthcoming, while the public positioning of the accusations and the substance of the supporting evidence damaged his national and international reputation and now form part of the historical record.

On another front, the continued mafia extortion of retail and manufacturing businesses in Palermo and the associated practice of loan sharking require consideration, if one is to believe that things have really changed. During the summer of 1999, several fires were set in front of businesses to send a message to their owners. In a few instances the perpetrators were arrested, but in most they could not be identified because the victims refused to collaborate with the police. Surprisingly, prosecutors seemed prepared to put a better face on this all too familiar pattern than they would have in the past. For one thing, it is now *illegal* both to pay the tribute and to withhold testimony. Doing so, businessmen risk being charged as mafia collaborators. This is so regardless of whether they pay the monthly tribute out of convenience or out of fear. To each and all, the state now claims that its institutions have been reformed to the point that local business operators can trust the police and the judiciary to protect them. Recently, the state has created programs to assist the victims of usury as well.

Furthermore, it is possible that increased extortionist activity is symptomatic not of the mafia's resilience but of its vulnerability. The maxitrial and successive prosecutions have confronted mafiosi with staggering legal fees and an untenable number of prisoners' families to support. Today's climate does not permit the solutions to this dilemma that emerged at the time of the Catanzaro trial in the late 1960s: kidnapping for ransom and trafficking heavily in drugs. And so, optimists reason, mafiosi are furiously turning to the only other way they know to raise money quickly: the increased extortion of their neighbors. In Jamieson's words, "when life becomes more difficult for the Mafia . . . these more primitive criminal activities take on greater importance" (2000: 227). This, of course, discounts the argument that as they were being repressed in Italy, financially savvy mafiosi made "off-shore" investments, entered into pacts with the Colombian cartels to exchange cocaine for heroin, established cocaine distribution networks in Europe, and moved money in global financial markets through increasingly sophisticated electronic transactions that defy investigation. And yet, the optimists respond, we may nevertheless see a weakening of the local base, a process of financial accumulation cut loose from the obligation to take care of and cultivate constituencies close to home. By going this route, the mafia risks being defined as an engine for greed and violence, devoid of the legitimacy it once enjoyed.

Yet another example of conflicting interpretations has to do with the whereabouts of Bernardo Provenzano, who remains at large. In the past, fugitives could live under the very noses of those who would arrest them in part because they benefited from dense networks of protectors and in part because the police and the judiciary were corrupt. If both of these conditions have receded, why has Provenzano (among some thirty other fugitives) not been found? More than this, what meanings should be read into his continued shadowing of the antimafia process? According to the embroiled confessions of Brusca and another justice collaborator, Riina's capture in 1993 took many strange twists and turns that are worth looking into. A deep look, they suggest, would reveal that the police who made the arrest were aided in their hunt by none other than Provenzano, who thereby inherited the mantle of capo of the capi. If this is the case, Provenzano has been a different kind of leader. Compared with Riina, nicknamed "the Beast," Provenzano is portrayed by the press and media as smooth and manipulative—the fox replacing the lion. Perhaps he called a halt to Riina's aggressive tactics: no more excellent cadavers or outrageous bombings against representatives and symbols of the state. Assuming that a succession in leadership did occur, it can account for the mafia's lower profile (referred to in the press as a *pax mafiosa*) since 1993.

Cynics attribute this lower profile to cunning strategy. Provenzano has restrained the *cosche* from throwing their weight around because the present climate is so repressive; relax the repression and he and his organization will be at it again, making up for lost opportunities with a vengeance. It has long been said that the countryside is the reservoir of the mafia in Sicily; in the postwar decades, mafia skirmishes in Corleone served as a training ground for the particularly aggressive small-town upstarts who infiltrated the Palermo *cosche*. Unless and until the machinations of small-town mafiosi become transparent, it is naive to conclude that a fugitive leader could not orchestrate such a scenario again. The implications for Palermo are considerable. As suggested in earlier chapters, many urban residents are also residents of a rural town where they may own property, engage in commerce, participate in local politics, and maintain an active presence in family, church, and other social institutions. It is there that they might be conditioned or provisioned by local mafiosi (or may have been in the past). For this reason, too, a lesser presence of mafiosi in Palermo does not necessarily spell less risk from the mafia overall.

All of which suggests that a lot is riding on the antimafia movements in the countryside, where a number of communities have elected progressive mayors (twenty of them women) and are promoting their own projects for political and cultural reform. We have noted that several of these mayors continue to endure menacing attacks—injuries to their automobiles and pets if not their persons. Yet it is also noteworthy that in Corleone, once considered the "rural capital of the mafia," a progressive mayor and town council were able to organize a research center and museum, the International Center for Documentation on the Mafia and the Antimafia Movement, that has drawn the attention of world leaders (see chapter 11, note 12).[3] Because of this and other initiatives, commentators in Palermo no longer see the countryside as so impenetrable. Meanwhile, the circle may be closing around the super-boss Provenzano. As of this writing, two of his closest associates have been taken into custody, and six persons originally from Cinisi (Badalamenti's hometown) have been arrested by the Finance Guard, acting on information from a *pentito,* on charges that include providing support to Provenzano. It would seem that without this capo—with the *cupola* finally decapitated—the continually regenerating small-town bosses have less chance of erupting into another round of scorched earth expansionism.

CONTINUED BACKLASH AND SOME POLITICAL TESTS

Besides measuring the antimafia process against the mafia, we must also assess its relation to the backlash it has provoked. As we have seen, the arguments at stake in backlash rhetoric are rather contradictory, on the one hand evoking *Sicilianismo*—the cultural defense of Sicily against outsiders—while on the other hand promoting *garantismo*—the universal values of individual rights and civil liberties. Counter-antimafia advocates further claim to champion employment opportunities for Sicilians, blaming the maxi-trial and the prosecution of political corruption for wrecking the regional economy. During the 1980s, positions like these were closely associated in Sicily with the Italian Socialist Party and Sciascia; after 1992 they became the battle cry of Berlusconi's personalized political party, *Forza Italia* (FI), which made an impressive showing in Sicily in the national parliamentary elections of March 1994. Winning 21 percent of the vote for the Chamber of Deputies nationally (enabling Berlusconi to become prime minister), its tally in the region was 30.4 percent and 34.8 percent in the island's western provinces. In Palermo, 50.2 percent of voters supported the coalition, *Polo per la Libertà,* made up of *Forza Italia* and the other main right-wing party, *Alleanza Nazionale*

(AN). Although the city's six electoral districts in every case include a variety of neighborhoods, making it difficult to compare them, party analysts claim that Palermo north delivered a much smaller vote to the *Polo* than the neighborhoods with well-known mafia *cosche*. Observers, of course, drew the conclusion that the *Forza Italia* clubs in such places were in *odore di mafia;* Gaspare Nuccio, the coordinator of Orlando's *La Rete* Party, went so far as to request that the Palermo Prosecutor's Office launch an investigation.

On the national level, the *Polo* coalition also included the Northern League of Umberto Bossi, but this proved to be an unreliable alliance for Berlusconi, named prime minister, to govern. By December 1994, Bossi had withdrawn his support and Berlusconi had to relinquish the prime ministership to an interim "technical" government. In the next round of parliamentary elections, in April 1996, the parties of the left and center left, under the umbrella of the *Ulivo* coalition, narrowly defeated the *Polo* (now minus the Northern League, which stood alone). Sicily voted the other way, handing a victory to the *Polo*. More to the point, whereas Berlusconi's party received 20.6 percent of the national vote, in Sicily its showing was 32.1 percent and in Palermo a resounding 37.5 percent. Here the next most successful parties were AN with 16 percent and the former Communist Party, the PDS, with 12.2 percent—a substantial gap.

Newspapers declared *Forza Italia* to be "the first party of Palermo" following the 1999 election to the European Parliament, in which it won 36.2 percent of the vote. The city that had once sent Salvo Lima to Strasbourg, moreover, was again offering persons with clouded reputations as EU deputies, in particular, Francesco Musotto, arrested in 1995 for collusion with the mafia (but then acquitted in 1998), and Berlusconi's close ally, Marcello Dell'Utri, placed on trial in 1997 for collusion and money laundering. Dell'Utri, who formerly managed Fininvest, proved himself an exceptional vote-getter.

During Berlusconi's brief tenure as prime minister in 1994, Fininvest came under scrutiny in the *mani pulite* investigations; then and afterward, he has fought several indictments through waging an energetic campaign of *garantismo,* advocating lighter sentences and reduced reliance on *pentito* testimony in criminal trials. His and his party's rhetoric pointedly target the leftist political leanings of the key Milan magistrates, defining their prosecutions as a maneuver to drive the rightist and centrist parties, above all the remnants of the Christian Democratic Party, from the Italian political scene. This argument was extended to the antimafia magistrates prosecuting Andreotti in Sicily, who were accused of pursuing a Communist plot left over from the Cold War (see Burnett and Mantovani 1998). That Sicilians flocked to *Forza Italia,* so adamant in its antimagistrate position, as the Christian Democratic Party fell apart, would seem to be an ominous sign for the antimafia process in the future. In the national parliamentary election of April 2001 and the regional election of May, *Forza Italia* did well enough, thanks to loyal Sicilian voters, to be able to name the prime minister (Berlusconi again) and to prevent Orlando from becoming president of the region. More recently still, the mayoralties of several rural towns including Corleone have fallen to FI candidates.

As might be imagined, many former DC politicians now comprise the raft of national and regional parliamentary deputies elected by FI in Sicily. The question is whether this recycling of the past is a sign that, in the end, nothing has changed, whether, as Paoli writes, "the window of opportunity, which was opened in the early 1990s, seems to be closing again" (2001: 18). We were residents of Palermo during the 1996 parliamentary election and observed at first hand the disappointment of PDS leaders as the votes were counted; they were especially embarrassed over their party's failure to mobilize a better showing in the city's popular quarters. When asked to interpret this outcome, they and other antimafia activists resorted to the long-standing framework of *clientelismo:* politicians of the *Polo, Forza Italia* in particular, had inherited certain locally entrenched, mafia-influenced clienteles. The campaign workers for one PDS candidate who ran in a "mafia-infested" district beyond the northern suburbs told the following story. About ten days before the election, young thugs appeared in the open-air market where he had been campaigning and pointedly told shoppers to tear up his campaign literature. One of his supporters, a doctor, received a menacing phone call. On the day of the election, four or five of the same youths patrolled the school that served as a polling place, exchanging words with those who entered in order to "control their vote." According to an analyst on the candidate's staff, his FI rival did especially well among the poorest voters. Perhaps most unsettling, upon the conclusion of the election, the defeated candidate received an anonymous letter of the type intended to seed doubt, recounting who, behind his back, had not voted for him.

The attribution of Sicily's aberrant (by national standards) 1996 vote to old-fashioned mafia-manipulated clientelism calls to mind Pierre Bourdieu's concept of "doxa"—the tacitly assumed way in which power operates because "every established order tends to produce . . . the naturalization of its own arbitrariness" (1977: 164). Yet, because of the influence—in Bourdieu's terms the "heterodoxy"—of the antimafia movement, and because of the ("orthodox") backlash that this influence has provoked, politics in Sicily have become considerably more ideological than was the case in the past. Berlusconi's pervasive television presence has also contributed to this shift, as has the increased role of television in Italian elections overall (see Laurence 1996). Using the TV, Sicilian candidates are able to troll for popular-class votes not only through the personalized promise of favors and menace of sanctions but also by articulating a message about the magistrates' "excessive powers" and threat to Sicilians' cultural integrity, civil liberties, and jobs.

Three days before the election, we attended a candidates' forum organized by Palermo's equivalent of the League of Women Voters and held in one of the gilded rooms of a restored *palazzo* in the historic center. Here, the PDS candidate accused the *Polo* of having created a crisis through their attacks on the magistrates. An AN candidate, to the loud applause of a small clique of FI and AN supporters (most of the audience was pro-*Ulivo*), brought up the controversial trial of the police spy and inspector Bruno Contrada (who, like Musotto, was eventually acquitted). "Why is it," he thundered, "that persons who testified in favor of Contrada were menaced? Because the mafia is not the only source of menacing acts! Europeans are dismayed with the sad state of human rights abuses in Italy, where the accused do not have the right to a defense." A *Rete* supporter seated in front of us nearly fell off her chair. Don't you know, she shouted from the audience, "that Bruno Contrada is *guilty*? To interpret his being prosecuted as 'nazi' is an outrage."

Our richest exposure to ideological fire came during the final election rally of a *Forza Italia* candidate campaigning in Uditore. Local supporters had organized a "farewell party" for her that, although announced in the newspaper, gave the impression of being a private event. We were, indeed, approached by a small group of her entourage who questioned us as to why we were there. The site of the party dramatized Uditore's 1960s transformation from an orchard zone to a patchwork quilt of apartment houses and postage stamp gardens. It was a two-story, gated, California-style *villetta* entirely walled in by buildings of ten to twelve stories except for a narrow passageway to the street. Beer and food were served from the first-floor kitchen to a crowd of perhaps two hundred, while the candidate held forth from the balcony of a bedroom on the floor above. Energetic and attractive, she had obvious charismatic appeal for her overwhelmingly male audience. Her message touched all the right bases from the perspective of a neighborhood full of construction workers: the magistrates and the Orlando administration were a threat to their very livelihoods, she told them, with their rigid approach to contractor-certification and future urban growth.

Mafiosi still seek political allies; and politicians have not ceased being tempted by the votes that the mafia controls. As Judith Chubb reminds us, the mafia's wholesale shift in endorsement from the separatists to the DC in 1948, and from the DC to the Socialists in 1987, are lessons learned (ibid.: 284). In 2001 Orlando, having just completed his mandated last term as mayor of Palermo, lost a bid for presidency of the Sicilian region. Disinclined to campaign for the leftist candidate in the mayoral election, he has seen the position go to a protégé of Berlusconi. Yet, as the vignettes of the 1996 election suggest, a shift may be in the making from an electoral system dominated by the clientelistic exchange of favors for votes to a system that is also based on persuasion—the ideological cultivation of opinion. It remains to be seen whether mafiosi are able to condition *Forza Italia* politicians as political friends and, more seriously, whether they can count on such friends to "adjust trials." Short of this, they are surely continuing to channel votes toward politicians who they think will work hard in Parliament to reform the tough sentencing laws and laws supporting the *pentiti*. In Chubb's words, "The public delegitimation of public servants committed in the front line of the struggle against corruption and organized crime cannot help but serve the interests of the Mafia" (1996: 285).

Underlying the ideological persuasiveness of *Forza Italia* in Palermo is the pending social exclusion of some portion of the city's working classes from the new "law and order" civil society, a problem that is likely to persist for reasons we have considered in this book: the crisis in the city's most important industry, construction; the mismatch between the civil society ideal of the worthy citizen and the moral as well as practical meaning of clientelism for poor people; the tendency for a great many activities that result from poverty, for example, the subsistence work of petty thievery, to be labeled proto-mafioso, and thereby severely criminalized. The old destiny of the mafia was built on its practice of proactively provisioning and conditioning the wider society across all of its social groups. Every group, from the top to the bottom of the social order, had members who became "connected," or "collusive," or "contiguous" with organized crime. Being in *odore di mafia* was neither the privilege nor the curse of any particular stratum. The most convincing

social analysts in Palermo today see a future in which criminal and criminalized activity is believed to be closely associated with the poorer
classes—undereducated as well as underemployed—and with neighborhoods of the city where these classes predominate. Such a Palermo would
thus be divided in the way that many contemporary cities are, between
a "civil society" and "others," considered a menace to that "civilization"
and unworthy of its entitlements (see Hall 1998). Although a sure foundation for the continued advance of the counter-antimafia backlash, this
development is not simply a recapitulation of "destiny."

LESSONS FROM THE "CAPITAL OF THE ANTIMAFIA"

In many respects, the antimafia process belongs to a genre of social activism that emerged worldwide during the 1980s and 1990s calling for
transparency and honest democratic government, exposing cronyism and
corruption, promoting "civil society." Implicated in these parallels is, we
believe, the shared experience of the Cold War era, when the super-power
rivalry between the United States and the Soviet Union, refracted through
the proxy states that each controlled, led to monstrous technological and
military experiments and the florescence of covert networks of power. In
many places—Eastern Europe, South Africa, Latin America—people have
been struggling, as in Sicily, to redress past excesses of illegal violence au-
thorized by Cold War regimes. Alison Jamieson compares the Association
of Women against the Mafia to the Plaza de Mayo mothers in Buenos Aires
(2000: 130–31). Italy, of course, was a democracy and not a dictatorship
during the Cold War era, yet this does not invalidate the comparison. Angry Sicilians want to know what sort of a democracy was it that consistently reinstated the same political currents with the help of mafia votes?
As Jamieson writes, "The permanence in power of the same coalition of
parties, the same party leaders and the same supporting bureaucracies,
cemented into place by virtue of their anti-Communist convictions, had
encouraged complacency and a sense of superiority to the law" (2000: 9).

Civil society rhetoric has also acquired enormous currency with international institutions since the Cold War ended: the United Nations,
the foreign policy establishments of the G-8 countries, the World Bank
and International Monetary Fund, and a vast array of nongovernmental
organizations and their corporate funders. Political and corporate elites
associated with these bodies define the concept by conjuring its oppo-
sites, whether in the form of "Islamic fundamentalism," the principal
bête noir in Central Asia and the Middle East, of terrorism, often por-

trayed as related to Islam, of "low trust" societies scarred by terrible histories, or of the uncivil forces of crime and political corruption. Eager to suppress elements of the world's societies that threaten civil order, a number of global leaders have recently identified Palermo as a model city. This book was written not to celebrate Palermo as a success story but rather to extrapolate lessons from its impressive, yet still inconclusive attempt to address what may be the world's most politically entwined, if not culturally embedded, organized crime tradition.

One lesson warns of the risk that "wars on crime" will become assaults on poor people. To the United Nations, among many other sources, the words "organized crime" imply not only the collusion or cooperation of "three or more people" to commit illegal acts on an ongoing basis but also the economic nature of these acts. The acquisition of economic resources through theft, extortion, loan sharking, the territorial control of legal businesses, and trafficking in illegal commodities are classic pursuits of organized crime. But, as we have seen, organized crime formations like the mafia characteristically grow out of earlier episodes of resource appropriation on a grander scale, for example, the legislated creation of a land market or the militarized invasion of a territory. Displacing and impoverishing whole groups of people, these dislocating events generate a complex array of responses, some of which are "criminal," others of which are retributive but defined as illegal through the broadening of criminal law.

As a general rule, such episodes of resource accumulation also provoke resistance—individual and collective action aimed at mitigating or overturning (as distinct from taking advantage of) the new, unjust situation. What the Palermo experience demonstrates is how hard it is to separate entrepreneurial criminals from social and political protestors of various kinds. A social theory that romanticizes these protesters while ignoring criminal entrepreneurs on the grounds that they have been "criminalized" is naïve. By the same token, however, the coincident and interrelated dynamic between resource accumulation, protest, and criminal opportunism renders crime fighting a threat to vulnerable communities, the more so if those communities are perceived as loci of trouble for the state.

The Palermo experience shines a further spotlight on the construction industry, a source of many challenges in the fight against organized crime. Widely recognized as organically permeable to mobsters and dependent for its viability on municipal-level corruption, this industry is often, also, a critical employer in urban areas. Cleaning it up entails undermining the livelihood of working people. In Palermo, the move to reform has been nourished by citizens' fury over violations of their built environment—by an awakening of their desire to rediscover abandoned references to a rich artistic history. Yet even these worthy motives cannot dispel the ripple effects of displacing construction workers, and casting them as the enemy to boot.

Another lesson derives from the tendency for organized criminals and traffickers to cultivate webs of complicity at the highest levels of power. Because these webs are not easily visible—and because "hot wires" are dangerous to touch—their contours must often be imagined or hypothesized, much as believers imagine the nodes and motivations in an occult universe of spirits. Herein lies a hornet's nest of difficulties. Hypotheses and imaginings inevitably partake of the analyst's wider theoretical and historical understandings. Brilliant minds might, indeed, come up with different maps, not to mention different strategies, for navigating uncharted terrain. It is always a question whether these differences can be taken at face value or whether the dissenting "cartographers" are motivated by, say, political goals or complicit relationships. The dawn of transparency, wonderful as it sounds, is everywhere clouded by "mysteries and poisons," pleas for healing that become divisive, moves to prosecute that lack support, and, tragically, the likelihood that some in the forefront of exposing "the truth" will be martyred. Nor do present-day theories of power offer much guidance in these respects. Whether they emphasize structural inequality (among classes, ethnicities, genders) or the discourses of the socially and politically dominant, they have little to say about the operations of hidden networks that are technically knowable but too dangerous to know—or about the consequences of imagining such networks where none exist.

Finally, if the antimafia process in Palermo is any guide, contemporary "wars on crime" will inevitably be influenced by the history of the Cold War. Many of the covert networks that sustain organized crime formations are a legacy of those decades when the United States and the Soviet Union, on their own and through proxy governments, recruited and financed shady groups, authorizing their illegal exercise of violence and allowing their illegal trafficking in the name of battling one another. In addition, the meddling ghosts of the Cold War era make for divisions among "antimafia" activists who have had to shed the polarizing (left versus right) political identities of the preceding decades in order to unite around the new task of building civil society. In the case of the Palermo antimafia movement, keeping the left-right axis submerged in the name of forging a broader coalition continues to require a great deal of political work.

There is also, many believe, a political cost—specifically, the cost of failing to attend to the circumstances of social and economic injustice. Because thorough attention was the pride and province of the old left, attempts to focus on injustice today are easily caricatured as evoking the divisive ideological politics of the Cold War. Yet, without sufficiently noticing, analyzing, and treating gross injustice—and without understanding its historical roots—crime-fighting movements can compound unjust effects, not to mention generate a retributive menace for the future. Palermo's grassroots activists understand this, but they were marginalized from the antimafia process after 1992 when, in the wake of the dramatic assassinations of Falcone and Borsellino, attention turned massively to cultural reform.

In today's world, social activists are ever more challenged by forms of economic dislocation occasioned by the global expansion of (neoliberal—some would say "turbo"—) capitalism. Serious and at times divisive arguments surround what to do about newly impoverished populations whose constituents include recruits for organized crime. Everywhere, we believe, advocates in favor of transparency and democracy, and opposed to crime, are encumbered by the depth of this problem, the more so if they define cultural transformations as the only transformations that matter. In the foregoing pages, we have sought to make visible the antimafia struggle of community activists in Palermo, not only those who have been martyred, or who wear the mantle of municipal authority, but those at the grassroots level whose efforts are often unsung. We have called attention to the excluded and how a few of them, at least, feel about being left out. Like the two girls who wrote to the Carabinieri, many want to recuperate, do not see themselves as "bad," but sense that (civil) society would like to be "liberated" of them and is saying so behind their backs. Their need, and the need of thousands like them, for a "new" urban economy in which they can find opportunities is, perhaps, Palermo's most important lesson.

Notes

CHAPTER 1. THE PALERMO CRUCIBLE

1. For a general discussion of international and European Union responses to the crisis of organized crime in Italy, see Jamieson 2000: 159–98.

2. Jean Strouse's biography of Morgan includes the details that Sicily's "royal splendor and eastern magnificence" inspired the furnishings of his student rooms and that he considered the Byzantine mosaics in the cathedral of Monreale to be "if possible, superior to St. Marks." He would have examined them until dark, he wrote, but for fear that local brigands would hold up his party for ransom on their descent into Palermo (Strouse 2000: 202).

CHAPTER 2. THE GENESIS OF THE MAFIA

1. The distinction is reinforced by some interesting features of the Calabrian counterpart to the mafia, 'Ndrangheta, which never made the quantum leap into normal politics and society, continuing to resemble a bandit formation in many ways. Significantly, mafiosi eventually condemned kidnapping as too "barbaric," although they continued to resort to this means of raising money in special circumstances. By contrast, ransom money remained the bread and butter of 'Ndrangheta. Clearly, if you want to cultivate relationships with the powerful—a mafia hallmark—better not to scare them with the constant menace of sequesters (see Paoli 1997).

2. La Duca proposes two religious brotherhoods as possible prototypes for the Beati Paoli: the devotees of San Francesco di Paolo (Palermo's second-most popular saint after the city's patron saint, Santa Rosalia), or the followers of Saint Paul, founder of the Christian Church (La Duca 1984).

CHAPTER 3. THE MAFIA AND THE COLD WAR

1. Upon first setting foot in the rural town of our 1965 fieldwork in Sicily, we encountered graffiti scrawled along the side of the town's central church proclaiming, "USA = SS; No to Gas." The message predated our arrival by months, but U.S. involvement in Vietnam was of grave concern to the Italian left, and we were inevitably suspected by some of being on a mission for the CIA. The graffiti and the suspicions were a small-scale, local manifestation of the tensions surrounding U.S. foreign policy in that time.

2. Mafiosi and party loyalists had ways of monitoring their clients' choices, the secret ballot notwithstanding. During elections held in the mid-1960s, we observed such persons waiting outside of the polling places. They said they could spot defections by the look in a voter's eye. The system of proportional representation enabled a more reliable check: distrusted voters were given a unique combination of preference votes to cast, a combination that could then identify the voter as each ballot was (publicly) counted and announced (Schneider and Schneider 1976: 164–65).

3. Alongi (1997: 81) gives the somewhat lower figure of forty-seven assassinations of left-wing leaders and peasants between 1945 and 1966 in Sicily as a whole.

4. Buscetta stated, however, in testimony in the Pizza Connection trial in the United States, that he was *posato* (expelled) for having dishonored his wife by living openly with another woman.

5. Among the victims was Vassallo, the favored contractor of the Palermo Christian Democrats, Lima and Ciancimino. Luciano Cassina, son of an impresario with major road-building and maintenance contracts, was another. Such disappearances disrupted the cozy relations that had developed between the mafia, the Palermo construction industry, and politics. A few of the sequesters were carried out in the territory of Stefano Bontade, exposing his lack of effective control despite his considerable prestige (Pezzino 1995: 255). Most audaciously, in 1975 the Corleonesi kidnapped Luigi Corleo, the father-in-law of Nino Salvo—one of the powerful Salvo cousins who held the tax-collecting franchise and who was the source of many financial and money-laundering favors for the Badalamenti-Bontade group.

6. Some of Riina's victims were mafia leaders who showed wet feet regarding the "scorched earth" removal of troublesome judges and police officials. As an example, Paoli cites Mariano Agate's murder of Vincenzo D'Amico and Ciccio Caprarotta. Agate was boss of the Mazara del Vallo *cosca* and an ally of Riina. He murdered his companions because they resisted his proposal to kill Paolo Borsellino, then chief prosecutor in nearby Marsala (Paoli 1997: 251).

7. According to Santino (1988: 238), in Palermo and its surroundings, 606 murders occurred between 1978 and 1984, excluding disappearances. The worst years were 1981 with 98, 1982 with 150, and 1983 with 113.

8. Now a *pentito*, Siino has described how he obtained a list of all the companies intending to bid on an important highway project linking Sciacca and Palermo from (then Euro-deputy) Salvo Lima (*Giornale di Sicilia*, September 9, 1999).

9. Contraband tobacco in the postwar period is a good example. In Italy, the state holds a monopoly on cigarette manufacture and sale, but Italians preferred to smoke Marlboros and other American brands. During the immediate postwar decades, sailors in cahoots with smugglers offloaded thousands of cartons of American cigarettes wrapped in plastic sacks from ships that were carrying them to countries where their import was legal. Posing as fishermen, the smugglers hauled up the sacks and brought them ashore near Naples and Palermo, entering their contents into Europe's thriving black markets.

10. See Jamieson (2000: 57), who cites the figure of 4,600 affiliates in 113 lodges. On July 26, 1992, the *Collegio* of the *Gran Maestri* of the Sicilian lodges refused to vote a position on the mafia, notwithstanding the assassinations of the judges Falcone and Borsellino only a short time before. A year later, Di Bernardo, the *Gran Maestro* of the *Grande Oriente d'Italia,* came under fire for having contributed to the preparation of the above-noted Cordova Report. Even though he publicly refrained from supporting Cordova's conclusions, claiming that they were too extreme, he was forced to resign. Di Bernardo went on to found a new network of lodges, the *Gran Loggia Regolare d'Italia,* and to arrange for English, French, and German masonry to break off relations with the GOI, whose leader, Armando Corona, was rumored to be close to Gelli and various secret service operatives (Forgione and Mondani 1994).

11. In the words of the *pentito* Mannoia, "Salvatore Inzerillo and Stefano Bontade had Sindona, the others [i.e., the Corleonesi] had Calvi" (quoted in Paoli 1996: 21).

CHAPTER 4. THE CULTURAL PRODUCTION OF VIOLENCE

1. Although prohibited by the Catholic Church, cousin marriage has long been a common way for propertied families to counteract the fragmenting effects of partible inheritance. Dispensations for such marriages are regularly granted upon presenting an application and paying a fee.

2. In his book on the *Camorra* trials in Naples, anthropological linguist Marco Jacquemet notes how a particularly violent faction, the *Nuova Camorra Organizzata,* hegemonic during the "long 1980s," funneled proceeds from racketeering into aid for prisoners and their families. Raffaele Cutolo, the faction's innovative head, called this form of assistance his "green cross" and used it to recruit more prisoners. In creating a verbally elaborate ceremony through which to induct them, Cutolo melded Catholic ritual with elements of nineteenth-century Cammoristic initiations that he purportedly dug up in the prison library (see Jacquemet 1996: 28–41).

3. He also related that, after his induction, he found himself asking whether the mafia were not "some sort of communism." No, he was told, "private property was recognized and everyone was free to do what he wants with it." But illegitimate business is particular: "before doing anything, one has to . . . ask . . . permission" of one's superiors (ibid.: 53).

4. We are reminded of Gaetano Mosca's turn-of-the-century account of the mafiosi who inserted themselves between the proprietor of an orchard and some lemon thieves; the former was asked to offer a small "gift" to the latter, who "did

it because they were hungry" (1949: 233–37). A classic description of extortion, written just after the Notarbartolo assassination in an effort to "explain" the mafia to northerners, it is reprinted in the *Encyclopedia of the Social Sciences*.

5. His (pseudo-)name is actually given as "Salvo" in the interview. We have replaced it with the generic "Tizio" to avoid confusion with the tax collectors, Ignazio and Nino Salvo, and the former DC mayor of Palermo, Salvo Lima.

6. It may be that this rule has changed. In 1999, a leading officer of the Palermo magistracy informed us that in response to increased police surveillance and the great number of mafiosi who have become justice collaborators, certain capi have taken to farming out some of these functions to street-level *picciotti* who are not mafiosi.

7. American mafia wives are often remarked upon for their materialism, even caricatured as princesses, their sights set on elaborate home furnishings and fur coats.

8. Inga Clendinnen, an Australian historian, has written a penetrating critique of representations of the Holocaust in which Nazi atrocities are interpreted as "absolute moral transgressions," indeed metaphysically evil, propelled by an exhilarating lust to kill born of identification with the Fuhrer and his projects (1999: 86ff). She is at the same time critical of Goldenhagen's argument that Germany's "centuries-long" history of eliminationist anti-Semitism rendered most Germans pre-adapted to participate in the rounding up and murder of Jews. Her close-up look at these bewildering, unthinkable events is in some ways more disturbing: ordinary men—family men bound by moral rules against, for example, theft and adultery—become executioners through a concatenation of almost familiar processes. Resonant with military training, whether in modern armies or among headhunters of other times, these include: being subjected to an ideological vision of a better, or purer future; the emergence of group loyalty; the fear of authority or of being punished; the efficacy of secrets and special codes in "sustaining the cohesiveness of an exclusive . . . elite"; the resort to alcohol or drugs as antidotes to faintness of heart or moral uncertainty; the dehumanization of victims. What initiates experience as difficult on their first try becomes with time and practice almost habitual; techniques and skills improve and formerly anxious or reluctant participants take pride in being respected by their comrades (ibid.: 119–31). Mafia studies are far behind Holocaust studies and concern a phenomenon of much lesser scale, yet they too might be illuminated by a broad, comparative approach to the normalization of cruel and vicious killing, especially as regards the "long 1980s."

9. The deposition of Vincenzo Marsala (1985) contains a similar description of the same events.

CHAPTER 5. SEEKING CAUSES, CASTING BLAME

1. As Marcello Cimino later clarified (1983), this did not mean that to be bourgeois in Sicily meant to be mafioso. There are other bourgeois elements. The point is to think of the mafia as a class fraction of the "grand, capitalistic bourgeoisie."

2. Gambetta has also been criticized for reducing a varied range of mafia

roles to one synthetic role, purveyors of protection (see P. Schneider 1994) and for overlooking the entrepreneurial involvement of mafiosi "in the construction industry, the refining as well as the transportation of heroin, and the recycling of illicit gains" (Chubb 1996: 280).

CHAPTER 6. MYSTERIES AND POISONS

1. This arrangement was made possible by the fact that both men were under indictment in the United States for violation of that country's laws.

2. Investigating magistrates, however, say that it is taboo—like "carrying water to your own mill"—to ask leading questions of one *pentito* based on prior knowledge from another.

3. As Richard Martin, then liaison between U.S. and Italian criminal justice, explained to us in 1987, it is common for the *pentiti* to want to protect certain areas, to claim not to know certain things. Buscetta, for example, seemed to want to protect Badalamenti. But to go too far in the direction of appearing to protect friends or hide information is to lose credibility.

4. Boris Giuliano was also an investigator, along with Giorgio Ambrosoli, into the fraud perpetrated on the Banca Privata Italiana by Michele Sindona. Ambrosoli's murder in the same year is noted in chapter 3.

5. This showed the tenacity and courage of Costa, who signed the indictments after virtually all of the other prosecutors in his office had declined to do so, a fact that leaked out of the office and led to his assassination.

6. A modification of Article 416 of the criminal code, hence known as 416bis, the Rognoni–La Torre law defines "Associations of a mafia type" as (to paraphrase) consisting of three or more persons who use powers of intimidation and the cover of extorted silence to commit crimes, gaining control of economic activities for unjust profits. To quote Jamieson, "The fusion of public-order concerns with economic controls and socio-criminological theory made the law unique in Italian legislative history. Investigations were no longer concentrated on 'the crimes of the Mafia' but on 'the Mafia as a form of criminality'" (2000: 28–29).

7. This notwithstanding periodic searches of his Ciaculli estate, one of which led to exaggerated reports of its having underground tunnels, as in the Beati Paoli (chap. 5).

8. An investigation of 1996 charged Carnevale with *concorso* in association with the mafia, for which he was tried and eventually was convicted. Several *pentiti* testified against him, among them Angelo Siino (the "public works commissioner of the Corleonesi"). Accusations also flowed from magistrates belonging to other sections of the *Cassazione*. Not only had Carnevale "adjusted" numerous trials between 1985 and his dismissal in 1993; he had made his colleagues feel uncomfortable by resorting to "dramatic and upsetting" tactics, for example, deploying a "rustic" and intimidating peasant near his office door in order to obtain their cooperation in overturning convictions. Perhaps five hundred cases were turned back, thanks to Carnevale finding small errors in the proceedings of the lower courts or announcing in advance that *qui non c'è niente*— "there is nothing here" (*La Repubblica,* April 9, 1998; *Giornale di Sicilia,* June

24, 1999). Most spectacularly, in February 1991 he ordered the release from prison of Michele Greco and forty-two bosses on the grounds that there had been a miscalculation in the number of days they could be held while awaiting trial. The public uproar that resulted brought about a reversal of the order by the president of the republic.

Fanatical about due process, Carnevale inveighed against the Buscetta theorem of the unity of the mafia, warning that the Constitution frowned upon magistrates in "military uniforms" rather than in "togas." Himself a Sicilian, from Agrigento Province, he heartily disliked his fellow islander, Falcone, whom he once referred to as a *cretino*. Apparently, he did not object to his own nickname, *Ammazzasentenza,* meaning "Sentence Killer."

9. To our knowledge, investigators never uncovered the author or motivation of this bizarre letter.

10. The Socialist leader, Craxi, who advocated the more radical step of moving to a presidential system, urged the voters to boycott the referendum, but 62.2 percent of them did not, and of these a surprising 95.6 percent supported the change.

11. The legislature also softened the edges of Article 41bis, allowing prisoners more contact with their families and the opportunity to "prepare their own meals on gas cookers at lunchtime (a privilege which had [previously] only been granted to Totò Riina for fear of his being poisoned)" (Jamieson 2000: 121).

12. Police inspectors have prepared a computerized identikit showing how he might have aged—an antimafia artist also caricatured Riina before his arrest. During the summer of 1999, we were told by a magistrate that Siino had just accused Brusca of playing a double game with respect to Provenzano—namely, that of exposing his whereabouts to the authorities but then informing him so that he could get away.

13. This court also convicted the *cupola,* and no one higher, for the murder of Pio La Torre, in his case as punishment for daring to promote legislation covering the confiscation of mafia assets. An interesting aspect of the decision was the court's statement, sure to bother skeptics, that the *"cupola* had to have been unanimous" because (1) all components were subordinate to the Corleonesi, (2) their interests converged, (3) no crime could be committed without permission of the capo in whose territory it took place, and (4) in the absence of unanimity, there would surely have been a violent reaction, and none was forthcoming (*Giornale di Sicilia,* July 27, 1999).

14. In fact, during a conference in 1988 he surprised us and the rest of his audience by saying, "Mind you, there is no third level of mafia!" He was arguing, we believe, that there was no hidden level within the mafia above the famed controlling *cupola.*

CHAPTER 7. THE ANTIMAFIA MOVEMENT

1. For an excellent review, see Edelman 2001.

2. In 1996, we attended the unveiling of a bust of Placido Rizzotto in the central piazza of Corleone, presided over by the town's recently elected antimafia mayor. Family members and perhaps two hundred well-wishers from Corleone

and surrounding towns were also present. Indicative of the way Cold War habits weigh on the antimafia movement of today, our companions, who were secular leftists, were dissatisfied that the ceremony was framed by the ringing of church bells. Rizzotto, they inveighed, would not have approved.

3. At the time a local priest active in DC politics in Villamaura quipped to us that Cardinal Ruffini had "died on the field of battle: on his way to vote!"

4. It was in this context that the student radicals, retailoring the left's anti-mafia perspective to an urban context, took on Mario Mineo's concept of a *mafia borghesia* (see chap. 5).

5. In northern Italy, radicalized members of Catholic Action also partici-pated in "transversal" grassroots mobilizations on behalf of the urban poor (see Tarrow 1988).

6. Italian law provides for victims to constitute themselves as civil parties to the state's prosecution of those who harmed them, but doing so in the case of mafia crimes was new. In 1987, interviewees thought it significant that funds were being raised to pay for attorneys for this purpose.

7. Fifty thousand signatures were required to force parliamentary consider-ation.

8. Consistent with their social mission, the activists named the room for Mauro Rostagno, a student radical of the 1970s who had set up a drug rehabil-itation center and gone on local television to denounce the mafia's drug traffick-ing, only to be killed on September 26, 1988.

9. The training took place through a region-funded, CGIL-administered course in "socio-cultural or community animation" (see Chiovaro 1981–82).

10. Galasso published a novel about this in 1988, which angered the regional leadership of the PCI, some of whom considered him "monomaniacal" about an-timafia.

CHAPTER 8. BACKLASH AND RENEWAL

1. The new generation of investigating magistrates and police are consider-ably more determined than comparable figures in the novels. In *Pirandello e la Sicilia*, Sciascia, convinced of the impossibility of "turning" a mafioso into a wit-ness for the state, elaborated on the duplicitous role of the informer or confidant. First a mafioso, sucked in by the police, begins to betray his companions, but they, finding this out, use him to feed the police carefully prepared *disinforma-tion*. In the end, the police become pawns in a factional dispute. Even the fascist system of exiling mafiosi worked to help certain factions get rid of their enemies, assisted by the police (1961: 175–78; see also Candida 1964). Such resignation hardly anticipated the singular success of Falcone and Borsellino in developing the phenomenon of the mafia *pentito*.

2. An interesting controversy surrounded the ultimately successful request of the *Giornale* to participate in the eventual trial of Francese's accused assassins as *parte civile*. Some observers, convinced that the paper was nudged by the Bontade-Inzerillo group to expose the Corleonesi, argue that it wittingly put Francese's life at risk and was, therefore, complicitous. On such grounds it would seem unconscionable to grant it the status of an aggrieved party. Others, though,

including the present head of the Palermo Prosecutor's Office, Piero Grasso, believe this line of thinking only opens old wounds and is unnecessarily divisive.

3. A temporary savior of *L'Ora* was Mario Rendo, one of the Knights of Labor of Catania, who, although close to the Communist Party, was in every way a contradiction to the paper's consistently antimafia editorial stance. At the time, journalists on the left defended Rendo as a source of jobs, even if he indulged in illegal methods.

4. Specifically the charge that Lima had been involved in the Mattarella killing. See chapter 6.

5. Revisiting Villamaura over the course of the "long 1980s," we were privy to people's deep discontent over the order, following the dalla Chiesa assassination, that horseracing be suspended at religious festivals throughout Sicily. Townspeople had always looked forward to three days of races up its main street in celebration of their patron saint. To substitute folk singers, which was what the festival planners resorted to, was risible and miserable in the eyes of just about everyone. Elsewhere, the ban on horseracing provoked huge demonstrations, dense with *umori Sicilianisti* (see Cimino 1983).

6. Close to a thousand tee shirts were sold. The proceeds, together with contributions collected during the day, gave the committee a cushion for its future activities.

7. The resulting ripples (followed in chaps. 10 and 11) garnered the attention of the Thorolf Rafto Foundation of Norway, which gave PAU its 1996 prize for contributions to human rights (see Jamieson 2000: 147).

CHAPTER 9. CIVIL SOCIETY GROUNDWORK

1. Later, Pappalardo criticized a group of priests who, along with Orlando, defined this killing as a "different sort of homicide" (*Giornale di Sicilia,* March 19, 1992).

2. We know of a small-town case where the doctor, having declared that a mafioso had a heart problem that justified moving him from prison to house arrest, then made regular house visits to "doctor" his EKGs. Consider, too, the physician who operated on the vocal chords of a mafioso so as to change his voice print.

3. *Segno* has published some exceptionally bold claims for Christian love and forgiveness—for example, an account of Emmanuel Levinas, a Jew born in Russia who suffered in concentration camps under Hitler and Stalin and who "emerged with the most profound compassion for those who mistreated him" (Haering 1985: 103–4). And of Korie ten Boom, a protector of Jews in Holland, who was betrayed and tortured but on her release cured the man who had betrayed her. After the war she founded two houses for the rehabilitation of concentration camp guards. The message is that anyone can be cured and pardoned to become a child of God—mafiosi included (ibid.: 104).

4. In 1994, Riina took advantage of a courtroom appearance to directly threaten sociologist Pino Arlacchi, along with Caselli and Luciano Violante, former president of the Antimafia Commission. "Signor Arlacchi writes," he said, "but what does he write? Communist things" (quoted in Jamieson 2000: 66).

5. A friend once corrected us for referring to the letters we write for students as "letters of recommendation." No, she said, those are "letters of reference," which is something else. With a recommendation, the receiver considers favoring the person who wrote the letter; a letter of reference is taken as introducing the person whom the letter is about.

6. Several ethnographers of the Mediterranean during the 1960s and 1970s recorded peoples' assumption that saints belonged in their social maps of worldly patronage (e.g., Boissevain 1965, 1977; Christian 1972; Kenny 1960).

CHAPTER 10. RECUPERATING THE BUILT ENVIRONMENT

1. In addition to the antimafia movement, groups throughout Italy engaged with drug treatment and rehabilitation have promoted the concept of putting properties acquired with contaminated money to "socially useful" ends. *Libera,* an organization headed by reformer-priest Don Luigi Ciotto, is perhaps the best-known example.

2. The Bank of Sicily has created a "Save Sicily" Committee that raises money in the United States for the restoration of particular monuments on the island, at the same time encouraging tourism.

3. The pedestrian experiments continue, in part as a response to national legislation addressing excessive automobile emissions in all Italian cities.

4. For more information on Palermo's immigrant communities see Cole 1997; Booth and Cole 1999.

5. Eberstadt describes Gioacchino Lanza Tomasi, cousin and adopted son of the author of *The Leopard,* rattling around in the Palazzo Lampedusa, "a shuttered hulk overlooking the sea . . . buying from the scattered descendants of its original owners the remaining jigsaw pieces . . . and propping them up . . . the doctor of an old house's aches and sorrows" (1991: 41).

6. The idea that *palermitani* might transform themselves from passionate automobilists to consistent bus and tram riders, let alone walkers and cyclists, has elicited a cynical response, even among many antimafia activists. Others, though—the "greenest" of the activists—are enthusiastic if less than hopeful. As they are quick to say, in 1962, it was totally unquestioned that private cars were the wave of the future; hence the construction of the multiple-lane ring road whose river of roaring vehicles, impossible to cross, bifurcated several outlying neighborhoods. In the new PRG of Cervellati, that road is to be submerged under malls and parks so that residents from the two sides of the "river" can interact.

7. By the same token, already in the 1960s, zones of new construction in Palermo were reaching a density of 21 cubic meters per square meter, in contrast to the national norm of 3.5 cubic meters per square meter in urban areas (see Chubb 1982: 134).

8. See chapter 6 on the sinister consequences that seemed to flow from investigating Calcestruzzi.

9. Giambrone, who initiated this project, claims to have been inspired by the use of these sheds in recent times for preparing the massive carriage that carries Santa Rosalia on her saint's day.

CHAPTER 11. "CULTURAL RE-EDUCATION"

1. This is not to imply that all of the middle schools are progressive; much depends on the principal. An interested, committed principal goes out of her or his way to recruit committed teachers, but principals who are inactive are satisfied with a staff of transients—teachers who, for whatever reason, land the school as their first job but cannot wait to move on.

2. Conversely, in 1999, we met a few working-class parents with antimafia convictions who did not let their children join the May 23 march to the Palazzo di Giustizia in honor of Judge Falcone because they feared the children might suffer reprisals.

3. The city government has recently decreed that the quarter be renamed for its parish church, San Filippo Neri.

4. Thirty-two households had no automobile.

5. The "dossier" of *Il Sole-24 Ore* (December 11, 2000), referred to in chapter 9, ranks the province of Palermo 88 out of 103 for reported purse and wallet snatchings, 99 out of 103 for reported carjackings, and 100 out of 103 for reported robberies. Its place on the list for break-ins is, however, forty-seventh.

6. After they are cannibalized for saleable parts, the cars are often burned. One sees their charred hulks on the edge of ZEN II.

7. On the effects of informal drug retail trade on poor communities, see Leeds (1996) and Venkatesh (1997).

8. Poor urban communities in which opportunities for youth are abysmal often manifest tensions between "the street" and "the school." The idea that the street generates resourceful and creative forms of culture in opposition to values represented by the school is especially well developed in Paul Willis's pioneering ethnography of working-class youth in England (1981).

9. Jamieson cites more discouraging figures. In southern Italy as a whole, the number of children who leave school before their mandatory fourteenth birthday is double the number in the north. Sicilian children drop out at a higher rate than in the other southern regions, while in Palermo's poorest neighborhoods, as few as 10 percent complete the minimum years. At the same time, Sicily has 25 percent of the institutionalized minors in Italy, considerably more than any other region (Jamieson 2000: 148–49).

10. Revisiting some of the families in 1999, we heard the refrain again ("when there was the mafia, there was construction," "the mafia *dava da mangiare*" [put food on the table]). People also commented spontaneously, as they had not before, on immigration, making note of television reports that more Sicilians were leaving, and of the government's overly generous approach to foreigners—described as "taking our jobs" or "working for too little pay." Gypsies, who "don't know how to live in apartments and expect handouts," were another target.

11. In January 2000, a newly built middle school named for Father Puglisi was inaugurated in Brancaccio. Since his arrival in the parish in 1990, it had been his goal to see middle school children educated in a proper school building rather than in rented spaces, which was the pattern that had prevailed.

12. Several groups of delegates were bussed to Corleone to visit a new mu-

seum and center for research and documentation on the mafia and to hear that town's antimafia leaders talk about their experiences. One, a city council member, used almost racial language to characterize what was new. For years, he said, we were depicted as "dark" *(scuri);* the media used to come and film us as a "strange dark people." Now we have ended the system that made us less "clean" *(pulito).*

13. Several antimafia activists considered these remarks to have a patronizing tone.

14. Typical of Orlando's rhetorical style, his speeches during the UN gathering paired economy and culture as if they were discrete, even opposite phenomena: our experience belies "economy produces culture" in favor of "culture produces economy." "We have built a culture of peace to promote an economy of peace." First the goal was for the city to be "less rich but more free, because we were illegally rich. Now we are more free and need to be more rich." "You have to have an identity to fight against the mafia, because the mafia is cultural, too." Interviewed by a Spanish newspaper, *ABC Domingo,* in September 2000, he referred to Palermo's postwar administration as having brought "the culture of death," whereas his brought "the culture of life." Palermo has become "an example of the culture of legality for the rest of the world." On a world book tour to promote his recently published (and translated) biography (Orlando 2001), he reiterated these black and white, before and after dualities.

CHAPTER 12. REVERSIBLE DESTINY

1. In Caselli's words, before the mafia behaved like a "vindictive father," exacting "ferocious punishments." Now it has changed strategy, "becoming a mother who understands and pardons" *(Giornale di Sicilia,* September 12, 1999).

2. Evidence here included the already noted photograph taken by Letizia Battaglia documenting Andreotti's presence at the luxury hotel of Ignazio Salvo in Bagheria, and testimony that he had given Nino Salvo's elder daughter a silver bowl as a wedding present.

3. In recent elections held after this chapter was first written, the progressive mayor of Corleone was replaced by a candidate of the center-right *Forza Italia* party. The new administration has showed less sympathy for the goals of the center, and a number of the members of the center's sponsoring committee have resigned.

References

Primary Sources

Buscetta, Tommaso. 1984. Transcript of Deposition, Parts I and II.
Centro Siciliano di Documentazione Giuseppe Impastato, and Comitato dei Lenzuoli di Palermo. 1996. *Eppur si avanza: 1985–1996, dieci anni di giustizia a Palermo tra emergenza e normalizzazione.* Pamphlet published by the authors.
Chinnici, Rocco. 1983. "Il diario del giudice Rocco Chinnici." In *Proceedings of the Commissione Parlamentare sul Fenomeno della Mafia,* Session of Wednesday, 28 September 1983, pp. 49–71.
Chiovaro, Marcella Contarella. 1981–82. *L'animazione negli asili-nido; appunti e schede di lavoro.* Palermo: ECAP—Istituto della CGIL per la Formazione Professionale.
Cipolla, Giuseppe. 1988. *Mafia cultura educazione: contributi alla didattica antimafia.* Partinico: Centro Jatino di Studi e Promozione Sociale "Nicolò Barbato."
Città di Palermo. 1998. *Interventi di ricupero nel centro storico di Palermo.* Palermo: Assessorato del Centro Storico.
Comitato dei Lenzuoli. 1992. *Nove consigli scomodi al cittadino che vuole combattere la mafia.* Pamphlet produced by the Comitato dei Lenzuoli.
———. 1992–99. Archive. Courtesy of Marta Cimino.
Commissione Parlamentare Antimafia. 1993. "Il partito trasversale delle logge irregolari." *Narcomafie,* October: 17–24.
Commissione Parlamentare d'Inchiesta sul Fenomeno della Mafia in Sicilia, ed. 1972. *Relazione sui lavori svolti e sullo stato del fenomeno mafioso al termine della V legislatura.* Rome: Stabilimenti Tipografici Carlo Colombo.

————. 1976. *Relazione conclusiva. Relazione sul traffico mafioso di tabacchi e stupefacenti nonchè sui rapporti fra mafia e gangsterismo italo-americano.* Relazione di Minoranza. Roma: Tipografia del Senato.

Folena, Pietro. 1993. "Il sistema sanitario in Sicilia tra affari, mafia e massoneria." Speech given to the Association "New Resistance," March 19, 1993, Palermo.

Gambetta, Diego, and Valeria Pizzini. N.d. "The Nicknames of Sicilian Mafiosi." Unpublished manuscript.

Grasso, Pietro. 2000. "Il ruolo della legge e degli organi preposti alla sua applicazione." Paper delivered to the International Symposium on "The Role of Civil Society in Countering Organized Crime: Global Implications of the Palermo, Sicily Renaissance," Palermo.

Gruppo Realtà. 1990. *Dossier Palermo: le realizazioni della amministrazione comunale di Palermo negli anni 1985–1990.* Palermo: La Sezione Studi Sociali del Gruppo Realtà.

Hitz, Frederick P. 1998. "CIA Inspector General's Investigation of Alleged Ties Between CIA, the Contras and Drug Trafficking." Unpublished paper. The entire two-volume report is available at www.cia.gov.

Informa Palermo. 1999. Periodico di informazione del Comune di Palermo.

La Fisca, Anna Maria, and Giovanni Palazzo. 1996. *Santa Maria dello Spasimo.* Palermo: Edizioni Guida.

Lo Dato, Enzo. 2000. "Palermo's Cultural Revolution and the Renewal Project of the City Administration." Paper delivered at the "Symposium on the Role of Civil Society: Creating a Culture of Lawfulness; The Palermo, Sicily Renaissance," Palermo.

Maddox, Richard. 1999. "The Politics of Space and Identity in a Europe 'Without Borders': Cosmopolitan Liberalism, Expo '92, and Seville." Unpublished manuscript.

Marsala, Vincenzo. 1985. Transcript of deposition.

Ministry of the Interior, Italy. 1993. *Rapporto annuale sul fenomeno della criminalità organizzata per il 1992.* May.

————. 1994. *Rapporto annuale sul fenomeno della criminalità organizzata per il 1993.* April.

Modello di gestione agricola in zona de periurbana. 1997. Città di Palermo, Ufficio di contratti. Contract number 10 with Coop. "il Nespolo." February 4.

Moody's Communique. 2000. "Moody's Assigns a First Time Aa3 Rating to the City of Palermo." Distributed at the International Symposium on "The Role of Civil Society: Creating a Culture of Lawfulness; The Palermo, Sicily Renaissance," Palermo.

Orlando, Leoluca. 2000. "From a Culture of Lawfulness to an Economy of Legality," Paper delivered to the Symposium on "The Role of Civil Society: Creating a Culture of Lawfulness; The Palermo, Sicily Renaissance," Palermo.

Paoli, Letizia. 1996. "The Integration of the Italian Crime Scene." Unpublished manuscript. April.

Provveditorato agli Studi. 1996–97. Protocollo d'intesa in materia di prevenzione e recupero della dispersione scolastica. Comune di Palermo, Procura della Repubblica per i minori, Tribunale per i minorenni di Palermo.

Terranova, Gilda. 1993–94. "Centro sociale San Saverio." Lauria thesis, Università degli Studi di Palermo.

SECONDARY SOURCES

Acuto, Santina, Alessandro Cestelli, Italia Di Liegro, and Marina Di Liegro. 1983. *Dimenticati a Palermo*. Palermo: Ila Palma.

Ajroldi, Cesare, Francesco Cannone, and Francesco De Simone, eds. 1994. *Lettere su Palermo di Giuseppe Samonà e Giancarlo De Carlo: per il piano programma del centro storico 1979–1982*. Rome: Officina Edizioni.

Alajmo, Roberto. 1993. *Un lenzuolo contro la mafia*. Palermo: Gelka.

Alcaro, Mario. 1999. *Sull'identità meridionale*. Turin: Bollati Boringhieri.

Alongi, Giuseppe. 1886. *La maffia nei suoi fattori e nelle sue manifestazioni: studio sulle classi pericolose della Sicilia*. Turin: Fratelli Bocca.

Alongi, Nino. 1997. *Palermo; gli anni dell'utopia*. Soveria Manelli: Rubbettino Editore.

Ambroise, Claude. 1989. "Cronologia." In *A futura memoria*, edited by L. Sciascia, 165–88. Milan: Bompiani.

Arlacchi, Pino. 1993. *Men of Dishonor: Inside the Sicilian Mafia*. New York: William Morrow.

———. 1994. *Addio cosa nostra: la vita di Tommaso Buscetta*. Milan: Rizzoli.

———. 1995. *Il processo: Giulio Andreotti sotto accusa a Palermo*. Milan: Rizzoli.

Arlacchi, Pino, and Nando dalla Chiesa. 1987. *La palude e la città: si può sconfiggere la mafia*. Milan: Arnaldo Mondadori Editore.

Armao, Fabio. 2000. *Il sistema mafia: dall'economia-mondo al dominio locale*. Turin: Bollati Boringhieri.

Backman, Johan. 1998. *The Inflation of Crime in Russia: The Social Danger of the Emerging Markets*. Helsinki: National Research Institute of Legal Policy.

Balibar, Ettienne. 1988. "Is There a 'Neo-Racism'?" In *Race, Nation, Class: Ambiguous Identities*, edited by E. Balibar and I. Wallerstein, 17–29. London: Verso.

Banfield, Edward C. 1958. *The Moral Basis of a Backward Society*. New York: Free Press.

Barbadoro, Idomeneo. 1966. *Le industrie di Palermo*. Palermo: Libri Siciliani.

Barbagli, Marzio. 1982. *Educating for Unemployment: Politics, Labor Markets, and the School System—Italy, 1959–1973*, translated by Robert H. Ross. New York: Columbia University Press. Originally published in Italian, 1974.

Barrese, Orazio. 1973. *I complici: gli anni del'antimafia*. Milan: Feltrinelli.

———. 1999. "The Ciaculli Massacre." A contribution to the CD-ROM "The Mafia: 150 Years of Facts, Figures and Faces." An initiative of the City of Palermo and the Tuscan Regional Authority, published by City of Palermo, Cliomedia Officina, 1999 (English version).

Bevilacqua, Piero. 1993. *Breve storia del Italia meridionale dal'800 a oggi*. Rome: Donzelli.

Birkbeck, Christopher. 1991. "Latin American Banditry as Peasant Resistance: A Deadend Trail?" *Latin American Research Review* 26: 156–60.

Blok, Anton. 1972. "The Peasant and the Brigand: Social Banditry Reconsidered." *Comparative Studies in Society and History* 14: 495–504.

———. 1974. *The Mafia of a Sicilian Village, 1860–1960: A Study of Violent Peasant Entrepreneurs.* New York: Harper and Row.

Boissevain, Jeremy. 1965. *Saints and Fireworks: Religion and Politics in Rural Malta.* London: Athlone Press.

———. 1977. "When the Saints Go Marching Out: Reflections on the Decline of Patronage in Malta." In *Patrons and Clients in Mediterranean Societies,* edited by E. Gellner and J. Waterbury, 81–96. London: Duckworth.

Bonanno, Joseph. 1983. *A Man of Honor: The Autobiography of Joseph Bonanno.* New York: Simon and Schuster.

Bonsignore, E. Midrio. 1994. *Silenzi eccellenti. Il caso Bonsignore; una battaglia per la giustizia.* Edited by B. Agnello. Palermo: La Luna.

Booth, Sally S. 1997. "Changing Geographies of Class and Gender: Earthquake Reconstruction in Western Sicily after 1968." Ph.D. dissertation, City University of New York.

Booth, Sally S., and Jeffrey E. Cole. 1999. "An Unsettling Integration: Immigrant Lives and Work in Palermo." *Modern Italy* 4:191–205.

Bourdieu, Pierre. 1977. *Outline of a Theory of Practice.* Cambridge: Cambridge University Press.

Brancato, Francesco. 1977. "Dall'unità ai fasci dei lavoratori." In *Storia della Sicilia,* edited by R. Romeo, 8: 85–173. Palermo: Società Editrice Storia di Napoli e della Sicilia.

Buongiorno, Pino. 1984. "La piovra con mille facce." *Panorama* (weekly magazine), July 23.

Burnett, Stanton H., and Luca Mantovani. 1998. *The Italian Guillotine: Operation Clean Hands and the Overthrow of Italy's First Republic.* New York: Rowman and Littlefield.

Calabro, Antonio. 1984. "I salvi non si toccano." *Panorama* (weekly magazine), May 14.

Campisi, Renato. 1994. *I ribelli.* Palermo: Rinascita Siciliana.

Cancila, Orazio. 1988. *Palermo.* Rome-Bari: Laterza Editori.

Candida, Renato. 1964. *Questa mafia.* Caltanisetta: Salvatore Sciascia. Originally published 1956.

Cannarozzo, Teresa. 1996. "Riqualificazione e ricupero del centro storico." In *Palermo tra memoria e futuro: riqualificazione e ricupero del centro storico,* edited by T. Cannarozzo, 23–71. Palermo: Publisicula Editrice.

———. 1998. *Dal ricupero del patrimonio edilizio alla riqualificazione dei centri storici: pensiero e azione del'Associazione Nazionale Centri Storici-Artistici in Sicilia, 1988–1998.* Palermo: Publisicula Editrice.

Caponnetto, Antonino. 1992. *I miei giorni a Palermo, storie di mafia e di giustizia raccontate a Saverio Lodato.* Milan: Garzanti.

Casarrubea, Giuseppe, and Pia Blandano. 1991. *L'educazione mafiosa: strutture sociali e processi di identità.* Palermo: Sellerio Editore.

Cascio, Antonia. 1989. "Donne e mafia." In *L'antimafia difficile,* edited by U. Santino, 99–102. Palermo: Centro Siciliano di Documentazione Giuseppe Impastato.

Caselli, Giancarlo, et al. 1995. *La vera storia d'Italia; interrogatori, testimonianze, riscontri, analisi. Giancarlo Caselli e i suoi sostituti ricostruiscono gli ultimi vent'anni di storia italiana.* Naples: Tullio Pironti Editore.

Catanzaro, Raimondo. 1992. *Men of Respect; A Social History of the Sicilian Mafia.* New York: Free Press.

———. 1993. "Recenti studi sulla mafia." *Polis* 7: 323–37.

———. 1994. "Domanda e offerta di protezione nelle interpretazioni della mafia: una risposta a Gambetta." *Polis* 8: 465–68.

Cavadi, Augusto. 1989. "L'esperienza del Centro Sociale S. Saverio." In *L'antimafia difficile,* edited by U. Santino, 155–58. Palermo: Centro Siciliano di Documentazione Giuseppe Impastato.

———. 1994. "Per una pedagogia antimafia." In *A scuola di antimafia: materiali di studio, criteri educativi, esperienze didattiche,* edited by A. Cavadi, 72–114. Palermo: Centro Siciliano di Documentazione Giuseppe Impastato.

Centorrino, Mario. 1986. *L'economia mafiosa.* Saverio Manelli: Rubbetino Editore.

Cervellati, Pier Luigi. 1995. *Palermo: le città nella città.* Palermo: Sellerio Editore.

———. 1996. "La normativa: Decreto Di Approvazione Della Variante Al PRG Relativa Al Centro Storico." In *Palermo tra memoria e futuro: riqualificazione e ricupero del centro storico,* edited by T. Cannarozzo, 117–68. Palermo: Publisicula Editrice.

Chatterjee, Partha. 1993. *The Nation and Its Fragments: Colonial and Postcolonial Histories.* Princeton: Princeton University Press.

Chilanti, Felice, and Mario Farinella. 1964. *Rapporto sulla mafia.* Palermo: Flacovio.

Chinnici, Giorgio, and Umberto Santino. 1989. *La violenza programmata: omicidi e guerra di mafia a Palermo dagli anni '60 ad oggi.* Milan: Franco Angeli.

Christian, William A. 1972. *Person and God in a Spanish Valley.* New York: Seminar Press.

Chubb, Judith. 1982. *Patronage, Power, and Poverty in Southern Italy: A Tale of Two Cities.* Cambridge, Mass.: M.I.T. Press.

———. 1996. "The Mafia, the Market and the State in Italy and Russia." *Journal of Modern Italian Studies* 1: 273–91.

Cimino, Marcello. 1983. "L'appropriazione mafiosa del sicilianismo." *Segno* 13: 11–19.

Cipolla, Giuseppe. 1989. "Tradizione e innovazione nell'esperienza educativa antimafia." In *L'antimafia difficile,* edited by U. Santino, 128–39. Palermo: Centro Siciliano di Documentazione Giuseppe Impastato.

Cipolla, Mariadele. 1995. *Vivi Villa Trabia: diario piccolo di vita cittadina.* Palermo: Gelka.

Clark, Martin. 1984. *Modern Italy, 1871–1982.* London: Longman.

Clendinnen, Inga. 1999. *Reading the Holocaust.* Cambridge: Cambridge University Press.

Cole, Jeffrey. 1997. *The New Racism in Europe: A Sicilian Ethnography.* Cambridge: Cambridge University Press.

Corleo, S. 1871. *Storia della enfiteusi dei terreni eclesiastici di Sicilia.* Palermo: Stabilimento Tipografico Lao.

Crisantino, Amelia. 1990. *La città spugna: Palermo nella ricerca sociologica.* Palermo: Centro Siciliano di Documentazione Giuseppe Impastato.

———. 1994. "Mafia: la fabbrica degli stereotipi." In *A scuola di antimafia: materiali di studio, criteri educativi, esperienze didattiche,* edited by A. Cavadi, 48–57. Palermo: Centro Siciliano di Documentazione Giuseppe Impastato.

———. 2000. *Della segreta e operosa associazione; Una setta all'origine della mafia.* Palermo: Sellerio Editore.

Cucchiari, Salvatore. 1988. *"Adapted for Heaven:* Conversion and Culture in Western Sicily." *American Ethnologist* 15: 417–42.

dalla Chiesa, Nando. 1983. "Gli studenti contro la mafia: note (di merito) per un movimento." *Quaderni Piacentini* 11: 39–60.

———. 1984. *Delitto imperfetto; il generale, la mafia, la società italiana.* Milan: Arnoldo Mondadori Editore.

Davis, John. 1969. "Honour and Politics in Pisticci." *Proceedings of the Royal Anthropological Institute of Great Britain and Ireland,* 69–81.

———. 1973. *Land and Family in Pisticci.* London School of Economics Monographs in Social Anthropology, no. 48. London: Athlone Press.

Davis, John A. 1998. "Casting off the 'Southern Problem': Or the Peculiarities of the South Reconsidered." In *Italy's "Southern Question": Orientalism in One Country,* edited by J. Schneider, 205–25. Oxford: Berg.

della Porta, Donatella, and Alberto Vannucci. 1994. *Corruzione politica e amministrazione publicca.* Bologna: Il Mulino.

De Lutiis, Giuseppe. 1991. *Storia dei servizi segreti in Italia.* Rome: Editori Riuniti.

Diani, Mario. 1995. *Green Networks: A Structural Analysis of the Italian Environmental Movement.* Edinburgh: Edinburgh University Press.

Di Bernardo, Giuliano. 1987. *Filosofia della massoneria: l'immagine massonica dell'uomo.* Venice: Marsilio Editori.

Di Lello, Giuseppe. 1994. *Giudici.* Palermo: Sellerio Editore.

Dombrowski, Kirk. 2001. *Against Culture: Development, Politics, and Religion in Indian Alaska (Fourth World Rising).* Lincoln: University of Nebraska Press.

Duggan, Christopher. 1986. *La mafia durante il fascismo.* Soveria Manelli: Rubbettino Editore.

Eberstadt, Fernanda. 1991. "Annals of Place: The Palace and the City." *The New Yorker,* 41–84 passim.

Edelman, Marc. 2001. "Social Movements: Changing Paradigms and Forms of Politics." *Annual Review of Anthropology* 30: 285–317.

Ellin, Nan. 1996. *Postmodern Urbanism.* Oxford: Blackwell.

Falcone, Giovanni. 1991. *Cose di cosa nostra.* Milan: Rizzoli.

Fentress, James. 2000. *Rebels and Mafiosi: Death in a Sicilian Landscape.* Ithaca: Cornell University Press.

Fentress, James, and Chris Wickham. 1992. *Social Memory.* Oxford: Blackwell.

Fiume, Giovanna. 1991. "Bandits, Violence and the Organization of Power in Sicily in the Early Nineteenth Century." In *Society and Politics in the Age of the Risorgimento: Essays in Honor of Denis Mack Smith,* edited by J.A. Davis and P. Ginsborg, 70–91. Cambridge: Cambridge University Press.

———. 2000. "Il rompicapo degli anni settanta." In *Mario Francese; Una Vita in Cronaca,* edited by G. Fiume and S. Lo Nardo, 31–43. Palermo: Gelka.

Forgione, Francesco, and Paolo Mondani. 1994. *Oltre la cupola; massoneria, mafia, e politica.* Milan: Rizzoli.

Franchetti, Leopoldo. 1925. *Condizioni politiche e amministrative della Sicilia.* 2nd ed. Firenze: Vallecchi Editore. Originally published 1876.

Gallant, Thomas W. 1999. "Brigandage, Piracy, Capitalism, and State Formation: Transnational Crime from a Historical World-Systems Perspective." In *States and Illegal Practices,* edited by J. McC. Heyman, 25–63. Oxford: Berg.

———. 2000. "Honor, Masculinity, and Ritual Knife Fighting in Nineteenth-Century Greece." *American Historical Review* 105: 359–82.

Galli, Giancarlo. 1995. *Il padrone dei padroni: Enrico Cuccia, il potere di Mediobanca e il capitalismo italiano.* Milan: Garzanti.

Galluzzo, Lucio, Franco Nicastro, and Vincenzo Vasile. 1992. *Obiettivo Falcone.* 2nd ed. Naples: Tullio Pironte Editore.

Gambetta, Diego. 1987. "Mafia: i costi della sfiducia." *Polis* 1: 284–305.

———. 1993. *The Sicilian Mafia: The Business of Protection.* Cambridge, Mass.: Harvard University Press.

———. 1994. "La protezione mafiosa." *Polis* 8: 291–303.

Giammarinaro, Maria Grazia. 1989. *Insegnare che cos'è la mafia.* Cosenza: Luigi Pellegrini Editore.

Giarrizzo, Giuseppe, ed. 1983. *La modernizzazione difficile: città e campagne nel mezzogiorno dall'eta giolittiana al fascismo.* Bari: De Donato.

Gibson, Mary. 1998. "Biology or Environment? Race and Southern 'Deviancy' in the Writings of Italian Criminologists, 1880–1920." In *Italy's "Southern Question": Orientalism in One Country,* edited by J. Schneider, 99–117. Oxford: Berg.

Gilbert, Mark. 1995. *The Italian Revolution: The End of Politics Italian Style?* Boulder, Colo.: Westview Press.

Ginsborg, Paul. 1990. *A History of Contemporary Italy: Society and Politics, 1943–1988.* London: Penguin Books.

———. 1998. *L'Italia del tempo presente; famiglia, società civile, stato, 1980–1996.* Turin: Einaudi.

Giuffrida, Romualdo. 1973. *Aspetti del'economia siciliana nell'ottocento.* Palermo: Edizione Telestar.

———. 1980. *Politica ed economia nella Sicilia dell'ottocento.* Palermo: Sellerio Editore.

Gouldner, Alvin W. 1970. *The Coming Crisis of Western Sociology.* New York: Basic Books.

Gramsci, Antonio. 1971. *Selections from the Prison Notebooks of Antonio Gramsci.* Edited and translated by Quintin Hoare and Geoffrey Nowell Smith. 2nd ed. New York: International.

Grimaldi, Aurelio. 1987. *Meri per sempre; l'amore la donna il sesso raccontato dai giovani detenuti del Malaspina di Palermo.* Palermo: La Luna.

Guarnieri, Carlo. 1992. *Magistratura e politica in Italia: pesi senza contrappesi.* Bologna: Il Mulino.

Guarrasi, Vincenzo. 1981. *La produzione dello spazio urbano*. Palermo: Flaccovio.

Guha, Ranajit. 1983. *Elementary Aspects of Peasant Insurgency in Colonial India*. Delhi: Oxford University Press.

Gulisano, Sebastiano. 1996. "Affari di cuore." *I Siciliani* February: 30–36.

Haering, Bernhard. 1985. "Una teologia siciliana della liberazione?" *Segno* 56–57:101–6.

Hall, John. 1998. "The Nature of Civil Society." *Society* 35: 32–41.

Handelman, Stephen. 1995. *Comrade Criminal: Russia's New Mafiya*. New Haven: Yale University Press.

Herzfeld, Michael. 1980. "Honour and Shame: Problems in the Analysis of Moral Systems." *Man* (n.s.) 15: 339–51.

———. 1985. *The Poetics of Manhood: Contest and Identity in a Cretan Mountain Village*. Princeton: Princeton University Press.

Hess, Henner. 1998. *Mafia and Mafiosi: Origin, Power and Myth*. New York: New York University Press. Original German edition 1970.

Hobsbawm, Eric J. 1959. *Primitive Rebels: Studies in Archaic Forms of Social Movement in the 19th and 20th Centuries*. New York: Praeger.

———. 1972 "Social Bandits: A Comment." *Comparative Studies in Society and History* 14: 504–7.

Humphrey, Caroline. 1999. "Russian Protection Rackets and the Appropriation of Law and Order." In *States and Illegal Practices,* edited by J. McC. Heyman, 199–233. Oxford: Berg.

Impastato, Felicia Bartolotta. 1986. *La mafia in casa mia; intervista di Anna Puglisi e Umberto Santino*. Palermo: La Luna.

Jacquemet, Marco. 1996. *Credibility in Court: Communicative Practices in the Camorra Trials*. Cambridge: Cambridge University Press.

Jamieson, Alison. 2000. *The Antimafia: Italy's Fight Against Organized Crime*. London: Macmillan.

Joseph, Gilbert M. 1990. "On the Trail of Latin American Bandits: A Reexamination of Peasant Resistance." *Latin American Research Review* 15: 7–55.

Joseph, Suad. 1993. "Connectivity and Patriarchy Among Urban Working Class Arab Families in Lebanon." *Ethos* 21: 452–85.

Kelly, Robert J. 1999. *The Upperworld and the Underworld: Case Studies of Racketeering and Business Infiltrations in the United States*. New York: Kluwer Academic/Plenum.

Kenny, Michael. 1960. "Patterns of Patronage in Spain." *Anthropological Quarterly* 33: 14–23.

La Duca, Rosario. 1975. *La città perduta: cronache palermitane di ieri e di oggi*. Naples: Edizioni Scientifiche Italiane.

———. 1984. "Storia e leggenda de *I Beati Paoli*," in *I Beati Paoli*, edited by L.Natoli, xv–xliii. Palermo: S. F. Flaccovio.

———. 1994. *Palermo ieri e oggi: la città*. Palermo: Sigma Edizioni.

La Licata, Francesco. 1993. *Storia di Giovanni Falcone*. Milan: Rizzoli.

La Rosa, Salvatore. 1977. "Trasformazioni fondiarie, cooperazione, patti agrari." In *Storia della Sicilia,* edited by R. Romeo, 9: 111–49. Palermo: Società Editrice Storia di Napoli e della Sicilia.

Laurence, Jonathan. 1996. "*Gridi E Sussurri:* The Role of Television in Italian Electoral Campaigns." *Cornell Political Forum* 11: 23–30.

Ledeneva, Alena V. 1998. *Russia's Economy of Favors: Blat Networking and Informal Exchange.* Cambridge: Cambridge University Press.

Leeds, Elizabeth. 1996. "Cocaine and Parallel Polities in the Brazilian Urban Periphery." *Latin American Research Review* 31: 47–83.

Légé, Bernard. 1993. "Un rehabilitation sociale." In *Urbanisme et rehabilitation symbolique: Ivri, Bologne, Amiens,* edited by G. Althab, B. Légé, and M. Sélim, 79–181. Paris: Editions L'Harmattan.

Leonard, Christopher D. 2001. "E' di moda la crisi." Ph.D. dissertation, The City University of New York.

Leone, Manfredi. 1998. "Il processo di ricupero del centro storico di Palermo: gli scenari possibili." In *Dal ricupero del patrimonio edilizio alla riqualificazione dei centri storici,* edited by T. Cannarozzo, 353–57. Palermo: Publisicula Editrice.

Linder, Marc. 1994. *Projecting Capitalism: A History of the Internationalization of the Construction Industry.* Westport, Conn.: Greenwood Press.

Linebaugh, Peter. 1991. *The London Hanged: Crime and Civil Society in the 18th Century.* London: Penguin Books.

Lodato, Saverio. 1999a. *"Ho ucciso Giovanni Falcone":* la confessione di Giovanni Brusca. Milan: Mondadori.

———1999b. *Venti anni di mafia: c'era una volta la lotta alla mafia.* Milan: Rizzoli.

Lo Picolo, Francesco. 1996. "The Historical Center of Palermo." In *Palermo tra memoria e futuro; riqualificazione e ricupero del centro storico,* edited by T. Cannarozzo, 71–91. Palermo: Publisicula Editrice.

Lumley, Robert. 1990. *States of Emergency: Cultures of Revolt in Italy from 1968 to 1978.* London: Verso.

Lupo, Salvatore. 1984. "Nei giardini della Conca D'Oro." *Italia Contemporanea* 156: 43–53.

———. 1990. "Tra banca e politica: il delitto Notarbartolo." *Meridiana; Rivista di Storia e Scienze Sociali* 7–8:119–56.

———. 1993. *Storia della mafia; dalle origini ai giorni nostri.* Rome: Donzelli Editore.

———. 1997. "The Allies and the Mafia." *Journal of Modern Italian Studies* 2: 21–33.

Mack Smith, Denis. 1968. *A History of Sicily: Modern Sicily After 1713.* London: Chatto and Windus.

Mancini, G. Frederico. 2000. "The Italians in Europe." *Foreign Affairs* 79: 122–34.

Mangiameli, Rosario. 1994. "Saggio Introduttivo." In *Sicily Zone Handbook 1943,* edited by the Foreign Office, v–lxxxiv. Caltanissetta: Salvatore Sciascia Editore.

McCarthy, Patrick. 1995. *The Crisis of the Italian State: From the Origins of the Cold War to the Fall of Berlusconi and Beyond.* New York: St. Martin's Press.

Melucci, Alberto. 1989. *Nomads of the Present.* Philadelphia: Temple University Press.

————. 1996. *Challenging Codes: Collective Action in the Information Age.* Cambridge: Cambridge University Press.

Mercadante, Vito. 1986. *La nuova mafia da Lucky Luciano a Michele Greco.* Caltanissetta: Vaccaro Editore.

Mineo, Mario. 1995. *Scritti sulla Sicilia.* Palermo: Flaccovio.

Moe, Nelson. 1998. "The Emergence of the Southern Question in Villari, Franchetti, and Sonnino." In *Italy's "Southern Question": Orientalism in One Country,* edited by J. Schneider, 51–77. Oxford: Berg.

Mola, Aldo A. 1992. *Storia della massoneria italiana; dalle origini ai nostri giorni.* Milan: Bompiani.

Montalbano, Giuseppe. 1949. *Sul ordine pubblico in Sicilia.* Palermo: Pezzino.

————. 1956. *La mafia è una piaga da estirpare.* Palermo: Grafiche A. Renna.

————. 1964a. *Mafia e banditismo politico in Sicilia,* 2: 104–16. Rome: Edizioni Montecitorio.

————. 1964b. "Natura politica, giuridica e psicologica della mafia: *Homo,* 1–8.

Montemagno, Gabriello. 1990. *Palermo: la primavera interrotta.* Palermo: Nuova Editrice Meridionale.

Mosca, Gaetano. 1949. *Partiti e sindacati nella crisi del regime parlamentare.* 2nd ed. Bari: Giuseppe Laterza e Figli. Originally published 1905.

Naselli, Benedetto. 1864. *I Beati Paoli o la famiglia del giustiziato.* Palermo: Officio Tipografico Clamis e Roberti, Teatro Drammatico Siciliano.

Natoli, Luigi. 1984. *I Beati Paoli.* Palermo: S. F. Flaccovio Editore. Originally published 1909–10.

Nicastro, Franco. 1993. *Il caso Contrada, le trame di boss, poteri occulti e servizi segreti.* Palermo: Edizioni Arbor.

————. 2000. "La sfida al cambiamento. La stampa palermitana negli anni di Francese." In *Mario Francese; Una Vita in Cronaca,* edited by G. Fiume and S. Lo Nardo, 43–57. Palermo: Gelka.

Notarbartolo, Leopoldo. 1977. *Il caso Notarbartolo.* Palermo: Editrice de "Il Vespro."

Orlando, Leoluca. 2001. *Fighting the Mafia and Renewing Sicilian Culture.* San Francisco: Encounter Books.

Padovani, Marcelle. 1979. "Presentazione." In *La Sicilia come metafora; intervista di Marcelle Padovani,* edited by L. Sciascia, vii–xiv. Milan: Mondadori.

Pandolfi, Mariella. 1998. "Two Italies: Rhetorical Figures of Failed Nationhood." In *Italy's "Southern Question": Orientalism in One Country,* edited by J. Schneider, 285–91. Oxford: Berg.

Pantaleone, Michele. 1962. *Mafia e politica, 1943–1962.* Turin: Einaudi.

Paoli, Letizia. 1997. "The Pledge to Secrecy: Culture, Structure and Action of Mafia Associations." Ph.D. dissertation, European University Institute, Florence.

————. 2000. *Fratelli di mafia; cosa nostra e 'ndrangheta.* Bologna: Il Mulino.

————. 2001. "Crime, Italian Style." *Daedalus* 130: 157–85.

Pardo, Italo. 1996. *Managing Existence in Naples.* Cambridge: Cambridge University Press.

Perriera, Michele. 1988. *Orlando: intervista al sindaco di Palermo.* Palermo: La Luna.

Petrusewicz, Marta. 1998. "Before the Southern Question: 'Native' Ideas on Backwardness and Remedies in the Kingdom of Two Sicilies, 1815–1849." In *Italy's "Southern Question": Orientalism in One Country*, edited by J. Schneider, 27–51. Oxford: Berg.

Pezzino, Paolo. 1992. *La congiura dei pugnalatori; un caso politico-giudiziario alle origini della mafia*. Venice: Marsilio.

——1995. *Mafia: industria della violenza. Scritti e documenti inediti sulla mafia dalle origini ai giorni nostri*. Florence: La Nuova Italia.

Piazzesi, Gianfranco, and Sandra Bonsanti. 1984. *La storia di Roberto Calvi*. Milan: Longanesi.

Pillitteri, Francesco. 1981. *Credito e risparmio nella Sicilia dell'unificazione*. Palermo: Palumbo.

Pino, Marina. 1988. *Le signore della droga; storie scellerate di casalinghe palermitane*. Palermo: La Luna.

Pirrera, Salvo. 1996. "L'attività del comune." In *Palermo tra memoria e futuro: riqualificazione e ricupero del centro storico*, edited by T. Cannarozzo,107–17. Palermo: Publisicula Editrice.

Principato, Teresa, and Alessandra Dino. 1997. *Mafia donna: le vestali del sacro e del'onore*. Palermo: Flaccovio.

Priulla, Graziella. 1989. "Informazione e mafia: dal silenzio al rumore." In *L'antimafia difficile*, edited by U. Santino, 69–79. Palermo: Centro Siciliano di Documentazione Giuseppe Impastato.

Puglisi, Anna. 1990. *Sole contra la mafia*. Palermo: La Luna.

Putnam, Robert D. 1993. *Making Democracy Work: Civic Traditions in Modern Italy*. New York: Beacon.

Ramella, F., and C. Trigilia. 1997. "Associazionismo e mobilitazione contro la criminalità organizata nel Mezzogiorno." In *Mafia e società Italiana. Rapporto '97*, edited by L. Violante, 24–46. Bari: Laterza.

Recupero, Antonino. 1987. "Ceti medi e 'homines novi' alle origini della mafia." *Polis* 1: 307–28.

Renda, Francesco. 1987. *Storia della Sicilia dal 1860 al 1970*. 2nd ed. Vol. 1. Palermo: Sellerio Editore.

——. 1991. "Prefazione alla seconda edizione." Preface to F. Renda, *I Beati Paoli; storia, letteratura e leggenda*, 7–11. 2nd ed. Palermo: Sellerio Editore. Originally published 1988.

——. 1993. *Resistenza alla mafia come movimento nazionale*. Soveria Mannelli: Rubbettino Editore.

Riall, Lucy. 1998. *Sicily and the Unification of Italy: Liberal Policy and Local Power, 1859–1866*. Oxford: Clarendon Press.

Roldan, Mary. 1999. "Colombia: Cocaine and the 'Miracle' of Modernity in Medellin." In *Cocaine: Global Histories*, edited by P. Gootenberg, 165–82. London: Routledge.

Rosengarten, Frank. 1998. "Homo Siculus: Essentialism in the Writing of Giovanni Verga, Giuseppe Tomasi Di Lampedusa, and Leonardo Sciascia." In *Italy's "Southern Question": Orientalism in One Country*, edited by J. Schneider, 117–135. Oxford: Berg.

Rossetti, Carlo. 1994. *L'attaco allo stato di diritto, le associazioni segrete e la costituzione*. Naples: Liguori Editore.

Sabetti, Filippo. 1984. *Political Authority in a Sicilian Village*. New Brunswick, N.J.: Rutgers University Press.

Santino, Umberto. 1988. "The Financial Mafia: The Illegal Accumulation of Wealth and the Financial-Industrial Complex." *Contemporary Crises* 12: 203–43.

———. 1989. "Mafia e lotta alla mafia: materiali per un bilancio e nuove ipotesi di lavoro." In *L'antimafia difficile*, edited by U. Santino, 19–37. Palermo: Centro Siciliano di Documentazione Giuseppe Impastato.

———. 1994. "Appunti su mafia e pedagogia alternativa." In *A scuola di antimafia: materiali di studio, criteri educativi, esperienze didattiche*, edited by A. Cavadi, 67–72. Palermo: Centro Siciliano di Documentazione Giuseppe Impastato.

———. 1997. *La democrazia bloccata. La Strage di Portella della Ginestra e l'emarginazione delle sinistre*. Soveria Mannelli: Rubbettino.

———. 2000. *Storia del movimento antimafia; dalla lotta di classe all'impegno civile*. Rome: Editori Riuniti.

Santino, Umberto, and Giovanni La Fiura. 1990. *L'impresa mafiosa; dall'Italia agli Stati Uniti*. Milan: Franco Angeli, Centro Siciliano di Documentazione Giuseppe Impastato.

Schneider, Jane, and Peter Schneider. 1976. *Culture and Political Economy in Western Sicily*. New York: Academic Press.

———. 1984. "Mafia Burlesque: The Profane Mass as a Peace-Making Ritual." In *Religion, Power and Protest in Local Communities*, edited by E. R. Wolf, 117–37. Berlin: Mouton.

———. 1996. *Festival of the Poor: Fertility Decline and the Ideology of Class in Sicily, 1860–1980*. Tucson: University of Arizona Press.

Schneider, Peter. 1994. Review of Diego Gambetta, *The Sicilian Mafia: The Business of Protection*. *Italian Politics and Society Newsletter* 42: 26–28.

———. 2000. "Putting a Good Face on a Bad Affair." In *Minature Etnografiche*, edited by H. Driessen and H. De Jonge, 46–50. Nijmegen, The Netherlands: Leo de Bruin.

Schneider, Peter, and Jane Schneider. 1998. "Il Caso Sciascia: Dilemmas of the Antimafia Movement in Sicily." In *Italy's "Southern Question": Orientalism in One Country*, edited by J. Schneider, 245–60. Oxford: Berg.

Sciascia, Leonardo. 1960. *Il giorno della civetta*. Milan: Einaudi.

———. 1961. *Pirandello e la Sicilia*. Caltanissetta: Salvatore Sciascia Editore.

———. 1964. *Mafia Vendetta*. New York: Knopf.

———. 1965. *Feste religiose in Sicilia*. Bari: Leonardo Da Vinci Editrice.

———. 1966. *Al ciascuno il suo*. Milan: Einaudi.

———. 1979. *La Sicilia come metafora; intervista di Marcelle Padovani*. Milan: Mondadori.

Scrofani, Serafino. 1977. "Gli ordinamenti colturali." In *Storia della Sicilia*, edited by R. Romeo, 9: 85–111. Palermo: Società Editrice Storia di Napoli e della Sicilia.

Siebert, Renate. 1994. *Le donne, la mafia*. Milan: Il Saggiatore.

Sorge, Bartolomeo. 1989. *Uscire dal tempio; intervista autobiografica.* Edited by Paolo Giuntella. Genova: Casa Editrice Marietti.

Spero, Joan Edelman. 1980. *The Failure of the Franklin National Bank: Challenge to the International Banking System.* New York: Columbia University Press.

Stabile, Francesco Michele. 1986. "Palermo, La chiesa baluardo del Card. Ruffini (1946–1948)." In *Le chiese di Pio XII,* edited by A. Riccardi, 367–93. Bari: Laterza.

———. 1989. "Chiesa e mafia." In *L'antimafia difficile,* edited by U. Santino, 103–27. Palermo: Centro Siciliano di Documentazione Giuseppe Impastato.

Stajano, Corrado, ed. 1986. *Mafia: L'atto d'accusa dei giudici di Palermo.* Rome: Editori Riuniti.

Stille, Alexander. 1995. *Excellent Cadavers: The Mafia and the Death of the First Italian Republic.* New York: Vintage Books.

———. 1999. "Palermo: The Photography of Death." *New York Review of Books.* July 15: 49–52.

Strouse, Jean. 2000. *Morgan: American Financier.* New York: Harper Perennial.

Tarrow, Sidney. 1988. "Old Movements and New Cycles of Protest: The Career of an Italian Religious Community." In *From Structure to Action: Comparing Social Movements Across Cultures,* edited by Bert Klandermans, Hanspeter Kriesi, and Sidney Tarrow. International Social Movement Research, vol. 1, 281–304. Greenwich, Conn.: JAI.

———. 1989. *Democracy and Disorder: Protest and Politics in Italy, 1965–1975.* Oxford: Clarendon Press.

Thompson, Edward P. 1975. *Whigs and Hunters: The Origin of the Black Act.* London: Penguin Books.

Tilly, Charles. 1974. Foreword to Anton Blok, *The Mafia of a Sicilian Village.* Oxford: Basil Blackwell.

Treverton, Gregory F. 1987. *Covert Action: The Limits of Intervention in the Postwar World.* New York: Basic Books.

Trombino, Giuseppe. 1998. "L'attuazione del piano particolareggiato esecutivo del centro storico di Palermo." In *Dal ricupero del patrimonio edilizio alla riqualificazione dei centri storici,* edited by T. Cannarozzo, 343–47. Palermo: Publisicula Editrice.

Vanderwood, Paul J. 1992. *Disorder and Progress: Bandits, Police, and Mexican Development.* Wilmington, Del.: Scholarly Resources Books. Originally published 1981.

Venkatesh, Sudhir. 1997. "The Social Organization of Street Gang Activity in the Urban Ghetto." *American Journal of Sociology* 103: 82–111.

Verdery, Katherine. 1996. *What Was Socialism, and What Comes Next?* Princeton: Princeton University Press.

Vitale, Salvo. 1989. "Dopo la morte di Peppino: resistere a mafiopoli." In *L'antimafia difficile,* edited by U. Santino, 91–98. Palermo: Centro Siciliano di Documentazione Giuseppe Impastato.

———. 1995. *Nel cuore dei coralli: Peppino Impastato, una vita contro la mafia.* Soveria Manelli: Rubbettino.

von Henneberg, Krystna Clara. 1996. "The Construction of Fascist Libya:

Modern Colonial Architecture and Urban Planning in Italian North Africa (1922–1943)." Ph.D. dissertation, University of California, Berkeley.

Willis, Paul. 1981. *Learning to Labor: How Working Class Kids Get Working Class Jobs.* New York: Columbia University Press.

Wolf, Eric R. 1966. "Kinship, Friendship, and Patron-Client Relations in Complex Societies." In *The Social Anthropology of Complex Societies,* edited by M. Banton, 1–22. London: Tavistock.

Index

ACLI *(Associazioni Cristiane Lavoratori Italiani)*, 176–77
Acquasanta neighborhood, 12, 13, 62, 107
administrative divisions (Palermo): 1980 districts, 166; "eight cities," 251–52, 256; *mandamenti*, 6; student survey of, 274
Albergheria neighborhood, 19, 183–86, 231, 271–74, 279
Alleanza Nazionale (AN; National Alliance party), 295–96, 298
Alongi, Antonino, 174
Alongi, Giuseppe, 30
Ambrosoli, Giorgio, 79
AMGOT (Allied Military Government of the Occupied Territories), 49–50
Andreotti, Giulio: DC current of, 56–57, 114, 157, 165, 190–91, 220; mafia and, 134, 147–50, 292; Sindona and, 79; trial of, 122, 134, 151–52, 213, 292–93, 297, 315n2
Annan, Kofi, 2, 286
Antimafia (journal), 177
antimafia judicial pool, 131–32, 146, 201, 210
antimafia movement, 3, 15, 90, 128, 159; activists, social background of, 3, 161–62, 218; Catholic activists in, 161–62, 165, 171–72; engaged in poor neighborhoods, 183–85, 187–89, 192, 205, 211, 258–59, 269–71; environmentalism and, 216–17; nineteenth

century forerunner, 38; response to assassinations, 203–10; women in, 161, 216–17
Antiochia, Roberto, 140, 177, 227
Arab (Islamic) architecture, 7–8, 269–70
ARCI *(Associazione Ricreativa Culturale Italiana)*, 204
Arcuri, Emilio, 179, 181, 186, 191, 242–43, 246, 257–58
aristocracy, 1, 6, 8–16, 35, 42, 131, 218; protectors of bandits, mafiosi, 30–31; role in unification, 26; Sicilian separatism and, 53–54
Arlacchi, Pino, 2, 175, 284, 312n4
Art Nouveau (Belle Epoque) style, 1, 12, 14, 18, 28, 57, 272
Association of Women against the Mafia *(Donne contro la mafia)*, 187–88, 213, 216, 300
Atria, Rita, 93–94, 158

backlash, counter-antimafia, 3, 127, 193, 263; discourse, 194–97
Badalamenti, Gaetano, 64, 66, 68, 88–89, 123, 169–70, 295
Bagarella, Antonietta, 154, 200, 225
Bagarella, Leoluca, 68, 154, 221
banditry, 24–26, 30–32, 51, 85, 305n1; brigand corridor, 25, 33, 38–39, 200; compared to mafia, 31–32, 46; in India, 44; in Mexico, 44
Banfield, Edward C., 110, 117

tangentopoli. See *mani pulite* (clean hands)
Tasca Bordonaro, Count Lucio, 51; Tasca family, 163
Terranova, Cesare, 69, 135, 138, 163, 174, 176
Terranova, Giovanna, 216
terrorism, terrorist bombings: extra-parliamentary extremists, 74, 130–31, 158, 164–65, 170, 177; mafia sponsored, 71, 148–49, 150; "years of lead," 164–65
third level of mafia, 53, 73, 133, 141, 150, 156, 159, 198, 310n14
tourism, 172, 183, 251, 287–88
trade unions, 188–89, 212; consortium of, 204; CGIL, 163, 166, 168–69, 176, 188, 192, 212, 225; CSIL, 188, 204; UIL, 188, 204
trasformismo, 27, 179

Ucciardone prison, 10, 25, 26–27, 127, 174, 195, 205, 225–28, 255; bunker courthouse in, 142–43; plan for transformation of, 255; "radio Ucciardone," 179
Uditore neighborhood, 19, 66, 155, 165, 271–73, 279, 298–99
UIL *(Unione Italiana del Lavoro)*, 188, 204
unification of Italy *(Risorgimento)*, 1, 25–27, 35, 39
United Nations, 290, 300; Convention against Transnational Organized Crime, 2, 244, 286
University of Palermo, 8, 90, 116–17, 208–9, 224, 228; architecture faculty

of, 181, 240–43; support for Ciaculli agricultural park, 254
urban planning: 1962 plan, 14, 156, 252; 1980s plan for historic center, 3, 181, 236, 239–44; 1990s PRG *(Piano Regolatore Generale)*, 251–58; design of ZEN, 271–72; and environmental activism, 256, 313n6; nineteenth century, 11–13; Paris as a model for, 12–13; under fascism, 235–36

Vassallo, Francesco, 56, 261–62, 306n5
Via Maqueda, 6, 11–13, 246
Via Notarbartolo, 13, 206
Via Roma, 11–12, 77
Viale della Libertà, 12–13, 14
Villa Igea, Hotel, 13, 35, 122
Villamaura, 20, 29–30, 121, 311n3, 312n5
Vinay, Tullio, 166
Vitale, Leonardo, 88, 91–92, 99, 132
Vizzini, Calogero, 49, 162

witness protection program, 132, 134
working classes, 189, 233, 258–59, 262, 287, 299–300
World War II, Allied bombing, 1–2, 9, 14–15

ZEN (Zone of Expansion North) neighborhood, 19, 271–73, 275–76, 279
Zisa: neighborhood, 12, 62, 107, 255; palace, 7, 10;

Compositor:	Rainsford Type
Text:	10/13 Sabon
Display:	Sabon
Printer and Binder:	Sheridan Books, Inc.